The Battle for Welfare Rights

MW00331292

POLITICS AND CULTURE IN MODERN AMERICA
Series Editors: Glenda Gilmore, Michael Kazin, Thomas J. Sugrue

Books in this series narrate and analyze political and social change in the broadest dimensions from 1865 to the present, including ideas about the ways people have sought and wielded power in the public sphere and the language and institutions of politics at all levels— national, regional, and local. The series is motivated by a desire to reverse the fragmentation of modern U.S. history and to encourage synthetic perspectives on social movements and the state, on gender, race, and labor, on consumption, and on intellectual history and popular culture.

The Battle for Welfare Rights

Politics and Poverty in Modern America

FELICIA KORNBLUH

PENN

University of Pennsylvania Press

Philadelphia

Copyright © 2007 University of Pennsylvania Press

All rights reserved. Except for brief quotations used for purposes of review or scholarly citation, none of this book may be reproduced in any form by any means without written permission from the publisher.

Published by
University of Pennsylvania Press
Philadelphia, Pennsylvania 19104-4112

Printed in the United States of America on acid-free paper

10   9   8   7   6   5   4   3   2   1

Library of Congress Cataloging-in-Publication Data

Kornbluh, Felicia, 1966–
    The battle for welfare rights : politics and poverty in modern America / Felicia Kornbluh.
        p.   cm. —(Politics and culture in modern America)
    ISBN-13: 978-0-8122-4005-4 (alk. paper)
    ISBN-10: 0-8122-4005-7 (alk. paper)
    Includes bibliographical references and index.
    1. Welfare rights movement—United States—History.   2. Welfare recipients—United States—Political activity.   3. Poor—United States—Political activity.   4. Public welfare—United States.   5. United States—Politics and government—20th century.   6. United States—Social policy.   I. Title.   II. Series.
HV91.K65   2007
362.5′56140973—dc22   2006052939

To Mom, Dad, and Anore

Contents

Preface

The Battle for Welfare Rights joins the scholarship on political, legal, urban, and social-movement history in the post-1945 United States. As in studies of such cities as Philadelphia, Oakland, Baltimore, Detroit, and Chicago, the evidence gathered here demonstrates that local conflicts led to profound changes in the tenor of municipal politics.[1] They transformed the electoral coalitions that supported both the Democratic and Republican parties. As in these other cities, what happened in New York was also a microcosm of changes that occurred at the national level. Grueling local battles over schools, housing, crime, and public aid reveal the complex progress of modern politics. Among other consequences, these battles made visible the redistributive implications of the movement for African American emancipation, and of other movements to overcome systematic injustice. *The Battle for Welfare Rights* is a contribution to the scholarly effort to clarify the discrete points at which many members of the voting majority came to understand these implications, and chose not to face them.

This work differs somewhat from other studies of postwar America. I critique the work of colleagues who have slighted the role of gender and sexuality in the conflicts that erupted within cities and political parties in the period between World War II and the mid-1970s.[2] Such concerns are central to the history of this period—as they are to the rest of U.S. history and, indeed, to all human history. By paying close attention to the debate over public welfare, it is easy to see that these issues are inseparable from the rest of the historical fabric and are tied particularly closely to the racial conflicts that many scholars have privileged in their portraits of twentieth-century movements for social change. The debate over welfare lay at the center of the political transformations in this period precisely because it linked popular anxieties about race, sex, and income, as well as migration, language, and the conventional work ethic. No account of the postwar American city, of the rise of conservatism from the radicalism of the 1960s, or of modern politics can claim to do justice to its subject if it omits questions about sex, gender, or sexuality.

The Battle for Welfare Rights also offers a corrective to histories of the postwar United States that treat the politics of race, ethnicity, and social hierarchy as simple black-white affairs. Puerto Ricans in New York City and elsewhere in the state, and Mexican Americans in California, played key roles in this history. The emergence of Latinos/as as recipients of public assistance was one sign of the so-called welfare crisis that politicians and journalists began to identify in the early 1960s. In New York, Puerto Rican leaders such as Frank Espada helped build the movement. Hundreds of welfare mothers and fathers, from heavily Puerto Rican neighborhoods in the boroughs of Manhattan, Brooklyn, and the Bronx, joined action groups that made demands on their local welfare offices.

In California, the same activists who spurred urban community organizing among Mexican Americans, and breathed new life into the farm workers' movement, created an organizing strategy for public assistance recipients. The Mexican American organizers César Chávez and Delores Huerta, working with Anglo-American activist Fred Ross, developed a strategy of "benefit-based" organizing that became essential to the development of a welfare rights movement in California and nationally.

Researchers have too often treated the history of politics and law as distinct from the history of grassroots protest. In fact, as chroniclers of the demand for Black Power and disputes over public housing have noted, the postwar evolution of politics and public policy was inseparable from the evolution of grassroots movements for social change. The arrival of new policies, such as those associated with the federal War on Poverty, dramatically changed activist social movements, shaping their strategies and largely determining whether or not they would be effective. The rise of new social movements, such as the movement for welfare rights, transformed municipal and national politics. The movements placed questions about racial hierarchy, the distribution of public power, and disparities in economic resources on the front burner of policy-makers' concerns. They also bred reaction: in response to social movement efforts, voting majorities began to withdraw their support for the expansionist post-New Deal state and its municipal equivalents, even in such famously liberal places as New York City.

This is a history of welfare rights politics at both the local and the national levels. The choice of New York as a center for investigation was both a principled and a practical one. New York was a key location in the history of the welfare rights movement. I discovered two rich bodies of information about the movement in this city. First, in search of information about the relationship between welfare rights and the law, I located the papers of Carl Rachlin, an attorney who had served as general counsel of the National Welfare Rights Organization (NWRO) and whose office was in New York. The papers contained transcripts of "fair hearings," administrative procedures that welfare recipients in New York and elsewhere brought when they had grievances. In these records, poor women and men explained how they felt about the public aid system, and described their daily experiences as clients of that system. Second, in search of an oral history interview, I visited Tim Sampson, former associate national director of NWRO, in California. I had heard rumors about the rich archive "in Tim's basement," which turned out to be a set of boxes he had deposited in the dank subterranean chambers of the Center for Third World Organizing in Oakland. Among other treasures, these boxes contained a complete set of copies of *Tell It Like It Is*, the newsletter of the Citywide Coordinating Committee of Welfare Groups, and a thick file of Citywide press releases, from which I could stitch together a more complete narrative of local events than had ever appeared in print. Beyond or before all these reasons, I am a New Yorker who was raised on the Upper West Side of Manhattan during the years chronicled in this book. My parents participated in local politics, including the conflict over urban renewal on the Upper West Side that spurred Beulah Sanders's entrance into activism. I know something about the fate of New York City, and I care about it deeply.

Thomas Jefferson and the Declaration of Food Stamps

I got food stamps
from the Department of Agriculture,
with the Liberty Bell
on the cover of the booklet.
I opened my booklet of food stamps
To see Thomas Jefferson
and the Founding Fathers
signing the Declaration of Independence
on every one dollar coupon.
At the back of the booklet,
I found instructions on how to shop
and a warning that I could not buy
cigarettes or beer or restaurant meals
with food stamps.

I never smoked or drank
or ate in restaurants.
I only wanted what Jefferson said he wanted,
but the back of the booklet told me
I couldn't buy that with food stamps, either.
While waiting at the welfare office,
I would open my booklet of food stamps
and talk to Thomas Jefferson.
Were you the inventor of the food stamp?
Did you give food stamps to Sally Hemmings,
the slave with all the children
who looked like Thomas Jefferson?
I was a history major in college.

So I wrote my Declaration of Food Stamps
proclaiming the right
to sit in a white linen restaurant,
eat as well as Thomas Jefferson,
then pay in piles
of clipped toenails
dumped into the tea.

—Martín Espada

Introduction

On May 13, 1970, Beulah Sanders of New York City became the acting secretary of Health, Education, and Welfare. Sanders, an African American woman, was the first recipient of public assistance to sit at the desk where decisions were made that affected millions of people like her. Immediately upon taking office, she called for an end to the U.S. war in Southeast Asia and a minimum income of at least $5,500 per year for every citizen. "Unfortunately," a contemporary source reported, "Mrs. Sanders's 'staff' of 150 [welfare] recipients from Baltimore and Frederick Md., Philadelphia, Rhode Island and Virginia, were unable to get inside the building to carry out her directives."[1] The would-be bureaucrats were outside chanting and carrying signs, blocked by a phalanx of police who had sealed off the building. Sanders and the others were members of the National Welfare Rights Organization (NWRO). Most were African American women; they were all public assistance recipients or other poor people. They occupied the building for nine hours before being carried out by police in an operation that Sanders described as "two cops to every woman."[2]

At the moment when she occupied the secretary's chair, Beulah Sanders was the elected leader of the City-Wide Coordinating Committee of Welfare Groups and first vice president of the National Welfare Rights Organization. The City-Wide Coordinating Committee, or "Citywide" in the shorthand often used in this book, was an organization of several thousand public aid recipients devoted to changing welfare in the city of New York. Citywide activists used tactics that ranged from demonstrations, sit-ins and other forms of civil disobedience, to legislative lobbying, registering voters to participate in elections, and suing welfare department officials in court. By 1970, the City-Wide Coordinating Committee of Welfare Groups had helped welfare families gain cash grants worth hundreds of thousands of dollars. Sanders and other leaders worked with an array of middle-class allies: social workers, attorneys, priests, nuns, and professional organizers. They built chapters in disparate neighborhoods throughout the city and created an interracial, cross-class coalition that made its presence felt powerfully at City Hall.

The welfare rights movement allowed Sanders and the women and men who joined her to articulate an ambitious political agenda and to broadcast it widely. The first item on this agenda was a national guarantee of income security. The idea of a guaranteed income challenged the conventional economics of the labor market. It promised that, if the private market failed to offer workers an adequate income, the government would supplement their wages. People who were unemployed, or who were not in the labor market because they were busy raising children, would receive enough money to raise them above subsistence. For a woman, a guaranteed income was better than a traditional welfare program because she did not have to prove that she deserved support in order to be eligible for it; she only had to prove that she was poor. A national guaranteed income would provide support to every poor person who asked for it, including unmarried women, divorced women, women leaving abusive relationships, those who combined parenting with low-wage jobs, and those whose partners were unemployed.[3]

The second item on the agenda Sanders pursued while at the helm of Health, Education and Welfare (HEW) challenged postwar U.S. foreign policy. By 1970, antipoverty activists had learned through bitter experience about the tradeoff between "guns and butter," or spending on foreign military projects versus spending on domestic social programs. The War on Poverty competed for federal dollars with the Cold War against the Soviet Union, the People's Republic of China, and Communist movements in smaller countries, such as Vietnam, that were believed to be their clients. Sanders opposed the conflict in Vietnam for its own sake, because it wrought destruction on people who appeared to pose little imminent threat to the national security of the United States. She also believed that it blocked progress toward a humane domestic economy.[4]

The welfare rights movement changed the national conversation about public benefits and thus about the heart and soul of government. The twenty thousand to thirty thousand card-carrying members and 540 local chapters merely hint at NWRO's influence at the peak of its strength. Even the most conservative estimates of its reach rank the National Welfare Rights Organization as the largest national organization of poor people in the history of the United States. The welfare rights campaign attracted thousands of African American women who were committed to social change. It also attracted Puerto Rican women and other Latinas, white women, Native American women, and low-income men. When Beulah Sanders and thousands of other public aid recipients made demands on the political system, they unsettled conventional power relationships based on sex, economic class, language, citizenship status, and race.[5]

The welfare rights movement challenged all these familiar hierarchies at once. By doing so, it raised questions that the other branches of the postwar civil rights movement, and the majority-white women's movement, had failed to pose. The African American civil rights movement, which is often referred to here by the more encompassing term "freedom movement," was a seedbed for many of the ideas and strategies of Citywide and NWRO.[6] Many welfare rights activists had participated in the campaigns of the Congress of Racial Equality (CORE), the leading civil rights organization in the urban North, before they discovered the cause of welfare rights. However, before the late 1960s, poverty and public benefits were not high on the agenda of the black freedom movement. By the time Martin Luther King, Jr., launched the Poor People's Campaign in 1968, some welfare rights organizations in New York City were already five years old. Not until the emergence of black feminism in the middle to late 1970s did issues of sexual difference and women's subordination came to the foreground in African American activist politics.[7]

The overwhelming majority of women in the feminist movement of the 1960s were middle-class whites. Many so-called "second wave" feminists discussed poverty, social class, and racism. Some individuals, including *Ms.* magazine founder Gloria Steinem and U.S. Representative Bella Abzug, openly supported the welfare rights movement. However, most white feminists privileged issues that activist welfare recipients saw as secondary to their concerns, such as gaining access to the labor market. Many women welfare recipients had worked as domestics or rural sharecroppers. They fought for a privilege that had traditionally been granted to respectable white women—to remove themselves from the workforce while raising children if they so chose—more than they did for the right to work.[8]

The conclusion of Beulah Sanders's occupation of the HEW secretary's office reveals the limitations of the welfare rights movement. Just as they could not hold the headquarters of a federal bureaucracy, recipients and their allies could not shape the public conversation about poverty for long. While they could issue directives to end poverty and stop the war, the women and men of Citywide and NWRO had little power to make federal officials listen to them. The most severe limitations they faced were political. Whenever welfare rights activists made their presence felt, whether testifying in Congress, bringing cases before the federal courts, or taking over buildings, working- and middle-class whites responded with hostility. Opponents of welfare rights insisted that the recipients be ejected from the halls of power. By the early 1970s, activist welfare recipients faced severe cuts in benefits and restrictions on their eligibility for aid. In New York City, they faced a set of new strategies by the city and state governments that undercut their organizing efforts and ultimately decimated their membership ranks.[9]

This is both a local and a national study. To chronicle this history in depth, *The Battle over Welfare Rights* emphasizes events in New York City, while also detailing struggles over welfare rights in other locales, and interactions between welfare activists and national politicians.[10] In the early 1960s, activist groups of welfare recipients began to sprout in the boroughs of New York City known as Manhattan and Brooklyn. At roughly the same moment, they grew in Northern and Southern California, in the city of Syracuse, and in a small number of other locations. All these groups were similar to one another, but the ones in New York City were the largest; they had the greatest network of support from middle-class professionals such as social workers, lawyers, and priests; and they were the most important sources of strategy and personnel for the national welfare rights movement. New York City in the 1960s and 1970s was the paradigmatic site of urban poverty and social welfare. Economic inequality in the nation's leading city prompted popular journalism as well as a steady stream of policy analysis. Mass-market books, such as *My People Is the Enemy* (1964), *Manchild in the Promised Land* (1965), *Down These Mean Streets* (1967), *The Black Badge: Confessions of a Caseworker* (1969), *The Enemies of the Poor* (1970), and *A Welfare Mother* (1977) all chronicled poverty and welfare in New York.[11]

As a location for studying the rise of political conservatism, New York City is uniquely revealing. The New York of Mayor John V. Lindsay (1966-73) was a notorious liberal outlier on the national political spectrum. But by the end of the 1960s, conflicts based on race, class, language, legal citizenship, and gender—and their electoral consequences—were clearly visible in New York as they were everywhere else in the United States. Social welfare policy, which threatened traditional relationships between whites and blacks, wealthy people and poor people, long-term citizens and migrants, speakers of English and speakers of Spanish, and women and men, became a special target of animosity. When Mayor Lindsay ran for reelection as an Independent in 1969, his opponents from the major political parties talked incessantly about welfare spending and charged that the mayor was allowing poor people to defraud the city. In the early 1970s, Lindsay himself made a commitment to cutting the public aid budget and demonstrating to voters who opposed government spending that his administration was putting welfare mothers and fathers to work.[12]

Beulah Sanders and the activists who joined her in Washington, D.C., were exceptional citizens of the postwar United States. However, the agenda they put forward in 1970 was far closer to the mainstream than it would have been ten years before or than it would seem ten years later.

Figure 1. Members of the National Welfare Rights Organization occupy the federal Department of Health, Education, and Welfare, 1970. Courtesy *Washington Star* photographic archives, copyright *Washington Post*, reprinted by permission of District of Columbia Public Library.

Figure 2. Welfare activists on their way to jail after the demonstration at HEW.
Courtesy, *Washington Star* photographic archives, copyright *Washington Post*,
reprinted by permission of District of Columbia Public Library.

Questions about public assistance were ubiquitous in debates over
domestic policy at the end of the 1960s and in the early 1970s. At the
moment when the women and men of NWRO occupied the HEW secretary's office, a majority in the U.S. House of Representatives had just
approved the Family Assistance Plan, a massive proposal for welfare
reform drafted by the Nixon administration. This plan competed for the
attention of Washington insiders with the recently issued findings of a
Commission on Income Maintenance that had been appointed by President Johnson shortly before he left office.[13] A long list of eminences,
from conservative economist Milton Friedman to liberal senator George
McGovern, pressed the government to guarantee incomes so that no
family in affluent America would be abjectly poor.

   The battle over welfare rights has been sidelined in narratives of political change in the twentieth century. This is an important lapse. The
questions welfare rights activists posed about poverty, employment, and

parenting, as well as about power and social hierarchy, were critical ones in the 1960s and early 1970s. They remained equally critical and painfully unresolved in the decades that followed. At the same time, it is easy to understand why historians have understated the place of the welfare rights debate in twentieth-century history. The grassroots social movement that took over buildings, along with its affiliate movements in law, social work, academia, and public administration, was almost totally vanquished by the end of the 1970s. When Senator McGovern made a modest income guarantee one plank of his 1972 presidential platform, Republican strategists turned the proposal and the candidate into laughingstocks.[14] The Social Service Employees Union in New York City, whose leaders demanded improvements for welfare recipients along with lower caseloads and higher salaries, lost much of its bargaining power when municipal unions and public assistance clients became scapegoats of the city's fiscal collapse in 1974–75. Lawyers who tried to persuade the Supreme Court that welfare rights were part of the U.S. Constitution lost decisive cases in the early 1970s.[15]

A few years after NWRO's brief takeover of the headquarters of the federal welfare bureaucracy, the welfare rights movement lay in tatters. In New York City, political opposition, benefit cuts, and new eligibility standards took virtually all the wind out of the sails of welfare recipients' activism. Enraged by policy changes, Citywide members attacked their neighborhood welfare offices, upending furniture, terrifying caseworkers, and stoking the fear and resentment of middle- and working-class whites. The National Welfare Rights Organization collapsed into a ring of local action groups.

The major social policy initiatives of the early 1970s rewarded other groups but did little to further the agenda of organized welfare mothers or fathers. With the notable exception of the U.S. Supreme Court decision in *Roe v. Wade*, which legalized abortion in the first two trimesters of a pregnancy, the feminist victories of the period were of limited importance to welfare mothers. Women on welfare, most of whom had little education and minimal economic security, did not benefit much from the bar on sexual discrimination in higher education contained in Title IX (1972), or from the protections contained in the Equal Credit Act (1974).[16] Other initiatives that might have helped low-income families never became law. In the early 1970s, legislation authorizing a universal national child care program, which would have extended benefits to all families regardless of income, passed both houses of Congress, but President Nixon vetoed it as part of his conservative turn. Congress approved the Equal Rights Amendment in 1972, but it was defeated in the states over the following decade. Among programs for the poor, the addition of an automatic Cost of Living Adjustment to Social Security pensions and the creation of Supplemental Security Income (SSI) raised living standards for the impoverished elderly and disabled but not for mothers and children. For its target groups, SSI supplanted previous forms of public assistance, raising the level of grants and making their administration less intrusive. The creation of SSI left women and children behind in old-style public assistance, with benefits that varied from state to state and procedures that often shamed their clients. Without elderly or disabled people as potential allies, impoverished parents and children became even more politically vulnerable than they had been before.[17]

The ideal of welfare rights received some of its harshest blows from a Democratic White House and Republican Congress in the middle 1990s. After Republican majorities came to both houses of Congress in 1994, President Clinton signed a bill to eliminate Aid to Families with Dependent Children (AFDC), the public assistance program for women and children that had existed since the New Deal. During debate, one member of Congress carried a placard that read: "Do not Feed the Alligators."[18] Instead of replacing AFDC with a more comprehensive and administratively simple system, the Personal Responsibility and Work Opportunities Act of 1996 created a new public assistance regime that was as cumbersome as its predecessor had been. In what appeared to be a direct attack on the welfare rights tradition, the authors of the 1996 law denied recipients formal entitlement to public assistance and thus undid one of the major victories the movement and its lawyers had won. The Clinton-era law described marriage and waged labor as the appropriate paths out of poverty for women. It capped each recipient's eligibility for financial help at five years over the whole course of her life and allowed individual states to curtail benefits even further.[19]

Despite its defeats, the idea of a right to welfare continued as a dissident strain in the politics of the late twentieth and early twenty-first centuries. In the summer of 2000, for example, the Kensington Welfare Rights Union, an activist group that was born in the middle 1990s, led thousands on a march through the streets of Philadelphia. Low-income mothers, disabled people in wheelchairs, and opponents of U.S.-led globalization had come to protest on the first day of the Republican National Convention.[20] In 2002, one-third of the Democratic caucus of the House of Representatives signed on to legislation that would have restored welfare rights to thousands by defining the uncompensated duties of mothers as "work" under federal welfare-to-work programs.[21] This legislation was introduced by Representative Patsy Mink, who had been the first woman of color in the U.S. House when she was first elected in the 1960s. In 2004, hundreds of welfare rights advocates, calling for a Basic Income Grant for all people, gathered in Barcelona,

Spain, to participate in a wide-ranging multinational conversation about the future of human rights. They learned about progress toward guaranteed incomes in countries such as Brazil, Belgium, and Spain, and in U.S. states such as Alaska.[22]

The legacy of welfare rights was evident in battles over wages as well as in those over public benefits. Under the leadership of a former Citywide staff member named Gary Delgado, the Center for Third World Organizing spurred activism among welfare recipients in Oakland, California, and trained organizers who joined an array of movements for social change. The Association of Community Organizations for Reform Now (ACORN), founded by welfare rights veteran Wade Rathke, helped low-income workers across the U.S. demand a "living wage" for their labor. Other efforts to create living wages were spearheaded by the Industrial Areas Foundation, an agency originally founded by the organizer Saul Alinsky. In the 1960s, Alinsky and his allies had trained welfare rights leaders and helped them develop strategies with which to build a movement.[23]

The questions that animated welfare rights activists from the 1960s through the early twenty-first century remain. Can we be citizens if we do not have enough to eat, or to clothe our children decently? When some members of a society prosper, shouldn't the rest of us gain as well? When disagreements arise about what poor people should receive from the government, who decides? And how?

The Battle over Welfare Rights explains how welfare rights came to the fore in both movement-oriented and mainstream politics. It argues that women and men who received public aid had long been dissatisfied. They were able to organize collectively in the early 1960s because the black freedom movement in the North and South, and the post-World War II government, made resources available that they had never had before. These resources were material, in the form of financial help, office space, and staff that came from local outposts of the federal War on Poverty. They were also rhetorical, in the form of the rights language that was popularized by the freedom movement and the U.S. Supreme Court under Chief Justice Earl Warren. The civil rights movement, the War on Poverty, and the language of rights made the City-Wide Coordinating Committee possible in New York City, and it enabled the formative welfare rights organizing that occurred elsewhere.[24]

Second, *The Battle over Welfare Rights* explores the ideas and strategies of Citywide and NWRO. This book treats poor women and men as thinkers as well as actors. Beulah Sanders and other activists created political theories from the materials available to them. They drew on, and transformed, Anglo-American legal and political traditions and the rights discourse of postwar United States. At the center of their approach to politics was a vision of citizenship. Welfare recipients and their allies believed that the rights for mothers that had been written into public policy in the New Deal period should apply to all low-income parents and not just to the respectable white women who had been their primary beneficiaries in the years between the New Deal and the 1960s. They saw the United States as an affluent society in which citizenship entailed access to the consumer goods that allowed children to hold their heads up in school and made women look and feel presentable. Citizenship meant full participation in the economic, legal and governmental institutions that shaped people's lives.[25]

Finally, this book explains why claims for welfare rights were pushed so far to the margins that they nearly disappeared from memory. Welfare recipients lost power and their ideas lost currency because local and national politics changed dramatically at the end of the 1960s. As the 1970s began, the black freedom movement was in disarray. The War on Poverty had been lost, thanks to federal squeamishness about the conflicts it inevitably inspired as well as the costs of the war in Vietnam. The culture of affluence that had reigned through the prior decade received a series of decisive blows: President Nixon devalued the dollar, imposed wage and price controls, and took the U.S. off the gold standard; oil prices soared after the 1973 war among Israel, Egypt, and Syria; and New York City teetered on the edge of bankruptcy. The Warren Court, which had encouraged a whole range of social have-nots to speak the language of legal rights and look to the courts for the redress of their grievances, came to an end when the chief justice retired in 1969. A new grassroots conservative movement made its presence felt powerfully, especially among Republicans. In New York, Governor Nelson Rockefeller, once the leader of the liberal wing of the Republican Party, turned toward the political Right. He chose welfare as an issue with which to build a bridge to increasingly conservative voters. Mayor Lindsay, also a liberal Republican, sought ways to mute what journalist Pete Hamill termed white lower-middle-class rebellion.[26] When this effort failed, he implemented new controls on welfare recipients and left the Republican Party.

When it is remembered, the welfare rights movement is usually treated as one of the great errors of postwar history. For example, Tommy Thompson, who served as secretary of Health and Human Services in the administration of George W. Bush, has claimed that welfare rights activists, who once seized the state legislature in Wisconsin to protest benefit cuts, succeeded only in persuading him that the U.S. was a society in trouble. The welfare rights movement, he has argued, turned him into a life-long opponent of public aid programs.[27] Former New York City official Charles Morris counted welfare rights activists as among

those who pressed "the costs of good intentions" on a Lindsay administration that could not afford them and proved tragically unwilling to say
no.[28] Journalists and policy analysts have seen the City-Wide Coordinating Committee of Welfare Groups and NWRO as militant organizations
that did much to tear the Democratic Party apart in New York and
nationally. Chroniclers of social welfare policy, beginning with former
Nixon administration official Daniel Patrick Moynihan, have made
NWRO a leading culprit in congressional defeat of the administration's
ambitious plan for welfare reform.[29]

Moynihan, Charles Morris, and other students of twentieth-century
politics have considered the welfare rights movement against the general background of social change in the 1960s. They have emphasized
such factors as the rights consciousness of the black freedom movement, the uses activist social movements made of law in the era of the
Warren Court, the culture of consumption, and the expanding national
government after World War Two. However, the point of emphasizing
rights, law, consumption, and the widening state has often been to
make a larger argument about what went wrong with postwar political
culture and social life. Rights, according to theorists such as Mary Ann
Glendon, have promoted individualism, weakening social identities and
community life. Political scientist Gerold Rosenberg has claimed that
twentieth-century efforts to create social change through the courts
embodied a "hollow hope" that could never have been fulfilled. In the
context of the postwar labor movement, historian Nelson Lichtenstein
has written, the language of rights led toward litigation and away from
organizing; it allowed workers to articulate grievances based on race,
gender, and age, but silenced those based on economic class. Political
historian Alan Brinkley has defined post-New Deal liberalism by its
simultaneous concern with rights and consumerism. A focus on consumerism, he has written, was a particularly faulty choice for liberals,
because it shifted attention away from employment and production and
narrowed political struggle.[30] The expanding postwar state is not quite
as unpopular among scholars as either rights or consumerism. But journalist Nicholas Lemann has argued that government efforts under the
War on Poverty, such as Community Action Programs, were at best mis-
guided approaches to solving the poverty problem. At worst, these
experiments starved funds and distracted constituencies from more
meaningful approaches to ending poverty, such as public employment
programs. Conservative writer Charles Murray has claimed that the
Legal Services Program, initiated under the War on Poverty, failed
because its employees sparked dissent among welfare recipients and
other people who were living on the margins of the affluent society.[31]

The history of welfare rights refutes some of these arguments about the modern United States and complicates others. Citywide and NWRO did not break up the Democratic Party. Reformist Republican John Lindsay would never have ascended to the New York City mayoralty in 1965 if the Democratic electoral coalition in the city had not already dissolved by that point. The main reason the Democratic Party fractured in New York was that its political machine was unable or unwilling to serve the needs of its African American and Puerto Rican constituents. At the national level, the Democratic Party split over civil rights and the war in Vietnam. This process began long before the first national welfare rights meeting. It was clearly visible in 1964, when members of the black freedom movement and white segregationists appeared at the Democratic National Convention and centrist Democrats failed to satisfy either of them. It became even more apparent after 1965, when domestic opposition to the war in Vietnam raged within the Democratic Party as well as between Democrats and Republicans.

The welfare rights movement did not defeat the Nixon administration's ambitious welfare reform plan. For this, the administration had mostly itself to blame. In 1969, President Nixon favored the plan, which would have added millions to the public assistance rolls. One year later, he told an advisor to be "sure it was killed," and three years later he publicly rejected a compromise on the proposal that had been reached by a hardworking group of U.S. senators and midlevel officials from his own administration.[32] Nixon changed his position because politics changed between 1969 and 1972. Urban riots and civil rights protests died down after 1969, and conflicts over the war in Southeast Asia escalated, especially after Nixon announced in the spring of 1970 that U.S. forces had crossed the border from Vietnam into Cambodia. Massive protests were followed by counter-protests. The result was a society more sharply divided than it had been when Nixon was elected. The welfare reform plan, which Daniel Patrick Moynihan and other members of the administration had originally framed as a boon to Southern whites whom they were courting for a new Republican electoral coalition, continued to have rhetorical value. But the administration ceased to make passage of it a priority.

In terms of rights, this book supports the tempered optimism of law professor Patricia Williams, who has written about the value of rights language for women of color and other relative outsiders to U.S. politics and law.[33] Within Citywide and NWRO, disenfranchised people formed a common agenda for social change—and even talked about economic inequality under capitalism—within a rights framework. Moreover, the history of welfare rights demonstrates that the promise that law could help achieve social change was more than a "hollow hope" for the members of at least one grassroots movement. For a period during the Warren Court era, formal legal strategies actively supported grassroots politics. Activist lawyers and activists in the black freedom movement ceased to make progress in the 1970s because historical circumstances changed, not because they allied with one another.

While mass consumption and a political economy built around it were hardly ideal, they were facts of life in the postwar United States. The history of welfare rights demonstrates that a culture and political economy of consumption did not forestall meaningful campaigns for social change. To the contrary, welfare mothers and fathers politicized their relationships with consumer society and entered the public stage as increasingly empowered citizen-consumers.[34]

The federal Community Action Programs and Legal Services Program, both of which were part of the War on Poverty, made enormous differences in low-income communities. Poor people often expressed frustration with the limitations of the War on Poverty. But even their frustration spurred action and organizing efforts that helped build social movements such as the one chronicled in this book.

In a very different work of storytelling from the past, historian Natalie Zemon Davis commented that her most basic ambition was to demonstrate that "astonishing things are possible."[35] While the events in this book occurred within the living memory of many of the people with whom I have discussed them, accounts of them have sometimes seemed to arrive on my desk not merely from a distinct moment in the past but from a distant planet. In sharing the history of welfare rights I, too, wish to recall that astonishing things are possible. The past does not exist to teach later generations a lesson. In the case of welfare rights, however, it offers an opportunity to see that astonishing things are possible even in modern U.S. politics. It also offers an opportunity to see that what has been done, no matter how astonishing, can be undone in the blink of an eye.

Chapter 1
Inventing Welfare Rights

By 1963 a version of civil rights had come to the northern slums and ghettos, a sort of version of rights talk, rights feeling, rights passion but it was very much economic rights. Nobody dared say welfare rights out loud before there was a welfare rights movement. But still these women were affected by that spirit.

—Frances Fox Piven, *welfare rights activist and scholar*

On June 30, 1966, fifteen hundred women and men gathered under the hazy sun at New York's City Hall to demand something they called "welfare rights." New York was hardly a stranger to protest or civic drama, but the city had not seen so many poor people demonstrating for decades. It had probably never seen a group like this, African American, Puerto Rican, and white, from all corners of the city. Beulah Sanders, a welfare recipient and one of the leaders of the event, remembered that she and her colleagues had recruited members to the new cause of welfare rights one at a time. They "walked the street, knocking on doors, talking to people, you know, saying, Miss, are you on welfare, are you low income, in order to get people to talk."[1] The event at City Hall was the achievement of the City-Wide Coordinating Committee of Welfare Groups, a coalition only a month and a half old. Its mandate was to represent more than fifty poverty rights organizations that had sprouted across the city in the prior three years. In addition to Sanders, an African American woman who had left New Bern, North Carolina, for New York with her twin boys in 1955, the group's leaders included community organizer Jennette Washington from the Upper West Side of Manhattan, an African American woman who had been in New York City since she was ten years old and had joined the welfare rolls because her mother was no longer able to provide child care while she was at work. Sanders and Washington were joined in the leadership of the new movement by Puerto Rican organizer, artist, and electrical worker Frank Espada from Brooklyn, and the white intellectuals Richard Cloward and Frances Fox

Piven from Columbia University and the Manhattan antipoverty project Mobilization for Youth.[2]

Beulah Sanders, Jennette Washington, and other members of the City-Wide Coordinating Committee of Welfare Groups proposed a wide range of changes in the welfare system. They asked for higher welfare grants and better access to the consumer goods that were ubiquitous in post-World War II America, plus jobs, job training, and day care for mothers who wanted it. They demanded that city officials pay burial expenses for everyone on public aid so that they and their loved ones would not wind up in paupers' graves. Members of Citywide argued that people who received public assistance were citizens who deserved the same legal safeguards that all other citizens deserved. They demanded that caseworkers stop investigating their homes and snooping into their personal lives, and that the welfare department give every recipient an opportunity to appeal a caseworker's decisions before losing benefits. Finally, they sought better social services: more hospitals, health centers, and clinics; caseworkers with smaller caseloads and more time to spend with clients; and regular meetings with the Commissioner of Welfare.[3]

In response to their demands, welfare commissioner Mitchell Ginsberg broke precedent. He heard the grievances and proposals of twenty-five Citywide members, led by Espada. It was the first time since public assistance became a national responsibility in the 1930s that a New York City welfare chief met face-to-face with his primary constituents. Ginsberg, a former dean of the Columbia University School of Social Work, sympathized with the recipients' situation and agreed with most of their proposals. In response to a request for supplementary grants for "decent school clothing" for children, he and Deputy Mayor Timothy Costello pledged to raise the clothing portion of the welfare budget by 10 percent. Ginsberg and Costello said they could not raise welfare grants across the board, but Costello promised to help get the change by lobbying the state legislature in Albany alongside the activists.[4] "They were very sympathetic," commented a picketer named Virginia Snipe; however, she added, "people on welfare can't eat sympathy."[5]

The demonstration on June 30, and its easy access to City Hall, announced the arrival of a new movement in New York City. At the same time, activists from coast to coast announced the arrival of a nationwide movement for welfare rights. In Ohio a "Walk for Adequate Welfare," from the racially divided city of Cleveland to the state capitol in Columbus, mirrored the black civil rights movement's long march from Selma to Montgomery and the James Meredith march in Mississippi.[6] As the marchers left Cleveland on June 20, Carl Stokes, who had just missed becoming the first African American mayor of a major U.S. city in a 1965 election, said that it was "more significant than the Mississippi march—

because it's here and it's about our problems."[7] When they arrived in Columbus on June 30, marchers asked their governor and state legislature to revise the "standard of need," the estimate of basic consumer prices on which social workers based welfare grants, to reflect increases in the cost of living. "Tramp, tramp, tramp," they sang, "we walk for welfare . . . 'Cause the children are in need / With checks to[o] small to clothe and feed . . . If we put shoes on the feet / Then there's not enough to eat / That's why we ask the Governor for more."[8]

Organizers reported twenty-five welfare rights actions in all on June 30, 1966, involving more than one hundred local groups and six thousand poor people and their friends. Farthest from Manhattan were the demonstrations in Los Angeles, Berkeley, and San Bernadino, California.[9] A group in Syracuse marched on the headquarters of the public aid department, demanding new furniture and an end to "night raids," or unannounced searches of women's homes by welfare department personnel. In Louisville, Kentucky, members of the West End Community Council asked that officials rescind "the policy which now limits welfare recipients to one can of meat per month."[10] Connecticut welfare recipients and middle-class activists, including members of the New Haven Congress of Racial Equality (CORE), marched to the state welfare office, demanding higher grants and the resolution of twenty-five complaints brought by individual clients. In Jackson, Mississippi, the Hinds County Freedom Democratic Party Welfare Committee sponsored a public meeting to coincide with the demonstrations around the country on June 30.[11]

Local welfare activism in New York and Los Angeles was remarkable. But a welfare rights movement that could coordinate political action across the country was an astounding development in the summer of 1966. The demonstrations kept questions about economic justice and public benefits on the national agenda at a moment when divisions over strategy among reformers, and a rising conservative movement, threatened to make them disappear. They also brought women's issues and voices to the fore in new ways. Both the "Second Wave" women's movement that began in the early 1960s and the postwar civil rights movement had often sidelined poor women and women of color. However, low-income women were at the center of a political movement about welfare. The protests offered hope to those who believed in the promise of the federal War on Poverty, which President Johnson and his advisers had instigated in 1964, but from which they had begun to retreat as soon as antipoverty programs became controversial.[12]

The nationwide welfare campaign was one extraordinary moment in the rights revolution that challenged so many traditional hierarchies in the 1950s, 1960s, and 1970s. As Citywide ally Frances Fox Piven later argued, this new movement was one manifestation of the passion for "economic rights" that mixed with more familiar civil rights demands in the middle 1960s.[13] It joined welfare with rights, bids for material well-being with those for political recognition, dignity, and respect.[14] It relied on the dissatisfaction of poor and working-class citizens, especially women of color. These welfare clients and would-be clients wanted to feed their children better. They also wanted access to decently waged jobs and better service at government offices. Beyond these discrete demands, the women and men of the welfare rights movement wanted first-class citizenship in the post-World War II United States. This meant gaining full access to its ballot boxes, its courtrooms, and its consumer marketplaces.

In the thirty years between the launching of federal aid to the poor under the New Deal and the emergence of welfare rights activism, poor women and men engaged in a variety of individual acts of protest against welfare department practices.[15] In the middle 1960s, what had been individual protest became collective and openly political. This happened because people's experiences in the late 1950s and early 1960s reshaped their expectations, and changes in government programs redrew the map of resources that were available to those who were dissatisfied. The black freedom movement inspired hope in African Americans, Puerto Ricans, Mexican Americans, and poor whites. The tactics and much of the nonviolent troop strength of the welfare rights campaign came from organizing efforts that preceded it, South and North. A largely forgotten prehistory of civil rights campaigns over schools, housing, police brutality, public benefits, and participation in urban political machines was especially important in building the fire that later activists set around welfare rights.[16] Government programs such as urban renewal and the War on Poverty promised to make major changes but ended up serving the middle class at least as much as they served poor people. These programs inspired optimism and disappointment in equal measure; they made it possible for many residents of low-income communities to organize politically; and they frustrated people in ways that often sparked even more organizing. The federal appellate courts, led by the U.S. Supreme Court under Chief Justice Earl Warren, helped popularize the language of rights, which welfare activists used to express their claims for economic well-being.

The forces that spawned welfare rights organizing were national in scope. They inspired poor women and men to mobilize all over the country. But New York City led the way. Welfare recipients in the boroughs of Brooklyn and Manhattan began to make collective demands on the public aid bureaucracy years before there was a national welfare rights movement. By 1966, more residents of New York than of any other city were committed to the cause of welfare rights. Beyond New York City, welfare recipients and their middle-class allies from the state of California and the city of Syracuse made the greatest contributions to the movement.

A Movement in the Urban North

On June 30, 1963, three years to the day before the national welfare rights demonstrations, journalist Gertrude Samuels published a prophetic article in the *New York Times Magazine*. The article, "Even More Crucial Than in the South," focused on the "economic and social discrimination" African Americans faced in five Northern cities. New York headed the list. Samuels warned that the city faced a "potentially explosive" situation and the likelihood of mass demonstrations.[17] She was right. Although New York City was free of legal segregation, racial tensions persisted over basic issues such as economic security, jobs, housing, education, and fair treatment by the police. Although Samuels did not notice it, New York was also rife with gender discrimination and tension over such issues as fathers' desertion of their families, sex-segregated employment, and mixed messages about women's proper roles.

Within the welfare system, the situation had become "explosive" well before 1963. Public welfare in postwar New York was a gathering point for negative political attitudes based on race, gender, and economic class. Beliefs about welfare also reflected popular concerns about women's sexuality, anxiety over South-to-North migration, and bias against those who spoke Spanish. In 1961, the city manager of Newburgh, New York, went on the offensive against public assistance, accusing "migrant-type citizens" of soaking up local funds. His proposals for cutting public assistance served to embarrass the Democrats who were in charge of the program at the national level and Nelson Rockefeller, the liberal Republican in the New York governor's mansion. The controversy in Newburgh became a favorite cause of anti-New Deal conservatives, including Senator Barry Goldwater of Arizona, who was preparing to run for President.[18]

Governor Rockefeller responded to the controversy by appointing a "Moreland Commission," or independent investigative body, on public welfare. As the commission discovered, the people of Newburgh were not the only ones who had reservations about welfare. A public opinion survey conducted for the commission found that "virtually one-third of the New Yorkers questioned said that they believed 40 percent or more of all relief recipients were chiseling 'in one way or another.'" Close to another third believed that "chiseling" prevailed among 11 to 39 percent of those on the rolls.[19] Individual citizens also complained about the welfare system. One New York City resident wrote to Mayor Robert F. Wagner, Jr., in 1962 to declaim against recipients, "the worst schemers you have seen . . . they love every thing for nothing, think we are good suckers, they are up looking at the real late show sleep to 1–2 o'clock Boy they got some racket."[20] The *New York Times* editorialized against "families that are coming to accept dependence as a way of life," and at least one member of the City Council demanded an inquiry into possible misuses of funds by the Department of Welfare.[21]

The Moreland Commission found that the welfare system was inadequate as well as unpopular. Its report described the state public assistance program as "one of the most narrow, restrictive, and complex in the United States."[22] According to the staff of the commission, clients received minimal information but were subjected to repeated investigations into their eligibility for benefits. In New York City, new caseworkers routinely went on the job with three and a half weeks of training. Slightly more than a third of welfare department staff members were satisfied with their jobs, a number that was among the lowest in the nation.[23]

Clients were no more satisfied than were their caseworkers. Hundreds wrote to Mayor Wagner to complain about their benefits and the way they were treated by officials. Brooklyn resident Fannie Blackwell, for example, told the mayor that her checks were delayed. "I need beds and mattresses the . . . floors are worn out the padding is coming out of the chairs and first of all I really want clothing for school," she wrote breathlessly. "I want to know why some thing cant be done for me."[24] Edward Powers asked Wagner to intervene to get him some warm clothes for the winter. "I have phone wrote & tried to get a ancer one way or another," he explained. "I have all ways voated Democrat & would love to voat this year can you help me. I want no special priveliges only justic."[25] Albertha White of Manhattan chastised the mayor. She held him to account for the bad meals she had to feed her three boys and the scraping she had to do to make ends meet on welfare. "Mr. Roosevelt did not intend for this to happen," she wrote. "This was a welfare for children. Now Mr. Mayor our Job is not in Mississippi" but in New York City.[26]

Of the issues journalist Gertrude Samuels highlighted in 1963, housing was the first to emerge as a cause for large-scale protest. After months of threats by the civil rights group CORE, a group of tenants in Harlem, the overwhelmingly African American and Puerto Rican Manhattan neighborhood, began a rent strike in September 1963 with the support of activist undergraduates. Its slogan, "No Repairs No Rent," had wide appeal. Under the leadership of community organizer Jesse Gray, the rent strike movement spread across Harlem and into the Lower East Side of Manhattan, the East Bronx, and other neighborhoods. By early 1964, the administration of Mayor Wagner had effectively ratified the strikes at several buildings and begun inspections on others. The mayor proposed expanding the system of special courts to hear housing-related complaints and tightening the penalties for landlords who violated the city housing code.[27]

Part of the appeal of the rent protest lay in the wide difference between its approach to housing problems and the approach typically taken by the Wagner administration. Like virtually all big-city mayors of the period, Wagner was in the thrall of "urban renewal," a federally funded program to transform city neighborhoods and increase their commercial value, which was authorized by the federal Housing Acts of 1949 and 1954. Under the urban renewal program, city governments were responsible for slum clearance; they took control of urban tracts through the municipalities' power of eminent domain, tearing down tenement buildings and displacing their tenants. Private developers or other government entities then built new structures on the cleared sites.[28]

As the writer Jane Jacobs argued poignantly about city neighborhoods including Harlem, the Upper West Side, and Morningside Heights, so-called urban renewal policies that replaced diverse communities with luxury housing or large public buildings diminished city life.[29] Urban renewal policy in theory served "the city as a whole," but often in practice served wealthy developers and established politicians at the expense of working-class people and communities of color that were displaced from the sites. Columbia University sociologist Herbert Gans reported that between 1949 and 1964, only one-half of 1 percent of federal urban renewal spending was devoted to relocating families and individuals from renewal sites to other homes.[30]

Among the most controversial urban renewal efforts in New York City was that on the Upper West Side of Manhattan. Tenants in the area south of Harlem and slightly west of Central Park fought a bitter, prolonged battle in the late 1950s and early 1960s for a neighborhood that would continue to serve their needs. Beulah Sanders and Jennette Washington were veterans of the protests on the Upper West Side. Their staunchest middle-class ally was Father Henry Browne, a Catholic priest at St. Gregory's Church in the urban renewal district and leader of a local antipoverty agency called the Strycker's Bay Neighborhood Council. Under a provision in the federal housing law, city governments were required to consult with local communities when they created urban renewal plans. The Wagner administration in City Hall chose to consult only with fairly elite New Yorkers. The Strycker's Bay group constituted itself as an alternative advisory committee.[31] When it became clear that city leaders wanted to build luxury and middle-class housing that would raise the neighborhood's tax yield but do little to improve the apart-

Figure 3. New York City activist Beulah Sanders. Courtesy *Washington Star* photographic archives, copyright *Washington Post*, reprinted by permission of District of Columbia Public Library.

ment stock available to working-class and poor families, Father Browne organized increasingly disruptive protests.[32] As a result of neighborhood pressure, the Wagner administration promised 2,500 low-income housing units—as well as 4,000 middle-income units and 2,500 high-income ones—on the West Side site.[33]

Hundreds of West Side residents, including Beulah Sanders and Jennette Washington, did not benefit even from the city's improved plan. Most of the new low-income housing on the site was not affordable to those poor enough to qualify for welfare. Even public housing had criteria (e.g., the absence of "illegitimate" children) that kept many families out. Bureaucratic mix-ups also interfered with families' efforts to relocate. Sanders, for example, moved with her children three times early in the urban renewal process, apparently because she received faulty information. "We're just like gypsies . . . except we don't have a covered wagon," she commented. Jennette Washington and her five children applied for admission to public housing but were rejected as a "potential problem" because they failed some of the Housing Authority's tests of good conduct. "You have to pass 28 standards of behavior, and I figure I could pass about three," Washington told a journalist.[34] In the initial stage of planning for the West Side site, Washington refused to move from her home. Someone from the Strycker's Bay Neighborhood Council invited her to the office and introduced her to activism on urban renewal and other issues.

Local struggles over housing, coupled with the national visibility of the black freedom movement, catalyzed a wave of demonstrations in New York City. In February 1964, African Americans and Latinos/as engineered a massive boycott of the city's public schools to protest racial segregation. The boycott became the largest civil rights demonstration in U.S. history until that time. Dr. Martin Luther King, Jr., commended its leaders for having "punctured the thin veneer of the North's racial self-righteousness."[35] Indeed, educational segregation had increased steadily in New York since the *Brown v. Board* decision in 1954; 74 schools in the city had student bodies that were 90 percent African American or Puerto Rican in 1958, but that number had risen to 104 by 1961 and to 117 in 1963.[36]

Another major explosion came on the opening day of the New York City World's Fair, April 22, 1964. Three local CORE chapters coordinated a "stall-in" of cars on the Long Island Expressway, a major artery to the fair, as well as protests at the fair site. They complained about African American and Latino workers not getting jobs building and staffing the fair and about the presence of particular companies that CORE accused of employment discrimination (e.g., Schaefer Beer). More generally, they objected that the fair, which included a Court of

Peace in the shadow of the "United States Steel Unisphere," plus two separate Fountains of Progress, misrepresented U.S. policies at home and abroad. Protesters shouting "Freedom Now!" drowned out part of a dedication speech by President Johnson. Civil rights leaders with national reputations, including Bayard Rustin, who had organized the 1963 March on Washington and coordinated the New York school boycott, opposed the demonstrations. But hundreds of CORE members participated.[37]

Frank Espada protested at the Schaefer Beer Pavilion. He was a committed community organizer, one of the architects of rent and school strikes in Brooklyn. However, Espada supported his family by working as a contractor for a company that did electrical wiring. By coincidence, Schaefer Beer hired that company to wire its World's Fair pavilion and the firm asked him to staff the pavilion on opening day. Espada left a few of the doors open to let protesters enter. "No one got hurt," he remembered, "but they were dancing on the bar—you know they had this beautiful bar. So everybody got busted."[38] His son Martín wrote a poem years later in which he admitted fearing that his father was dead when he disappeared after the World's Fair opening: "In 1964, I had never tasted beer / and no one told me about the picket signs / torn in two by the cops of brewery. / . . . That day my father returned / from the netherworld / easily as riding the elevator to apartment 14-F / and the brewery cops could only watch in drunken disappointment / I searched my father's hands for a sign of the miracle."[39]

The unresolved tensions around housing, schools, and economic inequality erupted into devastating riots the summer after the World's Fair opened. The July 1964 outbursts in Harlem and the Bedford-Stuyvesant neighborhood in Brooklyn were the first major urban riots of the 1960s. The chaos in Harlem started with the fatal shooting of an unarmed fifteen-year-old African American boy by a white police officer. Fifty to sixty people marched on the officer's police station, demanding his ouster. Police responded with a massive show of force, and black Harlemites swelled the ranks of protesters. Violence between citizens and police raged for over seventy-two hours. *New York Amsterdam News* correspondent James Booker found the roots of the riot in "civil rights doubletalk from City Hall . . . [and] slickly-written press releases . . . Too long, now," he wrote after observing the riots firsthand, "Harlem residents complain of being over exploited by both black and white politicians and businessmen, overstudied by the sociologists and do-gooders, and over-sensationalized by circulation-happy newspapers, and television stations."[40] In Bedford-Stuyvesant, a mass meeting about the shooting sponsored by Brooklyn CORE turned into two nights of "violence and vandalism."[41] The violence spread to Rochester, New York, and Patterson and Jersey City, New Jersey, after similar incidents of alleged police brutality.[42]

The riots shone a spotlight on the dissatisfaction simmering in many black and Latino/a communities. One consequence was that local political leaders went on the offensive against an innovative antipoverty initiative they accused of fomenting unrest. Mobilization for Youth (MFY) was a wide-ranging organization on Manhattan's Lower East Side. The participants in MFY projects were predominantly Puerto Rican and African American, with smaller numbers of Jewish, Irish, and Italian Lower East Siders who had stayed in the neighborhood after most whites fled to the suburbs. President Kennedy had inaugurated MFY personally by announcing from the White House lawn that the project would receive a federal grant of $13.5 million. MFY's efforts to prevent juvenile delinquency led to organizing among tenants of slum buildings and support for families that participated in the rent strikes Jesse Gray coordinated from Harlem. MFY also assisted parents and children who participated in the citywide school boycott. After the riots, a committee of the MFY board of directors joined Harlem leaders in calling for a Civilian Complaint Review Board independent of the Police Department, to investigate citizen charges of police misconduct.[43]

These developments provoked a political response. The Wagner administration stopped funding MFY and started investigating the agency as what one reporter called "a suspected Red honeycomb for leftists who have used its facilities—and juveniles—to foment strikes and racial disorders."[44] A study by the FBI, which former Kennedy administration staff member Daniel Patrick Moynihan took credit for initiating, found two Communist Party members and three "leftists" at MFY.[45] William F. Buckley's conservative *National Review* magazine took the red-baiting so far as to label the program "MFYovitch."[46] However, an attorney who conducted a review of MFY for its board found nothing worse than a low-level employee who had run for office with the Socialist Workers Party and "de facto support without pro forma endorsement" of the school boycott.[47]

Toward Citywide

Riots and grassroots protests had paradoxical effects. They inspired the controversy over Mobilization for Youth, but they also gave social change campaigns in New York City breathing room that they might not otherwise have had. The riots in particular terrified city officials, who wanted to prevent a recurrence more than they wanted to lambaste unconventional agencies working with impoverished African Americans and Puerto Ricans. MFY, the Strycker's Bay Neighborhood Council on the

Upper West Side, and the activist groups Frank Espada was coordinating in Brooklyn all weathered the storm of reaction.

MFY and one of the community groups Espada had organized in Brooklyn sponsored the first welfare rights organizing in New York City. Espada found that 80 to 85 percent of the people who asked his group for help were welfare recipients. Late in 1964, he and other activists established a Welfare Recipients League. Word spread about it, and chapters grew in other neighborhoods. By January 1966, there were at least ten Welfare Recipients Leagues around the city. Espada established contact with Richard Cloward, research director of MFY.[48] "We started talking primarily about rights, which is what that organization was about," Espada recalled. "The most important thing that happened as a result of that was that we found a lot of very strong leadership in women. I don't think we ran into any men in the Welfare Recipients League in that whole period, but we found some very strong leadership and these were women who took, essentially, the group that we had helped start and ran with it."[49]

Welfare rights activism emerged at MFY in much the same way it did in Brooklyn. MFY had opened its first Neighborhood Services Center in November 1962. The center was inundated with requests for material aid. The people who asked for help were eligible for public assistance but not receiving it.[50] Once residents of the Lower East Side had placed welfare issues on the front burner of their consciousness, the MFY staff made a major discovery: studying the records of families that sought help, as well as research about low-income New Yorkers, they concluded that for every family that received benefits another just as poor did not. Moreover, a majority of families on the welfare rolls received only their basic cash grants, although welfare regulations stipulated that they were eligible for a range of supplements in cash and in kind.[51]

Jennette Washington and Beulah Sanders at the Strycker's Bay Neighborhood Council came to welfare organizing slightly later than did Espada in Brooklyn and Cloward on the Lower East Side. In 1964, Sanders was employed as a nonprofessional "community worker" under a program established by the federal government. She began organizing welfare recipients as part of her job.[52] Sanders and Washington met for the first time at a poor people's conference. They decided to found the West Side Welfare Recipients League, borrowing the name from the groups in Brooklyn. Like Espada and the MFY staff, Jennette Washington discovered that welfare organizing was an immediate success. "Suddenly," she commented, people "said they were sick of conditions on welfare and were now ready to band together."[53]

Of all the factors that fueled the growth of the welfare rights movement in New York, the dissatisfaction of poor people was the most important. A steady stream of writers to the Harlem newspaper, the *New York Amsterdam News*, testified to sheer need and the wear and tear women felt from the mixed messages they received about their proper roles. "I am on welfare and believe me this is no picnic," announced one "Mixed up mother." She wanted to work for wages while ensuring that her children were well cared for. However, child care agencies were invariably too expensive, and their staff members asked why she wanted to be in the labor market instead of staying home full-time.[54] Another woman, who could not receive welfare because she owned a small amount of property, begged for help. "I have no money for food or medicine," or a telephone, Marie Gibbons wrote. "I don't feel safe with a young baby a month old in the house without a phone."[55]

The City-Wide Coordinating Committee of Welfare Groups grew from this seedbed of discontent. Citywide was a stitching together of the organizational efforts of the Brooklyn Welfare Recipients Leagues, the Strycker's Bay Neighborhood Council, MFY and other local agencies. Frank Espada, Jennette Washington, and Beulah Sanders first collaborated with the staff of MFY in December 1965. Together, they organized a meeting about the welfare system and the federally funded poverty programs, which they called the People's War Council Against Poverty.[56] In April 1966, they collaborated on a conference about welfare issues, the purpose of which was to help public aid recipients get their "full rights—what they are entitled to under the law, immediately."[57] This meeting culminated in the decision to create a City-Wide Coordinating Committee of Welfare Groups that would sponsor a demonstration at City Hall. Espada and Washington joined the Citywide Executive Board.[58]

Welfare and Its Workers

Simultaneous with the organizing among welfare clients and potential clients, hundreds of employees of the city welfare department left their trade union to join an independent, militant alternative. The Social Services Employees Union (SSEU) was formed by welfare workers who believed that their interests were not being served by their existing union, Local 371 of the behemoth District Council 37 of the American Federation of State, County, and Municipal Employees (AFSCME). After years of spadework, SSEU won an October 1964 election to represent a range of welfare department employees in collective bargaining. These welfare workers followed other public service employees in New York City in creating new unions. Hospital workers had recently formed Local 1199 of the Retail Drug Employees Union, and public school teachers had joined the independent United Federation of Teachers.[59]

New York's welfare workers went on strike in January 1965. The month-long action, called jointly by SSEU and Local 371, involved approximately 90 percent of the welfare caseworkers and 50 percent of the clerical workers, despite the fact that the state's Condon-Wadlin law forbade walkouts by public employees. The caseworkers and other employees demanded "Rehabilitation Not Humliation"—for themselves as well as for their clients.[60] To improve their working conditions, as well as their ability to serve poor families, they asked for substantial reductions in their caseloads. They also demanded salary increases, nicer offices and buildings, and better vacation and leave time. Local members of CORE encouraged welfare clients to think of the welfare workers' struggle as their own, to "keep the Welfare Centers busy" and overwhelmed by bringing problems to offices that were understaffed because of the strike.[61]

The Wagner administration responded by cutting strikers from the personnel roles. For only the second time since the Condon-Wadlin law took effect in 1947, the city sent strikers and their union leaders to jail. The welfare workers' action lasted longer than any previous mobilization up to that point by New York's public employees. It was resolved when the parties agreed to submit the unions' demands to a panel weighted in their favor and to remove all the penalties imposed on workers during the strike.[62]

The contracts signed months later by the unions and the city gave the welfare caseworkers much of what they wanted. The strike and negotiations established the start-up SSEU, alongside the established Local 371, as a legitimate bargaining agent vis-à-vis the city administration. The demands articulated by the new union widened the scope of issues that were subject to collective bargaining between the city and its employees, creating the possibility of a powerful alliance between organized welfare workers and organized clients.[63] If the workers demanded higher welfare grants and lower caseloads so that they could provide more attention to each client, while the clients created chaos inside welfare offices when their caseworkers were out on strike, then both would benefit.

Welfare and Rights in California

Outside New York City, welfare rights in the early 1960s took root most successfully in California. The movement there germinated at the same time that it did in New York. Its development followed similar patterns, inspired by the black freedom movement and by the promise if not the reality of government efforts to help the poor. However, the evolution of the welfare rights movement in California also differed somewhat from the evolution of Citywide. In Northern California, activists among the blind, who had fought the state government successfully to improve their public assistance benefits, were integral to the development of the movement. In Southern California, Mexican Americans and whites who were committed to improving the economic status of farm workers and Latinos/as in the cities played a similarly pivotal role. They contributed an approach to organizing among the poor, called "membership-based" or "benefit-based" organizing, which welfare rights leaders quickly made their own.

The most important activist in the California welfare rights movement was Johnnie Tillmon, an African American woman born in Arkansas. Tillmon came to Los Angeles in 1960 with her five children, leaving behind a husband from whom she was separated. She continued to work in laundries as she had in the South; it was, she said, "very hard work but we were free people," unlike sharecroppers or domestic servants, who worked under conditions much more reminiscent of slavery.[64] Tillmon became a shop steward for her union, secretary of a local Democratic Party club and a leader among tenants of her public housing project. She followed the progress of the civil rights movement, especially the effort to integrate Central High School in Little Rock.[65] In January 1963, Tillmon was ill and her daughter was cutting school. A middle-class friend whom she knew from her political activities suggested that she apply for welfare, or, as it was called in California, Aid to Needy Children (ANC).[66]

Shortly after she began receiving benefits, Tillmon organized a group of ANC recipients to help one another. She started with five like-minded women. They soon discovered, as Beulah Sanders and Jennette Washington had done in New York, that they shared a set of grievances. Within three weeks of their first meeting Tillmon and the other women had organized residents of two housing projects, elected officers, and named their group ANC Mothers Anonymous.[67]

Tillmon did not allow middle-class people at meetings of ANC Mothers Anonymous, but she developed middle-class allies. One of her early allies was Tim Sampson, a social worker on the staff of a private social service agency in Los Angeles. Sampson edited the local newsletter of the National Association of Social Workers, in which he advocated trade union organizing for caseworkers and the kind of protest action the New York City welfare employees staged in 1965. The "historic trend of 'professionalism'," he argued, "is a narrowing one and not socially responsible."[68] Sampson was a dissatisfied maverick within social work, an advocate for peace and disarmament who, as he recalled, was part of a group that "didn't give a damn about social work values, we just wanted to have peace and disarmament. And the other side said that in order to be professional, we needed to define . . . the professional social work aspects of peace and disarmament and I just found that to be . . . weird."[69]

Johnnie Tillmon and Tim Sampson became involved in welfare politics at a particularly auspicious moment. As in New York, social tensions in California were simmering just below the surface. In 1958, Californians had elected a progressive Democratic governor, Edmund "Pat" Brown. Brown won reelection easily in 1962 on a platform of greater social spending, increased trade union participation in public life, and nonpartisan cooperation among the political parties in the state legislature. (The bitter loser in that election was Republican nominee Richard Nixon.) But despite liberalization and public-sector expansion, the politics of race, class, gender, and migration continued to pull the state apart.[70]

County officials in California used the language of welfare reform to talk about their objections to migration and to the supposed failings of African American and Mexican American families. In 1962, Kern County officials created a program called "Operation Weekend," a series of investigations into the homes of welfare recipients. Pairs of social workers arrived at seven o'clock on Sunday mornings at women's homes and searched for evidence that they were having romantic relationships with men or breaking other welfare rules. Officials in Alameda County followed the Kern County example. Alameda welfare director Harold Kehoe said that his staff was seeking evidence of welfare fraud, defined as a man "in the house in a husbandly attitude."[71] Three days after the home checks, Kehoe removed four Alameda mothers from the rolls and prosecuted them for fraud, while continuing investigation of thirty-three others.[72]

Welfare recipients, social workers, and liberal members of Governor Brown's administration responded to Operation Weekend. When a caseworker named Benny Parrish refused to participate in the raids, Alameda County promptly fired him. Newly unemployed, he helped two women who had lost their benefits in the raids appeal the county's decision. While Parrish was pursuing these appeals, a friend of his founded the Alameda County Welfare Rights Organization, which devoted itself to research about clients' legal rights and advocacy for them at welfare offices.[73]

In addition to their effects on grassroots activism, the California welfare raids spurred legal action. The appeal of Benny Parrish's dismissal from the Alameda social work staff became a major case, which went all the way to the California Supreme Court. Parrish's brother-in-law, Tom Joe, who was at the time of the dismissal a welfare policy aide to state representative Phil Burton, found Parrish two attorneys affiliated with the American Civil Liberties Union. They treated the case as a proxy for one about Operation Weekend itself. Their ultimate argument was that Alameda County could not fire Benny Parrish because the county's policy violated the Fourth Amendment to the U.S. Constitution, which forbade summary searches and seizures of property.[74]

Welfare rights organizing in Northern California emphasized the legal rights of the poor. The idea that welfare recipients had meaningful legal rights derived in part from the work of scholar Jacobus tenBroek. TenBroek, who had lost his sight completely in childhood, led the National Federation of the Blind (NFB), the first national organization in the United States of and for the blind. He was also a lawyer, a professor at the University of California at Berkeley, and chair of the State Social Welfare Board under Governor Brown. Since founding the NFB in 1940, tenBroek and his colleagues had successfully pressed the state and federal governments to improve their treatment of the indigent blind. Fired social worker Benny Parrish and his friends in Alameda spoke to tenBroek soon after they began working with welfare recipients because they wanted to replicate the NFB's success.[75]

TenBroek combined his activism with a scholarly career. In 1955, a paper he presented at the National Conference of Social Work on "The Constitution and the Right of Free Movement" argued that people were free to move from one region of the U.S. to another even if they might ultimately become welfare recipients in their new communities; freedom to travel, he argued, was a fundamental right of U.S. citizenship. A series of essays in 1964 and 1965 responded to Operation Weekend and similar efforts to cut welfare rolls. Comparing public benefits law to conventional family law, tenBroek charged that the state of California systematically discriminated against the poor.[76]

In the early and middle 1960s, tenBroek was joined by others in calling the legality of welfare department procedures into question. A New Deal veteran named Elizabeth Wickenden believed that law could help save the U.S. welfare state from the likes of Harold Kehoe in Alameda. She drafted a paper titled "Poverty and the Law" and circulated it to a range of luminaries in the fields of law and social work. Wickenden outlined what she saw as violations of the U.S. Constitution and federal law in welfare practices.[77] She also contracted with Charles Reich, a professor at Yale Law School, to research the legal dimensions of social policy.[78] Reich suggested that aggressive searches of women's and men's homes were themselves illegal and could not therefore form the basis for denials of public benefits. In 1963, Reich published his findings in the *Yale Law Journal*. His article, "Midnight Welfare Searches and the Social Security Act," was read enthusiastically by those who were looking for ways to defend welfare from attack.[79]

Charles Reich made a second, more ambitious foray into theorizing a legal approach to social welfare in "The New Property," which appeared in the *Yale Law Journal* in 1964. Reich argued that those who relied on state benefits—whether direct money grants such as public assistance, broadcast licenses distributed by the Federal Communications Commission, or professional licenses in fields such as law and medicine—developed legally defensible property interests in them.[80] He believed that welfare was a form of "new property" that the government had created and could not simply withdraw at will. "These benefits," he wrote, were "based upon a recognition that misfortune and deprivation are often caused by forces far beyond the control of the individual."[81] Ten-Broek pronounced the essay a "whingdinger" and "a significant contribution to the most important democratic effort of modern times, namely the effort to bring the Constitution to the poor."[82]

Organizing the Poor

Conditions in California spurred new strategies for social movement organizing. Here, the key figures were César Chávez, Delores Huerta, Fred Ross, and Saul Alinsky. Alinsky was one of the progenitors of "community organizing," the mid-twentieth-century social change strategy that focused on mobilizing people in their neighborhoods rather than, for example, in the places where they worked.[83] In 1948, Alinsky helped organizer Fred Ross found the Community Service Organization in California. This organization focused on issues such as urban renewal, the treatment of Mexican Americans by welfare workers, and police brutality. Its leaders included Chávez and Huerta. Chávez left the Community Service Organization in 1962 to concentrate on organizing California's agricultural labor force. Ross helped him build the National Farm Workers of America and its successor, the United Farm Workers union.[84]

Ross, Chávez, and Huerta thought deeply about the impediments to organizing poor people. The main challenge they identified was the risk of economic retribution from employers or government officials, which could decimate a family if one of its members tried to join a movement. Farm worker organizations could offer the traditional returns of union membership: higher wages, better working conditions, and more of a say in the circumstances that shaped people's economic lives. However, in California the power arrayed against potential members was so formidable that these benefits often seemed impossible to win. Ross proposed that they experiment with membership- or benefit-based organizing, which ensured that anyone who joined received some benefits. In response to this suggestion, the National Farm Workers union and, later, the United Farm Workers opened service centers for members. They offered a credit union and burial insurance so that workers and their loved ones could have decent funerals.[85]

Welfare rights organizers soon learned about the strategies Chávez, Huerta, and Ross had developed. Veterans of the farm workers' and welfare recipients' movements together created the California Center for Community Development in 1965. Tim Sampson left his job in Los Angeles to become the director of field operations for the center, and social worker Benny Parrish joined him on the staff. Sampson contacted Johnnie Tillmon in Los Angeles and the welfare rights activists in Alameda County, and began building a statewide network of public assistance activists. Their model was tenBroek's California Council of the Blind, which had improved benefits and "acted as a watchdog" over the public assistance program Aid to the Blind.[86]

The End of Governor Brown

Democrats in Washington, D.C., and the Brown administration in Sacramento, promised to help poor people gain money and political power. However, they retreated from the conflicts that arose when poor communities asserted their new power. Administrators of the federal antipoverty programs, which were gathered under the umbrella of the Office of Economic Opportunity (OEO) at the national level but implemented differently in each locality, were especially prone to make promises that they were unable or unwilling to keep. Welfare rights activists in California were both inspired and discouraged by their experiences with government initiatives to help the poor.

Funds and personnel started to flow into poor communities in California after the U.S. government created the Office of Economic Opportunity in 1964. The California Center for Community Development received funding from OEO, which supported Benny Parrish and Tim Sampson while they informed public assistance recipients about the new welfare rights movement. But the center's funding evaporated within one year because of political opposition to their work.[87]

In 1965, the winds of California politics began to blow in a more conservative direction. Governor Brown tried desperately in the months before his re-election bid against conservative actor Ronald Reagan to distance himself from his record on issues such as welfare. Reagan won regardless of Brown's tactical retreat, by playing on fears that the Watts riot of August 1965 had ignited, as well as by opposing public welfare, housing desegregation, and the student Free Speech Movement at the University of California at Berkeley.[88] In the post-Brown era, liberals in the California Democratic Party lacked an obvious political home. Those who were interested in civil rights progress, and in defending welfare, moved ever closer to activist movements and further from mainstream party politics.

The welfare rights agenda kept advancing. California antipoverty activists had their first statewide meeting in February 1966. Representatives came from Johnnie Tillmon's ANC Mothers Anonymous and the Modesto Welfare Rights Organization organized by Benny Parrish. Delores Huerta of the United Farm Workers union spoke at their luncheon.[89] Jacobus tenBroek assumed leadership of a Welfare Rights Caucus that evaluated the convention and planned a second one. In June, activists created the California Welfare Rights Organization and tapped tenBroek as its temporary convener. This new federation combined the ideas and tactics of tenBroek's social movement of the blind, César Chávez's United Farm Workers, and the black freedom movement. "Operation Weekend" had emerged from the politics of fear and resentment. The California Welfare Rights Organization set out to build a counterpolitics of African Americans, Spanish speakers, recent immigrants and migrants, unmarried mothers, the poor and unemployed, disabled men and women, and various sympathetic, able-bodied, middle-class whites.

The Battle of Syracuse in the War on Poverty

The welfare rights movement in Syracuse emerged in much the same way as the movements in New York City and California had done. Urban civil rights protest and the War on Poverty brought people together, schooled them in tactics they could use to create social change, and frustrated them in ways that led to more activism. Syracuse also contributed something distinctive to welfare rights protest, a group of committed activists who ultimately joined the national staff of the welfare rights movement and became some of the movement's most important organizers.

One of the first projects to receive funding from the federal Office of Economic Opportunity was an effort to mobilize poor people in Syracuse, New York. Syracuse had two ingredients that recommended it as a laboratory in which to experiment with ways to reduce social strife. First, in 1964 it had nearly gone the way of Harlem, Bedford-Stuyvesant, and its neighbor Rochester; only a last-minute change in strategy by local police had kept African Americans in Syracuse from rioting. Second, Syracuse had already become the site of disciplined local organizing around issues of racial and economic justice. A local chapter of CORE had demonstrated the potential for community action among poor African Americans in a Northern city.[90]

The leader of the CORE chapter was George Wiley, an African American chemist who taught at Syracuse University. In the early 1960s, the chapter was rooted more in the university than in the African American community and had more white than black members. Under Wiley's direction, it opened an office in a low-income African American neighborhood and organized a school boycott by African American parents.[91] A local activist named Anna Mae Williams joined the boycott. "I had never met [Wiley]," she said, "but knowing that I lived . . . in bad housing and paying high rents and being very disillusioned because there was nothing I could do at that time about the conditions I was living in," she was ready to make the first gesture of protest CORE suggested.[92] Syracuse CORE organized demonstrations at downtown businesses that refused to hire African Americans, boycotted Woolworth's in sympathy with lunch counter protestors around the country, and mobilized against police brutality. The group waged a particularly tenacious campaign against the city's urban renewal plan. When riots threatened in 1964, Wiley and colleagues walked the streets pleading for calm and begging the police to avoid provocation.[93]

The Syracuse campaigns exemplified the vision CORE president James Farmer had for the organization. Not long after the near riot of 1964, Farmer asked Wiley to move to New York City as associate national director of CORE. Wiley's success at confronting urban economic and racial injustice recommended him above more experienced candidates for the post. Without dwelling on the decision for too long, Wiley took a leave of absence from his academic position, resigned from the Syracuse chapter, and persuaded a white former graduate student named Edwin Day to join him on the CORE national staff. The two men and their families picked up stakes and moved to New York.[94]

Federal antipoverty money arrived in Syracuse as Wiley left. OEO granted $314,000 for a Community Action Training Center at the Social Work School of Syracuse University. The project was under the direction of activist professor Warren Haggstrom, who hired community-organizing guru Saul Alinsky as a consultant. Alinsky sent his California colleague Fred Ross to Syracuse, where he trained social work students. The students helped African Americans and working-class whites make successful demands on the local public housing authority and led women welfare recipients in demanding grants for their children's school clothing.[95] In response, the mayor of Syracuse accused Ross, the students, and their federal funders of provoking "class warfare."[96] Federal officials retreated in the face of this opposition. OEO head Sargent Shriver defunded the Syracuse project in December 1965, despite poor people's lobbying to keep the doors open. OEO funded an alternative agency, which sponsored traditional programs such as adult education and instruction in household management techniques. By the beginning of 1967, the Community Action Training Center had disappeared.[97]

Two of the students who worked with Fred Ross, Rhoda Linton and William Pastreich, became leading welfare rights organizers within a few years of their experiences in Syracuse. A staff member of the Community Action Training Center named Bruce Thomas, a veteran member of the Syracuse CORE chapter, also later joined the leadership of the welfare rights movement. "What we were doing was community organizing," Pastreich remembered, including helping welfare recipients demand clothes that children could wear to church on Easter.[98] After the training she received, Linton recalled, she was alienated from most of her classmates:

When Malcom X was murdered, I remember Bill [Pastreich] and I went to this meeting that was like a vigil. . . . It came at a time when we were supposed to be in class, so we went directly from the vigil to class . . . and were booed when we got back to class. . . . That was not the way to do it—it was to become a professional and tell people one by one how to adapt.[99]

When Linton left Syracuse, she moved to New York City. By the middle of 1966 she was on the staff of a community agency in the Prospect Heights neighborhood of Brooklyn and organizing welfare recipients.[100] Pastreich, who had worked as a welfare caseworker in New York City before graduate school, also moved to the city after graduation. His first job was as a coordinator of the United Farm Workers boycott of California grapes. When Linton told him about her work with welfare recipients, he, too, joined the rising welfare rights movement.[101]

Before it totally ran out of funds, in January 1966, the Community Action Training Center hosted a Poor People's War Council on Poverty. This "War Council" was the first national convention of the poor, an expansion of the dialogue that had begun to occur statewide in California and citywide in the five boroughs of New York City. It gathered over six hundred delegates from twenty-one states, including civil rights veterans, welfare recipients, and a range of middle- and working-class people who had fought the local battles of the War on Poverty. Beulah Sanders and Frank Espada were present to represent the City-Wide Coordinating Committee of Welfare Groups.[102]

One observer at the Syracuse meeting was George Wiley, who had had a bruising few years since the heyday of local CORE activism. In 1965, CORE president James Farmer announced that he was resigning to take a job with the Johnson administration. Wiley battled attorney Floyd Mc-Kissick for the presidency, arguing that CORE should strengthen its focus on economic inequality and pursue the kinds of strategies that had worked in Syracuse. McKissick argued for greater black self-awareness, organizing primarily within African American communities, and focusing on economic development within those communities. McKissick won the election and Wiley and Ed Day both resigned from CORE. They were not sure where to go next. All the major civil rights organizations were either undergoing a transformation similar to that of CORE or casting about for new ideas; the urban organizing strategies and economic justice agenda Wiley had pursued in Syracuse were no longer the movement's avant-garde.[103]

By the time of the Syracuse conference, George Wiley was on the staff of the Citizens Crusade Against Poverty, the brainchild of United Auto Workers president Walter Reuther. The Citizens Crusade aimed "to couple the civil rights struggle with the poverty struggle."[104] Its members included liberal organizations based in Washington, D.C., such as Americans for Democratic Action, plus progressive labor unions, churches, and activist civil rights and student groups.[105]

In April 1966, conflict erupted at a meeting of the Citizens Crusade Against Poverty. The meeting's planners had invited sixty activists from the nascent welfare rights and antipoverty movements, including Johnnie Tillmon from Los Angeles.[106] OEO head Sargent Shriver promised to give the keynote address. However, after he began with relatively upbeat remarks on poverty in America, Shriver's low-income constituents interrupted with questions and testimonials. He abandoned the podium. "I don't know where we go from here," said a national leader of the auto workers union. "They have turned on the people who wanted to help them."[107] Although leaders of the Citizens Crusade attempted to put the best face on the situation, they were embarrassed and worried about the future.[108] For George Wiley, the confrontation between Shriver and disgruntled poor people hastened a change in direction that he had already begun, toward the poor people and away from national lobbying groups.[109]

Crisis and Strategy

After the Syracuse convention, the cause of welfare rights gained adherents and took off in new directions. George Wiley became increasingly enthusiastic about the possibility of injecting new energy into the civil rights movement by working with the people who had challenged Sargent Shriver's assessment of poverty in the United States. Richard Cloward from Mobilization for Youth and a colleague, Frances Fox Piven, furthered this process by sketching out a theory of welfare rights organizing. In February 1966, Cloward and Piven completed the first draft of a paper they called "Organizing the Poor—How It Can Be Done."[110] Addressing themselves to a civil rights movement that was seeking new direction, they circulated the article to activists all over the country.[111] They published a revised version of the paper in *The Nation* in May 1966.[112]

Piven and Cloward estimated that three out of five poor people who qualified for public assistance were not receiving it. Adding even a fraction of these people to the welfare rolls would create a bureaucratic and fiscal crisis in the cities and states. They predicted that the crisis would "impel federal action on a guaranteed minimum income plan," which would replace welfare with a unified system that helped all poor people. The steps through which Cloward and Piven proposed to create this major change were simple: advertise their "rights" to public assistance to the poor in terms they could understand; have organizers advocate for individual clients and coordinate demonstrations on common problems; and use lawyers to pursue formal appeals of welfare department decisions when informal means did not succeed.[113]

Although many veterans of the African American freedom struggle believed that their movement needed new ideas, few wanted to move into welfare organizing. Frances Fox Piven remembered meeting with all of the major leaders of civil rights organizations to explain her and Cloward's ideas. Wiley was the only one who wanted to pursue the welfare strategy.[114] Their article grabbed Wiley's attention because it described the campaigns members of Syracuse CORE had been pursuing since the early 1960s. Piven and Cloward argued that these efforts could produce major public policy changes.

Wiley left the Citizens Crusade Against Poverty. He had little in the way of an institutional base but was rich with contacts he made at the Syracuse convention with low-income activists. With his ally from Syracuse, Ed Day, Wiley founded the Poverty/Rights Action Center (P/RAC). Wiley and Day did not have any funding, but their wives agreed to support them financially by doing less glamorous jobs until the men were able to raise support from private foundations.[115] As Walter Reuther had done in founding the Citizens Crusade Against Poverty, they proposed to join the growing antipoverty movement with the live embers of the African American freedom movement. "The civil rights movement," Wiley wrote, "which once provided the unifying purpose and direction of activists, is now frustrated by financial problems and lack of agreement on immediate and long-range objectives . . . At the same time, new militant leadership is emerging in rural areas from Delano, California [the heart of the farmworker movement] to the Mississippi Delta, and in organizations in low-income neighborhoods in most major cities."[116] The Poverty/Rights Action Center, he insisted, was not a membership organization but "an office located in Washington, D.C." that would support activist groups and help them communicate with one another.[117]

The welfare rights movement took shape quickly in 1966. Cloward and Piven provided funds with which to send Ed Day around the country. His assignment was to discover whether the gap between the number of people eligible for welfare and the number receiving it was as wide outside New York City as within it. He was also to identify the people who were engaged in welfare organizing and create a national network linking them together. He told the activists he met, including Johnnie Tillmon, to travel to Chicago in May for a conference on the idea of a guaranteed national income. The conference had been organized by dissident student social workers at the University of Chicago's School of Social Service Administration.[118]

At the end of the conference, George Wiley convened a Welfare Action Meeting to coordinate future steps. This meeting brought together many of the people who had contributed to poor people's activism between 1963 and 1966. Espada had driven to Chicago with Jennette Washington and other leaders of the City-Wide Coordinating Committee of Welfare Groups. (Beulah Sanders was unable to attend.) He reported on the success of the Welfare Recipients Leagues in Brooklyn, which had organized between three and five hundred people in a single borough. Johnnie Tillmon could not travel to Chicago, but her ally Tim Sampson reported back to all the California groups. CORE member Anna Mae Williams attended, representing the poor people of Syracuse. She told the group about the Community Action Training Center, which had focused on housing and welfare "with considerable success, only to have their support cut off" by the federal government.[119]

The major decision of the Chicago conference was to coordinate a national day of action. New York City delegates pointed out that they were already planning a major protest in June. Representatives from Ohio explained that they had planned a ten-day walk from Cleveland to Columbus focused on the gap between welfare grants and the standard of living. The group decided to combine the New York and Ohio efforts. In New York, activists would proceed as planned in early June with local events that targeted neighborhood welfare offices. They would delay their City Hall protest until the 30th of the month. Activists elsewhere would tell their friends and allies to demonstrate on the same day, to coincide with the arrival of the Ohio marchers in Columbus.[120]

George Wiley, Ed Day, and the welfare recipients and organizers from around the country mobilized quickly to make the June 30 actions a success. They fanned the flames that had been rising since the early 1960s. When the New Yorkers finished demonstrating at City Hall and the Ohio welfare mothers arrived at their state capitol, Wiley and Day simply proclaimed the start of a national welfare rights movement. They distributed a mimeographed collection of newspaper articles on the demonstrations that they boldly titled "The Birth of a Movement."[121] No one disputed their claim.

Chapter 2

Citizens of the Affluent Society

"The Good Life"
As I travel
Day
by
Day
I meet different people
. . . Talking about the good life.
. . . Together
We will overcome
The hurdles of
Despair
and
Poverty
We will see the good life.

—Jennette Washington, leader, City-Wide Coordinating
Committee of Welfare Groups

In one of its first major protest actions, the City-Wide Coordinating Committee of Welfare Groups called a boycott of the New York City schools at the start of the 1966–67 academic year. This boycott differed from the one civil rights activists had organized in 1964 in that its leaders demanded that the city government spend money on clothing and supplies for schoolchildren as well as on school buildings, teacher salaries, and other educational needs. The focus of the boycott was less on the integration of schools than on the quality of schools, and children's access to goods that would help prepare them for school. Lily Mae Robinson, who sat in at the Department of Welfare for fifty hours in support of the boycott, wrote that she and her colleagues "dreamed of a better Welfare system for all those who need it, for jobs for those of us who can work, for decent housing and for *the best education we can give our children.*"[1] At the same time, she and other members of the City-Wide Coordinating Committee demanded supplements to their welfare grants to keep schoolchildren warm and decently dressed.[2]

Demands for material goods and claims to participate in what historian Lizabeth Cohen has termed the "consumer's republic" lay at the
heart of the movement for welfare rights.[3] Jennette Washington, Lily
Mae Robinson, and other activists asserted their right to the "good life"
promised by the affluent society.[4] They argued that full citizenship in
the postwar United States depended not only on having access to decent
schooling for their children, but also on being able to feed and clothe
their children decently, on having furniture in their homes, and on own-
ing decent goods.[5]

The school clothing protests led to the City-Wide Coordinating Committee of Welfare Groups' first arrests. Citywide activists picketed in support of the boycott at welfare department headquarters in lower
Manhattan. Robinson, with four other women and one man, spent two
nights sleeping on the floor of the office at 250 Church Street. By the
middle of the sit-in, she recalled, "we knew that we were now friends,
most of us with the same kinds of problems in housing, education, etc."[6]
Welfare Commissioner Mitchell Ginsberg, an important member of the
reformist administration of Mayor John Lindsay, ordered police not to
make any arrests. After two nights of sitting in and no progress in the
negotiations, "one group moved in on all entrances to the building,"
according to the newsletter of the City-Wide Coordinating Committee.[7]
Police arrested seventeen members of Citywide, including two members
of its Executive Board, and released them on bail later that evening.[8]

Picketing at the welfare department continued after the arrests. Those
the *New York Times* called "irate mothers" joined caseworkers from the
Social Service Employees Union (SSEU), who were attempting to
enforce provisions of the contract they had signed with New York City at
the end of their recent strike.[9] The social workers deposited thousands
of case files on the desks of their supervisors to protest what they saw as
the illegal action of assigning each of them many more families than
their contract allowed. Ultimately, members of the City-Wide Coordinating Committee declared victory and withdrew their pickets. Although
welfare recipients did not get a major boost in clothing allowances, the
group did claim a promise from social services commissioner Ginsberg
to help press state legislators to increase the clothing grants. The city
administration announced that it would hire hundreds of new caseworkers to manage case files that exceeded contractual limits.[10]

The kinds of demands that animated the school protesters, demands
for school clothing, winter coats, and other everyday goods, fueled the
expansion of the welfare rights movement. They reflected welfare recipients' longstanding grievances and ideas about what it meant to be a citizen of the post-World War II United States. Scores of parents had written
to Mayor Wagner in the early 1960s asking for the same goods that later

became the center of welfare rights protests. For example, public aid recipient Catherine Kerwin wrote to tell Mayor Wagner that her three nieces, whom she and her husband had rescued from public foster care after the death of their mother, had no winter coats, decent shoes, or galoshes to wear in the rain. "How," she asked, "can I possibly keep these girls going to school when I can't get them coats and shoes. Their school work is going to suffer and physically they will suffer because they can't get the proper fresh air and exercise that all normal children should have."[11] A study of New York City welfare families in the 1960s found that one-half of the mothers who received aid had children in school. Of these, approximately 30 percent reported keeping their children at home sometimes because they lacked clothing or shoes; 20 percent said they sometimes kept children out of school because they were ashamed of the children's shabby clothes.[12]

In welfare rights protests, as in the letters public aid clients wrote to the mayor, warm coats, rain gear, and school supplies were hardly trivial demands. They were the gateway to "what all normal children should have," linked not only to children's health but also to their educational success. In "our wonderful city," Kerwin insisted, no child should go "coatless and hungary."[13] Theresa Vasta, another recipient of public assistance, insisted to the mayor that she had "no time for games. My children are hungry and my oldest one is missing school because I have no money to send her." Despite her foreign-sounding surname, she added, "I am american born. I think I deserve the right treatment. Fair Treatment that is."[14] When Maria Ramos asked for clothing, she described herself as "a porto-riquen mother of the ones who are in your vote," and Julia Harrison told Mayor Wagner: "My husband is a Citizen of New York and he has a honorable discharge."[15] For these women, a public commitment to support parents who were trying to fulfill their responsibilities was the core of modern citizenship, the essence of the bargain between them and their government.

These demands had legitimacy within the welfare system. Caseworkers and supervisors in each public aid office had the authority to provide clients with supplements to regular welfare payments. New York City was under mandate from the state to maintain public assistance recipients at a minimum standard of health and decency. To comply, the city welfare department issued each caseworker a thick manual of procedures, which included lists of "minimum standards" items that clients might receive over and above their regular welfare stipends. Demands for children's coats, shoes, and other goods placed the welfare department on the defensive; since they appeared in the official manual of departmental procedures, welfare groups claimed it was "illegal" for caseworkers and bureaucrats to deny these items to clients who asked for them. It was up to the welfare department either to give clients what they said they needed or to explain why not. Demands for school clothes and other minimum standard items became part of an extremely effective "benefit-based" organizing strategy that mirrored the strategies César Chávez, Delores Huerta, and Fred Ross had used to organize farm workers in California.[16]

Of Liquor and Luxuries

Welfare recipients' demands for consumer goods coincided with postwar changes in local welfare departments. Ideas about proper parenting and spending had been woven into public welfare practice from the drafting of the Social Security Act of 1935 forward; they had been part of the practice of private charity agencies at least since the early twentieth-century experiments in "Friendly Visiting," which laid the groundwork for the modern profession of social work. However, as consumerism became more central in American society after World War II, it became more central in social casework as well.[17] Journalist Theodore H. White wrote in the mid-1960s that "it was if a radioactive dust, called money, was in the air, invisible but everywhere."[18] This radioactive dust fell on social workers and welfare recipients as much as it fell on anyone else.

In the 1960s, welfare mothers were judged more than they ever had been before on the way they spent their money. The Social Security Act Amendments of 1962, the last major changes to the law before the welfare rights movement began, contained a provision allowing local welfare departments to do what President Kennedy, in his statement upon signing the legislation, referred to "guarding against misuse of welfare funds paid for the benefit of dependent children."[19] The amendments permitted welfare departments to institute controls on clients who were thought to be spending their grants inappropriately. "In some instances," a Nebraska welfare director testified before the Senate Finance Committee, "this situation is a problem of poor household management, but in other cases the money is wasted on liquor and luxuries. . . . In some instances this means direct supervision of public funds to an individual family, where you may have low mentality, a lack of understanding of how to manage a household."[20] The 1962 amendments allowed states and localities to impose mandatory counseling or criminal prosecution on parents who neglected the "best interests of the child" when they spent welfare funds, or to replace their cash payments with vouchers for specific items. The voucher provision undercut a basic principle of the original Aid to Dependent Children program, the so-called "money payment principle" that public assistance grants must be paid in cash and without controls on recipients' spending choices.[21]

Social welfare liberals, who generally supported President Kennedy's amendments to the Social Security Act in 1962, voiced concern about the restrictions placed on poor families' spending. Welfare scholar Winifred Bell wrote confidentially that she believed "vouchers or other types of restricted payments would primarily cause hardship on large families—where I suspect the mothers are better buyers and planners than most welfare workers."[22] Advocate and New Deal veteran Elizabeth Wickenden saw in the provision the possibility for abuses of clients' civil rights. "The history of all efforts to apply moral judgments in a program intended to meet the needs of children on the basis of objective criteria of entitlement is closely related to the problems of minority groups," she wrote.[23]

Welfare department personnel in New York City were just as concerned with clients' spending patterns as were national policy makers.[24] Jennette Washington, Lily Mae Robinson, and every other welfare client had a personalized budget, which determined the size of her or his biweekly cash grant. This budget was based on a caseworker's assessment, which was sometimes made in consultation with a home economist on the welfare department staff, of the client's needs. Caseworkers had one major guide in making their determinations: the welfare manual that the local department issued to all employees. In New York City, this manual was full of details about the welfare budget, scaled to family size and children's ages, and dependent on whether the family in question received Aid to Families with Dependent Children (AFDC), Aid to the Disabled, Aid to the Blind, Old Age Assistance, or Home Relief; on what it paid for rent; and on such details as whether the family had a washing machine or needed to pay separately for laundry.[25] Individual welfare budgets varied widely from one another. The fortnightly budget of New York City AFDC recipient Louise Miller, for example, included allowances to cover her "estimated needs" for food, clothing, and rent for herself and her eight children. It also included smaller allocations for personal care and school expenses, household supplies, and both regular and diaper laundry. Miller and her children did not receive grants for some of the other items that appeared on the department's budget worksheet, such as ice, cooking fuel, and cod liver oil. Nor did Miller receive any grants for expenses related to "employment or rehabilitation," such as carfare, withholding taxes, or union dues.[26]

The items categorized as "minimum standards" in welfare department manuals were numerous and specific. The manuals specified that each adult woman required one hat, one "Dressy dress," one girdle, two cotton dresses, three pairs of panties, and two pairs of stockings. For living room furniture, the manual specified a couch, which was to have a "new cotton linters mattress," and a "drop leaf or extension (wood)" table. In the kitchen, normal family living supposedly required a dinette set and, for cooking equipment, a paring knife, an egg beater of the "rotary type," and a fruit reamer made of glass. Minimum standards in the category called "General Furnishings" included a shopping cart, alarm clock, towel rack, and toilet tissue holder, plus a "runner, 36" wide" for the hallway, and a washable bathroom rug.[27]

In addition to minimum standards for appliances, furniture, and clothing, welfare manuals itemized the various "special needs" that welfare clients might encounter, which the welfare department might pay for on a one-time-only basis or under specified circumstances. These ran the gamut from a special diet for a diabetic welfare recipient, to transportation for a doctor's visit, housekeeping services for a recipient who was physically unable to do her or his own housekeeping, and babysitting or child care help for an "overburdened mother" who was certified as such by a case supervisor. The amounts families or individuals received in their welfare checks were a combination of their basic budgets, plus any items the welfare department was providing to bring their cases "up to standard," plus payment to fulfill various "special needs," minus amounts earned from employment. Also subtracted from this total were any funds received in gifts, alimony or child support, or due the welfare department because of a prior overpayment.[28]

Welfare department administrators explained the standards as aids to "normal family living." Caseworkers had the duty and power to determine "the special items needed which are considered essential to the clients' comfort and well-being."[29] But activists challenged the welfare department on the basis of this mandate: why wasn't a mother the best judge of her family's comfort and well-being, or even of what she and her children needed in order to be "normal"? Why did the welfare department systematically fail to raise its clients to "minimum standards"?

Organizing for Minimum Standards

The idea of using minimum standards as tools for organizing was the brainchild of welfare department insiders. Many clients and all of their caseworkers knew about the standards. The letters clients wrote during the early 1960s indicate that some understood that arguments for minimum standards were hard for officials to refute. But even clients who knew that welfare offices occasionally helped them buy winter coats or school clothes did not know the wide range of goods the guidelines covered, because the welfare department deliberately kept information from them. When New York City leader Beulah Sanders met civil rights activist George Wiley for the first time, for example, he told her about the minimum standards system and the wide range of goods that were included in welfare department manuals. Sanders responded skeptically, demanding "to know how did he know, where did he get the information from."[30] Virtually no one outside the world of welfare knew about the system at all. The nascent welfare rights movement relied on dissident caseworkers, including those in the Social Service Employees Union, to share detailed information about minimum standards.

The organizers Frank Espada in Brooklyn and Ezra Birnbaum at Mobilization for Youth (MFY) on the Lower East Side of Manhattan started experimenting with minimum standards at roughly the same time. In the late summer of 1964 or early in 1965, Espada remembered, a friend who worked for the welfare department "dropped off some of the regulations that had to do with minimum standards."[31] Espada's group, East New York Action, and the Welfare Recipients Leagues it had been helping to create since 1963, began to pursue minimum standards for clients of public aid. At roughly the same time, Ezra Birnbaum of MFY created a simple checklist from the information about standards in the welfare manual. Clients who read the checklist learned about the minimum standards system at a glance. Virtually all of them saw that there was a wide gap between what they had in their homes and the array of goods the welfare department—in manuals it did not share with its clients—claimed were necessary for families to live at a minimum standard of health and decency. When he found out that MFY was working along the same lines as the Welfare Recipients Leagues, Espada visited Birnbaum and got a copy of the checklist. He remembered thinking it was "ideal, it was perfect" for recruiting new members and agitating with them at neighborhood welfare offices.[32]

Members of the Strycker's Bay Neighborhood Council on the Upper West Side approached the issue of minimum standards from their concern with urban renewal policies that displaced poor people from their homes. Jennette Washington of Strycker's Bay and the West Side Welfare Recipients League noted that people on welfare faced a financial crunch when urban renewal initiatives forced them to move from their apartments to temporary locations and then to public housing. Even when families resettled happily, she commented, "there were certain things they needed," such as furniture and kitchen supplies, which they could not afford on a regular public assistance budget.[33] A 1964 study of the West Side urban renewal area found that 52 percent of welfare families in that neighborhood lacked adequate furniture.[34]

The first major demonstrations of the potential of organizing for minimum standards came early in 1966. Birnbaum and other staff members from Mobilization for Youth fastened on the idea of winter clothing as a material benefit many welfare recipients wanted, and which they might

_____ Welfare Office

Date _____

Dear _____   ⊂○ Local Group
       social worker

The following are the furniture and household supplies items that I am lacking in my home and need in order to be brought up to minimum standards. I expect an answer to my request within one week.

KITCHEN

_____ table & 4 chairs	1 table per house		70.00
_____ extra chairs	1 chair per person		15.00
_____ high chair or low chair	as needed	durable quality	20.00
_____ refrigerator	family of 5 or less	11 to 12 cu ft.	150.00
_____ washing machine	family of 2 or more	12 lb. capacity	155.00 + installation
_____ range (gas on gas)		gas where available	150.00 + installation
_____ parlow heater	no central heating		(cost at local gas co.)
_____ dish cabinet	as needed		35.00
_____ utility cabinet	as needed		35.00
_____ floor covering	size of room-vinyl coated, hard surface $1.00-$1.40 per ft.		
_____ refrigerator	family of 6 or more	14 cu. ft.	200.00

BEDROOM

_____ bed (full or twin)	as needed		102.00 { metal frame 1 / head board 1 / innerspring 3 / mattress 3 }
_____ bunk bed	as needed	hardwood frame	125.00
_____ dresser or chest	1 per 2 persons	hardwood frame-4 drawer	60.00
_____ mirror	as needed		20.00
_____ crib	as needed	hardwood panels	30.00
_____ crib mattress	as needed		10.00
_____ playpen & pad	as needed	hardwood or nylon mesh	20.00
_____ stroller or convertible	as needed	steel frame, vinyl cover	30.00
_____ pillows	1 per person		3.00
_____ floor covering	size of room-vinyl coated, hard surface $1.00-$1.40 per ft.		

LIVING ROOM

_____ sofa	1 per home	durable quality	130.00
_____ sofa bed			140.00
_____ chairs	2 per home	hardwood frame	30.00 each
_____ tables	3 per home (2 end + coffee tables)		40.00 per set
_____ lamps-table or floor	1 per room & 2 per living room-as needed		12.50 each
_____ floor covering	size of room-vinyl coated, hard surface $1.25-$1.60		

HOUSEHOLD SUPPLIES

_____ bed spread	1 per bed	durable quality	6.00
_____ blankets	2 per bed-more if needed	washable	5.50
_____ sheets	4 per bed	durable quality	2.50
_____ pillow cases	1 pair per pillow	durable quality	1.25 per pr.
_____ bath towels	2 per person	durable quality	1.50
_____ hand towels	2 per person	durable quality	.75
_____ face cloth	2 per person	durable quality	.35
_____ table cloth	1 per family	durable quality	2.50
_____ rubber sheets	as needed	durable quality	2.00
_____ window shades	as needed	durable quality	2.00 per window
_____ curtains	1 pr. per window		3.50
_____ electric iron	1 per family		12.00
_____ ironing board	1 per family	durable quality	12.00
_____ clothes hamper	1 per family	durable quality	10.00
_____ pots & pans	as needed	durable quality	30.00 max.
_____ dishes	as needed	service for 8	22.00
_____ dishes	as needed	service for 4	13.00
_____ flatware	as needed	service for 8	24.00
_____ flatware	as needed	service for 4	12.00

OTHER _____

SIGNATURE _____
PRINT NAME _____
ADDRESS _____
CASE NUMBER _____

xNote: you may spend up to 10% more than these prices

Figure 4. Citywide created and distributed these forms, revealing the contents of welfare department regulations that described "minimum standards" of furniture and clothing for each welfare family. Courtesy NWRO Papers, Moorland-Spingarn Research Center, Howard University.

win from welfare offices. Dozens of clients arrived at the MFY offices to find out how to get coats for themselves and their children. They then requested winter clothing from their caseworkers and followed up on any unanswered requests or denials with group negotiations with welfare supervisors. The campaign netted hundreds of dollars' worth of winter clothing for New York City welfare recipients. It was so successful that Birnbaum, activist researcher Richard Cloward, and others decided to follow it first with a push for furniture "minimum standards" and then a campaign for all minimum standards. By the time of Citywide's inaugural demonstration at City Hall on June 30, minimum standards were a key part of the group's organizing strategy.[35]

Minimum standards campaigns drew people into the City-Wide Coordinating Committee of Welfare Groups. These campaigns attracted people because they built on the sense of entitlement to "the good life" that Jennette Washington expressed in her poem, a sense many others shared. A founder of the United Welfare League on the West Side explained how minimum standards piqued her interest and encouraged her to join the movement. Washington and another leader came to her home and asked if she was on welfare. "They asked if I thought the system was everything it was supposed to be. Did I have adequate clothing? Did I have any needs that the Department had not met?" When they first saw the minimum standards checklist, she and other people in her neighborhood "couldn't believe the things that were in [them]. Coats and sweaters. . . . There was a law in the books that said you were entitled to these things and we were going to try to get them."[36]

Local activists targeted welfare offices in dozens of different neighborhoods. The hope was to "show our strength" and "build POWER" by flooding the offices with requests for minimum standards and then, if the requests were not granted, either negotiating with administrators or picketing.[37] These efforts enabled individual welfare recipients to buy clothes and furniture for their children and themselves, helped build the membership of welfare rights groups, and strengthened Citywide. The Berriman Street Welfare League, for example, reported that its members had gotten $4,000 for clothes and household goods in the weeks between its creation on September 9, 1966, and early October. The Coney Island Welfare Rights Organization obtained over $25,000 for its members in this period by negotiating and picketing.[38]

The minimum standards campaigns confirmed the idea Chávez, Huerta, and Ross had developed working with farm workers, that concrete benefits were the key to attracting members to a poor people's movement.[39] Satisfied clients were the best possible advertisement for welfare rights activism. When members stood up at a Citywide meeting and announced their victories, they became object lessons in the value of joining the movement. The leaders of the City-Wide Coordinating Committee included Espada, the first chair of its Executive Board; Sanders, who succeeded him as chair; and Washington, a member of the board, plus advisers such as Birnbaum, Cloward, and researcher Frances Fox Piven. These leaders, and activists in neighborhoods across the city, built the New York City welfare rights movement one successful demand for minimum standards at a time.[40]

The Idea of a Guaranteed Income

With great momentum and many unanswered questions Jennette Washington, other New York activists, and their counterparts around the country met under the auspices of George Wiley and Edwin Day of the Poverty/Rights Action Center (P/RAC) for the first national welfare rights meeting. The goals of the meeting, in August 1966, were to capitalize on the energy these groups had generated in their local campaigns, to share information, and, from Wiley's and Day's perspective, to form a national welfare rights or poor people's movement that would have the Poverty/Rights Action Center as its headquarters.[41] For Johnnie Tillmon, who attended as an elected representative from the Los Angeles County Welfare Rights Organization, the spirit of the meeting "was just a buzz, buzz, buzz" with current and former welfare recipients from all over the country, almost all of whom were women, talking to each other intently and discovering how much they had in common.[42] She was especially impressed by Washington, whose stories made Tillmon believe that even liberal New York was stingy and disrespectful when it came to welfare recipients. Overall, the activists Tillmon met came from more than one hundred local action groups and twenty-four cities.[43]

The major question before delegates to the national welfare rights meeting concerned the long-term goal of the new movement they were creating. According to Hulbert James, a graduate of Howard Law School who had been organizing poor people in Louisville, Kentucky, since the early 1960s, they actively debated the idea of a guaranteed income, a direct payment from the national government to every citizen whose income fell below a certain level.[44] The guaranteed income advocates who provoked discussion at welfare rights meetings were part of a tradition in economic thought, the great exponent of which in postwar America was economist John Kenneth Galbraith. In *The Affluent Society*, Galbraith argued that many of the goods produced by modern businesses were useless. The private market, he claimed, was more successful at keeping people working, and therefore earning and participating in the consumer market, than at meeting human needs. By way of remedy, he urged "social balance" in the form of investments in public goods such as schools, hospitals, and roads that approached the level of investment in the private economy.[45] Since he believed that poverty was inescapable under modern conditions, Galbraith urged public investments in solving the poverty problem. In addition to making genuinely productive jobs available for people who lacked them, he believed that the government ought to find "a reasonably satisfactory substitute for production as a source of income."[46] The "substitute" Galbraith favored in 1958, when he first published *The Affluent Society*, was an expanded system of unemployment insurance; in its second edition, the book included a call for a national guaranteed income.[47] To those who thought it was immoral to give money to citizens who did not work for it, he asked:

if the goods have ceased to be urgent, where is the fraud? Can the North Dakota farmer be indicted for failure to labor hard and long to produce the wheat that his government wishes passionately it did not have to buy? Are we desperately dependent on the diligence of the worker who applies maroon and pink enamel to the functionless bulge of a modern motorcar? The idle man may still be an enemy of himself. But it is hard to say that the loss of his effort is damaging to society.[48]

Galbraith asked his readers to consider a "divorce of production from security," untying the knot between a worker's marketable output and his or her income.[49]

A slightly different but equally influential statement of the guaranteed income idea appeared in *Capitalism and Freedom* by economist Milton Friedman, with Rose Friedman, published in 1962. *Capitalism and Freedom* launched the idea of a negative income tax, or guaranteed income administered by the Internal Revenue Service, into intellectual and policy parlance. Friedman and Friedman judged virtually all antipoverty efforts by the government, especially those created under the New Deal, to be inefficient and corrosive of human freedom. They proposed to end such social welfare programs as public housing, which created and maintained goods that individuals with money to spend could more efficiently call into being through the private market. "If funds are to be used to help the poor," Friedman and Friedman asked, "would they not be used more effectively by being given in cash rather than in kind?"[50] They argued for a national system of payments to poor individuals and families, a negative tax that the government could simply send to those whose incomes were too low for them to owe any taxes. Although this negative tax payment might reduce the work ethic somewhat, Friedman and Friedman allowed for work incentives. "An extra dollar earned [would] always mean more money available for expenditure," they wrote, because the government would grant the worker a higher payment the more she or he participated in the waged labor market.[51]

Robert Theobald made an even more emphatic argument than Galbraith or the Friedmans had done for the income guarantee as a bulwark of modern citizenship. In a presentation he made at the national welfare rights meeting, and in his book *Free Men and Free Markets*, he argued that a minimum income guaranteed by the U.S. Constitution was essential to freedom. Theobald wrote that freedom was possible only if each individual had "*sufficient resources to enable him to live with dignity.*"[52] However, like Friedman and Friedman, he preferred direct payments from the national treasury to government programs such as public health care or housing. Theobald wrote that the United States had created in the postwar period "a productive system of, in effect, unlimited capacity."[53] He believed that the modern economy necessarily generated unemployment as well as growth and would, therefore, necessarily leave some people out. "This conclusion," he wrote, "implies the *complete* breakdown of our present socioeconomic system, which depends on the ability to provide jobs for all who require them."[54] He saw as the only answer to this situation a retreat from the idea of basing a citizen's income on his or her willingness to enter the paid workforce, or, as Galbraith had put it, "a divorce of production from security."[55]

The theories of Galbraith, Friedman and Friedman, and Theobald only half appealed to Beulah Sanders, Johnnie Tillmon, and other welfare activists. All four authors described conditions with which public assistance recipients were depressingly familiar: general prosperity simultaneous with high rates of unemployment; and jobs, when they were available, which did not produce much of value. They all argued that it was important to let every citizen participate in the public world of the consumer market. However, they wrote as though every citizen were the same. All four theorists seemed to assume that the typical beneficiary of the guaranteed income would be an unemployed man, but most welfare recipients were not men. They ignored the challenges mothers faced when they tried to combine waged work with parenting; the sex- and race-based discrimination that prevented women of color from securing decently waged jobs; and the fact that, in theory, the AFDC program already guaranteed minimal incomes for citizens who had children to raise. Theobald wrote eloquently about the value of participating in the consumer market for people's sense of dignity and social inclusion, but he certainly said nothing specific about children's school gear or a family's need for a bathroom rug. Galbraith did not mention mothers until the second edition of *The Affluent Society*, which appeared in 1969. In the end, although many of the intellectuals, organizers, and social workers involved in welfare rights favored the idea of a guaranteed income, the August 1966 meeting took no position on it.[56]

The other major debate at the national welfare rights meeting, according to Hulbert James, concerned the degree to which the new movement should involve itself in the politics of the War on Poverty. This was a serious question for poor people and their allies in the summer of 1966. Syracuse welfare recipients had already seen the generals of this war retreat from the political conflicts poor people caused when they organized in their self-interest. Activists from MFY in New York had been marked as Communists by the city's antipoverty bureaucrats because they supported rent strikes and school boycotts.[57] As with the guaranteed income idea, there was no consensus among welfare rights delegates on what they should do to improve the War on Poverty, or to save it from opponents who believed that it was already too closely tied to grassroots social movements.

"It's the Movement": Poor People March on Washington

Although the women and men who attended the national welfare rights meeting did not come to consensus after their discussion of federal anti-poverty programs, many of them nonetheless tried to make their voices heard in the congressional debate over these programs. The experience taught them that they were on stronger ground when they participated in local political battles over consumer goods and public assistance grants than they were in the national battles over poverty policy.

In September 1966, Frank Espada and other leaders in New York City decided to organize a Poor People's March on Washington. While helping to found the City-Wide Coordinating Committee of Welfare Groups, Espada had also taken a position with the Council for a Better East New York, a federally funded community action agency in Brooklyn, and helped create a Citywide Community Action Committee to represent participants in federally funded antipoverty programs before bureaucrats and members of Congress. The Community Action Committee called the march because the House of Representatives had thus far failed to appropriate funding for the key War on Poverty legislation, the Economic Opportunity Act of 1964, which was due to expire. Representative Adam Clayton Powell, Jr., of Harlem, chair of the committee that had jurisdiction over the legislation, had delayed action on it in order to pressure his colleagues into making improvements in it.[58]

George Wiley and Ed Day did not bid for the responsibility of coordinating the Poor People's March. To their considerable surprise, they discovered that the coalition planning the march chose P/RAC to manage it. "We're just sort of in it," Wiley offered in explanation. "It's the move-

Figure 5. Poor people march on Washington to save the War on Poverty, September 1966. Courtesy *Washington Star* photographic archives, copyright *Washington Post*, reprinted by permission of District of Columbia Public Library.

ment."[59] In a sign of changing grassroots politics, the group planning the march rejected Espada's proposal to ask Bayard Rustin to organize the march as he had the 1963 March on Washington and the 1964 New York City school boycott. A Harlem contingent "just attacked. They didn't want Rustin at all," presumably because Rustin was thought to be overly friendly to leaders of the Democratic Party and hostile to the new black militancy.[60] Wiley, with his background as a voice for economic justice and urban organizing in the Congress of Racial Equality and his new reputation as a supporter of welfare mothers and other poor people, was a more appealing figure.

With less than two weeks of planning time, Wiley, Day, Espada, and other organizers in New York managed to make a significant showing on Capitol Hill. Day calculated attendance at just over two thousand. People came from many of the places that had already become centers of welfare rights activism, including New York; Cleveland; Louisville, Kentucky; Fontana, California; Baltimore; Meridian, Mississippi; and a half dozen other cities and towns. Brownsville, Brooklyn, alone sent 250 people; Espada's home turf of East New York contributed 100; and Harlem 112.[61] A group of self-described poor people in Niagara Falls, New York, who could not afford the trip to Washington, sent 145 signatures on petitions supporting the War on Poverty that they hoped would "speak as lo[u]d as words."[62] The message of the Poor People's March was that the key agency of the War on Poverty, the Office of Economic Opportunity (OEO), was both imperfect and worth defending. "Perhaps," Wiley and Day wrote in materials they circulated to marchers, "some day we will have a good law and enough money. Then we must deal with the way OEO administers the program."[63]

The poor people's reception when they lobbied Congress was mixed.[64] In terms of its concrete goals, the Poor People's March was hardly a success. Chairman Powell and his colleagues finally ushered the antipoverty bill out of committee. When it reached the floor of the House of Representatives, however, Republicans and Democrats alike made disapproving mentions of the work of Mobilization for Youth in New York City and the Community Action Training Center at Syracuse University, which had organized welfare mothers and others to claim benefits. The House and Senate finally agreed to raise overall OEO funding slightly, but to place new controls on community agencies' use of the money, to eliminate the specific program that had sponsored the Syracuse effort and to place all War on Poverty employees under the Hatch Act that forbade government personnel from engaging in partisan politics. John Kifner of the *New York Times* described the effect of the new law in New York City as "confusion and dismay," as officials of the city Human Resources Administration, which oversaw both the welfare system and the War on Poverty, scrambled for the funds to keep existing projects alive.[65]

New York Was Where It Was At

The failure of the March on Washington to expand funding for community groups waging the War on Poverty contrasted sharply with the thousands of dollars Coney Island and Lower East Side mothers received every time they marched on a local welfare office. Minimum standards campaigns offered likely victories and material benefits as rewards for participation. While funding and staff from the War on Poverty helped make local organizing possible in New York, a national campaign to improve or save the War on Poverty promised likely defeats and only the distant possibility of long-term benefits.

The contrast was especially stark to those who knew what had happened in the New York welfare department since the minimum standards drives began in 1965. Even Human Resources Administration head Mitchell Ginsberg, the object of many of these drives, saw the wisdom in them. In an interview he gave after returning to academic social work in the 1970s, Ginsberg argued that the minimum standards strategy attracted participants in ways no other urban civil rights campaign or the War on Poverty had done: "That was understandable," he said, "because of all the other programs that any group could push for (housing, health, changes in education and so forth), none of those could be accomplished very quickly. You don't get new housing overnight. You don't change the school system"—indeed, African American and Puerto Rican New Yorkers had picketed and negotiated tirelessly since *Brown v. Board of Education* with precious little to show for it—"whereas a welfare benefit was almost immediately available to them. You could take a client down and the client could walk out with a check. The advantages of the welfare rights organization and membership were much more obvious and much more direct to the person involved than the participation in even" the War on Poverty.[66]

The contrast between the fireworks of the minimum standards campaign and the fizzling of the lobbying effort on behalf of the War on Poverty gave Jennette Washington, Beulah Sanders, Johnnie Tillmon, George Wiley, Ed Day, and others clear ideas about the next steps to take in their efforts to build a national welfare rights movement. The New York City campaigns for winter coats and children's school clothes, which combined welfare recipients' bids for citizenship with their beliefs about good parenting, drew people to the cause of welfare rights. Hulbert James, who was observing the New York situation closely and would soon join the Citywide staff, remembered thinking that "New York was where it was at in 1966 and 1967."[67] Echoing Mitchell Ginsberg, he argued that minimum standards were "an immediate thing. It is something people can deal with and relate to as against the theoretical question."[68]

The City-Wide Coordinating Committee of Welfare Groups stayed on the leading edge of the movement by reprising the winter clothing campaign on a wider scale. Citywide circulated a Winter Clothing Request

Form that gave members the opportunity to request such goods for men and boys as hats, snow pants, and polo shirts, and, for women and girls, cotton dresses, slips, and up to two pairs of stockings each. Parents could request special clothes for young children attending Head Start pre-school classes, and snow suits and mittens for their other young children. On December 12, 1966, neighborhood welfare groups submitted the winter clothing checklists by the hundreds. The strategy of demanding minimum standards, which reflected the striving especially of poor women of color for their families' well-being and for participation in the affluent society, was the yeast that made the welfare movement rise.[69]

Borough of Churches and Welfare Moms

The mobilization of welfare recipients and their success in obtaining material benefits were especially remarkable in Brooklyn. For years before community organizers arrived on the scene, Brooklynites had asked the mayor to help them get decent goods from the welfare department. Letter writers Catherine Kerwin and Theresa Vasta, both from Brooklyn, had made vehement demands for minimum standards in the early 1960s. When minimum standards were no longer solely individual matters but became the centerpiece of a group strategy, parents who received public aid came forward by the hundreds. Overall, the dollar value of special grants for minimum standards in Brooklyn rose from $142,759 in 1963 to over $3 million dollars in 1968. At the same time, membership in the Brooklyn Welfare Action Council (B-WAC), a coalition that linked local groups to the City-Wide Coordinating Committee, grew dramatically. Former Brooklyn welfare recipient and activist Jacquline Pope estimated the membership at its height at 8,000, or nearly 40 percent of the official membership of the national welfare rights movement.[70]

One great advantage enjoyed by the Brooklyn welfare movement was the backing it received from the Catholic Church. Late in 1965, a coalition of activists from different denominations observed the work Frank Espada had done in East New York and founded a chapter of the national group Christians United for Social Action (CUSA) in neighboring Brownsville. CUSA worked on housing issues and sponsored Neighborhood Action Centers devoted to welfare organizing. According to a leader of the group, the Catholic Archdiocese of Brooklyn donated the lion's share of its social action funds, which amounted to $32,000 in 1966 and $120,000 in 1967, to this new experiment in fighting poverty. Espada, meanwhile, moved up in the city's War on Poverty hierarchy and withdrew from daily welfare rights organizing. Late in 1966, he became the head of community organizing under the city's Community Development Agency, a post he held through June 1968.[71] CUSA became the lead organization mobilizing welfare recipients in Brooklyn.

Like other welfare rights organizations around New York City, CUSA relied on minimum standards to recruit people and keep them interested. Its staff members were dissident nuns and priests, who were influenced by the call of the Second Vatican Council to work among the poor. The priests and nuns held their first meeting, at which they told a group of twenty about minimum standards grants, in February 1966. Two weeks later, twenty-five welfare recipients, accompanied by a priest, delivered their request forms to the Livingston Welfare Center. When the recipients returned the next day, a $100 check was waiting for each of them. In October, another priest joined the group and CUSA opened its first storefront office in the middle of a commercial street.[72]

Brooklynite Joyce Burson joined the movement shortly after the priests and nuns arrived. She remembered someone handing her a leaflet about the new group at her local supermarket in the Bedford-Stuyvesant neighborhood and attending her first meeting shortly thereafter. The room was full of women welfare recipients, plus a few Volunteers in Service to America (VISTAs), whose small salaries were paid by the federal War on Poverty, and a priest named Father Duncan. "I felt good," she recalled, "because number 1 I was finding out that I was entitled to some things that I needed . . . I was hearing people say that you can do something . . . you don't have to be ashamed because you're on welfare, you know, you are okay, you're a person, and it's not your fault."[73] Minimum standards had drawn people to the meeting and were the main topic of discussion. Burson saw one of the minimums standards checklists designed by Ezra Birnbaum that night. She and the other women in the room were, she said, "shocked 'cause [this was a] legal fact sheet with all the items that you were entitled to . . . and you were just to check off if you needed these things. So we did."[74]

Rather than relying solely on priests, nuns, and VISTAs to lead the minimum standards campaign, the Brooklyn action groups were also led by their own members. Welfare recipients working as volunteers staffed the storefront offices of CUSA when they first opened. Burson volunteered at her very first meeting. The main jobs of the recipients were to compile minimum standards forms and use them to recruit more members. According to Jacqueline Pope, a volunteer who later became a college professor,and chronicler of the Brooklyn movement, "welfare recipients were in charge of the storefront's operations and were fast becoming experts in assisting their peers by completing forms, accompanying people to the welfare centers, and even making referrals to other community service programs."[75] When members of the groups accompanied newcomers to welfare offices to submit their minimum standards forms, they used these events to recruit even more members: "Each newly issued welfare grant was displayed and loudly discussed by the welfare rights organizers," Pope wrote, "sometimes followed up with testimonials by new members. Immediately, 20 or 30 people would inquire about welfare rights membership. Often, every client in a center would join."[76]

To supplement the efforts of the priests, nuns, and volunteers, the Catholic Archdiocese of Brooklyn paid the salary of a professional organizer. The first person to hold this position was former social work student Rhoda Linton. Linton had worked with Fred Ross and Saul Alinsky at the Community Action Training Center in Syracuse. After graduation, she had done welfare rights work somewhat illicitly while on the staff of a community agency in a gentrifying Brooklyn neighborhood. She remembered approaching the leaders of Catholic Charities, which she knew had supported the CUSA storefronts, and persuading them to hire her at roughly the same time that Burson was getting involved. From a small office at Catholic Charities headquarters in downtown Brooklyn Heights, Linton drove to neighborhoods around the borough telling anyone who was interested about welfare rights. She racked up $500 in parking tickets during the first year, visiting CUSA storefronts, Welfare Recipients Leagues, local groups funded by the federal antipoverty programs, and the leaders of established social welfare or charity agencies. Rather than seeing herself as an "organizer," Linton saw herself as a facilitator, a person who brought structure to "a movement waiting to happen." The most important ingredient in that movement's emergence was the draw of minimum standards. "When the money started flowing," she remembered, "people came from everywhere."[77]

The combination of minimum standards, archdiocesan funding, active participation by welfare recipients in running the campaign, and professional staff support brought new people into the movement and kept more experienced members involved. CUSA eventually oversaw five storefronts in East New York, Brownsville, and Bedford-Stuyvesant. The Brooklyn Welfare Action Council, a gathering point of all of the neighborhood welfare rights efforts in the borough, was born in 1967. B-WAC created its own leadership structure apart from the City-Wide Coordinating Committee of Welfare Groups. Burson, who felt like she had "never belonged to anything in my life," was elected president of the welfare rights group in her neighborhood.[78] Although she did not think that the priests saw her as a likely candidate for leadership, the other members voted for her anyway. She had helped create the largest welfare rights organization in Brooklyn, with over two hundred members. Shortly thereafter, she became the president of the Brooklyn Welfare Action Council and a member of the Citywide executive board.[79]

In Brooklyn as elsewhere in New York City, the minimum standards campaigns fulfilled the main goals of the new welfare rights movement. These were to build group membership in order to build power and to generate demonstrations that would pressure the welfare system to change. Local groups proliferated in number and grew in size, intensifying demands on welfare offices to distribute what they promised in their manuals, and keeping the movement on the radar screens of city officials. As the leaders of the City-Wide Coordinating Committee negotiated with Ginsberg, the stacks of requests for school clothing, winter gear, and furniture continued to accumulate in local welfare offices, serving as reminders that the negotiators had popular support. In the context of the urban riots of the middle 1960s, they also served as reminders of simmering, potentially combustible, dissatisfaction in African American and Puerto Rican neighborhoods of New York City.

"Just Beginning to Come But We Will Be Back"

The welfare rights movement grew by leaps and bounds. In areas where the movement had taken root before June 30 it spread its roots, adding chapters and members, and gaining influence. In December 1966, the Poverty/Rights Action Center counted 134 welfare rights organizations across the United States. These included established groups, such as Johnnie Tillmon's ANC Mothers Anonymous in Los Angeles and a long list of chapters of the Ohio Steering Committee for Adequate Welfare, as well as newer groups. By February 1967, the total was 188 groups, including 77 from New York City and 24 from Brooklyn alone. Month after month, the network expanded its geographic diversity and included more local and state groups, including a thriving California Welfare Rights Organization, a citywide ADC Parents Association in Denver and a League for Adequate Welfare (LAW) in St. Louis.[80]

These organizations were autonomous of one another and of the Poverty/Rights Action Center, but they were united by recipients' desires for what Jennette Washington called "the good life" and by minimum standards campaigns that helped them achieve it. Each had its own agenda, its own distinctive membership, and its own particular relationship with middle-class allies such as ministers, social workers, VISTAs, and lawyers. Ohio, for example, had an active statewide federation that predated P/RAC and received support from both the Protestant Inner-City Mission Against Poverty and the federal poverty programs.[81] However, the Ohio mothers and fathers faced many of the same issues that their counterparts did in New York. The Columbus Welfare Rights Organization took as its symbol an empty horn of plenty circled by the words "Welfare: a right, not a privilege." Activist poet

Mary Spurlock from Columbus addressed "Mr. Ohio" on the subject of children's winter clothes: "I'd like to see your face when your children would be cold / No winter clothes to wear, what they have are years old / With holes here and tears there / Yes, Mr. Ohio, it will cost you more: / We'll fight for our children / Till you open the door."[82]

National leaders of the welfare rights movement could not offer these diverse and dispersed local activists a great deal of help, but they tried to keep track of them and published a "welfare leaders' newsletter" to share reports of their progress with others across the country.[83] Meanwhile, the key activists and P/RAC staff continued building a national-level structure to support the growing movement that they could not fully direct. In February 1967, over 350 welfare rights activists came together to take the next steps in building an organization. The meeting marked the first encounter between Beulah Sanders and Johnnie Tillmon, the two most forceful local leaders of the movement.[84] The assembly nominated Tillmon to chair both the National Coordinating Committee (NCC) of the national welfare rights movement and the larger meeting. She had never played such a role before; the meetings of ANC Mothers Anonymous that she chaired typically had fewer than fifteen people in attendance.[85] Tillmon kept the proceedings relatively amicable by letting everyone air the grievances they harbored against local welfare departments and take credit for their achievements. Delegates heard, for example, from a group of welfare recipients who said that it was so difficult for African Americans to get benefits in Mississippi that the U.S. Civil Rights Commission had held a hearing on public welfare in their state.[86]

Immediately following the meeting a group of activists lobbied Congress and made the welfare rights movement's first visit to the Department of Health, Education, and Welfare. A delegation of five approached an assistant to the director of the Social and Rehabilitation Services division of the federal agency. However, once he had agreed to see them, another seventy-five women appeared to participate. The point, according to Tillmon, was "more or less to let folks know that we're here, just got here, you know, we just beginning to come but we will be back."[87]

The group planned to "be back" in the capital for a welfare rights convention over the summer that would officially inaugurate a National Welfare Rights Organization. Tillmon, Sanders, and the new National Coordinating Committee met twice to make preparations. Planning for the convention received a boost when Tim Sampson joined the staff of P/RAC. As Sampson had known it eventually would, the federal Office of Economic Opportunity withdrew funding from his statewide welfare rights and farmworkers' organizing project in California. He considered working for OEO in Washington, but George Wiley convinced him to accept the welfare rights post instead. Tillmon and Wiley went on a national fundraising tour, in which they learned about the possibilities for and limitations of outside support for their new welfare rights federation. They sought OEO funding but were unable to get it. Perhaps more surprisingly, they sought support from labor unions, such as the Amalgamated Meat Cutters Union, to no avail; although Wiley tried his best to describe the welfare rights organization as a "union of people," the trade unionists offered no support.[88]

More Money NOW!

In March 1967 George Wiley sketched out a plan for the future of the welfare rights movement. Building on the New York example, he, Day, and Sampson designed a National Action Campaign that would increase the number and size of local action groups by helping poor people gain some of the benefits of the affluent society. They provided minimum standards, or, as they were called within the movement, "basic needs" checklists that local activists could adapt to their circumstances. The slogan for this campaign was "More Money NOW!" Sampson, who took credit for creating the phrase, reflected years later that it was "really good on the street for welfare recipients," although it was "kind of a crass message. . . . It didn't clothe the idea of basic needs, you know, with very much dignity."[89]

After months of organizing across the country and logistical preparation work in Washington, D.C., the Poverty/Rights Action Center convened the inaugural meeting of the National Welfare Rights Organization (NWRO). Johnnie Tillmon and George Wiley issued a convention call that relied for its appeal on welfare recipients' desires to secure decent goods for their children and themselves, and their sense that they should receive all the benefits to which they were legally entitled. Wiley and Tillmon offered participants a chance to help found "the first national membership based organization of poor people." Together, they promised, welfare recipients could gain "justice, dignity, democracy, and MORE MONEY NOW!"[90] P/RAC publications sought to attract participants by suggesting that they would learn from one another how to obtain additional benefits. "Will *you* find out how the Columbus WRO fought and got an official copy of the State Welfare Manual? . . . How even recipients in Mississippi are getting their rights?" a writer, probably Ed Day, asked his audience of welfare recipients.[91] Alan Stone, a law student who worked at P/RAC that summer through an internship managed by the Law Students' Civil Rights Research Council, performed much of the hands-on logistical work for the convention. He remembered how eye-opening it was "for a few days to see country people, black and white" arrive.[92] Approximately three hundred delegates met to vote on creating a formal national organization out of their diverse welfare rights movement. They approved a constitution, created a permanent National Coordinating Committee, and chose four principles—Adequate Income, Dignity, Justice, and Democracy—as the official goals of the National Welfare Rights Organization.[93]

Tillmon and Wiley were correct when they labeled NWRO the first national membership organization of the poor ever formed in the United States. The hundreds of participants who showed up to make history in August 1967 had every reason to expect that NWRO would help them gain money, goods, and more: a seat at the table of public policy making, and respect from social workers, welfare department heads such as Mitchell Ginsberg, and mayors such as John Lindsay. The creation of NWRO was particularly remarkable in the context of the middle and late 1960s because the group was explicitly interracial and committed to economic justice for African Americans, Latino/as, and poor whites, rather than taking its cues from the increasingly polarized politics that prevailed at the time. Tillmon recalled a moment at the convention at which she and Beulah Sanders corrected Wiley when he referred to his audience as "black folks." Tillmon wrote Wiley a note saying, "will you please quit saying black and say poor, and Beulah stuck the note in front of George's face and when he went to say the first time [he said] 'poock' people. . . . 'Cause we [were] not talking in terms of black folks now."[94]

The convention culminated with a welfare rights rally on the Washington Mall and a march to the headquarters of the federal Department of Health, Education, and Welfare. Tillmon led a group of three hundred convention delegates, plus over a thousand activists from twenty-six states who had come to town expressly to participate in the action. She remembered that there were enough people to circle the building holding hands if they had wanted to do so.[95] This signaled the start of a new chapter in the history of welfare rights. Yet storm clouds appeared on the horizon as soon as federal officials reacted to the presence of organized welfare recipients and their allies. The group started out in the Senate Caucus Room in the U.S. Capitol building "to hear what our representatives had to say for themselves," in the words of the City-Wide Coordinating Committee newsletter. "Though many senators had been invited, none showed up."[96] Tillmon and Sanders, Wiley and Day, and their hundreds of allies then began the journey from the Capitol to HEW, ground zero of the national welfare bureaucracy. "And when we got to the HEW Building," Tim Sampson recalled, "there were cops or soldiers, I can't remember which, on the roof with guns and they had locked the doors against us." Sampson was "absolutely furious at my government that my government was reacting this way to women, you know, simply petitioning their government to change the system that affected their lives. And the women were astonished that I was angry and upset . . . it was like I was ignorant that I didn't understand that the government wasn't going to be helpful."[97]

In the early 1960s, Catherine Kerwin and other welfare mothers had been largely on their own when they wrote letters to the mayor of New York City asking for warm coats and galoshes for their school-aged children. Only a few years later, welfare recipients in New York had the opportunity to affiliate with other women and men like themselves and to get help from organizers, priests, lawyers, and social workers. They shared their problems with each other, discovered what they had in common, and learned how to turn individual requests for clothes and furniture into a political strategy for changing the balance of power between the welfare department and its thousands of constituents.

Eventually, with the backing of a National Action Campaign that shared the secrets of local governments with as many people as wanted to hear them, impoverished parents moved from supplication to demand, from individual items they claimed they needed to a collective claim for "More Money NOW!" As they organized a national movement, they began to ask national bureaucrats and politicians to hear what they had to say. "We will be back," Johnnie Tillmon promised. She and the other leaders of the rising welfare rights movement hoped that the U.S. Senate and the Department of Health, Education, and Welfare would not shut their ears and lock their doors forever.

Chapter 3
Legal Civil Disobedience

A lawyer is a very valuable piece of property in a poor community.
—*Stephen Wexler, welfare rights movement lawyer*

Joan Sunderland was a resident of the Bronx and an active member of the City-Wide Coordinating Committee of Welfare Groups.[1] In October 1967, after participating in the campaigns for clothing and furniture that had sparked a wildfire of protest against the New York City welfare system, Sunderland got a lawyer. The legal proceeding they initiated together was a "fair hearing," an appeal of a social worker's or supervisor's decision that occurred in a special tribunal organized under the state welfare department. By seeking help from attorney Stephen Nagler, Sunderland added force to the citywide and nationwide movement for welfare rights. She also gained her own day in court. Her hearing concerned a range of goods she had requested at the high point of the Citywide minimum standards campaign. Her caseworker believed she did not need some of these items, such as new dishes and drinking glasses to use at meals. When the hearing referee (the equivalent of a judge) asked about one of her requests, Sunderland openly disagreed with her caseworker:

THE REFEREE: Is it true she did not get those dishes?
MISS SORENSON [caseworker]: Yes, she has a full service for eight which she terms good china and doesn't think should be used in every day use.
MRS. SUNDERLAND: I sure do not with my children.[2]

At the very end of the hearing, the referee elicited Sunderland's perspective on her need for dishes:

THE REFEREE: One final question. Is there anything further, and I am talking to you [Sunderland] now as a gentleman to a lady that you wish to add to the record, any statement you wish to make?
MR. NAGLER: I have—

MRS. SUNDERLAND: Yes . . . Yes, because I feel that something that is given to me when I got married, I don't feel I should use it to serve my six year old, my two year old children with. These are dishes that a friend of my mother gave me when I got married. I don't think that this lady that spent her money would think for me to serve my kids on these dishes. Demitasse cups and saucers.
THE REFEREE: You are referring to the dinner set which Miss Sorensen has referred to, is that it?
MRS. SUNDERLAND: Yes.
MR. NAGLER: Do you use it for any purpose at all?
MRS. SUNDERLAND: Sure. When the Mother's Club [i.e., the welfare rights group] comes—
THE REFEREE: It is a decorative set more or less and when you have company?
MRS. SUNDERLAND: Yes.
MR. NAGLER: [And in regard to the] Glasses that she refused to give you.
MRS. SUNDERLAND: There the same thing. They are goblets and wine glasses. My mother was in the house when she said that I should use them. My mother gave me those things and I wouldn't dare give a two year old—she wouldn't. No one in this room would.[3]

While Joan Sunderland was explaining why she needed good dishes and regular dishes, glasses and "goblets," the fair hearing was coming into its own as a tactic of the national welfare rights movement. On October 20, 1967, NWRO announced a "new weapon" in the battle against poverty. The cover of the organization's newspaper featured a drawing of an old-fashioned bomb with a long fuse, marked "Fair Hearings."[4]

The welfare fair hearing, a formal legal proceeding authorized by the Social Security Act of 1935, had rarely been considered part of a revolutionary arsenal. It involved a single applicant for public aid who sought redress when she was denied assistance or when a caseworker refused to issue her a grant increase, special grant, or help moving to a new home. With little of the glamor that attached to famous cases in the federal courts, fair hearings were located in a corner of the law that well-trained attorneys and reform-minded social movements rarely visited before the 1960s. However, once activists discovered it, they turned this quiet neighborhood into the locus of some of the most hard-fought battles in the welfare rights movement.

Thousands of poor women and men pursued hearings and other legal remedies in order to gain "rights" and "welfare," full standing as citizens in the postwar United States and the material particulars that they believed underlay the good life. Every member of the City-Wide Coordinating Committee of Welfare Groups and NWRO talked about her rights and the rights of other welfare recipients. Members and their allies referred to virtually every contested action by a local caseworker or elected official as an "illegal" contravention of state regulations, the Social Security Act, or the U.S. Constitution. Joan Sunderland was only

Figure 6. NWRO newspaper introduces members to the fair hearing strategy.
Courtesy Periodicals Division, Wisconsin Historical Society.

one poor citizen out of many who used her hearing to call for the economic aid to which she believed she was entitled from her national, state, and city governments. Welfare recipients and their allies also participated in federal litigation and efforts at legislative and judicial law reform. As attorney and scholar Martha Davis has documented, welfare recipients and reform-minded attorneys together brought a string of cases before the federal courts at the end of the 1960s and beginning of the 1970s.[5] These efforts established important precedents. However, they were less important in the life of the welfare movement than day-to-day uses of legal language and strategies, including fair hearings.

Welfare recipients in Citywide and NWRO filed for fair hearings in part because they were relatively safe and accessible. When Joan Sunderland appealed the decisions of her local welfare office, she probably made her caseworker angry, but she was neither arrested nor physically assaulted, as she might have been if she had confronted the welfare department by less formal means. She placed her caseworker on the defensive and compelled the welfare department to spend time and money organizing the hearing, without taking huge risks herself. In the words of a welfare rights organizer in Mississippi, fair hearings were a form of "legal civil disobedience," which was safer than a public sit-in or a march on the state welfare office. Organizer Ted Seaver found that "The hearing was one of the few actions one could use to force the welfare department into a situation where it cost them more time, money and manpower" to schedule and staff the hearings, replace the caseworkers who left their regular jobs in order to participate, and transcribe the proceedings, "than it would cost the client organization."[6]

Civil Rights, Legal Rights, Welfare Rights

Members of the City-Wide Coordinating Committee of Welfare Groups and NWRO learned about "legal civil disobedience" from their predecessors in the African American freedom movement, South and North. The boundaries between the Southern and Northern movements were porous, and so were the boundaries between more familiar civil rights demands and demands for social or welfare rights.

The African American freedom movement had begun to use legal strategies early in the twentieth century. The National Association for the Advancement of Colored People (NAACP) had pursued legal action against racial segregation since the organization's founding. In 1939, executive director Walter White and staff lawyer Thurgood Marshall acknowledged the special significance of law in their overall strategy to defeat Jim Crow. They created a separate nonprofit organization, the Legal Defense and Educational Fund, Inc. (LDF), devoted solely to litigation. In the late 1940s and 1950s, the LDF started to win steady victories in the federal courts, in cases such as *Shelley v. Kraemer* (1948), which found that restrictive covenants forbidding property owners from selling to nonwhites were unenforceable, and in the series of educational equality cases culminating in *Brown v. Board of Education of Topeka, Kansas*.[7] Civil rights victories in court did not themselves produce integrated communities or classrooms, or end political exclusion by race and class.

But they were benchmarks of progress against the legal and political structures that undergirded segregation.[8]

Organizations devoted to civil rights law proliferated in the 1960s. The most important in terms of linking civil rights law to the welfare rights movement was the Lawyers Constitutional Defense Committee (LCDC), one of whose founders was Carl Rachlin, an anti-Communist labor lawyer who became the leading attorney for the Congress of Racial Equality (CORE). He served as legal director of CORE's rough equivalent of the Legal Defense and Educational Fund, the Scholarship, Education, and Defense Fund for Racial Equality (SEDFRE), and then as NWRO general counsel.[9] Rachlin was not especially interested in the sweeping appellate litigation that had become the specialty of the NAACP Legal Defense and Educational Fund. His goal in helping found LCDC was to support the black freedom movement "in motion"—in contrast to the long-term, appellate litigation the LDF had modeled in *Brown v. Board*—by designing legal strategies that dovetailed with direct action strategies.[10] Thanks to LCDC, dozens of attorneys went south in 1964 to support the students who were battling Jim Crow during the summer civil rights project known as Freedom Summer.

Southern civil rights law shifted over time toward welfare rights issues. After Freedom Summer, attorneys for the Lawyers Constitutional Defense Committee continued to take voting rights cases and to defend African Americans who had been accused of politically charged crimes. They also helped people access public assistance payments, veterans' benefits, and workers' compensation.[11]

The most important welfare case with which the LCDC attorneys became involved was *King v. Smith*, which began in the fall of 1966 when Mrs. Sylvester Smith arrived at the Alabama office of LCDC attorney Donald Jellinek.[12] Smith had lost her benefits because she was pursuing a sexual affair with a man who neither lived with her nor paid her bills. Under a statute that segregationist governor George Wallace had signed as the first Freedom Summer volunteers were arriving in his state, Alabama law treated this man as the "substitute father" of Smith's children. Local welfare officials withdrew her benefits; they argued that her lover should support her financially.[13] Like New York activist Joan Sunderland, Smith asserted her entitlement to aid and her equality with other women. She forbade the welfare department to investigate her sex life and, when her caseworker suggested she end her intimate relationship, she commented: "if God had intended for me to be a nun I'd be a nun."[14] The Justices of the U.S. Supreme Court essentially agreed with her, finding in *King v. Smith* that all eligible people were entitled to aid under the Social Security Act. Moreover, the Court found that recipients of government help had the same right to make choices about their intimate affairs as did other citizens.[15]

As the volunteer lawyers in the South shifted focus from other kinds of civil rights issues to welfare and public benefits, so did lawyers working with African American communities in the North. Carl Rachlin represented the New York City welfare recipients who were arrested for demonstrating and sleeping in at the welfare department in September 1966. In December of that year, he referred to his office as "a kind of legal aid organization to most of the poverty groups in New York." Rachlin claimed for himself and his staff "a kind of supervisory capacity over the legal problems that are developing rapidly in the welfare area."[16] At the request of George Wiley, whom he knew from CORE, he became general counsel of the National Welfare Rights Organization. Rachlin and attorney Stephen Nagler from the CORE legal office also became Joan Sunderland's lawyers. Between 1966 and 1968, they represented at least 365 welfare recipients in their fair hearing appeals and negotiations with the welfare departments of New York City and Westchester County.[17]

"The Poor Need Counsel"

Even before the emergence of the welfare rights movement, poor New Yorkers had combined welfare with rights, requests for material aid with their own understandings of the law. Those who had written letters to Mayor Wagner in the early 1960s had offered interpretations of their rights and of both constitutional and statutory law. Gloria Arce-Perez, for example, who claimed that she had been repeatedly propositioned by her male welfare investigator and lost benefits because she refused him, wrote that "as a citizen" she "must have the same rights and privileges of others . . . I and my children are victimize and my constitutional rights denied."[18] Charles Simmons from Harlem asked the Mayor, "for my sake and the law of the land," to raise his welfare budget."[19]

Although they talked about their rights, welfare clients in New York rarely brought their complaints before lawyers or judges. "The poor need counsel," commented an attorney who lived in East Harlem between the middle 1950s and early 1960s.[20] William Stringfellow observed that most Harlem residents' main interaction with law was through the police department. "The image of the police (and of the law)," he wrote just prior to the Harlem and Bedford-Stuyvesant riots of 1964, "is lamentably pretty much the same in New York as in Alabama, so far as Negroes and others who are poor or discriminated against are concerned."[21] Although roughly one-third of all lawyers in the cities of the United States were located in New York, almost none worked for poor people. Only a small fraction served African Americans or Puerto Ricans. On the basis of interviews with over eight hundred attorneys in private practice in Manhattan and the Bronx, political scientist Jerome Carlin concluded that poor people were, "for all practical purposes, denied access to and effective use of the legal system."[22]

While lawyers in private practice did not serve the poor, the nonprofit Legal Aid Society, founded in 1876, made a limited number of lawyers available to people who could not pay for them. Legal Aid lawyers attempted to bridge the gap between disaffected potential rioters and mainstream law. In 1964, there were 107 legal aid attorneys in New York City, 11 of them in Harlem. Critics charged that the Legal Aid Society simply could not meet the huge need of poor people and communities of color for legal assistance. They also claimed that legal aid lawyers treated the help they gave as a form of charity, not a right, and emphasized procedure over substance, assisting poor people in their efforts to locate lawyers but not helping them use law to become less poor.[23]

The map of legal resources available to welfare recipients changed dramatically in the middle 1960s. The staff of the Strycker's Bay Neighborhood Council focused on helping people assert their rights to welfare, health care, and other public goods. Strycker's Bay made an attorney available at its storefront office in the Upper West Side urban renewal district. Mobilization for Youth (MFY) on the Lower East Side responded to its constituents' complaints about the juvenile courts, police, and social service bureaucracy by opening a Legal Unit in 1964. MFY fielded nonlawyer welfare advocates who worked with clients who wanted to apply for, or maintain their eligibility for, public benefits. "Advocacy on behalf of the clients," writer Richard Elman and academic Richard Cloward argued, "was the bludgeon by which this city agency was made more responsive to a portion of its Lower East Side constituency."[24]

In 1965, the federal government began for the first time to hire lawyers to serve the poor. The MFY Legal Unit was a model for the federal legal services program, which Congress added to the War on Poverty one year after it began. Despite this connection, publicly funded legal services came slowly to New York City. Opposition from the organized bar, and the insistence of poverty warriors in Washington that there be "maximum feasible participation" by clients in the management of the program, blocked the Lindsay administration's application for legal services funds. Under the pressure of negative publicity, the city and federal governments and the lawyers finally agreed to a plan. In 1968, the Office of Economic Opportunity released $4.5 million to New York City for legal services, and local law offices flowered in low-income neighborhoods.[25]

Beyond the expansion of publicly funded legal resources, private-sector attorneys from both for-profit firms and nonprofit advocacy groups were more readily available to the poor in the middle and late 1960s than they had ever been before. Prompted by law students and young attorneys, probably embarrassed by Jerome Carlin's findings, and fearful of the effects of legal cynicism in Harlem and Bedford-Stuyvesant, elite private firms expanded their pro bono practices, which provided free counsel to people who could not afford to hire their own advocates. Nonprofit legal groups, such as the American Civil Liberties Union, also increased their focus on poverty. The Center on Social Welfare Policy and Law at Columbia University was established in 1965, when a private foundation decided to sponsor an "experimental center" to support lawyers who represented poor people.[26] Its director was the former MFY legal director, Edward Sparer. Another poverty law center opened at New York University in 1965, under the direction of attorney Norman Dorsen. It performed many of the same functions as the center at Columbia but sponsored more research and pursued no litigation.[27]

The use of legal strategies by members of the black freedom movement, the role lawyers and litigation played in the federal poverty programs, and the new availability of pro bono and nonprofit lawyers, transformed many New Yorkers' access to attorneys and courts. The cumulative effect of these changes was a huge shift in expectations of the legal system. Joan Sunderland and her colleagues at Citywide might never have sought justice through fair hearings if other poor people and people of color had not already developed faith in the capacity of legal institutions to answer their demands. A decade after *Brown*, as the walls of de jure segregation came tumbling down, these women and men viewed law as an arena in which they could fight for the economic goods that they believed were part and parcel of American citizenship.

Fair Hearings in Welfare Rights

Fair hearings were rarely used by clients of public assistance in the thirty years after passage of the Social Security Act. However, the hearings were not entirely forgotten in the period between 1935 and their discovery by welfare rights activists. A. Delafield Smith, assistant counsel to the Federal Security Agency, had argued in 1949 that the fair hearing was evidence of "enforceable legal rights of participation" in public aid programs. "All three of the federal [public assistance] titles" of the Social Security Act, Smith wrote, "require the state, as one of the conditions of the federal grants, to give the applicant the opportunity of a fair hearing before the state administrative agency. This generally brought applicants under the constitutional guaranty of due process."[28] Legal theorist Charles Reich made a similar point about the relationship between fair hearings and welfare rights in 1965. "The framers of the [Social Security] Act had a clear concept concerning the 'right' to public assistance," Reich argued, "and provided devices to protect these rights. Thus, in the program for aid to families with needy children, the Act requires that states afford an opportunity for a fair hearing to any individual whose claim is denied or not acted upon with reasonable promptness."[29]

Welfare rights organizers and attorneys learned about fair hearings from David Gilman, an attorney who worked for the Legal Aid Society on the Lower East Side of Manhattan. According to Gilman and social worker Ezra Birnbaum, attorneys and other advocates began representing welfare recipients in fair hearings in October 1965. Gilman told Carl Rachlin and other civil rights and economic justice lawyers about his experiences with the hearings. He and Edward Sparer of the Center on Social Welfare Policy and Law also began designing an appellate legal strategy focused on welfare rights.[30]

In 1966 and 1967, Rachlin and his staff at the CORE legal office began helping large numbers of welfare recipients bring hearings in New York City and nearby Westchester County. Jill Jackson, a welfare rights activist from Mount Vernon, a working-class city in Westchester County, was among the first of Rachlin's clients. She had suffered a fire in her home that ruined much of her furniture. Before bringing the appeal, Jackson had asked the Westchester welfare department for an array of replacement goods and for things she had never had before but believed she deserved, such as a telephone.[31] Jill Jackson brought her hearing in order to get these specific goods. She sought to defend her entitlement to a postwar standard of living, and to support the work of the welfare rights movement. Jackson described the visit of her caseworker, Miss Demo, as an exercise of power masked as compassion:

Miss Demo arrived at my home approximately eleven o'clock and she left at approximately ten after two in the afternoon. . . . Well, at my kitchen table we sat down and we talked about, of course, my children, the health of my children, the things that I needed in the apartment. She took a tour, accompanied by me of my apartment. She went into every closet, she ripped the sheets off every bed. . . . Of course, I let her do this. I had to open up the castroconvertible couch which was in my living room to show her what was on that. She asked me who was using it; I told her I was sleeping on it.[32]

When Jackson asked for a bed so she would no longer have to sleep on the couch, Miss Demo, she said, told her she could have new sheets but no new furniture. "I agreed with that," Jackson testified. "What could I do?"[33]

Like Mrs. Smith in the case *King v. Smith*, Joyce Jackson asserted a right

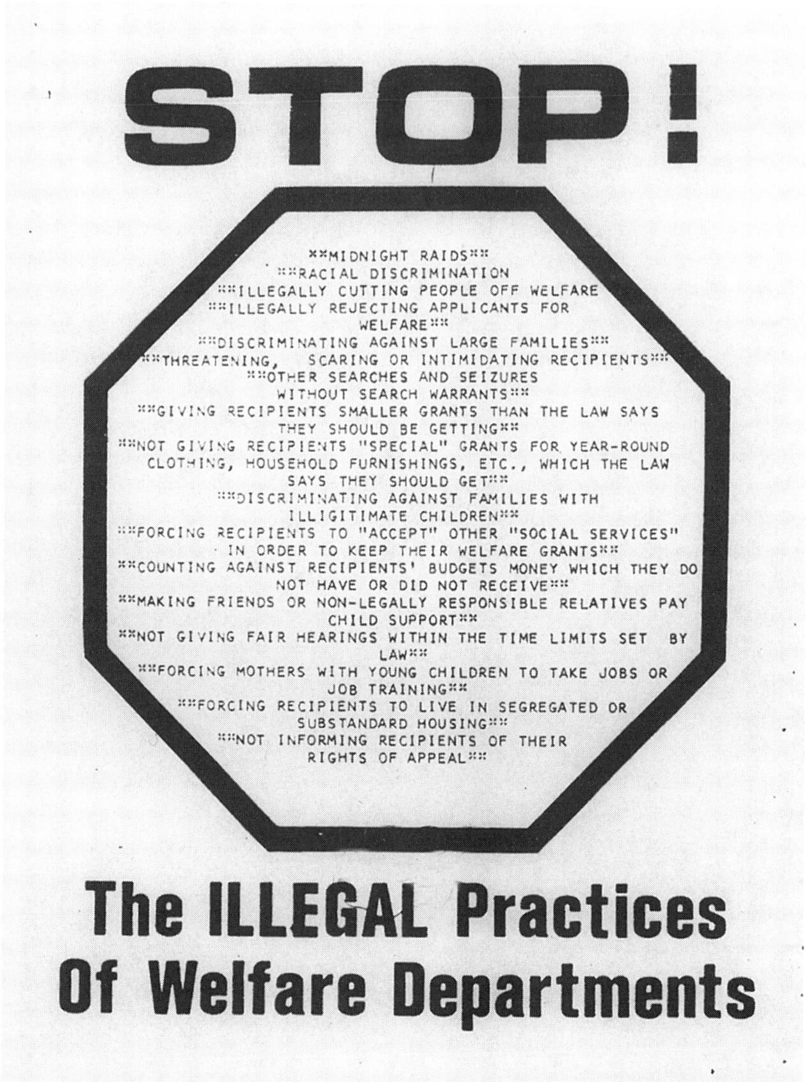

STOP!

MIDNIGHT RAIDS
RACIAL DISCRIMINATION
ILLEGALLY CUTTING PEOPLE OFF WELFARE
ILLEGALLY REJECTING APPLICANTS FOR
WELFARE
DISCRIMINATING AGAINST LARGE FAMILIES
THREATENING, SCARING OR INTIMIDATING RECIPIENTS
OTHER SEARCHES AND SEIZURES
WITHOUT SEARCH WARRANTS
GIVING RECIPIENTS SMALLER GRANTS THAN THE LAW SAYS
THEY SHOULD BE GETTING
NOT GIVING RECIPIENTS "SPECIAL" GRANTS FOR YEAR-ROUND
CLOTHING, HOUSEHOLD FURNISHINGS, ETC., WHICH THE LAW
SAYS THEY SHOULD GET
DISCRIMINATING AGAINST FAMILIES WITH
ILLIGITIMATE CHILDREN
FORCING RECIPIENTS TO "ACCEPT" OTHER "SOCIAL SERVICES"
IN ORDER TO KEEP THEIR WELFARE GRANTS
COUNTING AGAINST RECIPIENTS' BUDGETS MONEY WHICH THEY DO
NOT HAVE OR DID NOT RECEIVE
MAKING FRIENDS OR NON-LEGALLY RESPONSIBLE RELATIVES PAY
CHILD SUPPORT
NOT GIVING FAIR HEARINGS WITHIN THE TIME LIMITS SET BY
LAW
FORCING MOTHERS WITH YOUNG CHILDREN TO TAKE JOBS OR
JOB TRAINING
FORCING RECIPIENTS TO LIVE IN SEGREGATED OR
SUBSTANDARD HOUSING
NOT INFORMING RECIPIENTS OF THEIR
RIGHTS OF APPEAL

The ILLEGAL Practices Of Welfare Departments

Figure 7. Law lay at the center of the claims poor people made against welfare departments. NWRO newspaper. Courtesy Periodicals Division, Wisconsin Historical Society.

to sexual privacy. She claimed that she deserved to receive government benefits without relinquishing control over her intimate life. It was no longer routine in the late 1960s for welfare departments to catalogue their clients' sexual behavior or to base case work decisions on such behavior. However, judgments about clients' sexual practices still influenced welfare department personnel. One of Jackson's primary reasons for bringing her fair hearing appeal was her belief that, when Miss Demo visited, "all she was concerned with was whether Miss Jackson had a boyfriend and whether he was living with her."[34] The attorney for the Westchester County Welfare Department also raised the issue of whether she had a boyfriend, when he asked Demo:

Mr. McATAMNEY [Welfare department attorney]: Did she characterize her friend [who was helping to pay her bills] at that time? Oh, excuse me.
Mr. RACHLIN [Jackson's attorney]: Not only was it an interruption, but it was highly irrelevant.
Mr. McATAMNEY: I'm sorry; I was carried away.[35]

Jill Jackson and thousands of other welfare recipients in New York appealed their caseworkers' decisions in fair hearings. In 1964, there were 188 fair hearings in New York State. In 1966, when welfare rights groups and attorneys began experimenting with the hearings, the number jumped to 650. In 1967, the City-Wide Coordinating Committee of Welfare Groups made the hearings central to its strategy. New York State convened 4,233 hearings that year.[36] A single neighborhood chapter of Citywide brought one hundred appeals in the first three months of 1967.[37]

Fair hearings became an integral part of the strategy of the citywide and national welfare rights movements. As part of the NWRO National Action Campaign that began in the run-up to the welfare rights movement "birthday" on June 30, 1967, members of Citywide submitted more demands than ever before for minimum standards grants. Citywide leaders encouraged those whose requests were denied, or who faced delays in getting a response, to file for fair hearings within two weeks of their initial requests. "This was the first time," wrote Gilman and Birnbaum, "that Welfare Groups . . . had combined their requests for Minimum Standards and Fair Hearings in an essentially coordinated attack."[38] The hearings were part of a larger web of social movement strategy. They continued minimum standards demands by legal means, joining the formal right to appeal with nitty-gritty material issues.

"One Large, Massive Campaign"

The Citywide campaign aimed to submit a massive number of minimum standards and fair hearing requests to Mayor Lindsay. Leaders such as

Figure 8. Echoing the Supreme Court case *King v. Smith* (1968), welfare rights activists lampoon social workers who scrutinized recipients' personal lives. Courtesy *Washington Star* photographic archives, copyright *Washington Post*, reprinted by permission of District of Columbia Public Library.

Beulah Sanders and Jennette Washington, and middle-class supporters such as Carl Rachlin, intended to overwhelm the welfare department with requests in much the same way civil rights demonstrators had overwhelmed the Southern justice system with scores of people who refused to submit to Jim Crow segregation. They expected their joined demands for minimum standards and fair hearings to produce large cash grants for members of welfare rights groups and, therefore, to increase membership in Citywide and NWRO. By making organized welfare recipients visible through their mass demands and appeals, Citywide leaders hoped to make the Lindsay administration acknowledge the movement's "political muscle."[39]

Beulah Sanders and other Citywide members presented their requests for minimum standards and fair hearing appeals on July 21, 1967. The occasion was a public meeting state officials had convened to consider changes in fair hearing procedures. Citywide members packed the conference room; so many people asked to speak that the meeting was held over for an additional day. Sanders announced that Citywide was submitting about 1000 requests for fair hearings. She and other Citywide members continued to gather fair hearing requests through the summer and fall, asking welfare recipients to keep their request forms "pouring in."[40] In September 1967, the fair hearing campaign joined with the Citywide school clothing campaign. The two strategies "dove-tailed," according to lawyer Gilman and organizer Birnbaum, "and the City and State Welfare agencies treated all the F[air] H[earing] forms as one large, massive campaign."[41] Estimates of the number of hearing requests ranged from a low of six hundred to a high of two thousand for the period between August and October.[42] From September 1967 to January 1968, there were forty welfare hearings a day, five days a week, in administrative courtrooms in lower Manhattan.[43]

As a result of this "massive campaign," Citywide members accomplished most of their goals. In October 1967, Gilman and Citywide leaders estimated that fair hearings and minimum standards demands had pressured officials into giving clients hundreds of thousands, and possibly millions, of dollars' worth of grants. Women and men in the borough of Brooklyn alone received $150,000 in the first week of the campaign. Mass demands for minimum standards and legal appeals made the welfare rights movement an inescapable part of the political landscape in New York. Swamped with applications, representatives from the state and city tried to arrange a meeting with welfare rights lawyers. The lawyers refused to speak for poor people, so officials contacted Citywide directly. Sanders, Jennette Washington, and other members of the Citywide executive committee sat down with the welfare bureaucrats and walked away with agreements for babysitting expenses and carfare for those bringing appeals, hearings at night for those who needed them, and translators for Spanish-speaking appellants.[44]

In addition to supporting the organizational goals of the City-Wide Coordinating Committee of Welfare Groups, the "massive campaign" expressed the vision of citizenship that animated both Citywide and NWRO. By demanding fair hearings, Jill Jackson from Mount Vernon and Joan Sunderland from the Bronx claimed standing in the legal and political life of the postwar United States. They asked caseworkers, hearing referees, and city officials to take them seriously as mothers who knew how to care for their children and as shoppers with expertise about navigating the consumer marketplace on behalf of their families. At the high point of the affluent society and the rights consciousness of both the black freedom movement and the Supreme Court under Chief Justice Earl Warren, this group of welfare recipients, most of whom were women of color, demanded the political and material goods they believed were available to everyone else in their country.

When they sought and pursued fair hearings, welfare recipients expressed their desires for material aid and for recognition as members of the society in which they lived.[45] Mary Sellors, a welfare mother from the Bronx, was particularly eager to gain a financial boost for her family. "Oh, yes, I got some money that I wont you too get for me," she wrote to her attorney, explaining why she was demanding a fair hearing. At the same time, she wanted to use the law to make her caseworker listen to her. "A Woman came out here Tuesday," she complained. "I told her that the Children need there School cloths bad"—but money for the clothes still had not come.[46]

Welfare recipients sought acknowledgment of the hard work they did to make ends meet, despite welfare budgets that, they claimed, failed to cover their families' needs. As in the letters New Yorkers had written to Mayor Wagner in the early 1960s, and the demands Citywide members made for minimum standards, women who brought fair hearings spoke about the expertise they believed they had developed as mothers and consumers. Christina Mann, one of Carl Rachlin's clients, impugned the welfare department for making it difficult to negotiate the consumer market on behalf of her family. When the hearing examiner asked her to explain "how it is that you claim that you are not getting what you are entitled to from the agency with reference to your recurring grant," Mann exploded: "For $30 I can take care of her? A son that is as big as this man (indicating) and I got three more little girls behind him. Do you think I can do it on $30 [the clothing portion of her regular welfare grant]?"[47] Ann Freeman testified in her fair hearing about the distance between welfare department estimates of how long clothes would last and how long hers and her son's actually did last:

Q [Stephen Nagler, attorney for appellant]: What happened to the money which you received for Kevin for a shirt, pants, shoes, and socks?
A [Freeman]: This I bought him, right.
Q: In what condition are they now?
A: They are not in good condition. He wore them through the summer. . . .
Q: How come?
A: Because he's been wearing them continuously over and over and washing them and wearing them.
Q: What was he doing during the summer?
A: Playing a lot.
Q: Playing a lot?
A: Yes, and wearing the same things, you know. What they give you—I mean, the few things that they give you you have to be changing continuously, and you are washing and changing. For the little bit they give you to spend, it doesn't hold up.[48]

It might have helped Freeman's case if she had said that her family's clothing wore out in the course of some exceptional event; welfare department "special needs" grants were created to deal with such emergencies. However, Freeman emphasized the misfit between her and her son's ordinary experiences and the standards. By doing so, she suggested that welfare department policies themselves were off base.

Bargaining in the Shadow of the Hearing

The drive for fair hearings imposed major costs on the New York City welfare department. In addition to direct financial costs in the form of payments to clients, the department had to pay for the staff and space for night hearings and a translator's salary, and make daily disbursements for travel costs. To cover the huge jump in hearings, New York City hired four new hearing examiners and opened an Office of Fair Hearings in December 1967.[49] Virtually every welfare office in the city sent caseworkers and supervisors to defend their actions and departmental policies in fair hearings. Just as they were needed most to handle minimum standards demands, and the other grievances of clients who were inspired by the welfare rights movement, personnel were called away for hours at a time to welfare court.

The crunch in terms of personnel was worst at the very beginning of the Citywide fair hearing campaign in June and July 1967. With the campaign in full motion, the Social Service Employees Union (SSEU) called a strike. Caseworkers affiliated with the union stayed away from their jobs for nearly six weeks. The strike made conditions in welfare offices chaotic. "The treatment of welfare clients is horrible enough when the Department is operating normally," the leaders of the City-Wide Coordinating Committee said in a press release. "But during this kind of controversy, it's a nightmare."[50] Welfare recipients' fair hearings were also chaotic, because so many of the caseworkers who should have been testifying were out on strike.[51] In addition to familiar trade union demands, such as higher salaries and better fringe benefits, striking SSEU members demanded that the city add the costs of a telephone to every family's welfare check. Mayor Lindsay responded that the telephone demand was "clearly . . . not negotiable," and union members ultimately dropped the point.[52] However, the presence of the demand indicates the mostly symbiotic relationship between organized caseworkers and organized clients in New York City.[53]

Because of the many costs Citywide and the strikers imposed on the city administration, welfare commissioner Mitchell Ginsberg and those beneath him in the hierarchy were eager to prevent fair hearings. This often made them generous beyond the reckoning of low-income women and men. Of the three thousand appeals for which clients filed requests between September 1967 and January 1968, 90 percent never went to hearing.[54] A small portion of the requests was simply withdrawn. In the bulk of cases, however, local Welfare Centers contacted the appellants (or sometimes their lawyers) and started offering them furniture, back-to-school clothes, other goods, and cash, as incentives to abandon their fair hearing requests.

Informal negotiations occurred in exchanges among welfare recipients, their attorneys, and welfare department employees. In the days before her hearing, for example, Ann Freeman was offered over four hundred dollars in household goods and over one hundred in clothing—not everything she had asked for, but much more than she was used to getting. "We trust," an official wrote to Rachlin, "that this action taken by the New York City Department of Welfare answers Mrs. Freeman's request for a Fair Hearing satisfactorily."[55] Generally speaking, the longer clients held out and threatened the welfare department with a possible hearing, the more they got. Miriam Mitchell, a caretaker for her severely disabled brother, Timothy, continued to request a hearing until the welfare department met nearly all her demands. At the point when she first contacted Rachlin about a possible hearing, Timothy Mitchell was on the verge of being cut from the Aid to the Disabled rolls. Ultimately, however, the welfare department not only ceased to threaten a cutoff but raised Timothy Mitchell's grant, increased the number of hours and the rate of pay for his home health attendant, and released hundreds of dollars for items that were designed to make him more comfortable.[56]

The relationship between welfare department generosity and the desire to avoid hearings was usually submerged, but occasionally it became overt. In the morning before hearings started, or even after they had begun, welfare department staffs, clients, and attorneys sometimes haggled off the record to find arrangements that would satisfy both sides so they would agree to adjourn.[57] After she filed for a hearing, Martha Dickerson received a visit, a promise of material aid, and a suggestion that she might want to stay home from her hearing:

Q [Murray Gingold, Esq., Attorney for the New York City Department of Social Services]: You said you made a formal request to the Department for clothing?
A [Dickerson]: I wrote a letter.
. . . Q: What did you request in that letter?
A: I requested clothing for my children, my husband and myself.
Q: Did you get any answer to that letter?
A: I got no answer.
Q: Was there any refusal on the part of the Department to grant you those—
. . . A: Well, I called the Department several times and I couldn't get in touch with Mr. Dranoff [my caseworker] . . . So I think after Mr. Dranoff was informed that I was coming down here [for a hearing] he came to see me and he told me that the check would be coming along, that I could come down here if I didn't—I could come here or I couldn't.[58]

Rachlin wrote, tongue in cheek, to welfare commissioner Mitchell Ginsberg from the midst of one such negotiation: "Obviously, minimum standards are a part of the law and regulations and of course there is not nor should the[re] be any negotiations about them."[59] In fact, both sides knew that give-and-take over home health aides, spatulas, linoleum, and children's sweaters, in the shadow of potential fair hearings, was routine. The fair hearing campaign gave many poor people a taste of the negotiating power that wealthier individuals typically gained from raising the threat of litigation and settling their cases without going to court.

Despite all that Ann Freeman, Martha Dickerson, and Mary Sellors gained through fair hearings, the procedure was also costly for them. These women, who had young children and low incomes, invested their scarce time and energy in filing, preparing for, and presenting themselves at fair hearings. In order to participate, a mother had to get time off from her job, if she had paid work, or find a babysitter. She had to buy, borrow, or wash and press appropriate clothes and lay hands on enough cash for carfare and lunch (even if the welfare department later reimbursed her). The hearing might last much longer than planned. It might be stupefyingly dull. It would almost certainly involve public discussion of—and various judgmental suggestions about—the client's honesty, sexual practices, parenting skills, housekeeping abilities, and effectiveness as a money manager. A woman like Ann Freeman, who needed government aid to keep herself and her son Kevin afloat, might have decided not to pursue a fair hearing because she worried that her caseworker would cut her grant or close her case as retribution for challenging official decisions.[60]

Ann Freeman and Joan Sunderland discovered some of the limits to fair hearing participation as a strategy to improve their lot as welfare recipients. In Freeman's fair hearing, the referee micromanaged the testimony of all of the witnesses. Freeman had few opportunities to speak; when she tried to, she did not get far before the hearing referee silenced her.[61] Sunderland had to endure an almost literal airing of her dirty laundry in public during her fair hearing. She had asked the welfare department to bring her up to minimum standards for bathroom towels. Her attorney, Stephen Nagler, asked her caseworker how many towels she noticed at Sunderland's house. The caseworker replied that she had not counted them "because of the odor as much as anything," or, as the lawyer for the welfare department put it, "because they smelled."[62]

Beulah Sanders, Jennette Washington, and other leaders of the City-Wide Coordinating Committee of Welfare Groups could not assuage all of a public aid client's fears or concerns. But they did reduce the direct costs of the hearings by negotiating with the city administration for items such as carfare, and they protected their members from retribution by letting caseworkers know that the movement stood behind the hearings and the people who brought them. Citywide also protected Ann Freeman and the other appellants, and made it easier for them to navigate the appeals process, by ensuring that they had qualified advocates to represent them. Legal representation was never adequate for the crush of requests for hearings, but it was remarkably broad: Gilman and Birnbaum estimated that between September 18 and December 11, 1967, 90 percent of the people who arrived for hearings had lawyers or lay advocates to represent them.[63]

A New Weapon?

Fair hearings became an integral part of welfare rights strategy around the country beyond New York City. The hearing strategy was a powerful "new weapon" that could help resource-poor social movement groups increase their membership and raise their profiles. For individual clients, the hearings were opportunities to compel welfare departments to respond more quickly to their requests, obtain larger grants, and participate in a respectful public forum that recognized their rights. These benefits came with risks, but many welfare recipients' willingness to run these risks testified to their faith in law and belief in their right to participate in the affluent society.

Following the lead of the City-Wide Coordinating Committee of Welfare Groups, local welfare rights leaders everywhere in the United States adopted the combined strategy of demanding minimum standards and pursuing legal appeals. In Bridgeport, Connecticut; Binghamton and Rochester, New York; Cleveland and Pike County in Ohio; and Madison and Milwaukee, Wisconsin, various constellations of welfare recipients, middle-class allies of the movement, and attorneys placed the administrative fair hearing in the service of their organizing efforts.[64] In Louisville, a 300-member Welfare Rights Organization demanded over 100 fair hearings in its first year, with the help of attorneys funded by the federal Legal Services Program. By the end of 1967, welfare recipients in Louisville had requested between 1,400 and 1,500 hearings.[65]

Individual welfare recipients across the United States saw fair hearings as tools for winning benefits and gaining more just treatment from local welfare departments. Edward Donnelly of New Haven, Connecticut, wrote to NWRO seeking information about fair hearings because, he said, "I have hearing pending this month because of 57% cut in my A[id to the] D[isabled] benefits, and this information may be helpful towards surviving another Connecticut winter in one piece."[66] Elvira Jorgensen from Wichita, Kansas, wrote to NWRO seeking help and complaining that her local welfare office did not follow proper procedures when she sought a fair hearing. "Dear Sir," she began, "I know you are not going to do anything about this. you will throw it in the Waste Paper Basket if you have not allready done so. but I'm Leaving you Know anyway. The welfare did not have a hearing on this deal within 30 days and I do not even know why they cut this help off for in the first place they just cut it. I know I am just one small bearing in a mighty big wheel but. This little bearing likes to eat. so while your setting around not doing any thing. Help! Help! Help"![67] David Hensley filed for a hearing because a caseworker had removed him from the rolls. He believed the worker was retaliating against him for his efforts to organize recipients in his community, which, he offered, "is very badly needed. . . . The Welfare dept. Ontario [California] office has pushed the people here long enough."[68]

By offering information about fair hearings, access to lawyers, and updates on changing welfare laws, NWRO enhanced its ability to serve the local groups that affiliated with it. Like the California farm workers with whom César Chávez, Delores Huerta, and Fred Ross had worked in the 1950s and 1960s, welfare recipients were encouraged by the availability of concrete benefits to take the risks of joining an activist organization. Lawyers and legal information were themselves concrete benefits the movement could provide. They were also gateways to other valuable benefits, such as grants for minimum standards. "A lawyer is a very valuable piece of property in a poor community," NWRO staff lawyer Stephen Wexler wrote: "an organization that can command his [or her] skills for its members, and deny them to nonmembers has [a] powerful way to build its membership."[69]

Citywide and NWRO could count for legal assistance on extremely well-trained lawyers. Both organizations received personal assistance from Rachlin, who brought his years of experience in the labor and civil rights movements to bear on welfare problems, and from staff members of the Center on Social Welfare Policy and Law, who were at the cutting edge of legal strategy for the poor. NWRO and the District of Columbia welfare rights organization worked closely with attorneys at the federally funded Neighborhood Legal Services Program office.[70] Welfare rights groups across the country had allies in federally funded legal assistance offices and among public-interest attorneys. NWRO staff helped find lawyers for local activists who could not locate them on their own.[71] George Wiley and Edward Sparer from the Center on Social Welfare Policy and Law helped train entering Reginald Heber Smith Fellows, the most elite and politically progressive lawyers from the federal legal services program; they encouraged the "Reggies" to participate in the welfare rights movement.[72]

Lawyers showed a remarkable willingness to help welfare recipients mount their campaigns of legal civil disobedience. The visibility of legal contributions to the black freedom struggle, and the federally funded legal services program, helped lawyers believe that they could contribute to an active social movement without being ostracized from their profession. Even attorneys whose salaries were paid by the federal government showed little compunction about helping welfare recipients make their demands. Some OEO legal services attorneys reportedly established systems with welfare rights groups whereby they were openly "on call, particularly during actions or demonstrations."[73] When asked to respond to an attack against his agency by Senator Robert Byrd, the director of the Neighborhood Legal Services Program in Washington, D.C., replied: "We were scared to death by the Senator's attack, so scared that we only filed two suits against the Welfare Department that week."[74]

NWRO and affiliated attorneys helped welfare recipients access and interpret official documents or, in the words of Brooklyn organizer Rhoda Linton, helped them "get the law."[75] The most important documents welfare departments failed to disclose were administration manuals or handbooks, which contained information on minimum standards, about how caseworkers calculated families' grants, and about the procedures caseworkers were supposed to follow in their dealings with clients. Welfare activists in New York City made the manuals their "welfare Bible[s]" for organizing and collective self-education.[76]

Members of the Brooklyn Welfare Action Council made legal information and welfare regulations the heart of a Leadership Curriculum they created collaboratively with Linton and middle-class allies. "People began to understand that they could do a whole lot more if they knew a lot more," Linton recalled. "And the basic, basic, basic thing they needed to know was welfare law."[77] Women and men in Brooklyn found that they could "turn the tables on [case] workers if they just knew more than the worker which wasn't hard to do. [M]any, many people did the welfare law [course]. They saw the need for that."[78]

In addition to using existing welfare department materials, activists and attorneys wrote their own. They drafted alternative welfare manuals modeled on official ones but designed to be easy to understand. The Center on Social Welfare Policy and Law produced the first state-level manuals for the Georgia and Mississippi welfare rights organizations. The center's attorneys followed with a manual for Newark, New Jersey, and worked on one for New York with the City-Wide Coordinating Committee. These handbooks varied enormously. Most were written by a combination of attorneys, welfare rights staff, and recipients.[79] When she tested a draft of the Newark handbook, organizer Shirley Lacy noted that "Enthusiasm for the materials prepared has been very high among recipients. Some said that they did not even know that caseworkers had rules and regulations to follow. They thought everything was 'made up' as the situation presented itself."[80]

Leaders of NWRO and local welfare rights groups made legal information available to their members through publications and public meetings. George Wiley referred to the NWRO newspaper *NOW!* as "one of the principle organizing tools" of the movement in part because allied lawyers and staff attorneys contributed regularly to it. Lawyers also contributed to local newspapers, such as New York City's *Tell It Like It Is*, in columns titled "Our Lawyer Speaks" or "Welfare Law Corner" that explicated specific changes in welfare statutes or regulations.[81] Welfare rights organizers used workshops on welfare law and practices, and flyers or leaflets informing recipients of little-known aspects of the welfare rules, to recruit and retain members. For those who did not have the chance to enroll in one of the Brooklyn leadership classes, these workshops were the key means of improving their knowledge base, and gaining the information that would help them get more material benefits and build stronger groups.[82]

To the Cusp of Change

In 1968, the City-Wide Coordinating Committee of Welfare Groups continued to lead the rest of the movement in using fair hearings and working with attorneys. Beulah Sanders and Jennette Washington could count on hundreds of public-interest, pro bono, and federal legal ser-

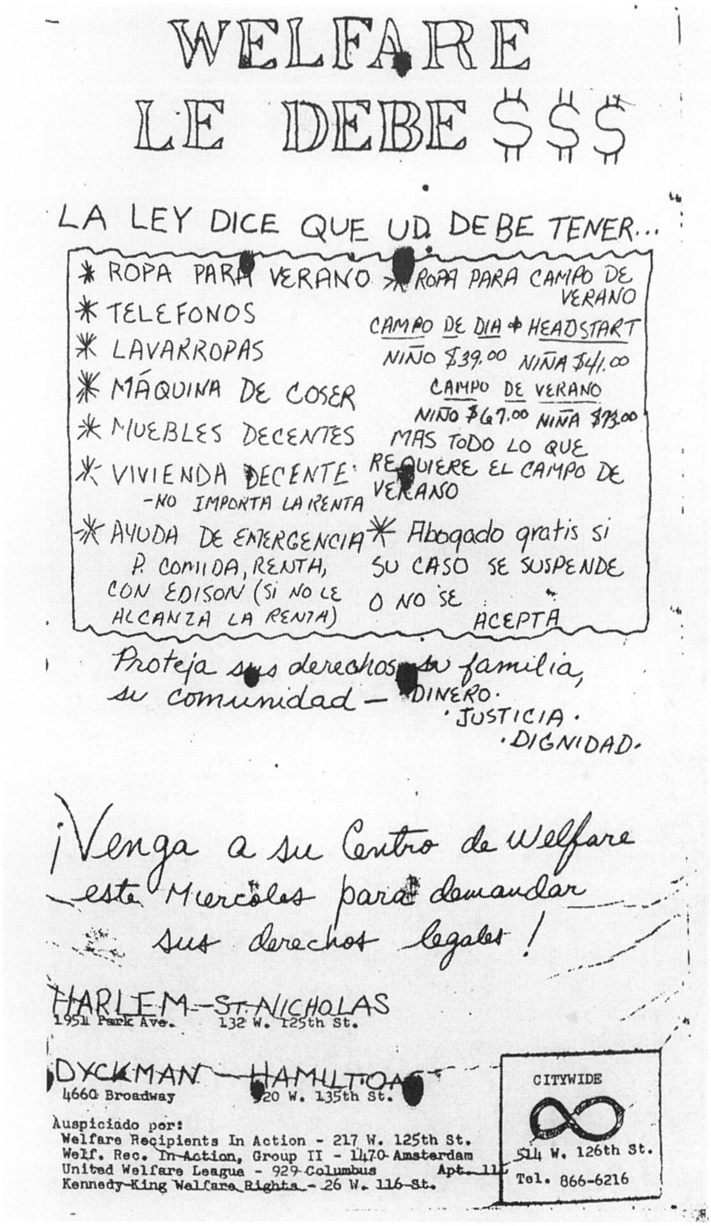

WELFARE
LE DEBE $$$

LA LEY DICE QUE UD DEBE TENER...

* ROPA PARA VERANO → ROPA PARA CAMPO DE VERANO
* TELEFONOS
* LAVARROPAS
* MÁQUINA DE COSER
* MUEBLES DECENTES
* VIVIENDA DECENTE -NO IMPORTA LA RENTA
* AYUDA DE EMERGENCIA P. COMIDA, RENTA, CON EDISON (SI NO LE ALCANZA LA RENTA)

CAMPO DE DIA ✦ HEADSTART
NIÑO $39.00 NIÑA $41.00
CAMPO DE VERANO
NIÑO $67.00 NIÑA $73.00
MAS TODO LO QUE REQUIERE EL CAMPO DE VERANO

* Abogado gratis si SU CASO SE SUSPENDE O NO SE ACEPTA

Proteja sus derechos su familia, su comunidad — DINERO. · JUSTICIA · · DIGNIDAD ·

¡Venga a su Centro de Welfare este Miércoles para demandar sus derechos legales!

HARLEM — ST. NICHOLAS
1951 Park Ave.   132 W. 125th St.

DYCKMAN — HAMILTON
4660 Broadway   920 W. 135th St.

CITYWIDE
∞
514 W. 126th St.
Tel. 866-6216

Auspiciado por:
Welfare Recipients In Action - 217 W. 125th St.
Welf. Rec. In-Action, Group II - 1470 Amsterdam
United Welfare League - 929 Columbus   Apt. 11
Kennedy-King Welfare Rights - 26 W. 116 St.

Figure 9. Citywide uses welfare department minimum standards and the right to a fair hearing to recruit new members. This flyer reads in part: "Welfare Owes You $$$. The law says you should have . . . spring clothes, telephones, washing machine, sewing machine, a free lawyer if you get cut off or your requests are refused. Come to your Welfare Center this Wednesday to demand your legal rights!" Translation by M. Anore Horton. Courtesy George Wiley Papers, Wisconsin Historical Society.

vices lawyers who were willing to place their expertise in service of the group's strategies. Citywide pursued a series of campaigns for minimum standards, one after another. Welfare rights activists used the hearings as backups to their other demands and won huge payments in cash and goods. While relying mostly on professional lawyers, the Citywide staff also trained fourteen members as paid "lay advocates" to represent others in hearings and negotiations. In July 1968, both the *Daily News* and *New York Times* reported that the campaign, with its combination of minimum standards demands and fair hearing requests, was costing New York City $10 million per month. The head of the New York State Board of Social Welfare estimated that each hearing cost the state $300 a day.[83]

The women and men who filed for fair hearings continued to ask for a mix of material aid and public recognition. Toni Stret from Brooklyn, for example, complained to Mayor Lindsay, social services commissioner Mitchell Ginsberg, and state welfare director James Louchheim that there was "no protection for people on welfare who trie to help themselves, or justice."[84] She wrote that her case had been closed without notice and asked: "WHAT LAW OR RULE IS THERETHAT SAYS A NEGRO WOMAN MUST USE ONE BOX OF SANITARY NAPKINS A MONTH AND NO MORE . . . WHAT LAW IN THE U.S. SAYS A PERSON RECEIVING HELP CANNOT HAVE VISITORS?"[85] Stret's letter did not spur any official action, so she sought "protection" and "justice" through a fair hearing. In addition to affirming her right to have visitors, and to have a budget that covered needs such as sanitary napkins, Stret brought the hearing in order to get school clothes for her children. When the hearing examiner suggested adjourning the proceeding, Stret protested: "do I understand that you are going to adjourn this hearing; am I right? . . . For how long? These kids here, they need shoes. The child has one dress that is too small for her, and I have been waiting since October for winter clothes. Now, how much longer can I wait?"[86]

The fair hearing tactic peaked with a "massive" campaign by Citywide for telephones for all welfare clients, with legal appeals for those who were denied.[87] Welfare department regulations treated the telephone as an emergency need, which caseworkers should add to clients' budgets only in exceptional cases. Beulah Sanders agreed that telephones were needed for emergencies. However, she claimed that all public assistance recipients were living under emergency conditions: "Without telephones," she said, "poor people on welfare in New York City can't even dial 911 when they have an emergency. And our people live in areas with the highest crime rates, the highest fire rate and with the most instances of children swallowing poisons and getting hit by cars."[88]

At the height of the campaign for telephones, public assistance clients in New York State filed 3,000 requests for appeals hearings in the single month of September 1968. At least 1,500 of the requests originated in New York City. Because convening hearings imposed a burden on the state and city, which made them bargain more generously, the Citywide newspaper reminded members that their "success depends on *everyone* going to their hearing."[89] Success was very nearly theirs. The chair of the state social welfare board concluded that the minimum standards and fair hearings demands in 1968 came "close to breaking down the system."[90] Legal civil disobedience—swamping the system with demands for welfare rights, like filling the jails and clogging the courts with demands for civil rights—had the effects that movement strategists had hoped it would have. Aided and abetted by attorneys who were inspired by the role of law in the civil rights struggle, women and men who received public assistance brought social welfare policy to the cusp of change. Citywide caused so much havoc in the New York City welfare department that Mayor Lindsay began to press for a uniform national welfare system that would be fairer and possibly more generous than any policy poor people in the United States had ever seen.[91]

The experiences of Joan Sunderland and other welfare recipients who sought fair hearings pose challenges to the gloomy picture of the recent legal past that has appeared in some scholarly works.[92] Welfare recipients used legal tactics to pursue their personal aims and the goals of their movement. For women and men who were accustomed to being denounced by state and federal legislators, impugned by governors during elections, and systematically underbudgeted by their caseworkers, courts and hearings appeared flexible and generous by comparison with other institutions. Like their predecessors in other branches of the black freedom movement, activist welfare recipients did not believe that they had to choose between direct action and legal action; they saw the two as mutually supportive. They treated fair hearings as extensions of the movement's other tactics.

Joan Sunderland and many others used law to pursue their particular citizenship claims as women. Welfare rights activists claimed equality with other women and mothers who were not poor. They made class- and race-conscious demands for sexual privacy. When Sunderland told a room full of middle-class female welfare department employees that she refused to serve her two-year-old child meals on her good china, and added, "she wouldn't. No one in this room would," she was claiming a particularly gendered form of equality with other women in the postwar United States. When Jill Jackson insisted on a fair hearing in part because her caseworker was more interested in her personal life than in her material needs, and Mrs. Sylvester Smith argued that being a "nun" was not a legitimate criterion for receiving public aid, these women were demanding public recognition of their rights to sexual self-determination.

"Can the courts bring about social change?" an important skeptic has asked.[93] In the movement for welfare rights, the contributions of lawyers and legal tactics were significant. Fair hearings were not an ideal weapon in welfare recipients' battles for social recognition and material advancement. The logic that made thousands of members of Citywide and NWRO pressure welfare departments by seeking hearings was the particular logic of the middle and late 1960s, informed by the legal and social changes brought by the black freedom movement and the Supreme Court under Chief Justice Warren. Moreover, Citywide members took their battle for welfare rights into hearing rooms and courtrooms because of particular local circumstances, including the sheer number of available attorneys in New York City, the fears sparked by the Harlem and Bedford-Stuyvesant riots in 1964, and the related rise of public-interest, pro bono and government-funded legal aid for the poor.

Fair hearings alone did not conquer people's fear or apathy, build the membership of local groups, or strengthen the hand of the movement vis-à-vis its perceived antagonists. But they were part of the process by which Citywide and the National Welfare Rights Organization accomplished these ends. Alongside demands for participation in the affluent society, legal proceedings helped this poor people's movement succeed temporarily against enormous odds. With fair hearings as one tool among many and each appeal as one hearing among thousands, welfare recipients such as Beulah Sanders, Joan Sunderland, and Toni Stret gained access to material goods and to a measure of respect from public authorities. Their creative legal strategies certainly do not prove that law was or is necessarily a friend to the poor, or to African Americans, or to women—only that under particular historical circumstances and constraints it provided unique resources to welfare recipients who were intent on claiming their rights.

Chapter 4
On a Collision Course

How can a rich man know the needs of the Poor?
. . . He wouldn't dare pick up a mop, or a broom, to do a floor
He wants the poor people to be his slave forever more.
He don't care what form, fashion, or color they come
As long as they keep him comfortable, and supply him with a clean home.

—*Nancy Gooding, Citywide member*

In July 1968, Beulah Sanders sent a telegram to New York City mayor John Lindsay. With demonstrations raging at local welfare centers, City-Wide Coordinating Committee president Sanders predicted that her group and the city government were on a "collision course."[1] She promised more disruption until New York City and State increased welfare benefits, and either they or the federal government increased the minimum wage. "It's not a group of lazy, shiftless women" on welfare, she said. "It's a question of decent jobs."[2]

The prophecy Beulah Sanders offered to the leaders of New York's government was a credible one. In addition to massive demonstrations for minimum standards, which were continuing to net millions of dollars in new benefits for welfare clients, and the fair hearings that added force to clients' demands, Citywide had entered a new phase of militancy in the summer of 1968. Only a few days before sending her telegram to Lindsay, Sanders had led a delegation of welfare recipients to a meeting with social services commissioner Jack Goldberg that turned into a prolonged sit-in at his offices. Irene Gibbs, who was part of the delegation, insisted to Goldberg that her "children be decently clad, decently fed, and decently housed—like your children and Mr. Lindsay's." Gibbs tied her opposition to low welfare grants to her feelings about waged work for welfare mothers; "if everyone tries to tell Mrs. Gibbs she has to go to work or take counseling under 'Operation Compass'," the city's employment program, she said, "I'll send them to 'Operation Hell'!"[3] After Goldberg heard the group's demands and

Gibbs's plea, he left for the day. Sanders sat down at his desk and took the title "Commissioner of People Services." She stayed at her post from Friday afternoon until Sunday night, when she and other Citywide members were arrested.[4]

Welfare recipients in New York City were on a collision course with officials at the state level, as well as with Mayor Lindsay and Commissioner Goldberg. In June 1968, New York governor Nelson Rockefeller, the national leader of the liberal wing of the Republican Party, formally proposed changing the welfare system in ways that threatened to decimate the Citywide movement. He suggested eliminating most extra grants, giving each welfare recipient instead a $100 annual supplement. The "flat grant" threatened to make the two central strategies of the Citywide movement, the fight for minimum standards and the pursuit of fair hearings, irrelevant.[5] Before Rockefeller put the proposal forward, he, Mayor Lindsay, and the Democrats who controlled Congress and the White House, had all committed themselves to cutting welfare. National Democrats and New York's liberal Republicans began to argue that mothers should be in the waged labor market and that the purpose of government social policy was to help them get there. This was part of a sea change in the philosophy behind public assistance.[6]

Sanders, Gibbs, and other welfare rights activists were completely opposed to the flat grant, which they saw as an assault on welfare rights. However, they disagreed with one another about the place of the labor market in the life of a welfare mother. While Sanders wanted higher minimum wages for people who might choose waged work over public aid, Gibbs fiercely opposed a government-funded "compass" that claimed to point her in the right direction while also limiting her options. Citywide member Nancy Gooding feared a mandatory work program that would place her and other women in domestic service, as the "slave forever more" of a middle-class family.[7] When Democrats in Congress mandated employment or job training for mothers, and prescribed group day care for their children, the NWRO staff and top leadership described the proposals as regressive, racist, an abrogation of mothers' natural roles, and a danger to the young. Citywide leaders such as Gibbs and Sanders joined the chorus of opposition. However, the strident rhetoric masked disagreements among welfare rights activists about mothers' proper place. Many opposed the compulsion in the amendments more than they opposed paid work or group child care as such.

Welfare and the Voters

The term "backlash" entered the political lexicon during the 1964 presidential election season. The term was used to describe the reaction against progress in civil rights that propelled the candidacies of Barry Goldwater and George Wallace. It is tempting to describe the emerging antiwelfare consensus of the late 1960s as the product of an anti-welfare rights backlash that resembled the anti-civil rights backlash of the middle 1960s. However, opposition to welfare programs predated the welfare rights movement; public spending for social welfare had always been controversial, especially when the beneficiaries were African American and female. In New York City, there was an antiwelfare movement before there was a welfare rights movement at which to lash back. The shift in the late 1960s was, therefore, one of degree rather than of kind.

The politics of welfare were closely tied to the politics of integration. The movement to integrate schools began as early in New York City as it did anywhere in the United States and met with equally concerted resistance. According to historian Joshua Freeman, organized opposition to educational integration first appeared in New York in 1959 as a response to an effort by the city government to bring African American students from Bedford-Stuyvesant in Brooklyn into an overwhelmingly white school district in the borough of Queens. The anti-integration movement grew in every part of the city; its leaders created a network they called Parents and Taxpayers (PAT). In September 1964, after African Americans and white allies who wanted integration had organized a massive school boycott, PAT organized its own two-day boycott to protest integration; one-quarter of students in the city stayed home.[8]

PAT members and sympathizers, many of them white homeowners in the boroughs of Staten Island, Queens, and Brooklyn, resembled whites in Chicago, Detroit, and other cities who mobilized to block post-World War II efforts at housing and employment integration. These hardworking people struggled toward middle-class security with help from a wide array of public benefits, such as Veterans Administration mortgages, federal mortgage interest deductions, and publicly funded highways. Although their economic mobility was built on unacknowledged help from the postwar welfare state, these white New Yorkers viewed public assistance at least as negatively as they viewed government-mandated integration of their neighborhoods or workplaces. Welfare carried the same racial tinge as the other issues, and it flew in the face of a work ethic that many believed had delivered them from the depths of immigrant poverty.[9]

The first notable signs of change in electoral politics occurred in 1964. From a close study of local patterns in the presidential election, political analyst Kevin Phillips concluded that Republican candidate Goldwater won nearly 40 percent of the tally among Irish Americans, Italian Americans, and other white ethnic voters in New York.[10] The next sign of conservative strength came a year later. The 1965 mayoral election was a paradoxical event. John Lindsay, a Republican who had spoken on behalf of civil rights while in the U.S. Congress, and who relied on African American and Puerto Rican votes, won decisively—a remarkable achievement for any Republican in the New York of the 1960s. He was widely described as a likely candidate for president in 1968. At the same time, however, the newly formed Conservative Party mounted a spirited mayoral campaign by William F. Buckley, a conservative Catholic writer and editor of the magazine *National Review*. Buckley's running mate was Rosemary Gunning, a leader of Parents and Taxpayers, the anti-integration group. Buckley and the Conservative Party were less interested in running New York City than in depriving Lindsay of the mantle of the future. They focused on racially charged hot-button issues such as welfare, crime, and schools.[11]

Welfare was central to the Conservatives' argument against Lindsay and their bid for votes. Buckley promised, if elected, to impose a one-year residency requirement for public assistance, to hunt for fraudulent claims in the Aid to Dependent Children program, and to compel all able-bodied recipients who were not raising children to report for street-cleaning duty. "No workee, no dolee," he later quipped in reference to the proposal.[12] He suggested a "pilot program . . . to explore the feasibility of relocating chronic welfare cases outside the city limits" in rehabilitation camps.[13] Buckley's proposals, and the vociferous response to them by Republican liberals and Democrats, energized and divided the electorate. Over 80 percent of eligible New Yorkers voted for mayor in 1965; of these, 13.4 percent chose Buckley. Among them, by Kevin Phillips's calculations, were 25–30 percent of voters in white ethnic neighborhoods.[14]

The Visible Poor

Antiwelfare sentiment never disappeared from public life in New York City. However, it was somewhat submerged early in the Lindsay administration, when reform groups such as the City-Wide Coordinating Committee of Welfare Groups and public-sector unions such as the Social Service Employees Union largely set the agenda by protesting and negotiating with City Hall. Three major social changes made the recessive strain of antiwelfare sentiment into a dominant force in the city's political life by the late 1960s. First, a gradual but dramatic decline in the portion of blue-collar jobs simultaneously challenged working-class financial security, white racial privilege, male dominance, and the privilege many married women enjoyed of being able to withdraw from the waged workforce to raise children if they so desired. The proportion of stable, blue-collar, male-dominated jobs fell from approximately 41 percent of all jobs in New York City in 1946 to 27 percent in 1970.[15] Because this change occurred simultaneously with the rise of the black freedom movement, it produced competition between whites and people of color for a shrinking share of the employment pie. At the same time, white New Yorkers saw welfare recipients, a disproportionate number of whom were African American and Latino/a, receiving government grants that rose in value over the decade. Between 1961 and 1971, welfare grants for mothers and children in New York rose in real terms by more than 37 percent while average wages were nearly stagnant.[16]

Economic change had the potential to challenge conventional relationships between men and women, and this also stimulated opposition to welfare programs. The jobs that were siphoned away in postwar New York were precisely those most likely to pay a "family wage" that would enable a male wage-earner's wife to stay out of the formal workforce, underwriting a sharp sexual division of labor. In the years after World War II, the family wage system eroded, and working-class white women with school-aged children entered the labor force in nearly unprecedented numbers. A rising number of white women with employed husbands began to juggle wage-earning with child-rearing, as African American women had routinely done in the past.[17]

The second major change was a remarkable increase in the welfare rolls. As Mayor Lindsay put it, "If the 'other America' was once invisible, it [was] so no longer."[18] The rise in welfare caseloads initially had little to do with the organized movement for welfare rights, but was the result of an inchoate social movement that inspired people to leave the South or Puerto Rico for the northeastern United States, and then induced recent migrants and longer-term residents to apply for public aid when they fell on hard times. According to one study, over half of the nonwhites living in New York City in 1960 had been born outside the state.[19] Moreover, by 1960, 4.9 percent of the population of the City was receiving public assistance of one kind or another.[20] As wealthier people moved out of the city and poorer ones continued to move in, the fraction of the population receiving public aid jumped to nearly 10 percent in 1967 and to 14 percent by 1970. The most rapid growth in welfare use occurred in the middle to late 1960s. In 1966, over 568,000 people in the city claimed public assistance; by 1967, the number had risen to over 700,000. By the end of the decade, over a million people were receiving cash benefits in New York City.[21]

These numbers surprised many New Yorkers, who felt like they lived in a prosperous city at a prosperous time. The rise in "welfare dependency" was grist for the mill of political candidates who followed in William Buckley's footsteps and were ready to blame the welfare rights movement for the increase. However, before 1968, the City-Wide Coordinating Committee of Welfare Groups had little effect on the welfare caseload. The most thorough study of welfare data in New York City in this period found that until 1968, the rising numbers simply reflected rising poverty in the city. The percentage of poor people who were getting benefits had barely changed since the beginning of the decade. From the early 1960s until February 1968, only about one-half of all the people who qualified for welfare actually received it. "What happened after February appears to have been a very different matter," argued Larry Jackson and William Johnson from the Rand Corporation. "From February 1 to September 1, 1968, New York City's AFDC caseload rose by 17 percent. At the same time, the eligible population in the City appears to have remained more or less constant. Because of this . . . the percentage of eligible families on AFDC rose from 53 percent on February 1 to nearly 62 percent on September 1."[22] The percentage continued to rise from that point forward, through the end of the decade.[23]

Organizing by the City-Wide Coordinating Committee was responsible for approximately one-quarter of the rise in the welfare rolls at the end of the 1960s. Jackson and Johnson concluded that increased applications for welfare were the single variable that best explained the rise in the overall caseload (as opposed, for example, to lower rates at which caseworkers closed cases, or a greater readiness than previously to open them). And they concluded that the welfare rights movement spurred rising applications. Citywide's activism publicized the availability of welfare, reduced the stigma associated with it, and therefore encouraged more people to apply.[24]

The third change that affected public attitudes toward welfare was an increase in the costs of the program in the course of the decade of the 1960s. It did little good to point out, as some statisticians for New York State did, that the percentage of personal income devoted to public assistance actually declined between the 1930s and the late 1960s; the gross numbers concentrated the fears and resentments of many working- and middle-class New Yorkers.[25] In 1961, New York City spent over 50 percent more on public assistance than it had in 1951; by the end of 1966, public assistance costs had increased by another 70 percent (see Table 1).[26] Looking only at cash expenditures, the U.S. Census Bureau calculated that New York City's spending on categorical public assistance programs more than doubled between 1961 and 1966. It more than doubled again by the end of the decade (see Table 2).[27]

In 1968, the total budget for the Human Resources Administration topped the billion-dollar mark. This was the largest item in the New York City budget, more expensive than the public schools. In 1969, Ginsberg, the head of the agency that was responsible for both the welfare pro-

TABLE 1. TOTAL PUBLIC ASSISTANCE EXPENDITURES FROM ALL SOURCES,
1951–1966 ($000)

Year	New York State	New York City	Rest of state
1951	240,827	164,056	76,771
1952	238,887	159,567	79,320
1953	229,801	152,779	77,022
1954	247,548	165,016	82,532
1955	260,692	171,140	89,552
1956	262,159	172,993	89,167
1957	276,315	184,898	91,418
1958	312,089	206,113	105,976
1959	333,547	213,975	117,572
1960	339,057	218,783	120,274
1961	382,479	250,952	131,528
1962	423,160	276,734	146,427
1963	488,349	325,026	163,324
1964	563,601	379,557	184,044
1965	644,656	444,835	199,821
1966	592,714	427,961	164,753

Source: New York State Office of Statistical Coordination.

TABLE 2. NEW YORK CITY CASH ASSISTANCE PAYMENTS, 1949, 1961–1973 ($000)

Year	Total public welfare	Categorical cash assistance	Other cash assistance
1949	172, 874	n/a	n/a
1961	294,688	172,590	26,746
1962	320,710	171,408	18,248
1963	395,830	211,270	26,657
1964	510,030	255,085	33,596
1965	558,446	296,634	42,996
1966	716,125	393,456	65,437
1967	1,127,169	538,150	98,037
1968	1,516,791	774,173	149,219
1969	1,627,768	827,251	119,638
1970	2,005,812	1,003,040	131,225
1971	2,215,469	1,075,273	112,761
1972	2,485,575	1,149,901	140,475
1973	2,587,434	981,487	119,317

Source: U.S. Census Bureau.

gram and the local War on Poverty, asked for a budget of $1.7 billion. An
estimated 91 percent of this sum was to be spent on public assistance.[28]

Even before the full flowering of the welfare rights movement, New
York City officials were desperate to reduce these costs, which they saw

as political as well as fiscal poison. But there was little they could do. As an assistant explained to Mayor Lindsay in April 1966, public assistance combined federal, state, and local funds as well as federal, state, and city-level administrative rules. Any time city officials tried to bend the rules in order to save money, they risked losing funding from the state and federal governments. Costs would never come down significantly, Lindsay's deputy concluded, "so long as the caseload continues to rise."[29] By November, Mayor Lindsay was "increasingly concerned about public attitudes [toward welfare costs] and therefore public responses."[30]

The Lindsay administration was especially vulnerable because New York City, compared with other local governments, paid a very high share of total welfare costs. The federal government contributed a lower percentage of the welfare budget in New York State than it did in virtually any other state; and New York State gave its localities a lower portion of public assistance costs than any other state. By the end of the 1960s, local governments across the United States were paying on average about one-fourth of the cost of public assistance not covered by the federal government, or one-tenth of the total. New York cities and counties paid 46 percent of the budget not picked up by Washington, or one-fourth of the total.[31]

These trends in the welfare caseload and the cost of public assistance did, indeed, set the welfare rights movement and the city government on a "collision course." Beulah Sanders, Irene Gibbs, and Jennette Washington depended on rising grants and expanding welfare rolls to attract new members to Citywide, and to give veteran members reasons to stay involved. The group's benefits-based strategy, with its campaigns for minimum standards and fair hearings, necessarily imposed new costs on local government. And the "crisis strategy" Piven and Cloward had outlined early in the history of the welfare rights movement was designed to provoke exactly the kind of "concern about public attitudes" that Mayor Lindsay expressed at the end of his first year in office. The men at the top of the Lindsay administration believed that, unless they could persuade the state and federal governments to pick up more of the city's public assistance budget, they would either have to limit the number of people who actually received the aid to which they were legally entitled or raise city taxes enough to cover the costs. Neither option was particularly appetizing.[32]

Work, Compulsion, and Dissent

The first stage of the Lindsay administration's effort to slow down the increase in the welfare rolls was couched in the language of expanding women's opportunities. "The central focus here in 1967," Mayor Lindsay reported in his Annual Report to the City Council and the public, "was to find effective ways to counter the steadily rising trend in the number of persons receiving public assistance . . . through various job incentive and guidance measures."[33] These measures included stationing an employment counselor at each welfare office, offering financial incentives to clients who worked for wages, and expanding child care availability "to enable mothers receiving public assistance to work during the day."[34] The Lindsay administration put welfare mothers to work caring for the children of other women who had enrolled in employment training or joined the formal work force. It created places in group child care centers for 1,500 children of welfare mothers.[35]

Leaders of Citywide and the National Welfare Rights Organization fought the Lindsay provisions. However, welfare rights activists were not necessarily opposed to waged work. From the beginning of the movement, opinion within it was divided about employment, training, and child care. Some of the most vocal members, such as Irene Gibbs, demanded the freedom to be full-time mothers without juggling childrearing with waged labor outside the home. In a society that privileged child-rearing as the primary responsibility of middle-class women, it seemed unfair to these activists to deny that role to poor women. Moreover, it appeared to Gibbs and other Citywide and NWRO members that there was a cultural double standard in the United States, which allowed many white mothers to devote themselves entirely to motherhood while African American and Latina mothers had less time to spend with their children.

Members of the NWRO staff, especially white men such as associate director Tim Sampson and African American men such as executive director George Wiley, articulated a position similar to Gibbs's but with a sexist twist: they argued that women should not be forced to work outside their homes, but that the federal government should create jobs for men that would allow them to assume their natural roles as the heads of their families. Of course, this approach would work only if poor families were headed by married couples, which was often not the case. By contrast, Beulah Sanders and many other women active in welfare rights demanded government help to obtain respectable jobs with decent wages for themselves. Although they disagreed on some of these fraught questions, welfare rights activists shared a resistance to forced work, compulsory job training, and child care arrangements that parents could not choose for themselves.[36]

Mayor Lindsay's moves in the direction of reducing welfare costs and expanding employment opportunities for women were consistent with federal policy. In response to fears about a national welfare crisis, Democratic majorities in both houses of Congress and a Democratic White

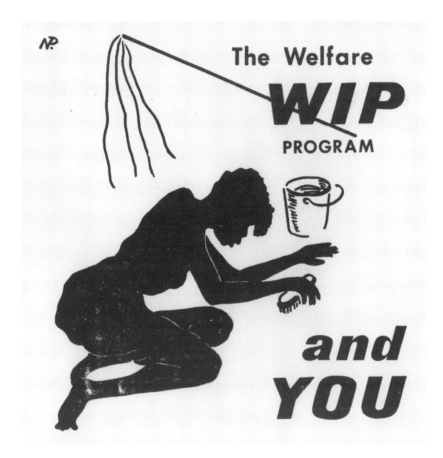

Figure 10. Congress calls its welfare-to-work initiative the Work Incentive Program (WIN), but NWRO members call it WIP. Courtesy NWRO Files, National Center for Law and Economic Justice.

House cobbled together a self-contradictory package of amendments to the Social Security Act, the landmark antipoverty legislation that had been passed as part of the New Deal. The centerpiece of these amendments was a mandatory work program for mothers who received public assistance, the first ever in the history of the program. Its proponents called the new policy "WIN," but welfare rights activists called it "WIP."

WIN/WIP was one of three major components of the Social Security Act amendments of 1967. Under the program, every adult welfare recipient who was judged suitable for placement would be required to work for wages or enroll in a training program, provided that appropriate employment and child care services were available. If she failed to find a job or to participate in training, then she would lose a portion of her family's welfare grant. Alongside WIN/WIP, members of Congress offered a financial work incentive. It allowed recipients to add the first $30 that they earned from paid work, plus one-third of the rest of their earnings, to their grants without losing their eligibility for benefits.[37] The second major component of the 1967 amendments was a cap on the percentage of a state's population that could receive federal public assistance. The cap was an even more direct response to the so-called welfare crisis than WIN/WIP or the proposed work incentive. NWRO members referred to this attempt at chilling entitlement to welfare as the caseload "freeze."[38]

The third major proposal before Congress in 1967 was a requirement that states raise their standards of need, or estimates of the income families needed to live decently. State standards of need were important to welfare recipients because they were yardsticks against which legislatures and welfare departments judged the adequacy of the grants they gave to the poor. Raising the standard of need was a liberalizing move that spoke to welfare recipients' demands for first-class citizenship in the affluent society. If consumer prices rose, then standards of need should also rise, and welfare mothers should receive higher cash grants so that they could continue to navigate the marketplace on behalf of their families. The idea of revising the standard of need sat uneasily with the more draconian portions of the 1967 amendments.[39]

NWRO opposed the amendments vehemently from the moment they were introduced in Congress, dubbing the legislation that included them "the anti-welfare bill" of 1967. With the support of Representative Wilbur Mills, the powerful Arkansas Democrat who chaired the Ways and Means Committee, the bill quickly passed the House. NWRO mounted concerted opposition when it came before the Senate.[40]

Critics of the amendments from the welfare rights movement emphasized the coercive aspects of WIN/WIP. Several years after the battle over the "anti-welfare bill," Beulah Sanders commented that it and similar top-down government employment programs were shams, "just something to keep your mouth closed . . . [I]f they want us off the welfare rolls," she asserted, "come up with the training program and the jobs. You know, the women would be glad to take it."[41] She and other women in welfare rights feared that the federal government would use WIN/WIP to slot them into work as domestic servants in the homes of whites. Domestic work was low-paid, onerous, and often demeaning labor, with which women of color in the 1960s were already all too familiar. NWRO president Johnnie Tillmon, for example, had her first job as a maid at age eighteen. After that experience, she promised herself, "God and Moses that I was through working in anybody's kitchen but my own."[42]

While women in the welfare rights movement resisted government programs that mandated mothers' employment, they were equally skeptical about the arguments of white, middle-class feminists who thought paid work would make them free. Well-educated women with opportunities for professional careers seemed not to understand the limited options available to less privileged women; white women destined for "pink collar" jobs seemed unaware of the racial discrimination that excluded women of color from even these lower-paid but relatively stable and respectable positions.[43]

These divergent views became visible when Beulah Sanders and George Wiley were invited to testify before congressional hearings on "income maintenance." Representative Martha Griffiths, a Michigan Democrat who described herself as "the most dedicated feminist" in the House of Representatives, tried to persuade Sanders and Wiley of the wisdom of her position in favor of work requirements for welfare mothers.[44] Wiley interrupted her:

Mr. WILEY: Mrs. Griffiths, may I turn that around a minute? . . . Our feeling is that a good number, in fact the vast majority, of the welfare recipients and many of the other people who need income support legitimately should not be in the labor force, because they have other important responsibilities at home, to take care of their families . . . [T]he important thing is that the men, that the people who are able to be heads of households or ought to be legitimate heads of households be the ones that get those jobs.
. . . Representative GRIFFITHS: You say that this work incentive program [will] be used to force mothers to work. Well, [the Department of Labor] will have a choice as to which mothers work and which do not. But if you do not say anything about mothers working, then they are going to see to it that none work. They are not going to be given any chance to work. And in my opinion, this is wrong . . . I am a woman, Mr. Wiley, and I know the kinds of discriminations that have been used against women.[45]

Beulah Sanders's perspective had something in common with Wiley's, in that she, too, feared that welfare mothers who wanted to spend most of their time raising children would be forced to do something else for a living. At the same time, she shared Griffiths's concern about enhancing women's choices and opportunities for gainful employment. She opposed WIN/WIP *and* hoped for a government program that might offer welfare mothers more of what they wanted:

Mrs. SANDERS: Could I say one thing before you go, woman to woman?
Representative GRIFFITHS: Yes.
Mrs. SANDERS: . . . One of the things we are concerned about is being forced into these nonexisting positions which might be going out and cleaning Mrs. A's kitchen. I am not going to do that because I feel I am more valuable and can do something else. This is one of the things these people are worrying about, that they are going to be pushed into doing housework . . . But they do not have the

training, they do not have the experience, they do not have the college degree [to get better jobs].[46]

Sanders and Griffiths agreed on the importance of increased federal funding for child care. Although both thought that women should have access to waged work, Sanders's concerns about being funneled into use-less training programs and relegated to domestic service made her oppose WIN/WIP, while Griffiths's fears about women not being treated equally with men made her support this mandatory work program.

The best efforts of Beulah Sanders, Johnnie Tillmon, and George Wiley were not enough to keep Congress from passing WIN/WIP and the other amendments into law. Welfare rights activists saw the amend-ments' passage as a betrayal by the Democratic Party and a president who had started out as a champion of the poor. The NWRO staff pro-duced a report titled "The Welfare WIP Program and YOU" that fea-tured the image of a black woman, barefoot, on her hands and knees, scrubbing the floor with a hand brush. A scrub bucket stood nearby and a lash hovered over her back (see Figure 10).[47] NWRO members pro-tested at the home of Representative Wilbur Mills, calling the amend-ments "regressive and racist."[48] They took Mills as their "Public Enemy #1," and accused leading members of the House and Senate of back-room chicanery to get the law passed.[49]

They Had a Dream

When she finished battling in Washington over work requirements for welfare mothers, Beulah Sanders returned to New York City. The local situation was more promising than the national one. In 1967, there were nearly eighty local action groups under the Citywide umbrella; by the middle of 1968, there were over one hundred local groups, with about six thousand dues-paying members.[50] Citywide leaders mobilized against the new welfare amendments locally and regionally. In an open letter to Governor Rockefeller, Jennette Washington asked what he planned to do to make up for the lapses in the federal legislation, and pledged her-self, as mother of six, not to "take this sitting down."[51]

While organizing against WIN/WIP, Citywide leaders were also pre-paring to participate in the Poor People's Campaign, a massive effort spearheaded by Rev. Martin Luther King, Jr., to focus the black freedom movement on economic inequality. When King originally announced that he planned to gather poor people to demand some of what an affluent society had to offer, George Wiley and the elected leaders of NWRO responded with skepticism. They saw King as a middle-class pro-fessional man who did not comprehend the issues that mattered most to them. He settled their concerns somewhat by coming to meet with NWRO's National Coordinating Committee, which included Johnnie Tillmon, Sanders, Carmen Olivo from New York, and three other representatives from Citywide.[52] Hulbert James remembered that Dr. King sent "Bernard Lafayette who was the coordinator of the [Poor People's] campaign, and immediately the ladies at George's urging, said 'No, we are not talking to Bernard Lafayette. We are talking to Martin. We don't want [Ralph] Abernathy, we want Martin King.' Talk about power at a bargaining table. King, Abernathy, Andy [Young, the three top leaders of King's organization, the Southern Christian Leadership Conference] flew to Chicago."[53]

When King arrived, the women peppered him with hard questions about class and gender in the civil rights movement, the role of whites and Latinos/as in the Poor People's Campaign, and the Social Security Act amendments. Mamie Hall from Citywide started off by asking "where he had been from 1966 until now."[54] A representative from Illinois asked whether there were any welfare recipients on the board of the Southern Christian Leadership Conference (SCLC). King answered, not very satisfyingly, that SCLC was a group of preachers and "had no women on its board."[55] Carmen Olivo, an NWRO officer as well as a member of Citywide, reminded King that "not only Negro[e]s were poor but many Puerto Ricans are very upset over how they have to live in this country," and Tillmon underlined that there were "more white people on welfare than non-whites."[56] King won over these welfare rights veterans by committing himself to the fight against the public assistance amendments. At the end of the meeting, King and the NWRO leaders convened a press conference. He came out publicly against the "anti-welfare bill," and they endorsed the Poor People's Campaign.[57]

Citywide proceeded with its local campaigns for minimum standards and fair hearings, its efforts to repeal the new federal legislation, and its support for the Poor People's Campaign. Sanders called on everyone in Citywide to support Dr. King and "help him do his job."[58] At the end of March 1968, King came to New York City to spark enthusiasm for the Poor People's Campaign. He defended strategies of nonviolence, which had recently been derided by the embattled Harlem Congressman Adam Clayton Powell, Jr. A weary Dr. King spoke about poverty and "that evil, unjust war" in Southeast Asia.[59] He connected the struggle against what he had recently termed "racist imperialism" with the struggles of poor whites in Queens and African Americans in Harlem.[60] Among the places he visited was Citywide headquarters. Beulah Sanders met him there and appeared with him publicly at a series of meetings.[61]

Nine days after his visit to Citywide headquarters, Martin Luther King, Jr., was shot dead in Memphis. Unlike African Americans in Washington, D.C., and a score of other cities, New Yorkers did not riot in response.[62] Sanders, who traveled to Atlanta for King's funeral with a Citywide delegation, reflected that "Anyone who stands up and speaks for poor people is a target anywhere, any time . . . What's the country coming to?" she asked. "What are we to do?"[63] Wiley, a moderate who had helped lead NWRO into alliances with white liberals and officials of the federal government, was shaken by the assassination. He found himself "prepared to cheer secretly when people are planting bombs in Macy's."[64] NWRO staff responded to the murder by proposing a "living memorial" to King that included repealing the 1967 amendments, "the most regressive and racist piece of social legislation in the history of the country."[65]

On April 22, 1968, the day on which King had planned to start his Poor People's Campaign, District of Columbia police arrested welfare rights activists at the U.S. Capitol building. The activists had come, they explained, to honor the memory of Dr. King and to demonstrate against the 1967 amendments. Of the thirty-nine arrested, thirty-two were NWRO officers and regional representatives, including Johnnie Tillmon, Mamie Hall from Brooklyn, and Beulah Sanders.[66] In Sanders's words: "We let everybody know that we won't be forced to work, leave our children or accept coun[selling]."[67] Irene Gibbs from New York City thought the event communicated to Congress that welfare recipients were serious about demanding their "just rights." Following King, she linked the welfare crisis with the war in Vietnam, imploring members of Congress to "Take the money from Vietnam and feed our children."[68]

The first event of the Poor People's Campaign was a Mother's Day march sponsored by NWRO. Over three thousand people walked in the rain, past buildings that rioters had reduced to charred skeletons and piles of bricks, in the heart of Washington's African American community. Coretta Scott King joined Beulah Sanders, Johnnie Tillmon, and the other NWRO leaders to underline her opposition to the 1967 welfare amendments and lend support to the effort to memorialize her late husband as a crusader for economic justice.[69] Everyone in America, she said, has a "right to live," meaning they were entitled to either jobs or guaranteed incomes.[70] Welfare recipients, middle-class black clubwomen, black male civil rights leaders, and wives of congressmen called on "Mother Power" to defeat WIN/WIP and the caseload freeze, and to create a national minimum income.[71]

In June, four busloads of Citywide members joined hundreds of NWRO activists in the Solidarity Day demonstrations organized by the Southern Christian Leadership Conference. After listening to a long

JOIN WITH
MRS MARTIN LUTHER KING
as she leads
welfare mothers on a
MOTHERS DAY
protest march through
Washington's black community
SUNDAY, MAY 12, 1968

Gather for March
John F. Kennedy Playground
7th and P Streets NW
2:30 p.m.

Rally
Cardozo High School
13th and Clifton Streets NW
4:30 p.m.

SPONSORED by the NATIONAL WELFARE RIGHTS ORGANIZATION and the POOR PEOPLES CAMPAIGN

Figure 11. Coretta Scott King marched through riot-torn neighborhoods with NWRO to kick off the Poor People's Campaign. Courtesy NWRO Papers, Moorland-Spingarn Research Center, Howard University.

lineup of speakers, including Johnnie Tillmon and Coretta Scott King, Jennette Washington was left with a combination of optimism and pessimism, "deep down within asking myself do they really mean it. . . . Will they all go home forgetting so quickly yesterday, or did the spark come alive to really search to the depths to find answers?"[72]

Resurrection Undone

The doubts Jennette Washington expressed about the depth of public policy makers' concerns and the lasting influence of Solidarity Day turned out to be well founded. When NWRO claimed "Mother Power" and maternal entitlement to a decent standard of living, the organization gained allies, but it also touched a nerve of working- and middle-class white anger. After a profile of Johnnie Tillmon appeared on the "About Women" page of the *Washington Post,* exasperated women readers wrote to insist that she should work for wages and practice sexual restraint.[73] "The American dream," one wrote, "is one of being able to WORK for what you get, not one of self indulgence, of physical satiation everytime that desire wells in ones heart."[74] "What do the negroes expect?" asked another; "that all the white should help them—why not the rich colored people help the colored. They don't want to work."[75]

On June 24, 1968, police and federal government employees tore down Resurrection City, the shantytown on the Washington, D.C., mall that was the primary symbol of the Poor People's Campaign. As journalist I. F. Stone pointed out, that same day the U.S. Senate voted in favor of an antiballistic missile system, the costs of which could amount to $50 billion. The Poor People's Campaign was widely considered a failure (although not by Stone, who found it "inspiring . . . [with] the same hope and the same will to rebuild" that he had seen in Jewish refugee camps after World War II).[76] The campaign left SCLC in disarray.[77] Through protests and lobbying, the campaign had successfully negotiated changes in federal food programs, including a major expansion in food stamps. But its gains were a far cry from the goals of Dr. Martin Luther King, Jr., and Coretta Scott King. Despite months of pressure from the Poor People's Campaign, Citywide, and NWRO, the public welfare amendments of 1967 remained on the statute books.[78]

Welfare rights activists faced disappointments in New York as well as on the national stage. Governor Rockefeller moved to end the disorder in the public aid system by floating the idea of a "flat grant" in the state legislature. Eliminating minimum standards payments for public assistance promised to halt the rise in the welfare budget, and tame the social movement the governor held responsible for increasing it. Under the Rockefeller proposal, a welfare client would receive one yearly supplement of $100 for items not covered in her or his regular grants.[79]

Citywide members responded to the flat grant proposal with an increasingly militant effort to stave off the change, or, failing that, to wring the maximum amount of money possible out of the welfare department before the flat grant became law. A dozen members of the Citywide Executive Board, including Sanders and Irene Gibbs, sat in at

the office of Social Services commissioner Jack Goldberg.[80] Next, Citywide celebrated the second "birthday" of NWRO with a demonstration
at the United Nations on June 30, 1968. Gibbs and Executive Board
member Eladio Mendez left the sit-in at Goldberg's office to join this
symbolic appeal to the world on behalf of the forgotten poor of the
United States.[81] Finally, Citywide members demanded to be included in
a meeting about the flat grant between the State Board of Social Welfare
and federal officials. After their request was denied, forty activists took
over the offices of the state commissioner of Social Welfare. When the
officials locked themselves in a conference room, the welfare recipients
banged on the door and walls in an effort to gain admission; some of
the women took off their shoes, Khrushchev-style, and used them to
pound on the door.[82]

None of these tactics helped Citywide make friends or influence people at City Hall or in the state capitol in Albany. However, in the short
run, the new militancy did defeat the flat grant. After the news about sit-
ins, sleep-ins, and shoe-ins by welfare mothers hit the media, state legislators moved to block Rockefeller's proposal. A majority in Albany
favored the flat grant but blanched at the governor's effort to sweeten
that proposal by offering supplements to basic cash grants. Rather than
seeing the Rockefeller proposal as a punitive response to the welfare
rights movement, these opponents saw it as a form of guaranteed
income that rewarded out-of-control welfare militants.[83]

With the flat grant temporarily retired to the wings, Citywide leaders
reached out to Coretta Scott King and, through her, to women's organizations like those that had supported NWRO's Mother's Day March.
Referring to Citywide's efforts as "the real war on poverty," Scott King
exhorted the leaders of other women's groups in New York City to support the embattled movement for welfare rights.[84]

A Mirage in Miami and a Liberal Lament

At the same time that that they were embroiled in the politics of welfare
in New York, Governor Rockefeller and Mayor Lindsay were both seeking the Republican nomination for President of the United States.
Rockefeller proposed the flat grant, and Lindsay accepted it, in large
measure because they were attempting to demonstrate their credibility
to Republicans who believed that both men were too liberal to succeed
on the national stage.

Only days after the New York State legislature defeated Rockefeller's
flat grant, the Republican National Convention opened in Miami.
Although Rockefeller was far behind Richard Nixon in the delegate
count, he was still seeking the nomination as the convention began.

Lindsay was also a nominal candidate for the presidential nomination and, more credibly, was in the running for the vice presidency. When Nixon won the nomination on the first ballot and named Maryland governor Spiro Agnew as his vice-presidential nominee, the New York liberals learned how far the geographic center of their Party had shifted to the South and Southwest and how far its ideological center had shifted to the right.[85]

Lindsay's comeuppance at the Republican National Convention was especially humiliating, and instructive. Citywide activists were dissatisfied with the mayor's antipoverty efforts and his responsiveness to their agenda. But Republicans from the rest of the country knew him as a pro-civil rights liberal who was partially responsible for the Kerner Commission Report, which blamed urban riots on racial and economic inequality as much as on individual lawlessness.[86] By the traditional logic of regional and ideological balance on a presidential ticket, Lindsay would have been an ideal running mate for either Nixon or California governor Ronald Reagan. However, the politics of the convention made this logic instantly moot. As the convention began, Nixon hurried to make peace with Southern opponents of civil rights and the Goldwater wing of his Party. He secured the presidential nomination and protected himself against challenges from Rockefeller and Reagan. In private meetings, Nixon handed Strom Thurmond of South Carolina and Barry Goldwater veto power over his vice-presidential nominee. The two rejected Lindsay and approved Nixon's choice of Spiro Agnew, a Governor of Maryland who had made antipathy to African American militants a centerpiece of his politics. With Thurmond's and Goldwater's blessings, the only thing Nixon offered John Lindsay was the opportunity to stand before the convention and second Agnew's nomination. Lindsay accepted the offer.[87]

Beulah Sanders and other leaders of Citywide were just as disappointed by the Democratic National Convention in Chicago as Lindsay and Rockefeller had been by the Republican meeting in Miami. Sanders, George Wiley, and Etta Horn of the Washington, D.C., welfare rights alliance were invited to testify before the Democratic Platform Committee. They asked that the platform include their goals of higher welfare grants, repeal of the 1967 amendments, and, "beyond welfare," a national minimum income adequate to support a family.[88] Juliet Greenlaw, a welfare rights leader from Indiana, was invited to speak at hearings on the Democratic platform. She insisted that a compulsory employment program like WIN/WIP was unnecessary; the federal government, she argued, would not have to force welfare mothers to work if there were jobs available that would pay them adequately, and if they could be sure that their children were safe. "We think the real reason for this bill," Greenlaw explained, "is to force black people to take the maid and hardman jobs that no one else wants to do and that don't pay enough to support a family. We have our own kitchen floors to scrub and our own children to look after!"[89]

The Democrats listened politely to the Citywide and NWRO leaders. However, they did not include any of the major welfare rights demands in their platform (much as they resisted the demands of other dissidents and protesters who came to the Democratic National Convention in 1968).[90] The platform merely committed the Democrats to the vague goals of advocating public "assistance free of . . . indignities and uncertainties," and promised a "thorough evaluation" of programs for the "working poor," such as a guaranteed income or children's allowance.[91]

The Democratic Party's lack of interest in their agenda was only the first of the disappointments Citywide leaders experienced in Chicago. "Stuff was just cut out from under us," Citywide Director Hulbert James recalled. "We picked a newspaper [up] at the convention in Chicago and read where the city was instituting this flat grant to be effective that September."[92] After quiet negotiations among members of the Lindsay administration, federal officials, and emissaries from Governor Rockefeller's office, New York City was poised to initiate a "simplified payments system" that closely resembled the flat grant proposal and yet did not require legislative approval to be enacted.[93]

This new flat grant would eliminate most of the leeway caseworkers had to provide for their clients' minimum standards. It would raise basic welfare grants by 6 percent, give clients $100 per year in supplemental funds, and leave only a few provisions in the regulations for special grants. Lindsay administration officials claimed that the plan was not designed to save money but was intended "to help relief recipients plan better for their own needs."[94] On the day it was announced, approximately 150 Citywide members rallied at City Hall, pledging "massive resistance" to the new policy and calling Mayor Lindsay a hypocrite.[95]

Two days of nearly continuous protest at City Hall followed. On August 27, six hundred welfare recipients and their allies returned to Mayor Lindsay's front yard, where they were confronted by two hundred New York City police officers and nine "mounties" on horses.[96] When a group tried to enter the grounds of City Hall Park, the mounties charged at them, and other police pushed women and men back with nightsticks. Thirteen people were arrested, including Jennette Washington and Hulbert James, who were charged with inciting a riot. Attorney Carl Rachlin commented that there was "no excuse for the horses"; outraged African American and Puerto Rican women demonstrators asserted that the police "wouldn't do this to white people."[97] On the next day, the police arrested eighteen more Citywide activists, including

Beulah Sanders. Martin Morgenstern, president of the Social Service Employees Union, joined the welfare recipients in City Hall Park. At the end of the week, Sanders pledged her "undaunted" commitment to fighting the flat grant and to holding John Lindsay responsible for the unrest that would surely follow from his policies.[98]

Citywide activists may have been undaunted, but they were frustrated. Gaining nothing but arrests from their choice to target Mayor Lindsay and the physical premises of City Hall, they returned to the local welfare centers. They began a new wave of demonstrations. These were fueled by the anger about the Lindsay and Rockefeller administrations' efforts to withdraw the supplemental grants that had brought many New York families within reach of adequate incomes.

New York City began implementing the flat grant on September 1. For the next three and a half weeks, women and men affiliated with Citywide ran roughshod over neighborhood aid offices.[99] Joyce Burson, who was opposed to these tactics, remembered occasions on which she would organize members of the Brooklyn Welfare Action Council for a peaceful protest, and Jennette Washington or another leader would help the infuriated clients tear up a welfare office instead. "It wasn't so much that we ever sat down and planned to go in and tear up a center," she remembered, but "it happened."[100] Seventy-five recipients overturned furniture, ripped telephones from the walls, intimidated employees, and scattered the official papers of three welfare centers that were located in the same building in Brooklyn.[101] To a reporter on the scene, one woman cried out: "It's not funny. . . . You sleep on the floor and feed your children with 33 cents a meal and see if it's funny."[102] The incident was widely reported. A front-page story about it in the *New York Times*, Hulbert James later lamented, "did more than any other news story to discredit the movement in New York. It was all downhill from then on."[103]

While Citywide members blamed the Lindsay administration for capitulating to antiwelfare forces, many New Yorkers thought their mayor was too lenient. One particularly controversial city policy forbade Welfare Patrolmen (a specially organized corps of public servants, who were paid less than other city police forces and were not permitted to carry firearms) from intervening in demonstrations or arresting the demonstrators.[104] A staff member from the Fulton Welfare Center complained to the mayor about the no-arrest policy: "Employees of the Department are told they have a responsibility to meet the needs of recipients, not their *demands*. . . . If because of his policy of 'NO ARREST,' I must wonder everyday how I will get out of the building, maybe the day I cast my vote for John V. Lindsay I should have 'stood in bed'."[105]

After the Citywide protests in Brooklyn, Lindsay, who was no doubt thinking back to the Republican Convention in Miami and ahead to his mayoral re-election campaign in 1969, gave the order to arrest welfare demonstrators. The *Times* gave its full-throated support. "It is wrong for police to 'overreact' to incidents," the newspaper editorialized. "It is also wrong for them to 'underreact'."[106]

In the weeks and months that followed, Citywide activists carried on their fight against the flat grant. They risked arrest, and courted the disapproval of working- and middle-class New Yorkers, by disrupting welfare centers and demonstrating in places where they thought Mayor Lindsay might notice them. Hundreds of welfare families came close to eviction when they participated in a Citywide "spend-the-rent" campaign that protested the flat grant by using rent money for clothing, shoes, and household goods that were no longer covered under the new policy. The Citywide leadership enlisted Carl Rachlin and lawyers from the Center on Social Welfare Policy and Law to help them sue New York City and New York State for the backhanded way they created the new welfare system.[107] A group from Citywide even demonstrated against the flat grant at Macy's Thanksgiving Day Parade, handing out leaflets that read, simply: "Thanks for Nothin."[108]

In April 1969, as the state legislature prepared to pass major cuts in the social services budget, welfare recipients gathered one more time for a huge rally in Manhattan's Central Park. It turned into a spontaneous march down Fifth Avenue. For the first time since the City Hall Park demonstrations that followed Mayor Lindsay's announcement of the flat grant, mounted police charged the demonstrators. There was confusion and violence in the streets.[109]

The increasingly confrontational tactics of the citywide welfare rights movement bred a firestorm of reaction against the welfare system and against women and men who relied on its benefits. Members of the New York City Council jostled one another for posts on a commission to investigate alleged improprieties at the welfare department. As the number of New Yorkers on the welfare rolls passed 900,000, Council members competed with investigators from the federal Department of Health, Education, and Welfare, and private researchers on the payroll of the Teamsters Union, to ferret out supposed welfare frauds. Rockefeller submitted a budget for 1969 that proposed cutting benefits per family by 10 percent, eliminating the $100 annual supplement that had been the silver lining for recipients around the dark cloud of the flat grant, and stiffening eligibility requirements for all forms of public aid.[110]

John V. Lindsay described the final months of 1968 as "the worst of my public life."[111] Infuriated welfare recipients were only one of his problems. He also faced striking teachers and enraged parents in the

Figure 12. New York City Mayor John Lindsay (left) with pictures of Richard Nixon and Spiro Agnew in background. Lindsay had hoped that Nixon would ask him, not Agnew, to be his running mate in 1968. Courtesy John V. Linsday Papers, New York City Municipal Archives.

battle over community control of the public schools, a police force that used a work slowdown as a negotiating tool to improve its wages and working conditions, potential walkouts by sanitation workers and firemen, and a threatened epidemic of the "flu."[112] As Lindsay began his reelection campaign, working- and middle-class white people in most of the city seemed to regard the mayor with special antipathy. Journalist Pete Hamill's April 1969 essay on "The Revolt of the White Lower Middle Class" quoted an iron worker who asked: "What the hell does Lindsay care about me?"[113]

The mayor attempted in 1969 to demonstrate that he cared about white New Yorkers. He took a somewhat harder line on issues that caused race-based resentment, including welfare. His administration brought the rate of increase in new welfare cases down dramatically, allegedly by directing social workers to reject applications or to delay the opening of new cases. The mayor promised that he would use savings in the welfare budget to put more police and sanitation workers on the streets.[114] Lindsay faced two challengers in the 1969 mayoral race, a Republican and Democrat, both of whom sounded at times like they were reading from the playbook of William F. Buckley's 1965 campaign. Lindsay ultimately won because they divided the increasingly hostile white vote, because communities of color continued to back him, and because he shifted his political profile enough to neutralize part of the lower-middle-class revolt.[115]

Nelson Rockefeller nearly met his comeuppance in 1968 at the hands of the political Right. Nixon's victory in November came close to shattering Rockefeller's last, lingering hopes of ascending to the presidency. Political strategists in the Nixon campaign, such as Kevin Phillips, demonstrated that a Republican could win office without so much as the New York governor's blessing. They built a victorious electoral coalition out of middle- and working-class whites in the Midwest, Southwest, and South, along with voters from the Northeast who could no longer abide the trend toward racial integration or the other consequences of Democratic and Republican liberalism. In the aftermath of the 1968 election, the governor's biographers opined: "The time had come for Nelson Rockefeller to move irrevocably rightward."[116]

Welfare activism in New York never fully recovered from the imposition of the flat grant or the negative publicity generated by Citywide's furious attacks on the welfare system. After Rockefeller and Lindsay curtailed the expansion of public assistance, it became clear that the benefit-based organizing the welfare movement had learned from César Chávez and Fred Ross was key to its strength at the grassroots. For Jennette Washington, Irene Gibbs, and thousands of other welfare parents, children's clothes and home furnishings were important in themselves. They were also vitally important signs of family well-being and citizenship in post-World War II society. Without the opportunity to gain these extra benefits, there was far less reason for poor mothers and fathers to join Citywide. Moreover, the flat grant deprived Citywide members of their opportunities to appeal, both practically and rhetorically, to law. It became more complicated to charge the welfare department with "illegal" treatment of clients when caseworkers were no longer bound to distribute information about extra grants or issue them to people who needed them.

The confrontations over public welfare that occurred in New York City were pivotal to the evolution of U.S. politics. They were of course significant for the politics of welfare. Poor women and men in New York had led the nation in forming a mass movement for welfare rights. Citywide was the incubator of this movement's most important tactics. The wreckage that followed imposition of the flat grant portended welfare cutbacks elsewhere.

The conflicts surrounding welfare that became visible in the late 1960s both revealed important political cleavages and helped generate realignments in local and national politics. When they moved against Citywide, Rockefeller and Lindsay were responding not only to popular opinion among working- and middle-class whites in New York; they were answering the rise of a vocal, powerful new movement within the Republican Party. In the words of Kevin Phillips, this increasingly powerful subgroup of Republicans was not in favor of any ideology so much as "*opposed* to welfare and the Establishment."[117] When Rockefeller floated his plans for welfare reform and Lindsay unleashed the police against protesters, both were playing to a national audience within the Republican Party as well as to local audiences of antiwelfare New Yorkers.[118]

Welfare policy and the issues it inevitably raised about gender, race, work, and the power of the poor was central to the political transformations that occurred in New York and elsewhere as the power of the black freedom movement diminished and the many reactions to it gathered strength. Citywide's minimum standards and fair hearing campaigns advanced the claims of African American, Latina, and poor white women, as well as low-income men. Citywide and NWRO members argued that they deserved the option to be excused from the paid workforce when their children were young, and that their families should enjoy a decent standard of living whether or not they were earning wages. These claims ran counter to racist traditions in U.S. social policy: for decades, respectable white women had been discouraged from participating in the labor force while everyone else was told to work for low wages.[119] The Rockefeller and Lindsay administrations cut the benefits that had allowed poor parents to negotiate the consumer market somewhat powerfully on behalf of their families, and that had promised to let them raise children without also juggling jobs and child care outside the home.[120]

Despite Beulah Sanders's and Jennette Washington's best efforts, the welfare rights movement in New York City began to collapse in the late summer and fall of 1968. This was not, as Frances Fox Piven and Richard Cloward argued retrospectively, because the movement shifted focus from mass organizing or disruptive tactics to lobbying for new legislation or maintaining the organizational integrity of either Citywide or NWRO.[121] Quite the contrary: the capsize of the Citywide movement came in the wake of its biggest push into the streets and welfare centers. Strategic missteps by Sanders, Washington, and George Wiley were not the cause of the movement's collapse. The welfare rights movement lost power because most white voters opposed everything it stood for: the political enfranchisement of African American, Puerto Rican, and poor white women; the expansion of the consumer society to those who had been excluded from most of its benefits for the half century since World War I; a revolution in individual and social rights that included widespread access to law; and alternatives to the waged labor market, or dependence on a man, when these notoriously unreliable sources of economic well-being failed to provide what women and children needed. Energetic opposition to these fundamentals of welfare rights ideology, especially by working-class and middle-class whites, changed politics in New York City. Opposition to these same principles in other parts of the country transformed national politics in ways that ultimately turned liberalism on its head.

Chapter 5
Give Us Credit for Being American

> *We are not going to steal anything. We want you to share some of it, you understand? We can have paradise here, all of us. There is enough wealth.*
>
> —*Mildred Prem, welfare rights activist, Buffalo, New York*

In June 1969, Brooklyn welfare rights leader Jackie Pope told readers of the *Welfare Righter* about a recent political demonstration that had taken her by surprise. In the middle of the National Conference on Social Welfare in Manhattan, she reported, three hundred social workers walked out of the proceedings, marched down Seventh Avenue, and joined a picket line in front of the Sears & Roebuck store on Thirty-First Street. Responding to claims by members of Citywide that Sears discriminated against welfare recipients by denying them credit, the social workers "burned" their charge cards (or, more likely, cut the plastic cards in half) and followed welfare mothers and fathers into the store. Women and men who had, under recent statewide cuts in public benefits, lost access to special grants for items such as children's school clothes and furniture, "applied for credit, ordered merchandise with the credit applications, and sampled the floor samples—that is, they sewed, vacuumed, played records and listened to stereos."[1]

In the aftermath of the flat grant, Citywide activists held on to their dreams of first-class citizenship in the United States, including their vision of participation in the consumer market and of gaining a fair hearing in public agencies and courtrooms. The battle for credit at Sears and other department stores was, according to Brooklyn leader Joyce Burson, "a case of clients running the show." Ordinary members of welfare rights groups demanded a form of citizenship in the affluent society that she, a seasoned leader, had hardly contemplated. The Brooklyn welfare rights movement "started out . . . to just hassle the down town businessmen's association to try and get them to intercede for us" on public welfare policy, but rank-and-file AFDC mothers and fathers turned the

Figure 13. The NWRO newspaper shows the consumerist tactics the movement pursued after New York and other states began cutting welfare in the late 1960s. Courtesy Periodicals Division, Wisconsin Historical Society.

effort toward making demands on the private sector itself. They "decided we ought to be fighting for credit because we need credit. . . . We tried to talk them out of it," Burson remembered, but the members insisted.[2]

Consumerist demands were constitutive of welfare rights politics throughout the history of the movement. However, before 1968, these demands had treated public-sector institutions as almost solely responsible for meeting welfare recipients' needs. By 1969, the climate in public institutions had changed: Governor Rockefeller and Mayor Lindsay had begun to change their liberal stripes and Richard Nixon was President. In the federal courts, the Warren Court era of expanding the rights of minorities was coming to a close. NWRO activists across the country shifted some of their protest energy from government agencies to private companies in order to "force the most powerful segment of the society—big business—to yield."[3] Mildred Prem from Buffalo and other welfare recipients perceived a "paradise" of private wealth in the United States, and they asked major corporations to "share some of it."[4]

In a multi-faceted campaign to join the affluent society, Citywide members and other activists not only tried to get credit cards for welfare recipients, but they also fought for changes in the federal Food Stamp program so that they would have more liberty in the daily spending decisions they made for their families. They pursued a "Private-Sector Family Allowance Plan" under which large companies were asked to transfer some of their profits directly to impoverished families. At the same time, they asked local school districts to disburse compensatory education funds directly to low-income families, instead of to school officials who might or might not make sure that the money was used for children's most immediate needs, and they battled utility companies over what activists claimed was unequal treatment of welfare families.

The Poor Pay More

The Sears campaign that Jackie Pope and Joyce Burson observed in New York grew from longstanding problems in the relationship between impoverished people and consumer markets. One of the few empirical sources on poor people's consumption in the 1960s was a study cosponsored by several settlement houses on Manhattan's Lower East Side and in Harlem, which focused on African American and Puerto Rican public housing residents. The resulting book, *The Poor Pay More*, argued that low-income consumers often paid more than higher income ones for goods of equal or inferior quality. Author David Caplovitz claimed that this occurred because low-income consumers, who had limited cash on hand and limited geographic mobility, and who lacked "shopping sophistication," purchased the goods on credit.[5] These consumers could not receive credit at stores that sold low-priced goods or offered credit on fairly good terms, and so they purchased from peddlers who came into their homes or at local stores that offered high prices, poor merchandise, and installment credit with very high rates of interest. The installment system allowed customers to take goods home if they made small initial payments—and signed sales contracts in which they promised to make relatively high regular payments long into the future.

The Poor Pay More offered dramatic examples of consumer exploitation by sales people. Sales contracts were worded confusingly or misleadingly, and the goods purchased were of such low quality that they fell apart before they were paid for. Store owners might overlook a few missed payments but might also be quick to repossess the furniture or appliances of customers who were delinquent in payments. When they did not repossess, store owners could garnish the customer's wages, that is, arrange to receive a portion of the consumer's wages directly from her or his employer. Such a course of action let employers know that their employees were delinquent customers and could lead to them being fired.[6]

Despite all of these negatives, low-income African American and Puerto Rican families in New York City participated in the consumer economy. Ninety-five percent of the families Caplovitz studied had televisions in their homes, 41 percent owned washing machines, and 23 percent had colored telephones.[7] He concluded from these figures that "*need*, as indicated by family size" shaped consumption patterns with little regard to income. For poor families, like other American families in the postwar era, "Bridging the gap between current income and extensive needs and aspirations is the institution of credit."[8] While middle-class families used credit cards that they received from major department stores, poor consumers used installment credit from local merchants. Even the 15 percent of families in Caplovitz's study who received welfare were able to purchase goods on credit for their homes.[9]

The conditions Caplovitz described in the early 1960s moderated somewhat under the pressure of legal reform efforts later in the decade. The consumer credit squeeze, and the procedures retail firms used to either collect or repossess from their delinquent customers, were high on the short list of priorities for the nascent poverty law community of the middle 1960s.[10] Attorneys who worked out of storefront legal services offices represented clients in their dealings with local installment merchants. Others tried to use the courts to control the system of installment sales by bringing cases under Section 2-302 of the Uniform Commercial Code of the United States, a model statute concerning "unconscionable" contracts, which individual jurisdictions wrote into law beginning in the middle 1960s. An "unconscionable" contract was so one-sided—and relied so heavily on the vulnerability or ignorance of one of the parties—that courts need not enforce it.[11]

The idea of "unconscionability" was the centerpiece of an important 1965 decision by Judge J. Skelley Wright of the U.S. Court of Appeals for the D.C. Circuit. The plaintiff in the case was a welfare recipient from

Washington, D.C., named Ora Lee Williams. In 1962, Williams purchased a stereo priced at over five hundred dollars. She defaulted on her payments soon thereafter. The Walker-Thomas furniture company repossessed all the goods Williams had acquired over a five-year period, arguing that the company had a right to repossess because one densely worded clause in its contract with Williams kept "a balance due on every item purchased until the balance due on all items, whenever purchased, was liquidated."[12] Judge Skelley Wright refused to enforce the contract because he deemed it unconscionable, a term he defined in sweepingly ambiguous terms. He recognized "gross inequalit[ies] of bargaining power" between low-income African American female welfare recipients and aggressively profit-seeking firms.[13]

Black (Buying) Power

The welfare rights movement may have been the only social movement that demanded credit cards from Sears, but it was not alone in its focus on the consumer dimension of the economy, or on questions about discrimination and the availability of credit. Historically, women's movements in the U.S. have often targeted consumer issues, perhaps because women have had particular responsibilities for negotiating the consumer market in order to care for their families.[14] Consumption has also been a vital part of black political protest and the assertion of dignity, human rights, and civil rights by African Americans.[15] The claim to ladyhood, a gendered demand for dignity and decency, which welfare rights activists expressed in their campaigns for credit, clothes, and home furnishings, recalls individual and collective acts by African American women from at least the middle nineteenth through the late twentieth centuries.[16] Among Latino/a activists, the outstanding examples of consumer protest were the boycotts of California grapes and lettuce that César Chávez and Delores Huerta of the United Farm Workers coordinated in the 1960s and 1970s.[17]

A new, largely middle-class consumer movement emerged in the 1960s. This movement converged at points with the women's and civil rights movements, federally funded antipoverty programs, and both government-funded and independent legal reform efforts. Its patron saints were Rachel Carson, whose *Silent Spring* (1962) raised concerns not only about the fate of wildlife but also about the safety of produce for consumers, and Ralph Nader, whose *Unsafe at Any Speed* (1965) took as its target the automobile industry, the signal consumer industry of the post-World War II era.[18] One major consumer concern of the 1960s was access to consumer credit for women and racial minorities. Second-wave feminists, for example, joined their demands for women's equal employment opportunities with demands for equal credit opportunities, including credit cards in their own names for married women and improved credit access for single and divorced women. These efforts resulted ultimately in passage of the Equal Credit Opportunity Act of 1974.[19]

New Yorkers had a tradition of pursuing politics at the point of consumption dating from at least the early twentieth century. Jewish housewives on the Lower East Side protested inflated food prices during World War I in a series of pickets and boycotts that resulted in cost controls on meat, milk, and other staples. Harlem was a center of the "Don't Buy Where You Can't Work" campaign during the Depression, which pressured white business owners on the central business strip of 125th Street to hire African Americans for visible positions that offered some hope of upward mobility. It was also the center of a consumer cooperation movement, which aimed to bypass mainstream merchants and merchandising. Ella Baker, who later became the director of branches for the NAACP and the guiding force behind the Student Nonviolent Coordinating Committee, cofounded the Young Negroes Cooperative League in 1930, educating Harlem consumers about the possibility of building an economy not based on the profit motive. After World War Two, Harlemites continued to organize cooperatives and to agitate for affordable prices, job and ownership opportunities, and high-quality goods in local stores.[20]

In the 1960s, consumer politics of all kinds thrived in Harlem and other African American neighborhoods. A new cooperative movement continued the work Ella Baker had begun, to educate consumers about the benefits of co-ops and the mechanics of creating them. In one protest over high food prices in African American neighborhoods, welfare recipients and wealthier women joined together to picket chain stores and shop en masse at cooperative grocery stores. Members of the Harlem Consumer Education Council planned the action for a day on which welfare recipients were to receive their fortnightly checks.[21]

Consumer boycotts and pickets aimed to increase job opportunities for African American workers. They also aimed to improve the treatment of black consumers in the public space of the grocery aisle or sales floor and to raise the quality of goods available to black families. Grassroots campaigns, such as one aimed at grocery stores that activists nicknamed "Operation Lambchop," conducted spot checks of sales practices and prices in Brooklyn and Manhattan to prove that poor and African American consumers did, indeed, pay more for food and furniture than did wealthier whites. Harlemites, Brooklynites, and other New Yorkers complained about their limited access to consumer credit and the myriad problems they faced when they signed installment sales contracts.[22]

Nationally, consumer complaints became central to the African American freedom movement in the late 1960s. Of the major civil rights groups, the Congress of Racial Equality (CORE) had the greatest impact on the consumer politics welfare rights leaders pursued in the aftermath of the New York flat grant. CORE coordinated national boycotts of department stores and discount retailers that refused to hire or serve African Americans. Local CORE chapters also developed the tactic of the "shop-in." In a "shop-in," roughly comparable to a labor union "sit-in," activists would disrupt the sales floor of a particular store in order to pressure the company that owned it to negotiate on civil rights demands. In 1964, CORE chapters organized "coin-ins" at branches of the Bank of America during which activists interfered with bank operations by standing at tellers' windows demanding large amounts of change. Combined with 100 days of picketing, this tactic persuaded the bank to hire a significant number of African American employees.[23]

When he worked for CORE, attorney Carl Rachlin had tried to use some of the organization's resources to pursue consumer litigation. He tried unsuccessfully to generate a class-action lawsuit using Section 2-302 of the Uniform Commercial Code. Rachlin argued that the consumer credit issue was "not an individual problem but a large socio-economic problem and as lawyers we should attack it in that way."[24]

By 1967, consumer issues and other economic concerns were ubiquitous in African American movement circles. In their book *Black Power*, Stokely Carmichael and Charles Hamilton made an analogy between white-black relationships and relationships between European colonial powers and their African colonies. The flow of consumer capital out of African American communities, and the credit practices of white store owners in black neighborhoods, was central to the comparison. Similar calls for economic self-determination were heard among leaders of traditional civil rights groups. Faced with stalled campaigns for housing, school, and job integration in the North, and a potentially vast new constituency of underemployed urban youth, leaders intensified their focus on economic causes and solutions for what ailed black America. In his last book, *Where Do We Go From Here?* Martin Luther King, Jr., profiled strategies that utilized the power of urban African Americans as consumers. Even as he distanced himself from the slogan "Black Power," King endorsed a vigorous use of black "buying power."[25] He singled out the "vicious circle" that low-income consumers encountered: "You are condemned to the jobs and shops which are closest to your home," he wrote. "Once confined to this isolated community, one no longer participates in a free economy, but is subject to price-fixing and wholesale robbery by many of the merchants."[26]

After King's assassination, the Southern Christian Leadership Conference focused on black consumers and black-owned businesses through Operation Breadbasket, a national campaign of consumer boycotts that had begun in 1961 but expanded dramatically in the late 1960s when it came under the direction of Reverend Jesse Jackson.[27] Operation Breadbasket boycotts reportedly produced one thousand new white-collar jobs for black Philadelphians in the early 1960s, and spurred selective buying efforts in Chicago, Detroit, Pittsburgh, Cincinnati, and Wilmington, Delaware. In New York City, Operation Breadbasket combined employment demands with consumer-oriented ones; a boycott of the A&P grocery made demands including that the chain stop raising its prices on welfare recipients' "check day."[28]

The Kerner Commission Report of 1968 argued that consumer practices were responsible for much of the fury of young African Americans that had led to rioting in Northern cities. New York City mayor Lindsay and other members of the commission found that, in eleven out of twenty cities they studied, grievances about treatment by white store owners fueled urban riots. The Kerner Commission report argued that many of the grievances began with the problem of consumer credit in low-income, racially segregated communities, and the exploitation of inner-city residents by installment merchants who offered them low-quality goods on terrible terms.[29]

Perhaps because they were afraid of more riots, the President and Congress aired the same concerns about credit for black consumers and entrepreneurs that animated the writing of African American activists and scholars and the Kerner Commission. Richard Nixon began speaking in support of "black capitalism" during the 1968 campaign. As President, he created an Office of Minority Business Enterprise in the Small Business Administration to increase opportunities and access to credit for African American, Mexican American, Puerto Rican, and American Indian entrepreneurs. Although the office was funded at low levels, by the time of Nixon's resignation in 1974 it had an annual budget of $242 million.[30] In the same year that President Nixon created the Office of Minority Business Affairs, Congress considered dramatically expanding access to credit for poor people. In the Senate, William Proxmire (D-Wis.) and a few colleagues sponsored a "Community Credit Expansion Act," to improve access to "consumer credit, mortgage credit, and business credit in urban and rural poverty areas." Citing the Kerner Commission report, Proxmire spoke out against the "credit gap" that he believed privileged wealthier neighborhoods at the expense of low-income ones, and the trap of the installment system.[31]

Citywide and NWRO members asserted families' need for consumer credit to acquire large consumer durables such as furniture and home appliances, which they could not afford all at once. They argued, as King had done, that welfare recipients were in an even weaker bargaining position vis-à-vis exploitative local merchants than were other low-income people. Beulah Sanders, Jackie Pope, and many others sought credit at what they termed "reputable" working- and middle-class department stores such as Sears, Montgomery Ward, Lerner, and Lane Bryant, which catered to working-class and middle-class customers.

Collective campaigns for credit at Sears, the paradigmatic American consumer emporium, and for access to all-American consumer products, were expressions of welfare recipients' desire for citizenship in the affluent society. For Jackie Pope, Joyce Burson, Beulah Sanders, Jennette Washington, and other women of color, the private-sector consumer economy was a particularly significant arena in which to assert membership in postwar society. An increasing proportion of married women with children, white as well as black, were working for wages by the mid-1960s. At the same time, women were still responsible for negotiating the consumer marketplace on behalf of their families.[32] As in their battles over minimum standards and special grants, women welfare recipients who fought for rights in the private sector were seeking recognition as citizen-consumers who negotiated the market on behalf of their families just as other women did.

Critical Consumerism

The idea for a consumer credit campaign originated with welfare rights activists from Philadelphia. In the summer of 1968, Roxanne Jones and Margie Jefferson of the Philadelphia Welfare Rights Organization, with the help of Volunteers In Service To America (VISTAs) whose small salaries were paid by the federal government, devised the idea of seeking credit at major downtown department stores exclusively for members of their group.[33] The campaign was a great success. By August 1968, they had negotiated credit agreements with the Wanamaker, Lerner, Lit Brothers, and Lane Bryant stores. The Philadelphia activists later gained limited credit access from other stores, including Sears. In their agreement with the Lerner Shops, applicants for credit showing evidence of their membership in a welfare rights group would not even undergo credit checks but would receive credit automatically. Jefferson lauded the credit agreements as a way to release people from the hold of exploitative stores: "No longer are we restricted to buying inferior merchandise at high prices in the ghetto," she commented.[34] The Philadelphia WRO saw its membership double after it publicized its agreements with the stores.[35]

The credit idea spread quickly from Philadelphia to New York City. In November, 150 members of the Brooklyn Welfare Action Council

(B-WAC) demonstrated at the E. J. Korvette store in their borough's downtown. They demanded credit. In language that mirrored the claims they made against the welfare department, they asked for the right to represent all welfare recipients in their dealings with the department store chain.[36] B-WAC leaders Joyce Burson and Jackie Pope practiced a good cop/bad cop routine on the credit manager of the Korvette store. Burson remembered that in the middle of negotiations, Pope would stand up and say: "Well listen, isn't no sense us sitting here 'cause this man is not going . . . to deal with us, so let's just go, let's just tear up the store . . . and she'd get up and everybody would get up and they'd follow her out the door." Burson would pretend that she could not control Pope and the other women, and would start to leave, before the store's representative would conciliate "and I'd finally let him convince me that we could talk again."[37] Korvette's management offered twenty-five dollars' worth of credit, which Joyce Burson and the other activists refused because they were holding out for a more complete credit deal. Managers from Abraham & Straus, across the street from the Korvette store, hastened to open negotiations with the B-WAC leadership.[38]

The City-Wide Coordinating Committee of Welfare Groups picked up the credit campaign from its members in Brooklyn. Beulah Sanders, Sadie Jackson, and Archerie DeLeon of Citywide soon found themselves negotiating credit deals simultaneously with Abraham & Straus, Korvette, Sears, Gimbel's, Lane Bryant, and the Lerner stores. In April 1969, a coalition of welfare mothers demonstrated at a Bronx Sears store, demanding credit and threatening a boycott.[39] In early July, welfare recipients and their allies returned to the Manhattan Sears store that they had previously visited with the social workers from the National Conference of Social Welfare. Ninety welfare recipients entered the store, asked for credit applications, and demanded that these be processed immediately. They then listened to "music on expensive Hi-Fi's [and] had a dance session," according to a report by Citywide and B-WAC member Mamie Hall.[40] Although Sears refused to consider a citywide credit agreement with the welfare coalition, the other stores saw what had happened at Sears and took preventive action: active members of Citywide received coupons for credit at Gimbel's, Abraham & Straus, and Korvette.[41]

The most disruptive tactic New York welfare recipients used in their effort to get consumer credit was a "shop-in." Citywide borrowed the shop-in concept from CORE. However, CORE shop-ins aimed to get black people hired, while welfare rights shop-ins focused exclusively on the treatment of shoppers.[42] The most detailed description of a shop-in is that of Jackie Pope, written years after one of the demonstrations at the Brooklyn Korvette store: first, she wrote, she and Burson assigned members various roles to play. They asked one group to negotiate with the store, another to stand outside explaining the action to passersby, a third to confront Korvette's employees on the sales floor, and a fourth to impersonate ordinary shoppers who were either sympathetic to the welfare recipients or irate about the delays they caused. "On the day of the demonstration, members impersonating customers selected hundreds of dollars' worth of goods and took them to the cashiers, who proceeded to tally the items on their registers. When asked for payment, each 'customer' produced her welfare identification card and said, 'Charge it to the Welfare Department'."[43] By mentioning the welfare department, the demonstrators linked the credit campaign with their opposition to the flat grant. Before New York State cut the "extras" from public assistance payments, they might have been able to use welfare money to shop for these extras; with flat grants and tight family budgets, they turned to private-sector consumer credit as a second-best alternative.

In response to the slowdowns and long lines that resulted from their actions, the women and men who had chosen to pose as ordinary customers complained loudly about the situation and created even more disruption by gathering in crowds around the cash registers. "By the time police reached the demonstration floors," Pope remembered, "everything had returned to normal except for piles of unbought clothing surrounding most of the cash registers. 'Customers' were browsing alongside actual purchasers, waiting for the police to leave and the signal to begin the demonstration anew."[44]

The basic aim of the credit campaign was to make local welfare rights groups, such as B-WAC and Citywide, intermediaries between their members or potential members and the stores. This represented an effort to continue the benefit- or membership-based approach to organizing, which welfare rights organizers had originally learned from Chávez, Huerta, and Fred Ross, in an increasingly hostile political environment. Even as Beulah Sanders and other leaders fought to maintain welfare clients' access to special grants and fair hearings, they also saw credit cards as new benefits that Citywide could help its members access.

The key to the credit campaign was that local welfare rights groups, rather than merchants, would evaluate potential customers and offer lists of credit-worthy consumers to the stores. The Abraham & Straus store in Brooklyn, for example, accepted pre-approval from B-WAC as adequate proof of a customer's credit-worthiness, without the usual financial background checks that it conducted on credit applicants. With a letter from the chair of the local group, and certification by Mamie Hall from the B-WAC leadership, a woman or man could receive a maximum of one hundred dollars in store credit.[45] Local welfare rights groups became the consumption-side version of trade union hiring halls, able to choose who would have access to credit and therefore to high-priced goods poor customers could not pay for all at once.

Shop-ins around New York City were effective ways to convince large retail companies to reconsider their credit policies for welfare recipients. Although it is difficult to know for sure, it is likely that the credit benefit helped recruit new members to Citywide and slowed the exodus of members that had begun after the flat grant became law. However, the credit campaign was disastrous for welfare rights activists' efforts to build bridges to working- and middle-class New Yorkers. According to a report in the *New York Times*, stores that extended credit to welfare mothers and fathers were flooded with telephone calls. "Why make credit that easy?" many asked. "People on public assistance shouldn't get credit at all! Are we going to have to pay higher prices to support welfare recipients on credit like we are paying higher taxes? What about people like me—people who work for a living but can't get credit because our income is too low—aren't we entitled to get credit at least as much as the welfare families?"[46] One of journalist Pete Hamill's informants for his meditation on "The Revolt of the White Lower Middle Class" was similarly provoked: "every time I turn around," this white working-class father commented, "one of the kids needs shoes or a dress or something for school. And then I read about . . . some fat welfare bitch demanding—you know, not askin' but *demanding*—a credit card at Korvette's. . . . You know, you see that, and you want to go out and strangle someone."[47]

In response to the hostility, Citywide executive director Hulbert James defended the credit campaign by underlining the fact that low-income people already received credit, albeit from unscrupulous merchants. To those who feared welfare recipients would default on their credit accounts, James argued that public assistance was in fact a form of "guaranteed income"; although most members of the City-Wide Coordinating Committee of Welfare Groups lacked wages, they did receive income, and were therefore able to repay their debts.[48]

Credit for Being American

National welfare rights leaders and staff members were impressed with the credit campaigns in Philadelphia and New York. In February 1969, Beulah Sanders, Carmen Olivo from New York, and the other members of the NWRO National Coordinating Committee (NCC) voted to make demands "on both the Federal government and the private sector."[49] The centerpiece of the private-sector part of their strategy was a national boycott of Sears, Roebuck, which the committee members promised to initiate during the Easter shopping season if Sears did not reverse its policy and begin offering credit to welfare recipients. Sears, remembered NWRO deputy director Tim Sampson, "was the really great connecting link" in the credit campaign, a focus for local agitation all over the country and for national-level protests as well.[50] The NCC appointed a five-member committee, chaired by Washington, D.C., leader Etta Horn, to coordinate the boycott and negotiate with retail firms.[51]

Welfare rights activists used a range of different arguments to pursue their claim for consumer credit. They assumed the ubiquity of credit sales, even for poor people, and focused on the practices of local merchants and high-interest installment contracts. NWRO members and staff also described the credit plan as an answer to "discrimination" against welfare recipients. By this, they meant three things at once. The first was racial discrimination, which played a major role in welfare rights thinking although not all NWRO members were black or Latina/o. The second was status or caste discrimination, based on the position of the credit-seekers as recipients of particularly despised government programs. Third, and most ambitious, was income-based discrimination comparable to what poverty lawyers were theorizing in the late 1960s and early 1970s. The legal thinkers who attempted to introduce income discrimination into the American political vocabulary wanted to enshrine in legal doctrine the idea that poor people as a class needed the equal protection of the laws promised under the Fourteenth Amendment to the U.S. Constitution. To realize the promise of equality, they believed, the U.S. government must grant citizens at least subsistence income, a right to welfare, or, as they also called it, a "right to life" that could not be vitiated by a tightfisted legislature.[52]

Welfare recipients and movement allies made arguments about income-based discrimination and equality between the poor and rich. At the start of the national Sears campaign, Etta Horn expressed her frustration at Sears president Arthur Wood in these terms: "We feel that president Wood is a part of the sick society that is prejudiced against the poor. This whole society is run on credit, especially for the rich man. So why can't we have it. The poor need it more than the rich."[53] In a letter to Sears management, the head of a citizens' group in Appalachia affiliated with the welfare rights movement expressed his concern about "discriminatory credit policies followed by Sears stores. We do not believe a person should be refused credit for the simple reason that he is a recipient of public assistance. People on welfare," he added "must be allowed the same rights and opportunities as other American citizens."[54] The NWRO staff underlined this view of consumer credit as a right in a list of proposed slogans for the Sears campaign: "The Rich get cash & credit at least give the poor credit"; "How Many credit Cards do you have? We only want ONE a SEARS credit card for all poor people"; and "Give us Credit for being American."[55]

Welfare rights activists saw themselves as entitled to consumer credit because they were entitled to participate fully in a consumer-oriented society. Particularly for white working-class women and women of color, the right to buy decent goods for oneself and for one's children was bound up with postwar ideas of womanhood and motherhood. Members of the Chicago Welfare Rights Organization expressed the link between consumer credit and their roles as mothers and decent women in a leaflet they distributed at a protest of a Sears fashion show. Credit cards, they argued, "will give us the opportunity to 'buy better' clothing for our loved ones and children." They complained that their own clothes were "current fashions 5 to 8 years ago."[56] Dorothy Perry, the twelve-year-old daughter of the "Action Chairman" of the Sears campaign in Newark, New Jersey, wrote: "One thing I can truely say is that while I am on welfare my mother is learning her rights and believe me she is getting them. We have had many Demostrations and they have made a Lot of change to Blacks and whites and have given them more courage to Fight For there rights," she continued. "Today we went to Sears to ask them could we have credit in there store they don't want any part of us welfare people. They don't know what it is to be poor and to try to have the better things in Life."[57]

The combination of militancy and propriety that the Chicago group expressed in its protest appeared in representations of the Sears boycott from the national welfare rights office. In a report to local activists on the progress of the Sears campaign, an NWRO artist represented the organized welfare recipients as a black woman in a dress, with conservatively styled low-heeled shoes on her feet and a prim hat with a ribbon and feather on her head (see Figure 14). The woman carried a sign reading "BOYCOTT EAR" and raised her formidably strong-looking right arm and fist at a chicken labeled "SEARS."[58] The Sears chicken had been sitting on an egg marked "credit for recipients."

"You Got To Be Kidding"

At the national level, welfare rights leaders asked Sears management to enter into an agreement that would be binding on all of its stores. The details of the plan closely resembled the one Sanders and other New Yorkers had negotiated with Abraham & Straus. It stipulated that "a letter of reference from NWRO should be adequate proof that the recipient is a good credit risk, and there [should] be no other investigation."[59] Sears was asked to ensure that welfare recipients were not charged any additional interest rates above the 1.5 percent per month ordinarily

Figure 14. An artist represents the NWRO demand for credit cards at Sears as a battle between African American women and a greedy company sitting on a nest egg of profits. Courtesy NWRO Papers, Moorland-Spingarn Research Center, Howard University.

charged to credit customers, and not to hold NWRO or its local chapters responsible for any late or missed payments. Etta Horn's committee and the NWRO staff advised local activists to insist that stores make access to credit dependent on certification by a welfare rights group.[60]

Tim Sampson and George Wiley in the NWRO headquarters office believed that the credit campaign might help organized welfare recipients recover somewhat from their political isolation at the end of the

1960s. They thought that a focus on Sears and other major companies offered valuable opportunities for participation in welfare rights activism to middle-class "Friends" of the movement, such as the social work conferees who destroyed their credit cards in the name of equality. In the midst of a season of flat grants and statewide cuts in welfare budgets, the Sears campaign was an opportunity for NWRO to "dramatize welfare recipients' need for clothing and furniture," and gain publicity for local action groups "so that other welfare recipients will join."[61]

Sampson's and Wiley's calculation was only half correct. The Sears campaign did, indeed, involve middle-class allies in the work of NWRO. "Friends," including Betty Younger, the widow of a Cleveland minister who had helped organize welfare rights protests before his death in 1968, and leaders of the Women's Division of the Methodist Church, were pleased by the Sears campaign because it offered them concrete ways to support NWRO that went beyond writing checks.[62] But some middle-class people otherwise sympathetic to NWRO disliked the Sears campaign, and it caused genuine rage among a few.[63] As it had in New York City, the demand by welfare recipients for credit cards touched a particular nerve in some antiwelfare whites. NWRO activists asked people they encountered at demonstrations in front of Sears stores and elsewhere to mail in postcards affirming their support for the campaign, and pledging financial contributions. "Dear NWRO," the cards read:

I support the NWRO boycott of Sears. I do not believe that welfare recipients should be discriminated against and not receive credit.
____ I have notified Sears that I will not buy from Sears until an agreement with NWRO is reached.
____ I would like to do more to help welfare recipients gain equal rights. Please send more information.
____ I am enclosing a contribution to help in the cause.

Of the twenty-two cards that survive in the archives, twenty were supportive and one was ambivalent. But one, received April 7, 1969, was doctored to read: "Dear NWRO":

I **DO NOT** support the NWRO boycott of Sears. I do believe that welfare recipients should be discriminated against and not receive credit.
THEY Get ENOUGH!
____ I have notified Sears that I will buy from Sears
____ I would **NOT** like to do more to help welfare recipients . . .
____ I am enclosing a contribution . . . **You got to Be Kidding!**
Let them go to work
like we all do!
Signed
Disgusted Harder Worker
Struggling-Middle Classer![64]

The Sears campaign provoked an even more irate response from a correspondent who identified himself only as "an outspoken wage earner."[65] Welfare, and the organized demand for consumer credit, drove this self-described worker to distraction. He complained, in terms that were already clichés, about the supposed spending patterns of women who received public aid. "Did you ever count the number of 'Cadillacs' that pull up at the stores to cash their 'Welfare' checks? I know of one case where the woman had to wait for the cashier for a few minute's to cash her 'Welfare check,' and became very 'imprudent' because she had to get 'back to her cottage' on the lake, while her boyfriend sat in a new 'Cadillac' in front of the store waiting for her! She was dressed in clothes that I never could afford to buy for my wife!"[66]

NWRO members were never able to persuade Sears management to enter into a national agreement covering their full credit plan. However, in Philadelphia, Memphis, Pontiac, Michigan, and Portsmouth, Ohio, welfare rights groups received some access to credit at Sears. In Cincinnati, the local Sears store agreed to the entire NWRO credit plan. In Boston, certified welfare rights group members received $50 credit lines at Filene's, Gilchrist, and Jordan Marsh in the wake of a major demonstration at Sears.[67] At least three thousand welfare recipients and other poor people received credit from Montgomery Ward as a result of NWRO negotiations with the company's national management. Probably hundreds of others received credit through informal agreements between their groups and various consumer emporiums, and many more poor people received credit on what the companies claimed was an individual basis but was more likely leniency shaped by the companies' fear of NWRO actions.[68]

The credit campaign spread across the country. In twenty-nine areas, including Rochester, New York; Des Moines, Iowa; Hinds County, Mississippi; and Pomona, California, welfare rights organizations reported that they either had negotiated with Sears or were planning to do so. Groups in sixty-two areas, ranging from West Helena, Arkansas, to Bakersfield, California, had conducted Sears actions of some kind by April 9, 1969. As they did in New York, these actions ran the range of disruptiveness. They included passing out leaflets in front of busy Sears stores, filling out credit applications collectively and creating long lines for service, and having numerous "Friends" with Sears credit destroy their credit cards and deliver them to the store management.[69]

Local welfare rights organizations maximized disruption by timing their shop-ins to coincide with some of the heaviest shopping days in the year. Etta Horn and George Wiley suggested that the groups demonstrate on the Saturday before Easter and offered detailed suggestions on how to carry out protests. "If you have any problems," they suggested, "raise hell," call Sears headquarters in Chicago, and alert the press.[70] Welfare rights groups also organized demonstrations at department stores to coincide with the heavy shopping period between Thanksgiving and Christmas.

A Private-Sector Family Allowance

A second foray into the private sector by the welfare rights movement was the "private-sector family allowance plan" that NWRO offered to major consumer-product companies. This strategy transposed the Western European idea of a family allowance, a grant from the national government to help parents raise the next generation of citizens, to the private consumer market.[71] Utilizing the rhetoric of the incoming Nixon administration, Etta Horn, NWRO chair Johnnie Tillmon, Tim Sampson, and George Wiley sought the help of profit-making firms to secure welfare rights.

NWRO leaders proposed that large national firms enable poor people to buy their products by donating vouchers, or coupons, for the products to the National Welfare Rights Organization. NWRO would then distribute the vouchers to its members and, as with the Sears credit plan, gain a concrete material benefit the organization could provide to members as a reward for their participation. Horn, Tillmon, Sampson, and Wiley offered their national network of local action organizations "as a distribution system for these coupons."[72] They suggested that the companies provide packages of $5.00 or more of coupons for the family of each NWRO member, distributed in small denominations and redeemable, like sales coupons, in local grocery and drug stores. "If a number of companies participated," NWRO publications argued, "this could amount to a significant direct subsidy of poor people without any intervention or involvement of government agencies."

The exchanges between welfare rights leaders and officials of various firms about the private-sector family assistance plan illuminate the wide berth that social movement activists of the late 1960s believed they had to reinterpret standard economic practices. They also reveal the distance between the thinking of welfare rights activists and that of the people who ran profitable corporations. Requesting a meeting with J. F. McFarland, the president of General Mills, Wiley and Tillmon argued that corporations had a responsibility to ameliorate poverty. They also presented their request as a corporate opportunity. Tillmon and Wiley proposed the welfare rights movement as a particularly apt partner for the behemoth marketer of brand-name household products because of its unique position as a movement of poor people and its consumer orientation: "NWRO," they claimed, "is the only nationwide organization of, by and for poor people vigorously striving for a fuller share of the abundance of our affluent society."[73]

As they expressed their belief in the Nixon administration's ideal of private-sector rather than governmental solutions to problems such as poverty, the welfare rights leaders also called into question the morality of limitless profits. "Since poor people do not have enough *money*," they wrote, "we ask that your company distribute a share of your great wealth to those poorest of the poor."[74] Appealing to corporate self-interest, they assured the General Mills executive that donating products to NWRO members would help in accessing the low-income market. Tillmon and Wiley argued that this would happen both because the NWRO vouchers would make General Mills products more visible in low-income communities and because NWRO would create its own "honor roll of participating companies and their products."[75] In their outline of the voucher plan, NWRO leaders added that, despite their poverty, welfare recipients had buying power estimated at $10 billion per year. Finally, they pointed out that, because of charitable giving laws, "The cost of this program would be largely born[e] by the federal government through tax write offs."[76]

The response to Tillmon and Wiley's request came from the General Mills company's chief community relations officer rather than from its president. His letter revealed befuddlement about the arguments made by NWRO and resistance to the idea of giving away products that his firm might otherwise sell for a profit. "Dear Mrs. Tillmon," he wrote, "although your letter outlines in general terms a cooperative approach toward solving the problems of poverty, I must confess that I remain confused as to the exact means."[77] He invited Tillmon to send additional information about the plan, but General Mills and NWRO never made any progress in designing a joint program. Welfare rights leaders had no more success with the other corporations to which they offered the private-sector family allowance "opportunity."[78]

Cash, Not Food Stamps

In addition to their efforts to gain credit and goods, welfare recipients in New York City and elsewhere fought to maintain control over how they would spend their public assistance grants in the consumer market. One of the hallmarks of the public assistance programs created during the New Deal was the "money payment" principle, by which local welfare departments were supposed to dispense grants in cash rather than in kind and leave each client free to spend her money as she saw fit.[79] As previously noted, this principle was weakened by the 1962 amendments to the Social Security Act, which allowed caseworkers to restrict the spending of clients they believed were mismanaging their money. It was also weakened by the rise of food stamps, an alternative to cash welfare that recipients could spend only for goods that appeared on a federally approved list.

Welfare recipients never accepted the limitations federal and local authorities placed on their purchasing power. However, their battles against these limitations became more difficult over time; one manifestation of the crescendo of conservatism surrounding public welfare was the increasing recourse policy makers and caseworkers in the late 1960s and early 1970s made to restrictions on recipients' spending.

Thomasina Lewis, Jean Younger, Ann Freeman, Miriam Stevenson, and Toni Stret, all clients of Carl Rachlin, demanded fair hearings in part because their social workers had restricted their cash grants. Several of the women had been given two-party rent checks, which local officials wrote out directly to landlords so that clients could not spend their rent money on something else. Others had the amounts they were instructed to spend on electricity, heat, or food removed from their welfare grants and distributed in the form of vouchers that could not be cashed.[80] A caseworker placed Lewis "on voucher" after she received an emergency cash supplement to fill a budget gap she explained by saying that she was robbed. When a welfare department supervisor had asked if she wanted to receive vouchers or cash, Lewis wrote, "I told him that I wanted the cash grant." However, her caseworker had explained that she would henceforth receive vouchers. Thomasina Lewis decided to bring a fair hearing because, as she put it, "I do not think this is fair."[81]

Lewis and the other women who brought fair hearings with Rachlin's help were fighting for control over their public assistance grants. In addition to two-party rent checks and vouchers instead of cash, they objected to the welfare department practice of assigning a "shopper" to a client who was believed to have trouble managing her money or who suddenly received a large sum. Julia Lopez and her husband, for example, won eleven checks (presumably for minimum standards items), totaling nearly seven hundred dollars, from the Melrose Welfare Center in the Bronx. Their caseworker insisted that they endorse the checks and leave them with the welfare department. When the couple protested, the answer they received was that their worker "was taking the checks 'til he could get a shopper for her. Both Mrs. Lopez and husband insisted that they could do the shopping alone" and asked for their money.[82]

The City-Wide Coordinating Committee of Welfare Groups did not wage a collective campaign against vouchers or mandatory shoppers, but it did protest against food stamps. The food stamp program was originally authorized by Congress on a limited basis in 1939. It expanded dramatically in the 1960s and early 1970s, reaching ever larger numbers of poor people in a widening range of counties across the United States.[83] Unlike public assistance, the only criterion for receiving food stamps was economic need. Anyone who was poor could get stamps, if she or he was able to purchase them (they were worth more than they cost, but were not free) and was willing to shop within their restrictions.

The federal government implemented the stamp program in a limited number of New York counties in 1968, but New York City did not get food stamps until the summer of 1970. According to welfare director Mitchell Ginsberg, the delay was largely due to Citywide's vigorous opposition.[84] Beulah Sanders was an especially vehement foe of food stamps because she believed they restricted clients' spending and narrowed their ability to respond to emergencies. She argued that the program grew out of an alliance between antipoverty activists and the farming lobby, which promoted the program as a benefit to the agriculture industry more than as help for parents and children. She suspected that the rise of food stamps was part of an effort to take cash out of the hands of poor people. "I'll take Green Power any day," Sanders wrote, "instead of food stamps."[85] Other Citywide members protested against the creation of a local food stamp program because of the limited range of goods consumers could buy with the stamps. Puerto Rican members were especially exercised about the prospect of receiving stamps instead of cash, since the rules excluded imported foods, such as "Spanish products" that were staples of their diets.[86]

Welfare rights activists around the country shared these concerns. Marty Green, who chaired the food stamp committee of the Washington, D.C., welfare rights group, echoed Beulah Sanders's critique of U.S. agriculture policy and the favoritism it showed toward large-scale farmers. Many poor people, she explained, "in dire need of food," could not afford to buy the stamps. Others faced emergencies and wanted the flexibility to redeem their stamps for cash when crises arose.[87] Fifty women and children demonstrated in Houston against food stamps, arguing that the program deprived them of "the right to spend their money as they see fit" and made it hard for them to afford necessities such as "laundry supplies, household cleaning supplies, toilet tissue, [and] sanitary napkins," which were not covered under the food stamp regulations.[88] Annie Smart from Baton Rouge, Louisiana, found shopping with food stamps "embarrassing," and argued that it "strips you of your dignity."[89] Joe McDermott, who was part of a poor people's coalition from South Carolina that traveled to Capitol Hill to discuss problems in the program, insisted that it wasn't "right to give food stamps to me and then tell me how I can use them."[90]

In New York City, the battle over food stamps was inseparable from

the battle over flat grants. In August 1968, on the eve of the implementation of the flat grant, two hundred members of the Brooklyn Welfare
Action Council demonstrated at the headquarters of the Board of Elections, demanding access to the vote even for those who could not read
and insisting: "We do NOT want FLAT GRANTS or FOOD STAMPS.
These are the goals of City Hall."[91] Rather than accepting food stamps
as inevitable, Citywide members tried to preserve and improve the system of free surplus food distribution, which New York welfare recipients
generally preferred to food stamps. Citywide members were arrested at
commodity distribution centers around New York as they passed out
leaflets informing people of their rights as clients of the program, and
they demanded that the centers make a wider range of foods available.[92]

Demonstrations and debates between Citywide activists and city officials helped to hold the food stamp program at bay. However, Governor
Rockefeller ultimately proposed state legislation to bring food stamps to
every county in New York, and both the state legislature and City Council approved the move.[93] Food stamps finally came to New York City on
August 31, 1970. The Lindsay administration abolished the commodity
distribution system and encouraged the 775,000 people in "working
poor" families, plus over one million welfare recipients, to apply for the
stamps.[94]

As they campaigned for credit cards and against food stamps, Citywide
and NWRO members took arguments and tactics from these campaigns
into other arenas. In 1968, Citywide announced a march on the welfare
centers to protest budgets that "cheated" clients by granting them less
than they actually paid for utilities and thus forced them to use money
from their strained food budgets for gas, electricity, and water. By 1969,
welfare recipients from all over the country had taken their protest
directly to the utility companies, accusing them of discriminating against
the poor by demanding high deposits from low-income people and
charging higher rates in poor neighborhoods than they charged elsewhere.[95] While they fought to keep the food stamp program out of many
U.S. counties, activists also fought to bring in the school lunch program,
which made federally subsidized food available to schoolchildren. Members of NWRO argued that schools offering subsidized lunches should
not discriminate against poor children by making them stand in separate lines, or hold food stamp-like chits that marked them as different
from everyone else.[96]

One of the most creative strategies NWRO sponsored was an effort to
compel local school districts to distribute the money they received for
poor children's education directly to the families of those children. This
strategy began with complaints by low-income parents about the fees
public schools charged for gym suits, class trips, and other educational

expenses. Such charges, argued attorneys affiliated with NWRO, placed poor people systematically at a disadvantage when they attempted to access education, and therefore violated the equal protection clause of the Fourteenth Amendment. Their solution was to end the programs school districts had created to serve poor children under Title I of the federal education law, and distribute the money Congress had allocated for educating the poor directly to parents.[97] Through what lawyer Gabe Kaimowitz called "the *proper* application of Title I," parents would be able to pay school fees, and welfare recipients could buy their children some of the clothes and shoes that had disappeared from their budgets when New York and other jurisdictions created flat grants.[98]

In their Sears campaign, efforts to gain a "private-sector family allowance," and opposition to food stamps, Citywide and NWRO members ventured into politics as American consumers who deserved fair treatment although they were poor, black, brown, female, and recipients of government benefits. Beulah Sanders, Jennette Washington, and Etta Horn linked their agenda for reforming the welfare state with an agenda for reforming the supposedly private realm of the profit-oriented market.

Welfare rights activism illuminated the fuzzy boundaries between the public and private sectors, raising hard questions such as why the government should permit a company like Sears to acquire limitless profits at a time when the city of New York could barely afford its welfare costs. What, the women and men of the welfare rights movement asked, did lucrative companies, which benefited from government regulation or even subsidies, owe to everyone else? In the food stamp controversy, they underlined the ways public policy makers shaped and directed the spending decisions of low-income families. They pointed out the fact that politicians used public tax revenues to sustain the market for agricultural commodities, and complained that there were not enough public resources devoted to ending hunger. Why, these activists wondered, did federal planners get to choose what poor families would eat, or how much of their limited income they would spend on food as opposed to other goods? Why were poor people treated differently from rich ones, by companies and governments alike?

Chapter 6

Nixon, Moynihan, and Real Live Welfare Moms

If you can (1) get out of Vietnam, and (2) put through a Family Security System, the Republicans will become the majority Party in the United States.

—*Urban affairs adviser Daniel Moynihan to President Richard Nixon*

When Mitchell Ginsberg resigned from his position at the helm of the New York City welfare department, he could have recovered from the tumult of the late 1960s by lying on a beach in the Caribbean. Instead, he went to Washington, D.C., to help President Nixon negotiate with Congress over welfare reform. Desperate for a solution to the city's nascent fiscal crisis, which was inseparable from its welfare crisis, Mayor Lindsay had dispatched Ginsberg to the Capitol in an effort to pass a welfare law that might help New York avoid bankruptcy. "I would love to write a book on this experience," Ginsberg commented, "but first of all nobody would believe me and secondly I would get run out of the country. It is indeed amazing how national policy gets made."[1]

The welfare reform effort in which Ginsberg became enmeshed was the Family Assistance Plan (FAP). President Nixon first announced the FAP proposal in August 1969. It finally failed in Congress in October 1972. FAP would have established a national minimum welfare grant of $1,600 for a family raising children. The plan would have cost the federal treasury approximately $4 billion. By offering income supplements to those who were working but poor, it would have added roughly 10 million people to the assistance rolls.[2] Like the Work Incentive Program that had been the hallmark of welfare reform in 1967, FAP also included a work requirement. The program would have transformed welfare, especially in the poorest states. The Nixon administration initiated this ambitious proposal because the President and a few key advisers were convinced that it would further the project they had begun in 1968, of drawing new white voters from the Democratic Party into their electoral coalition.

For members of the City-Wide Coordinating Committee of Welfare Groups, FAP did not seem like a generous departure from prior policy. It seemed, instead, like a cross between the New York flat grant and the worst aspects of the Social Security Act Amendments of 1967. Since their average benefits already exceeded the $1,600 level, the Nixon plan did not have much to offer New Yorkers. The FAP work requirement posed the same problems from their perspective as the Work Incentive Program (WIN/WIP): it devalued the work women did as mothers, potentially endangered their children's well-being, and either trained people for jobs that did not exist or pushed them into domestic service, which they had only recently begun to escape after a one-hundred-year struggle. Moreover, the Nixon plan emphasized the so-called working poor, a group the President and his advisers understood as disproportionately male and white. This was felt as a slap in the face to Citywide members, and especially to the women who formed the bulk of the membership. Women welfare recipients believed that they should receive benefits in their own right rather than as the economic dependents of male workers, or as badly compensated wage workers who juggled their parenting responsibilities in the interstices of their lives.

For officials of New York City and New York State, FAP was a glimmer of hope on the horizon. If the federal government assumed responsibility for welfare, then the Lindsay administration might balance its budget without imposing such heavy taxes that it would enrage middle-income voters and drive businesses to the suburbs.[3] If city officials were no longer making daily decisions about welfare benefits, then they would no longer be targets of attack by the City-Wide Coordinating Committee of Welfare Groups. At the state level, FAP promised to defuse the conflicts that had begun to occur with increasing frequency as Lindsay begged Governor Rockefeller and legislators in Albany to help meet New York City's rising social benefit costs. Under a nationalized system such as FAP, Rockefeller would no longer be a protagonist in the welfare drama. With welfare out of the way as a topic of political debate, Mayor Lindsay and Governor Rockefeller stood a chance of saving their political careers.

Antiwelfare Politics

As the New York State government instituted ever harsher cuts in welfare budgets, and New York City administered them, Citywide activists kept trying the tactics that had served them in the past. They lost nearly every round of the fight. When the legislature in Albany followed Governor

Rockefeller's recommendation and passed an 8.5 percent cut in welfare budgets, Carl Rachlin and other lawyers brought suit on behalf of City-wide. They claimed that the cuts violated the equal protection clause of the Fourteenth Amendment and a portion of the 1967 Social Security Amendments, which required states to adjust the "standards of need" on which they based public assistance grants to reflect changes in the cost of living. One federal judge issued a temporary injunction that for-bade the state from implementing the cuts, but a three-judge panel deemed them legal and the U.S. Supreme Court affirmed this ruling.[4]

After the cuts went into effect, Citywide members demonstrated at local welfare centers throughout the city. The Lindsay administration had the police arrest unprecedented numbers of them. The cuts affected all the categories of public assistance, including disability bene-fits and aid to the aged poor. Welfare rights activists protested reduc-tions in all the programs only to see them rescinded for the disabled and aged but retained for parents and children. In September and October 1969 Citywide organized a school boycott in which parents kept their children home to protest the lack of funding for school clothing and other goods.[5] Jennette Washington pledged to maintain the protest "until we get clothing for our children"; activists in Brooklyn chanted: "Lindsay and Rockefeller you just lost our vote because you took from us our overcoat."[6] But the city administration arrested hundreds of women and men, and the boycott eventually petered out.[7]

In addition to familiar tactics, the leaders of Citywide also tried new ones. In July 1969, they joined the NWRO "live on a welfare budget" campaign, which invited middle-class women and men to try feeding their families on the amounts state and federal governments allocated for poor families.[8] The campaign had special resonance in New York because of the flat grant and subsequent state budget cuts, which left welfare families with just sixty-six cents per person to spend per meal. *New York Times* food critic Craig Claiborne advertised the tactic by offer-ing menus for the middle-class ally of the movement who was at a loss as to what to prepare. A sample day included

Breakfast
Unbuttered Toast
Instant coffee
   or
Reconstituted milk
Lunch
Minestrone
Dinner
Leftover chili
With macaroni
Cabbage salad[9]

Claiborne offered recipes as well, which were useful for those who were attempting to survive on a welfare budget for the first time because the government's cost estimates assumed that everything was prepared "from scratch." A recipe for Chicken Broth and Boiled Beef included "3 pounds cracked beef bones (procured, if possible, without cost from local butcher), 2 1/2 pounds brisket of beef, 8 cups cold water, Salt and pepper to taste."[10] Citywide and NWRO invited the families of members of Congress to participate in the campaign. June Bingham and her husband, Representative Jonathan Bingham of the Bronx, informed the press at the end of their week on a welfare budget of their "repeated edginess . . . inability to apply themselves fully to work, and repeated daydreaming about food," as well as about the long hours June Bingham spent shopping to get nutritious food from sympathetic grocers for free, or at a price she could afford.[11]

With progress stalled in New York City and New York State, many Citywide activists left to join the national NWRO staff. Rhoda Linton, the organizer for the Brooklyn Welfare Action Council, departed in September 1968. Linton had helped make the movement in Brooklyn the strongest in the United States, with more members than any other local area and a leadership development curriculum that enabled individual activists to become effective advocates for other welfare recipients. Two graduates of the Brooklyn curriculum, Joyce Burson and Jacqueline Pope, followed Linton to NWRO headquarters in 1969.[12] Burson became a liaison between recipients across the country and NWRO—a vitally important job, given the gap between the mostly middle-class, largely male, and disproportionately white staff and the African American women who predominated at the movement's grassroots. Pope, who had edited the Citywide newsletter, became the editor of the NWRO monthly publication (a job that had once belonged to Wiley's colleague from CORE, white activist Edwin Day).[13] Hulbert James, the executive director of Citywide, left for Washington, D.C., in March 1969. He became the director of field operations for NWRO. James later succeeded Tim Sampson, who was white, as NWRO associate director.[14]

While Citywide was fighting the flat grant in New York, welfare recipients across the country were battling similar cuts. NWRO members faced, and fought, changes in the public assistance programs in New Orleans; Fayetteville, North Carolina; Phoenix; Houston; and the states of Kansas and Rhode Island.[15] Under the leadership of Ethel Mae Mathews, Atlanta mothers fought a series of reductions in the Georgia welfare rolls and the creation of a statewide mandatory work program. "I am still on the job organizing poor people and letting them know that they do have a right to a decent life and an adequate income," Mathews wrote to Bertha Cavanaugh of the NWRO staff. "We are still

Figure 15. Father James Groppi of Milwaukee and other welfare rights advocates in the chamber of the Wisconsin state legislature, 1969. Image ID # 4933, courtesy Visual Materials Division, Wisconsin Historical Society.

having fair hearing[s]" to appeal individual cases in which recipients were dropped from the rolls, she reported, "and we are still being cut."[16]

The most dramatic confrontation over a state budget cut occurred in Wisconsin. The governor called a special session of the legislature to consider repealing a recently passed multimillion-dollar drop in welfare funding. With NWRO support, welfare recipients and their allies spent a week marching from Milwaukee to Madison to demonstrate at that special session. Father James Groppi, a white Catholic priest who was renowned for advocating African American civil rights, led approximately one thousand protesters into the State Assembly at the start of the session.[17] Women and men stood in the legislative chamber, testifying about how difficult they found it to make ends meet and how hungry their children would be if the cut was not rescinded. The Assembly voted, 71–24, to find Groppi in contempt of the legislature. Police arrested him while he sought sanctuary in the chapel of the Catholic students' center at the University of Wisconsin.[18]

The letters Groppi received after he became publicly identified as a friend of the welfare rights movement offer glimpses of Northern white attitudes toward welfare recipients. Although he received friendly mail, largely from Catholics outside Wisconsin, most of it was ferocious.[19] The letters illuminate the uphill battle Citywide and NWRO faced in trying to recruit "working poor" whites into a common front against poverty. "HEY GROPPI," one began. "Why don't you make your body black and then you will be like the rest of your black ones the lazy bums they allways want a hand out."[20] Another asked: "If these A.D.C. mothers can have more than one out of wedlock child . . . why can't they work, don't give me this baloney they have to be home with their children."[21] Rejecting the spirit of the Second Vatican Council (1962–1965), which pledged to fight poverty across the globe, several writers advised Groppi that public aid for African American women was not what the Church had in mind. "Christ . . . never made trouble," one correspondent advised."[22] Another insisted that "Jesus . . . did not intend for equality of all people, equality in material possessions."[23]

Groppi's correspondents tied their rejection of public aid for African American mothers and children to crass sexual stereotypes and fears of intimacy across racial lines. One anonymous letter expressed the hope that the authorities would hang Groppi for his sins, and instructed him to "tell those lazy no good people that live out their lives in adultery – to quit having kids out of wedlock – get out & get a job and earn their money by the sweat of their brow . . . How would you like it," the author asked, "if you [or] your mother was raped by a negro. How would you like it to have a negro 1/2 bro or sister."[24] The writers made particular efforts to counter arguments about the inadequacy of family welfare grants. Another anonymous correspondent assured Groppi that she or he "personally [knew] welfare women who have private telephones."[25] A range of writers complained about the choices welfare recipients made in the consumer marketplace, especially in what was described as widespread spending on alcohol, cigarettes, and other luxuries.[26] "Get those people to work," implored a self-described "Quiet, Sideline Observer." Rather then seeking the bounty of the affluent society, she or he counseled, Groppi should teach the poor to "live peaceably and thriftily, and to conform with the way of life that is ours in America."[27]

Guaranteed Adequate Income

The politics of budget cuts, and persistently negative attitudes toward welfare recipients, led NWRO and Citywide to focus on the guaranteed income as a unifying goal and a way to reach new allies. In the aftermath of the Wisconsin conflict, Jennette Washington and Irene Gibbs from New York City, and other members of the NWRO National Coordinating Committee, pledged to "*expose* such cutbacks."[28] They promised to fight the cuts by reaching out to new allies among the middle class and among low-income workers.

NWRO advocated an income guarantee that would meet the needs of people without any earnings as well as those who earned low wages.[29] "Poor people," insisted one publication, "have never been able to secure enough income from the wages they earn to enable their families to live decently. Yet every man, woman, and child has the right to live."[30] The NWRO plan for guaranteed income was designed to cover all of the basic needs of a family, whether or not the adults in it were participating in the labor force. However, the $5,500 basic income figure in the proposal did not allow for "life insurance, out-of-town travel, a car, long-distance phone calls, cigarettes, dry-cleaning," or other arguable necessities.[31] The NWRO plan also included work incentives so that recipients who earned wages were better off financially than those without wages.[32] All adult citizens were eligible for benefits under the program. Eligibility was not contingent on personal behavior and did not need to be certified by a caseworker. The NWRO guaranteed income would have replaced all of the public assistance programs administered by localities, states, and the federal government.[33]

The experience of the City-Wide Coordinating Committee of Welfare Groups with the flat grant shaped the NWRO guaranteed income plan. The staff of the national welfare rights office, which included New York veterans Rhoda Linton, Joyce Burson, Jacqueline Pope, and Hulbert James, was determined to prevent what had happened in New York from occurring on a national scale. As a result, the guaranteed income plan included both a basic cash payment for families and a system of special or emergency grants. Although including special grants made the plan more complex, the whole experience of welfare rights organizing since 1963 was bound up with these kinds of incentives. The first generation of welfare rights activists had learned from César Chávez, Fred Ross, and Delores Huerta that discrete benefits built a poor people's movement. They could hardly imagine a welfare rights movement without them, and the post-flat grant scene in New York certainly seemed to confirm their worst fears of what happened in the absence of such benefits.

The NWRO plan also built on the experiences of welfare rights activists with legal appeals or fair hearings. Since recipients needed to know the law that governed a program before they could appeal, the proposal included a provision for distributing all of its regulations "to all participants, potential participants, and organizations of participants."[34] The NWRO Guaranteed Adequate Income allowed fair hearing appeals not only *after* a social worker or bureaucrat had dropped someone from the rolls or cut her benefits but also *before* she or he lost benefits. The plan made special monetary grants available to appellants so that they could hire attorneys and could place their children in child care during the hearings.

While welfare activists were refining their guaranteed income plan, Mayor Lindsay and Governor Rockefeller also began to endorse the idea of a national guaranteed income. In their experiences, the "welfare crisis" in New York City was first and foremost a crisis in financing. As Mayor Lindsay had discovered to his dismay, the city of New York was responsible for a larger portion of welfare costs than almost any other city in the U.S.[35] At the same time, the mayor had little power to effect remedies. Lindsay and other local officials could not write new eligibility criteria for public assistance programs because these came down to the local level from federal bureaucrats at the Department of Health, Education, and Welfare. They could not set the level of welfare grants because this was under the control of the state government. And they could not raise the taxes they needed to meet the welfare budget because these, too, lay in the province of Governor Rockefeller and state legislators. "A Mayor," Lindsay lamented, "is the chief executive of a step-child form of government . . . the creature of a state, subject to its mandate."[36]

With so many of the relevant cards in the hands of state and federal governments, Lindsay asked Governor Rockefeller and President Nixon to assume fiscal responsibility for the welfare program. Lindsay argued that the situation was so grave that cities like New York could not "wait for a reluctant Washington to act," but needed immediate relief from welfare costs by the state.[37] However, at hearings on the Nixon welfare proposals before the U.S. Senate Finance Committee, Lindsay argued that the "single most far-reaching reform would be complete federal financing and administration of the welfare system."[38]

Governor Rockefeller wanted less responsibility for public assistance, not more. As costs rose and hostility toward welfare heightened, Rockefeller, too, began to look for a solution at the national level. To clarify his options, he had organized a conference on welfare reform in March 1967. The meeting debated the merits of a negative income tax versus those of a European-style family allowance, with economist Milton Friedman speaking for the former and Daniel Patrick Moynihan, a veteran of New York politics and the controversy over Mobilization for Youth in the early 1960s, for the latter.[39] Although Rockefeller had not expressed support for a national guaranteed income in his effort to win the presidential nomination, Republicans close to him did float similar ideas during the 1968 primaries.[40] When the Nixon administration introduced its welfare reform plan in 1969, Rockefeller enthused that the proposal was perhaps "the most significant Federal domestic legislation put forward in a generation."[41]

The Nixon Plan

For President Nixon, welfare reform was one way to reach his administration's over-arching goal, which was to create and solidify a new electoral coalition.[42] Pursuit of this goal led the President to support FAP in 1969 and early 1970 and then to abandon it. The war in Vietnam, a rising conservative movement, the decline of the welfare rights movement, and the flagging of the black freedom movement shifted the political map at the very end of the 1960s and beginning of the 1970s. The Nixon administration changed its plans for welfare reform accordingly.

President Nixon had begun to show an interest in welfare reform even before taking office. During the transition period after winning the election, the President-elect assigned Richard Nathan to head a Task Force on Public Welfare. The Task Force was ecumenical in composition: Mitchell Ginsberg from New York City was a member, and both Nathan and member James Sundquist were employed by a centrist think tank, the Brookings Institution. The Task Force proposed compelling states to pay public assistance to "Unemployed Parents," that is, adult men, and striking the caseload freeze on Aid to Families with Dependent Children from the 1967 Social Security Amendments.[43] In a bow to the fiscal concerns of Lindsay, Rockefeller, and other local leaders, the Task Force also proposed increasing "federal financial responsibility for Public Assistance and the establishment of national minimum standards for benefits."[44]

When he came to office, Nixon handed the welfare portfolio to HEW secretary Robert Finch and Daniel Moynihan, who headed a new entity called the Urban Affairs Council.[45] After months of study, Moynihan and Finch became convinced that a moderate approach to welfare reform was insufficient. A Welfare Committee of the Urban Affairs Council offered a complete reform plan that began to circulate in the White House early in April 1969. The heart of this proposal was a minimum income stipend for all poor families, a "Family Security System."[46]

Moynihan sold "Family Security" to Nixon on racial and gendered grounds. In the report of the Welfare Committee of the Urban Affairs Council, Moynihan called "incentives for family stability and work . . . the entire basis of our proposal."[47] The key to the Urban Affairs Council draft was its emphasis on the "working poor."[48] Extending relief to such people would, in Moynihan's phrase, relax "a very serious inequity in the present system" by which female parents benefited from it disproportionately. Moreover, while the Aid to Families with Dependent Children (AFDC) rolls were 46 percent black, Moynihan pointed out, "families designated as poor, but which were headed by a male not eligible for welfare were 70 percent White."[49]

Moynihan promised that the new program would redistribute federal dollars not only to whites but also to the South. The minimum payment under Family Security would meet or exceed the public assistance benefits paid in sixteen states, most of them southern. At the same time, the committee draft acknowledged that states with relatively high welfare benefits would be "worse off, unless those states supplement" the $1,600 national minimum.[50] The Urban Affairs Council proposal emphasized men in the South in particular. In 1969, the proposal specified, only one state in the region had a public assistance program for "Unemployed Parents," typically low-wage male workers. "The lack of an [Unemployed Parent] program means that payments will go to female-headed families, but not male-headed families, unless the male is disabled. This is an incentive to desertion, even in low payment states."[51] Family Security payments, Moynihan reasoned, could put money in the pockets of Southern men, and might allow men who were considering deserting their families to remain with their wives and children.

In the case Moynihan made to Nixon, electoral calculations were never distant. In one especially brazen case, the President's urban affairs adviser reported on a meeting he and Finch had conducted with corporate leaders to discuss the potential family security program. The executives, Moynihan reported, were "immensely impressed" with the proposal he outlined. Moynihan added that the vice chairman of the Ford Motor Company had taken special pains to "let [the President] know, for what it is worth, that in his opinion . . . if you can (1) get out of Vietnam, and (2) put through a Family Security System, the Republicans will become the majority Party in the United States. 'You'll be in for twenty years,' he concluded."[52]

In the particular political circumstances that surrounded his administration in 1969, President Nixon chose to support the family security plan. With the exceptions of Finch and Moynihan, virtually all of the high-level White House staff and cabinet members opposed the ambitious proposal, with its millions of potential new beneficiaries and its particular vision of family restoration.[53] Nixon unveiled the welfare proposal on August 9. He framed it as a response to a social problem and a crisis in gender relations for which the public assistance system was itself responsible. He echoed Franklin Roosevelt's second inaugural invocation of "one third of a nation, ill-housed, ill-clad, ill-nourished"[54] with a negative verdict on "A third of a century of centralizing power and responsibility in Washington . . . A third of a century of social experiment . . . A third of a century of unprecedented growth and change" that left government hamstrung and ineffective.[55]

In the short term, Nixon's characterization of public assistance was a political winner. He reached out to both poles of popular sentiment about welfare, to those whose main complaint was "dependency," and to critics of a busybody national program that threatened poor people's "dignity."[56] The President spoke to local administrators, including Lindsay and Rockefeller, who desperately wanted federal fiscal relief. Finally, the national income plan promised material and what Moynihan later called "symbolic" patronage to working-class and lower-middle-class whites, a group that Nixon was determined to reach.[57] By signaling regard for the work ethic, faith in two-parent heterosexual family life, and skepticism about both the programs of the 1930s and the people who benefited from them, President Nixon made those he had dubbed the "silent majority" feel like he was listening.[58]

Following President Nixon's presentation of the Family Security System to the public, the proposal began a bumpy ride through Congress. The program was renamed the Family *Assistance* Plan, since the emphasis on "security" in the August statement reminded some Nixon aides too much of the New Deal.[59] White House allies introduced the Family Assistance Act to Congress in October 1969.[60]

The plan promised both change and continuity in the welfare status quo. Its centerpiece was a national minimum income of $1,600 for a four-person family with children. Those without other income would receive simply this base payment. Parents who also worked for wages would receive income supplements that declined gradually as their incomes increased. A recipient could earn as much as $3,500 per year and still get financial help from the federal government. Families without children, and financially well-off families, got no help. The plan granted benefits to all the groups that had received public assistance since the mid-1930s: impoverished women and children, the aged poor, the blind, and the disabled. As before, women and children in what President Nixon called a "typical welfare family" received less per capita than members of the other recipient categories.[61] Although FAP would have been more uniform across the U.S. than traditional public assistance, benefits would have continued to vary; the thirty states in which the FAP minimum was lower than average AFDC benefits were required to continue supplementing clients' grants.[62]

FAP included work requirements for welfare mothers. Nixon described his program as shifting from "welfare" to "workfare."[63] However, the FAP work requirement was a partial and gendered one, and no more stringent than the Work Incentive Program that had been sponsored by the Democrats. Mothers with children under age six were completely exempt from the work requirement, as was "the mother or other female caretaker . . . if an adult male . . . who would have to register is there."[64] The program exempted men or women working full-time with incomes below the FAP ceiling, and those who cared for ill household members. The work program under FAP also had the same weaknesses as WIN/WIP, with bare-bones funding for training, job creation, and child care.[65] In the end, the weight of the administration's argument that FAP promoted waged work was borne by the financial incentives in the plan—its coverage of "working poor" families and its relatively high income ceiling for those who were earning wages and wanted to continue receiving benefits—rather than by its work requirement.

The Nixon administration made two gendered arguments about FAP. The first was that AFDC and, by extension, the whole New Deal state system, discriminated against men. The purpose of FAP was, therefore, to undo the "blatant unfairness"[66] in public assistance, the "inequitable . . . treatment of male-headed families as opposed to those headed by a female."[67] The single greatest innovation in the legislation was its extension of federal public assistance to men and to two-parent couples. The target population for FAP was the "working poor," defined by Secretary Finch as "families in poverty headed by men working full time."[68] The second, related, argument was that AFDC broke otherwise workable nuclear families asunder. Public assistance programs that made male absence a criterion of eligibility unwittingly drove men away. FAP was designed to undo the damage by allowing low-earning men to stay with their wives (or girlfriends) and children without endangering the family's access to aid. The Nixon administration went so far as to hope that FAP would promote cohabitation or marriage.[69]

Cambodia Broke Our Stride

In April 1970, FAP was approved by a lopsided vote (243–155) in the House of Representatives. The Los Angeles Times editorialized that there was "little doubt" the Act would soon become law.[70] Mitchell Ginsberg, who offered regular bulletins on the progress of the legislation to Mayor Lindsay, believed that the Senate would vote on the measure by the beginning of May.[71] However, Ginsberg was mistaken. The Family Assistance Act did not even make it through the Senate Finance Committee by the end of December, much less through the other legislative roadblocks it would have to pass before becoming a law. The committee deadlocked over the president's plan. Rather than calling it welfare reform, Finance Committee chairman Russell Long charged, it "would be more appropriately entitled the 'Welfare Expansion and Mess Perpetuation Bill'."[72] The ranking Republican on the Finance Committee repeatedly asked whether FAP would discourage people from participating in the labor market.[73] Senator Fred Harris, a liberal whose family had participated in NWRO's "live on a welfare budget" campaign, pushed the administration to explain how families were supposed to survive on $1,600 per year.[74]

Behind the scenes were social and political conflicts that affected everyone in the United States and had special resonance within the Senate. The two most important points of conflict concerned civil rights and the war in Southeast Asia. In the civil rights arena, Nixon made a concerted effort to place a white Southern conservative, first Clement Haynsworth and then G. Harrold Carswell, on the U.S. Supreme Court. The Senate refused both men. The President pressed the Justice Department and Department of Health, Education, and Welfare to drag their heels on civil rights enforcement, particularly after the Supreme Court decision in *Swann v. Charlotte-Mecklenburg* (1970), which approved busing students to schools outside their neighborhoods to remedy segregation.[75]

In addition to civil rights, the war in Southeast Asia helps explain what happened to the welfare plan in the Senate. FAP passed the U.S. House on April 16, 1970. On April 19, a Senate subcommittee released portions of its investigation into U.S. bombing and combat operations in Laos. On April 30, Nixon informed a national television audience that he was preparing to send troops into the nominally neutral territory of Cambodia. Protests over the expanding war drove over a third of college campuses to shut down. National Guardsmen killed protesters at Kent State and Jackson State on May 4 and May 6 respectively.[76] On May 8, there was the first in a series of violent confrontations between construction workers in hard hats and antiwar activists in lower Manhattan—a stone's throw away from City Hall Park, where Citywide members had protested the flat grant. The most raucous of the pro-war demonstrations that followed was sponsored by the construction trades union and featured a group of workers on a cement mixer with a sign reading: "Lindsay for Mayor of Hanoi."[77]

War in Southeast Asia and conflict at Kent State took the Senate's attention away from welfare policy. On May 5, the Foreign Relations Committee charged that the President had violated the Constitution by sending U.S. troops into Cambodia "without the consent or knowledge of Congress," and called for repeal of the Gulf of Tonkin Resolution that had initially authorized the Vietnam War. Commentators across the country saw a constitutional crisis in the works.[78] The Finance Committee hearings on FAP were unavoidably shaped by these events, which dimmed the incentive of Democrats to work with the administration on a compromise and dampened the desire of Republicans to support FAP simply because Nixon was the leader of their Party. "Cambodia," Moynihan later reflected, "broke the Administration's stride."[79]

Amid these enormous social and political conflicts, the ideological spectrum within the White House narrowed. Those who had advocated the welfare proposal lost power, while those who continued to oppose it, especially those who could speak effectively to construction workers who hated John Lindsay, rose in prestige. Moynihan and Finch, whom Nixon called "eunuchs" and "poets," were both eased out of their positions.[80] Moynihan had become a roving counselor to the President in October 1969, with continued responsibility for FAP. When he threatened resignation in the spring of 1970, Nixon offered him the post of Ambassador to the United Nations. Nixon's top staff invited Finch to resign from HEW in June 1970. His replacement was Elliot Richardson, who appeared less "captive" (in John D. Ehrlichman's phrase) to groups that sought help from HEW.[81] Finch became an adviser to the President with a limited domestic policy portfolio. The Urban Affairs Council was abolished in July 1970, its work folded into a new Domestic Policy Council under Ehrlichman's direction.[82]

Simultaneous with the eclipse of its liberal wing, the sun rose on the Nixon Administration's conservatives. Nixon increasingly appreciated Vice President Agnew's value among white ethnics and Southerners. He also valued Patrick Buchanan, the most conservative of his speechwriters, as a spokesman for the new politics of the 1970s. As the President and his advisers picked up the pieces from the social conflicts over the war in Vietnam and opposition to it, Buchanan drafted vitriolic speeches for the Vice President against students, criminals, welfare recipients, and political protesters. Nixon was delighted by these rhetorical outbursts, and saw them as vital to his Party's appeal in the coming congressional elections as well as the presidential battle of 1972.[83]

The social fracturing that occurred in 1970 changed the political calculations within the White House. Nixon had once been persuaded that ambitious welfare reform could help him reach white working- and middle-class voters. He began seriously to doubt whether this was true. With the legislation facing deadlock in the Senate and Spiro Agnew becoming one of the administration's most popular spokesmen, the President backed away from his welfare proposal. On July 13, 1970, presidential adviser H. R. Haldeman confided to his diary that Nixon had emphasized the importance of "basing all scheduling and other decisions on political grounds." He wanted the White House staff to choose its audiences carefully, to "emphasize Italians, Poles, Elks and Rotarians, [and] eliminate Jews, blacks, youth. About Family Assistance Plan," Haldeman added, President Nixon "wants to be sure it's killed by [the] Democrats and that we make a big play for it, but don't let it pass."[84] This was not a final verdict on the plan; many of the impromptu Nixon directives Haldeman recorded were later rescinded. But it signaled a change in thinking about welfare reform at the top of the political pyramid. Nixon and his advisers continued to talk about FAP, and chastise

Senate Democrats (but not the equally intransigent Republicans) for opposing it. However, they spent only a deliberately limited amount of political capital to pass the bill.

Despite the administration's ambivalence, members of Nixon's staff amended FAP and reintroduced it to Congress. For liberals, the administration increased the minimum income for a family of four to $2,400; for conservatives, it increased work requirements for those who were not already "working poor." In 1971, President Nixon named FAP the first among "six great goals" for the United States.[85] In his 1972 State of the Union address, he described the legislation as the first item on the unfinished agenda of his administration.[86]

The electoral agenda of the Nixon White House made FAP a lower priority in practice than it was in the President's rhetoric.[87] Shortly after the 1972 State of the Union speech, some HEW staff members and advisers to Senator Ribicoff of Connecticut developed a compromise plan. In June, Democratic presidential candidates George McGovern and Hubert Humphrey debated on national television. McGovern outlined his proposal for a national minimum income of $1,000 per U.S. citizen.[88] Political observer Mitchell Ginsberg remembered that Ehrlichman and Haldeman then wrote a memorandum to President Nixon arguing that "with the possibility of McGovern as a candidate, the Democrats are going to be vulnerable on welfare. You would be much better, in our judgment, to be advised not to go" for the Ribicoff-HEW compromise on FAP.[89] Nixon responded to this advice by indicating at a press conference that he would not make the same concessions his HEW staff had made to pass the welfare reform legislation. "And that," Ginsberg commented, "was the complete debacle."[90] In October, the Senate voted down the compromise proposal and a less generous alternative endorsed weakly by the President.[91]

FAP partisans were disappointed. They placed blame for the loss squarely with the Nixon administration. The *Washington Post* charged the President with abandoning welfare reform for a "marginal political benefit he did not even need."[92] The *New York Times* stated as a matter of fact that the welfare measure had been "garroted" by the administration that originally advocated it.[93] And the *Nashville Tennessean* blamed the administration for the failure of FAP, insisting that, "At almost any point, Mr. Nixon could have used the full power and prestige of his office to get welfare reform."[94]

NWRO and FAP

Unlike the editorial writers from the *Post* and the *Times*, welfare recipients from Citywide and NWRO opposed the Family Assistance Plan.

Beneath the superficial similarities between the Nixon-Moynihan plan and their own plan for Guaranteed Adequate Income, they saw major distinctions, especially in the treatment of women who headed families. As with the flat grant in New York, Beulah Sanders, Jennette Washington, and other leaders believed that the Nixon administration's proposal was designed to help someone other than them, and that it might well end up hurting them.

The initial reaction of leading welfare rights activists to the Nixon welfare proposals was cautious but not wholly negative. The leaders of City-wide and NWRO had been searching for a national solution to the political deadlocks they faced. However, the Nixon proposal was not intended to benefit Northern urban welfare mothers, who were the grassroots base of NWRO. The $1,600 minimum income was too low to improve their material situation. Citywide members worried that the FAP minimum would in fact become a maximum in states like New York that were bending under the burden of welfare financing. Welfare rights activists objected to the White House's appeals "to hate, anger, and racism of middle class Americans with 'work or starve' talk . . . buying some political credit by providing some benefits for the working poor . . . channeling money to the Southern states and also [potentially] allowing the northern, industrial states to spend less on welfare."[95]

The welfare rights movement's approach to guaranteed income and the Nixon administration's approach embodied different ideas about poverty and its solution. NWRO members argued that the way to deal with women's poverty was to let them decide whether they preferred to receive their income directly from the government, from a private employer, or from a combination of the two. The way to address men's poverty was to let them, too, make choices between government grants and wages. Moynihan and Nixon argued that the preferable way to solve women's poverty was to have them form long-term intimate partnerships with men who had private-sector jobs, and to have the national government subsidize those jobs. If women were unable or unwilling to find men to "head" their families, then they would have to work for low wages while raising their children, and the federal government would provide them with income supplements. Men, the intended beneficiaries of FAP, could best provide for themselves and their wives and children by working for wages and receiving income supplements.

Beulah Sanders and George Wiley explained the differences between their approach and the White House plan to members of the Committee on Ways and Means of the House of Representatives, during the first Congressional hearings on FAP. Sanders conceded "that something is wrong with the welfare system," and that reform was necessary.[96] However, Wiley argued, the administration proposal failed "to go to the heart of the matter, which is the inadequacy of the income which is provided and available to poor people to raise and nurture their families."[97] Sanders expressed her frustration over the work requirement in FAP. "This country," she claimed, "is too rich for . . . saying rather than give [welfare recipients] more money they should be going and get a job when you know for a fact that this country has failed to provide the jobs that poor people need."[98]

NWRO leaders offered amendments to the FAP proposal rather than rejecting it out of hand. These amendments revealed philosophical and political differences between welfare rights activists and the administration. In an April 1970 version of the NWRO Guaranteed Adequate Income plan, the activists offered a list of principles that they saw as essential to national welfare reform, beginning with adequate income as a "national goal" and a timetable for reaching a basic income level of $5,500 per year. They sought the addition of emergency grants and regular cost-of-living increases to the "flat" guaranteed income in FAP. NWRO members insisted that the benefit be administered uniformly at the national level and be genuinely universal, to cover "all poor people, not just families with children."[99] They asked for access to jobs, while insisting that they should not be forced to work outside their homes. Finally, they demanded the same procedural rights that they had won under the public assistance system, especially access to information and opportunities to appeal in fair hearings.

Although NWRO spoke in one voice in its policy statements, the welfare rights movement was internally divided over the Nixon plan. When welfare rights activists had fought against the federal Work Incentive Program, women in the membership and the NWRO staff had disagreed with one another on the question of whether jobs should be primarily for men or for both women and men. There was more unanimity about FAP than there had been over WIN/WIP. Virtually all NWRO members argued that a guaranteed income had to be "adequate" to free them from dependence on fickle men or labor markets. They therefore saw FAP as a move in the wrong direction. However, some affiliated lawyers and NWRO staff members opposed the views of the recipients, not because they believed women should necessarily be dependent on men but because they believed that mothers should be willing to accept mandatory work assignments.

NWRO's affiliated attorneys were ambivalent about the Nixon plan. Even before President Nixon unveiled the proposal, NWRO counsel Carl Rachlin expressed a willingness to negotiate about including an employment requirement in a welfare reform package.[100] At a meeting at the Center on Social Welfare Policy and Law, attorneys who worked closely with Citywide and NWRO worried about the negative consequences of opposing FAP. Edward Sparer, the center's founder, asked: "should we help FAP to get passed?" He answered his own question by insisting that they should lobby for the Nixon plan only if the welfare recipients asked them to do so. However, he added, "client decision-making . . . isn't that big a hurdle"; poor women's and men's opposition to FAP might be overcome in time.[101]

George Wiley and other NWRO staff members sought ways to negotiate over FAP, even while publicly denouncing it. Wiley attempted to maintain lines of communication with liberals in Congress and a few Nixon administration officials as the war of rhetoric over FAP escalated.[102] Hulbert James remembered that he and virtually all of the middle-class staff members believed that the proposal was destined to succeed no matter what they did. "Here," he thought, "was something whose time had come."[103]

On May 13, 1970, with the FAP proposal under heated discussion in the Senate Finance Committee, welfare recipients took over the Department of Health, Education, and Welfare. Beulah Sanders became the movement's secretary of HEW. According to *Washington Post* reporter Haynes Johnson, who was an eyewitness to the takeover, Sanders and her colleagues "railed against American intervention in Cambodia and the lack of money to deal with domestic problems . . . 'What would you do if one of your children had been one of the Kent students'?" one woman asked Secretary Finch.[104] This was not the work of a group that believed it was time to break bread with the Republican White House or accept the moderating influence of its lawyers. Sanders and the activists who followed her leadership were frustrated by the unwillingness of the White House and Congress to take their perspectives seriously.[105]

The demonstration sharpened opposition to the welfare rights movement. The editors of the *Post* referred to Sanders, Wiley, and their colleagues as an "army of occupation," and added: "we would not be unhappy to see the arrests take place a little sooner next time. . . . For there is no argument—none—that can rationalize this childish and abusive performance as some sort of socially beneficial protest or some acceptable form of 'dissent'."[106] The most controversial representations of the takeover were photographs showing Sanders sitting at Secretary Finch's desk and George Wiley with his feet on the desk.[107]

For Beulah Sanders, the takeover of HEW headquarters was tied to her opposition to the widening war. After participating in a U.S. delegation to the Paris peace talks in 1968, Sanders had run for state senate in New York as a candidate of the Freedom and Peace Party. She appeared frequently as a speaker at antiwar demonstrations.[108] Sanders was the only African American speaker at the first national rally following the shootings at Kent State and Jackson State, days before the HEW take-

Figure 16. Johnnie Tillmon (left), Beulah Sanders, and HEW Secretary Robert Finch during the NWRO takeover of Finch's office. Courtesy *Washington Star* photographic archives, copyright *Washington Post*, reprinted by permission of District of Columbia Public Library.

over. "We are fighting against death in Vietnam and death in Cambodia," as well as for freedom from hunger in the United States, she told a crowd of thousands.[109]

Other members of the City-Wide Coordinating Committee and NWRO joined the issue of the war with the cause of a guaranteed income. Citywide and welfare rights groups in fifty cities participated in demonstrations on April 15, 1970, the "New Priorities Day" declared by the peace movement. At a rally outside the Manhattan office of the Internal Revenue Service, Jennette Washington linked the issue of the war with a call for adequate income by arguing that the federal government was misusing the tax revenue it collected.[110] "Adequate Income for all Americans would cost $50 billion," an NWRO report noted in preparation for the demonstrations, the same amount as the war in Vietnam and other military spending.[111]

Zapping FAP

Welfare rights activists simultaneously pushed for their own guaranteed income proposal and expressed their opposition to FAP. On April 30, the day Nixon announced the imminent arrival of U.S. troops in Cambodia, Eugene McCarthy of Minnesota introduced a version of the NWRO plan to the Senate as "the Adequate Income Act of 1970."[112] At the annual NWRO convention in July, delegates from all over the country approved a resolution firmly opposing FAP. "The Nixon Plan," it read, "is a direct attack on poor people," a flat grant that would eliminate "emergency needs, cost-of-living increases, and surplus food commodities."[113] NWRO members especially opposed the work requirement, which they described as undercutting parents' ability to make important decisions about their children's care. They also objected that FAP deprived "poor people the due process of law."[114] "Zap FAP" became the new slogan of the welfare rights movement.[115]

Beulah Sanders and other movement veterans increasingly refused to sugarcoat their critiques. The leaders of NWRO were especially forceful when they testified before unofficial congressional hearings sponsored by Senator McCarthy in November 1970. Sanders suggested that the interests of capitalist employers lay at the heart of the FAP proposal. Welfare reform, she insisted, "must not be a vehicle for subsidizing slave wage employers at the expense of poor people."[116] She insisted that welfare recipients be treated the same as middle-class women, and that African Americans and Latinos/as be treated the same as whites. Sanders called Senator Abraham Ribicoff "a nut" because he had once proposed that Mayor Lindsay cut the New York City welfare rolls by putting women to work cleaning the streets. "Senator Ribicoff," she said, to applause,

"I would be the first welfare recipient to volunteer to clean up New York's streets if your mother and your wife were beside me."[117] Alma Perry from Newark testified that she would never work in domestic service; indeed, she had no intention of working for pay until her children were completely grown: "I intend to have [welfare] until my children have a better job," she reported. "I'll be on welfare a long time before I would scrub anybody else's floors. I ain't ironing no shirts."[118]

Sanders and the other leaders opposed FAP in part because of the assumptions it contained about men, women, and sexuality. Eliza Williams from Connecticut objected to the President's efforts to unite welfare mothers with "working poor" fathers because some of those men were abusers. Women and children, she argued, were better off without them. Any suggestion that "my ex-spouse, whose integrity is only to inflict cruelty on others as well as to himself, be returned to my household," she emphasized, "this should be folded up and buried, not six feet under, but 100 feet down in the ground."[119] Gladys Rivers from Michigan objected to the President's focus on male wages and two-parent families as a form of discrimination against women who did not have husbands.[120] And Sanders claimed that women who received welfare deserved to have adult intimacy as much as wealthier women did. Under the FAP legislation, stepfathers were financially responsible for their stepchildren. If this initiative became law, she argued, "the woman stands a chance of losing out on a husband which she could have had through the man not being forced to take care of those kids. We feel our mothers need husbands as well as any other citizen."[121]

The women who spoke at the McCarthy hearings linked their opposition to FAP to the war in Southeast Asia. Roxanne Jones from Philadelphia asked, audaciously: "Who is it that had the audacity to sit down over scotch on the rocks . . . pills or methadone or whatever it was, to even consider in this affluent and rich country, where we waste over $80 billion a year in military, and suggest that a family of four should live on $1600?"[122] Shirley Rivers from Maryland went beyond objecting to the cost of the U.S. war in Vietnam and, "from a mother's viewpoint," called the cause itself into question: "Our children," she testified, "especially the boy children, we have to raise them, then they are taken from our homes and sent over to some foreign land to fight a battle that we don't know a thing about, ain't none of our people."[123]

By turning up the volume of their attacks on FAP, the welfare recipients made it ever more unlikely that a compromise would emerge, or that they would be parties to any high-level negotiations about it. However, the White House itself had already turned away from FAP; what support remained for the proposal in the Nixon administration was mostly rhetorical. Opposition by administration officials and senators from both major parties had a much greater effect on FAP than the opposition of Beulah Sanders and other welfare recipients. Asked a few years after the events occurred, Mitchell Ginsberg and HEW welfare expert Tom Joe both argued that the recipients were not powerful enough politically to defeat FAP. Insofar as Citywide and NWRO affected the debate, their influence was limited to Senate liberals. Given the Nixon administration's record on civil rights and the war in Vietnam, these liberals might well have opposed the plan even if welfare recipients had not encouraged them to do so.[124]

From the time of the informal hearings organized by Senator McCarthy through the final defeat of the Family Assistance Plan, the debate over welfare reform remained much the same. Despite moments at which compromise appeared possible, the minimal support for FAP from the White House, the continued polarization of U.S. politics, and the special place of welfare in that polarization obliterated the incentives to compromise. John Gardner, a former secretary of HEW and leader of the advocacy organization Common Cause, organized a conference that he hoped would reignite negotiations over FAP. Gardner invited both HEW secretary Richardson and George Wiley, who was asked to bring two or three welfare recipients. When Wiley asked that the forum be open to one or two hundred NWRO members, Richardson indicated he would not attend and Gardner cancelled the event.[125]

Beulah Sanders was elected chair of NWRO at the organization's 1971 convention, which focused on the campaign against FAP more than it focused on any other single issue.[126] Activists across the country mobilized angrily against President Nixon's proposal. Elizabeth Perry and other women in the Washington, D.C., Family Rights Organization coordinated three public hearings "to inform the community about FAP—Nixon's Family Destruction Plan which is designed to enslave poor people."[127] California Welfare Rights Organization head Catherine Jermany reported that 250 members of her group appeared at state legislative hearings on a welfare cut proposed by Governor Ronald Reagan, and explained to legislators "how Reagan's Bill is just one step from Slavery (F— America's Poor) Bill."[128]

Catherine Jermany, Roxanne Jones, and Beulah Sanders got part of what they wanted as a result of their lobbying, demonstrating, and testifying. Although their opposition was just one small piece of the puzzle that produced the defeat of President Nixon's FAP, they treated the defeat of the bill as a victory for NWRO.[129] At the same time, there was much that the organized welfare recipients were not able to accomplish through their political efforts: FAP or no FAP, the flat grant still stood in New York State. Neither "hardhats" nor politicians like Nelson Rockefeller softened in their views of impoverished women and children who accepted public aid. Despite the best efforts of Jermany and Los Angeles resident Johnnie Tillmon, Ronald Reagan succeeded at vilifying welfare mothers and passing major cuts in California antipoverty programs. An October 1971 study in the NWRO newspaper found thirty-one states in which legislatures and governors either had implemented or were planning reductions in benefits to the poor.[130]

In the years that followed the contentious battle over the Family Assistance Plan, a range of commentators insisted that welfare recipients had made a terrible mistake in opposing it. In the book he wrote shortly after leaving the White House, urban affairs adviser Daniel Patrick Moynihan could hardly find enough bad things to say about the welfare recipients who helped derail the Family Assistance Plan, or the liberals who agreed with them. He accused welfare mothers of invidious self-interest for opposing a public assistance system that would have raised Southern benefit levels even as it left benefits in states like New York stagnant. Moynihan also charged that NWRO members stubbornly misread FAP as an inadequate substitute for waged work or conventional marriage. Instead, he argued, they should have understood that the heart of the plan was a generous supplement to "working poor" male wages.[131] In the late twentieth century, a new generation of historians studying President Nixon argued that the welfare recipients misunderstood his administration, which despite Watergate and the war in Vietnam pursued ambitious domestic initiatives such as the income guarantee contained in the Family Assistance Plan.[132]

Welfare rights partisans and opponents alike have overstated the role of NWRO in defeating FAP. They have downplayed the significance of other actors, such as White House officials and both Democrats and Republicans in Congress. By far the most significant opposition resided in the Nixon administration itself—in a Cabinet that was overwhelmingly opposed to the proposal, as well as a President who cared more about fashioning a new political majority than he did about reforming the welfare system.

Moynihan and other commentators who favored the legislation have suggested that welfare recipients' efforts to "zap FAP" obliterated the last, best hope for positive reform in U.S. social policy in the twentieth century. However, passage of FAP would not have ensured a different history for welfare. Beginning with the flat grant in New York, and extending to Wisconsin and at least twenty-nine other states, welfare cuts were popular public policies before, during, and after the battle over FAP. There is every reason to believe that cities and states would have continued cutting benefits with or without a federal policy change in the early 1970s.[133]

Those who claim that welfare recipients were on the wrong side of the FAP debate miss the fact that poor women and men had philosophical, political, and economic objections to the plan. Beulah Sanders believed that the point of the welfare rights movement "was to see that we got a guaranteed adequate income for every human being." She wanted in particular to see that "every A[F]DC mother with children . . . would have an adequate income regardless" of whether she married or worked for pay.[134] The NWRO Guaranteed Adequate Income proposal reflected Sanders's priorities. As paltry and incomplete as it was, the AFDC program itself reflected her desire that women and children have alternatives to conventional employment or marriage. The FAP legislation, with its work requirement and low basic income level ("no money for anybody to live on," in Sanders's words), would never have done as much for unmarried women as the NWRO guaranteed income plan promised to do.

Chapter 7

End of an Era

Unless current trends in Albany and Washington are reversed, the future of our jobs is dim indeed.

—*Social Service Employees Union, New York City, Official Statement*

In the fall of 1971, Beulah Sanders, the new chair of the National Welfare Rights Organization, headed a meeting that took her back to her political roots. Its subject was the increasingly dire welfare situation in New York City. After hearing from executive director George Wiley on the details of recent cuts in benefits, Sanders and the other elected leaders of NWRO authorized Wiley to establish a headquarters in Manhattan for "Operation New York."[1] "What happens in New York," Sanders wrote, "often sets the pattern for the rest of the country. Because of this fact, the NWRO Executive Committee has decided we must make a major fight in New York."[2]

Operation New York was a response to a wave of changes in the politics of welfare in the early 1970s that made the harsh rhetoric and benefit reductions of previous years seem like mere surface ripples. Politicians and bureaucrats from New York were taking ever more ambitious measures to bring welfare costs down. By making welfare less generous, they hoped to quiet both the welfare rights movement and the widening movement against welfare.[3] Even moderate participants in the welfare debate of the early 1970s called on welfare recipients to work harder and argued that the crux of the crisis in public benefits was the number of poor people who were receiving the aid to which they were legally entitled. In 1971, welfare rights lawyer Carl Rachlin, who lived in New York City, wrote a letter to Wiley in which he noted the antiwelfare mood and concluded that they had reached "the end of an era."[4]

As Sanders had feared they would, policy changes in New York inspired a cascade of changes throughout the United States. Senator Herman Talmadge of Georgia proposed an amendment to the Social

Security Act extending the Work Incentive Program to more people and imposing harsher penalties on those who did not participate in it. The Talmadge bill passed, and the President signed it in December 1971.[5] In the Supreme Court, progress toward welfare rights was reversed with a series of decisions that rejected the claims of NWRO and its lawyers to a constitutional "right to life," or a minimum standard of material well-being to which every citizen was entitled. Following the New York example, scores of states and cities cut benefits and tightened their eligibility criteria.[6]

Beulah Sanders, George Wiley, and other activists responded creatively to the antiwelfare wave of the early 1970s but their efforts were no match for the forces arrayed against them. The NWRO national headquarters office ultimately closed in 1974. Despite Operation New York, Citywide closed its office in Harlem in 1975.[7] These events were the culmination of processes that had been in motion since Governor Rockefeller first proposed the flat grant in New York State. The militancy of antiwelfare politicians and voters discouraged welfare mothers and fathers who might otherwise have mobilized for improvements. Repeated rhetorical assaults undermined people's faith in the possibility of social change.

Across the country, welfare recipients were blamed for the tight municipal and state budgets of the early 1970s. The situation was especially acute in New York City. The city still possessed what Mayor Lindsay had called a "stepchild form of government," without the power to determine welfare benefit levels or raise the revenue necessary to cover its budget. The public assistance caseload and costs of the program continued to rise. Moreover, New York City was still paying the bills for the public-sector building boom of the 1960s and faced new fiscal obligations, such as relatively generous union contracts for public-sector employees and "Open Admissions" to the City University of New York.[8] If nothing changed, the city was destined to run out of money. Governor Rockefeller, continuing a turn to the political right that had begun during his bid for the Republican presidential nomination in 1968, refused to twist any arms in Albany to bail out the New York City welfare department. Instead, he called for administrative innovations to reduce expenditures and drive people from the assistance rolls. The Lindsay administration protested on only a few points.

Operation New York

The national welfare rights movement launched Operation New York because the policies of the Rockefeller and Lindsay administrations were seen as threats to welfare recipients throughout the country. The events that led to NWRO's New York campaign began in the final months of 1970. The Human Resources Administration estimated total costs for the coming fiscal year at $2.4 billion. The lion's share of this money was to be spent on public assistance, and $663 million of it would have to be raised from municipal taxes. Mayor Lindsay refused to approve the budget and filed a legal suit against the state and federal governments for imposing an unbearable fiscal burden on the people of New York City.[9] At the same time, the Lindsay administration began a concerted effort to lower costs by reorganizing the welfare department, turning the job of "income maintenance," or the issuance of assistance checks, over to low-paid employees and a first generation of office computers, while leaving "social service" functions in the hands of a limited number of college-educated caseworkers.[10] The administration's hope was that these efforts would save money and help the welfare department survive with fewer employees. Lindsay and his top officials may have been especially eager to limit their reliance on unionized caseworkers, whose willingness to organize independently and to strike had placed them in a strong bargaining position vis-à-vis the city.[11]

From the perspective of the welfare rights movement, the aftermath of the Lindsay administration's declaration of war against the state and federal governments was even worse than the budgetary problems that precipitated it. The governor and legislators in Albany responded to Lindsay's legal action against them by charging that welfare costs were higher than necessary because New York City let thousands of clients defraud the program. These accusations persisted despite reports that the city's economy was in decline, and that low wages and unemployment were causing rising numbers of working-class whites and blacks to depend on public assistance.[12]

The wrath of politicians at the state level led to a host of benefit reductions and new eligibility standards. These included a 10 percent cut in cash benefits in Aid to Families with Dependent Children (AFDC); a $500 drop in the income cutoff for Medicaid eligibility, which made 25,000 families ineligible for health care coverage; and a new rule that required employable Home Relief recipients to appear at a state government office every fortnight to certify their eligibility and pick up their checks. Governor Rockefeller introduced legislation that would have reinstated a one-year residency requirement for benefits and created a "voluntary relocation program" to drive poor people out of New York. Rockefeller and the legislators also created a Public Service Work Opportunities Project that promised to cut assistance rolls and weaken municipal unions by putting welfare mothers and fathers to work in lower-level government jobs. Even mothers of very young children who failed to appear for work assignments were to be removed from the rolls.[13]

Mayor Lindsay made extraordinary efforts to expand New Yorkers' access to child care, and he spoke out publicly against the proposed residency rule.[14] But he and his top advisers did what they could to implement the directives from the state regarding Public Service Work Opportunities.[15] By August 1971, the city government had referred nearly 21,000 people to the state as "employables" and had taken action to close two thousand public assistance cases.[16] City bureaucrats worried about how to limit the number of recipients placed in office jobs, and increase the number working in the parks and on duties such as rat control. The budget director warned Mayor Lindsay: "Instead of having large numbers of people in the parks and lots giving public evidence of our effort to use these people according to the priorities we agreed upon, we are placing larger numbers of them in indoor, clerical tasks which makes them largely invisible to the [antiwelfare] public." Lindsay underlined his "full support" for any efforts to correct this problem.[17]

Eventually, the Lindsay administration went beyond implementing state laws that narrowed access to social welfare and became an antiwelfare innovator in its own right. The city opened a fraud control unit within the Human Resources Administration in October 1971. Welfare department staff referred to the District Attorney hundreds of women and men who had supposedly pretended to lose their checks in order to get more money.[18] In June 1972, Human Resources Administration official Charles Morris asked Mayor Lindsay for nine hundred new employees with whom to interview every existing welfare client and reestablish her eligibility for aid, and to prevent "illegal work stoppages" (strikes) and the taking of too many vacation days by the employees of neighborhood welfare offices.[19] The point of these efforts was both political and fiscal; a well-staffed welfare crackdown might diminish public aid costs or it might not, but it would certainly signal to irate taxpayers that something was being done about the welfare problem. In the midst of this spending in the name of fiscal responsibility, Mayor Lindsay quietly rejected the budget for the Community Action Program in New York City and thus ended the flagship program of the local War on Poverty.[20]

The Lindsay administration's twists and turns on welfare policy would have been surprising to many of the mayor's supporters, especially those outside New York City. Lindsay's reputation as a social policy liberal had been cemented by his leading role in producing the Kerner Commission Report on urban riots. Lindsay had been an outsider in the increasingly conservative Republican Party since 1968. He finally left his longtime political home to run for President in the Democratic primaries of 1972.

Lindsay's campaign platform included his commitment to a guaranteed adequate income for all citizens. The mayor's departure from the Republican Party cost him political allies without helping him leave New York for the national arena; his campaign petered out shortly after it began. In the end, exhausted by the enormous social and political upheavals of the 1960s as well as his own feints to the right at home and to the left outside New York, John V. Lindsay decided to step down at the end of 1973 rather than face another uphill battle to hold the mayor's office.[21]

Jennette Washington, George Wiley, and other leaders of the welfare rights movement saw the policy changes in New York as part of a larger pattern of racism and a disregard for the poor on the part of white politicians. The NWRO newspaper referred to Governor Rockefeller as a "Five-Star General" in the war against the poor. Washington called him "the slavemaster of New York State" because of his punitive proposals, and because of the brutal ending he had authorized to the takeover by inmates of the Attica state prison.[22]

"People Before Property"

Beyond Attica, there were plenty of reasons for Jennette Washington to be bitter toward city and state officials in the early 1970s. One of the most immediate was a series of reports indicating that the problem that had launched her political career—the housing crisis that resulted from the racially discriminatory, class-biased pattern of urban renewal—was as acute as it had ever been. Eight years after Jennette Washington and Beulah Sanders had been displaced from their apartments on the Upper West Side of Manhattan by urban renewal, welfare recipients faced an acute housing shortage. Increasingly, caseworkers met their clients' needs for living space by booking them into "welfare hotels," unappealing and impermanent lodgings that cost more per night than did semi-decent living spaces but were not bound by the city's maximum rent guidelines. In December 1970 and January 1971 alone, six children died in the welfare hotels as a result of fires, falls out of windows, and falls into elevator shafts.[23]

A demonstration by welfare rights and tenants' rights activists culminated in an occupation of a new but still untenanted apartment building on the Upper West Side. More than 500 mourners, including George Wiley, marched behind the hearse of the latest child who had died in a derelict hotel and held a brief memorial service in front of City Hall. Then, shouting "People before property!" and "No more murders of our children!" about 150 of them boarded buses headed for a building on West 90th Street. Seventy-five families, complete with their children and belongings, moved into attractive apartments on the very site from which some of them had been displaced a decade earlier. "Now that the new building is finished," the *Welfare Fighter* reported, "it is to be out of bounds for most welfare recipients. Only 10% (15 out of 179) of its units are designated for poor people."[24] After three and a half hours, over one hundred policemen arrived to evict Wiley, welfare recipients, and their supporters from the building.

The immediate provocation for Operation New York was a series of waivers the federal Department of Health, Education, and Welfare (HEW) granted New York State to experiment with new ways to cut welfare costs. Governor Rockefeller and legislators in Albany proposed to limit cash benefits in certain parts of the state to the revised FAP level of $2,400 per family. In addition, state officials would offer recipients financial incentives to engage in behaviors they deemed salutary, such as raking leaves in a public park, helping authorities locate and prosecute a spouse who had deserted, or cooperating with school authorities. NWRO leaders termed this a "brownie point" system and argued that it interfered with poor people's autonomy. Faith Evans, an African American welfare father and the Eastern regional representative to NWRO, described the proposals as violations of "the Constitution of the United States, the Bill of Rights, and the Emancipation Proclamation."[25]

When it sent George Wiley to New York, the National Coordinating Committee of NWRO gave him a wide mandate to press for reversals in the new policies. His overarching goal was to build a new political coalition of "welfare recipients, unemployed workers, Vietnam veterans, youth and senior citizens" to challenge the increasingly conservative mainstream politics of the early 1970s. According to Wiley, this coalition would not focus primarily on public welfare but on waged work, demanding "that all who are able to work can get jobs. Jobs that provide an income adequate to meet their needs."[26]

Wiley did not succeed at building a new political coalition in New York City or at bringing low-wage workers into the welfare rights movement. The main achievement of Operation New York was the defeat of the "brownie point" program. Community protests organized by members of Citywide, the Black Panthers, and other Harlem activists pushed Rockefeller to end the experiment.[27] Operation New York garnered public attention when Wiley and Citywide members demonstrated against the presentation of an honorary degree to HEW secretary Elliot Richardson. In place of Richardson's official commendation, Citywide granted Richardson a "Doctor of Laws in Social Oppression. . . . For your cooperation above and beyond the call of duty with Governor Rockefeller in assisting him to secure waivers of federal regulations to clear the way for the implementation of New York State Demonstration projects which would impose undue hardship on welfare recipients and violate their rights."[28] The Secretary refused the welfare rights version of an honorary degree, a roll of toilet tissue tied with a blue bow.

Against the Tide

Everywhere in the United States, the odds were overwhelmingly against the survival of welfare rights groups in the early 1970s. Still, local activists and national leaders such as Jennette Washington, George Wiley, and Beulah Sanders struggled to sustain their organizations. This fighting spirit allowed the movement to score some unlikely victories.

Until at least the end of 1972, local and state-level welfare rights organizations recruited members, opened new chapters, brought legal suits, lobbied legislatures, arranged demonstrations, spread information, published newsletters, and raised money—although it was never enough. Leaders who rose from the ranks, as Sanders and Washington had done in New York City, worked hard to maintain their groups and plant the roots of welfare rights in firmer soil. NWRO received letters and reports from grassroots activists in at least twenty-five states plus the District of Columbia in the early 1970s.[29] During one six-week period in 1972, Connecticut welfare recipient Eliza Williams held meetings across her state, helped bring over nine hundred people to Hartford for a demonstration, sat in on the lawn in front of the capitol building for two weeks, and led the group in commandeering the office of the federally funded city poverty agency. All of this activity persuaded the Connecticut legislature to restore rent and utility payments to welfare budgets.[30] Cassie Downer, who headed the Milwaukee affiliate of NWRO, reported that her group had one thousand members, had successfully defeated proposed restrictions on welfare eligibility, and made "me and other recipients begin to realize and feel our dignity."[31]

Although the welfare rights era had nearly passed, organizing continued even in parts of the country that had been fairly weak centers of NWRO activism, such as the South. Huntsville, Alabama, for example, had a welfare rights organization that was strong enough to challenge official plans for implementing the food stamp program in December 1972. Birmingham organizer Ruby Williams reported on welfare rights workshops for people in far-flung regions of the state, a plan for challenging Governor George Wallace's legislative priorities in the legislature, and a new affiliate composed entirely of senior citizens who wanted better medical benefits. Marie James and other welfare recipients in the Midlands area of South Carolina lobbied against a federal program that singled out South Carolina (and counties within the state with disproportionate African American populations) for a mandatory work demonstration project.[32]

Buoyed by the activism that continued at the local and state levels, and buffeted by the nationwide hurricane of antiwelfare sentiment, the NWRO staff and elected leadership experimented with creative efforts to sustain the movement. One new idea, which appealed particularly to male staff, was to begin aggressively recruiting men and low-wage workers in part by emphasizing jobs, as Wiley had done in Operation New York. This was a controversial departure for NWRO. In 1967, Wiley had opposed the Social Security Act amendments on the grounds that the government should provide employment for men and keep women who were raising children out of the labor market. Beulah Sanders had argued that mothers themselves should choose whether and how to combine waged work with parenting. When Wiley shifted his focus to waged work for everyone, he did so in the hope of broadening the reach of NWRO, from public aid recipients to all poor and working-class people. He believed that the movement could attract anyone who demanded government intervention to meet his or her needs, whether that person wanted welfare narrowly construed or other benefits from the welfare state, such as economic planning to support job creation, minimum wages that kept pace with inflation, or protection for workers who wanted to bargain collectively.

These initiatives faced obstacles within and outside NWRO. Many whites were reluctant to join what they considered an African American welfare mothers' movement. The overwhelming majority of male trade unionists were allergic to collaboration with welfare mothers; if their members were so poor that they qualified for public aid, union leaders were reluctant to broadcast the fact.[33] And the women who served on the National Coordinating Committee of NWRO did not want to pour resources into efforts to organize low-wage working men and others who were not welfare recipients. Johnnie Tillmon remembered that she wanted to recruit non-recipients to NWRO. But she recalled that Beulah Sanders and other women fiercely resisted the idea.[34]

The efforts to recruit working men to NWRO failed, but they generated new organizing outside of the welfare rights movement. With NWRO backing—and apparently without the approval or even the knowledge of the organization's elected leadership—white staff member Wade Rathke began experimenting with organizing low-wage men and women in Little Rock, Arkansas. Rathke's project began as part of an NWRO "southern strategy" to support leaders such as Annie Smart in Baton Rouge and to place pressure on congressional leaders such as House Ways and Means chairman Wilbur Mills of Arkansas. However, Rathke soon resigned from NWRO. He renamed his organization, which focused on the working poor, Arkansas Community Organizations for Reform Now (ACORN).[35]

For George Wiley, the conflicts between NWRO staff and elected leadership, combined with the frustrations he faced in trying to reconcile welfare rights with the mainstream work ethic, ultimately caused him to resign as executive director. He resolved at the very end of 1972 to start a new Movement for Economic Justice.[36] "The fact that NWRO is made up mostly of AFDC mothers, who comprise only 3-million of the 50-million poor people in the country, highlights the necessity to broaden the movement," he wrote.[37] His new initiative acceded to the antiwelfare spirit of the time by demoting the issue of public assistance from first place to merely one issue among many. At the same time, however, it was a continuation of the commitment to interracial organizing on economic issues that had animated Wiley since his days as a Syracuse civil rights leader in the middle 1960s.

In addition to explicit attempts to expand NWRO membership to include low-waged men, Beulah Sanders and other leading members and staff made a range of efforts to broaden the coalition in support of welfare rights. They attempted to work more closely with the Southern Christian Leadership Conference (SCLC), which was still reeling from the loss of Dr. Martin Luther King, Jr. NWRO and SCLC had worked together on the Poor People's Campaign of 1968. In 1971, Wiley and SCLC's Ralph Abernathy joined in a "spring offensive" against poverty and the war in Vietnam. They issued a set of political demands with César Chávez of the United Farm Workers. In Washington, D.C., NWRO members met an SCLC mule train, which revived the iconic tactic of the Poor People's Campaign. Sanders and Abernathy led a rally in the lobby of HEW headquarters. When police constructed a barrier to keep demonstrators from accessing other parts of the building, Jennette Washington and Philadelphia's Roxanne Jones led the crowd in tearing it down bit by bit. Two hundred and seventy-six NWRO and SCLC activists were arrested.[38]

The meetings between NWRO and SCLC did not produce a unified new organization. However, they became the basis for a working coalition among poor people's organizations, which included the United Farm Workers and the National Tenants' Organization, headed by former Harlem rent strike leader Jesse Gray. According to NWRO sources, the members of this coalition turned out the vote for candidate George McGovern in the 1972 Nebraska and California primaries. They gained concessions from the Democratic National Committee by threatening to demonstrate on the evening the Democratic convention opened in Miami.[39] The Poor People's Platform they formulated called for a guaranteed income for all, a minimum wage that covered more workers, rec-

Figure 17. Children's March for Survival, 1972. Courtesy *Washington Star* photographic archives, copyright *Washington Post*, reprinted by permission of District of Columbia Public Library.

ognition for poor people at future Democratic conventions, and
challenges to such "slanders as that the reason for welfare is that some
people simply do not wish to work . . . [and] that welfare is the good life
of color TV's and cadillacs."[40] Their $6,500 per year adequate income
plan received nearly one thousand votes from convention delegates,
two-thirds of the votes needed for passage.[41]

NWRO leaders and staff made another large-scale effort to build bridges to new allies when they orchestrated a Children's March for Survival
on March 25, 1972. The march called President Nixon to account for
his recent veto of national child care legislation, as well as for the possible effects on children of work requirements for welfare mothers. An
additional goal of the march was to link NWRO to feminists, child advocates, and a range of other possible allies. NWRO estimated that fifty
thousand people participated in the D.C. march, which had the backing
of seventy-five organizations and such well-known activists as Dr. Benjamin Spock, Gloria Steinem, Reverend Jesse Jackson, and feminist and
peace advocate Representative Bella Abzug.[42] New York City welfare
rights groups organized a "children's fair" for the day before they were
to leave for the capital, and fifteen other cities created children's
marches of their own. The Social Service Employees Union in New York
organized buses to take its members to the march, arguing that "unless
current trends in Albany and Washington are reversed, the future of our
jobs is dim indeed."[43]

The Children's March united diverse constituencies behind the goals
of the welfare rights movement for one day. But these constituencies did
not work together for long. Some NWRO members and staff were ambivalent about the whole idea of building coalitions, which would necessarily dilute the welfare rights message. They feared that public aid
recipients would be forced to compete for resources, even within the
organization, with people who were wealthier and better educated than
they were.[44] To those who believed that new coalitions were essential to
NWRO's survival, perhaps the greatest disappointment of this era was
the welfare rights movement's failure to build ongoing ties with wom-
en's organizations. Tim Sampson remembered a moment in his career
as associate director of NWRO when he "realized, for the first time," in
light of the rising women's movement of the late 1960s, "that I was working for a women's organization." He wrote letters to the officers of all
of the major women's organizations with offices in Washington, D.C.,
from the Daughters of the American Revolution to the National Council
of Negro Women. The only group to respond was the National Organization for Women (NOW), the paradigmatic "second wave" feminist
organization.[45] In 1970, NOW endorsed the idea of a guaranteed
income and expressed solidarity with NWRO. However, NOW did not

offer activist welfare recipients the thing they needed most, financial support.[46]

Court Action and Direct Action

Amid all of their political challenges, local activists and NWRO leaders scored some impressive legal victories in the early 1970s. In New York, a suit that bore the name of the leader of the Upstate Welfare Rights Organization ended in an order from a federal district court forbidding different counties to pay public aid clients different amounts of money. This resulted in the raising of welfare grants in upstate New York, a boon to clients of thousands of dollars.[47] In *Dublino v. New York State Department of Social Services*, another federal district court ruled that the work program instituted by Rockefeller and the state legislature violated the federal Social Security Act. Although the court rejected the most ambitious arguments put forward by the welfare recipients' attorneys, it ruled that recipients of *federal* programs did not have to comply with mandatory work rules established by the *state* government.[48]

The most significant legal victory for welfare rights in the early 1970s was Justice Brennan's majority opinion for the U.S. Supreme Court in the New York City fair hearing case *Goldberg v. Kelly*. The issue in the case was whether the Fourteenth Amendment's promise of "due process" implied that all welfare recipients deserved a fair hearing before being dropped from the rolls. From the perspective of the welfare rights movement, pre-cutoff hearings were important for the same reasons that fair hearings were generally: they imposed the cost of conducting the hearings on welfare departments and required the continuation of benefits to those recipients whose cases were successful. Therefore, they raised the incentives to negotiate with clients, or even to refrain from cutting people off of the rolls. A pre-termination hearing, like any other fair hearing, was a benefit the welfare rights movement could help its members access.

Justice Brennan's decision suggested that welfare recipients possessed what legal theorist Charles Reich had termed a "new property" interest in their benefits.[49] If government agents could not withdraw welfare grants without explaining why, or offering opportunities to contest the decision in a trial-like setting, then the relationship between recipients and their benefits might indeed be viewed as similar to the relationship between an owner and her or his property. "It may be realistic today," Brennan wrote, "to regard welfare entitlements as more like 'property' than a 'gratuity'."[50] He argued that public assistance was "not mere charity, but a means to 'promote the general Welfare'" by preventing unrest and allowing impoverished citizens to participate fully in their society.[51]

In another area of law, NWRO provoked HEW to convene conformity hearings to determine whether individual states were violating the Social Security Act. Welfare activists won the right to participate in these hearings as the representatives of all public aid clients. As a result of pressure from NWRO, HEW officials called administrators from Nevada and Connecticut to account for the way they were managing the AFDC program; if the state administrators refused to participate in the conformity hearings, their states might lose huge amounts of federal funding.[52] Although an opinion by Judge J. Skelly Wright of the U.S. Court of Appeals for the D.C. Circuit had already granted welfare recipients standing to participate in the conformity hearings, federal officials hesitated to let them do so. HEW cancelled the Nevada hearing and tried to keep a rowdy group of welfare recipients from participating in the Connecticut hearing. Finally, through a combination of what an anonymous writer for the NWRO newspaper termed "court action and direct action," the welfare recipients were allowed to participate.[53]

NWRO's strategy of provoking and participating in conformity hearings rocked the ship of state, much as the legal civil disobedience of Citywide members had done in New York. In the summer of 1970, NWRO successfully pushed HEW to hold hearings on several states' failure to revise the "standard of need" on which welfare grants were based, in violation of the 1967 Social Security Act amendments.[54] The federal official in charge of the hearings informed NWRO's old antagonist, former HEW secretary Robert Finch, about a request by the head of social services in California for "a 'secret meeting'" to discuss ways to avoid a public hearing without forcing the state to change its standard of need. "He said," the letter continued, "the substantive decision will be made at San Clemente," that is, at the western White House, suggesting that President Nixon would never allow his administration to cut off federal aid to the politically important state of California.[55] However, the HEW official warned:

Great care must be taken in arriving at an acceptable alternative to a hearing since under the recent decision by the D.C. Court of Appeals a copy of the proposed material resolving the issue, together with a statement outlining the Administrator's reasons for accepting it, must be submitted to all parties (and NWRO has already asked to be a party). If a party is dissatisfied with the decision of the Administrator, it can go directly to Federal Court. I have no doubt that if California proposes an alternative which does not fully comply and if we accept it, the NWRO will immediately take us to Court. Thus, any proposal should be considered on its merits or else we will be left in an extremely vulnerable position.[56]

Faced with the possibility that NWRO would take them to court, officials of the Nixon administration chose to ignore the political pressure from the California government and hold the hearing, to which NWRO and the California Welfare Rights Organization were both parties.[57] Testimony from women and men on welfare and from sympathetic social workers "demonstrated" to hearing examiner J. Andrew Brooks "that public assistance payments by California had not kept pace with rising costs of living. . . . Technically, such evidence may have been superfluous," he editorialized, "but it . . . focused attention upon social problems which are urgently in need of solution."[58] Brooks decided that California was violating the law and that his superiors in Washington, D.C., were free to suspend millions of dollars in public assistance payments to the state if they so chose.[59] Finally, in response to this threat, Governor Reagan and the California state legislature complied with the law and raised the state's standard of need.

"Human Rights Isn't in the Manual"

The pressure NWRO placed on states by participating in conformity hearings produced gains for welfare recipients. But legal tactics, such as conformity hearings and individual fair hearings, were less powerful tools for welfare recipients in the early 1970s than they had been a few years earlier. One reason for the change was that the availability of free and low-cost legal assistance diminished in the early 1970s, in part because the federal legal services program contracted. The factors that had delayed arrival of the program in New York City, especially skepticism about public funding for legal work on the part of the organized bar, persisted everywhere in the United States. Moreover, the close relationships between many legal services lawyers and militant social movements aroused suspicion among politicians who were their targets. In 1974, this opposition drove Congress and the White House to eliminate the Legal Services Program and create instead a semiprivate Legal Services Corporation with limited public funding. Law students and attorneys whose salaries were not funded by the government largely moved on to other causes once the welfare rights movement faltered and poverty litigation stalled in the high courts. Some withdrew altogether from the effort to use the law for social change.[60]

In this climate, women and men who participated in welfare rights battles were increasingly conscious of the weaknesses of legal strategies such as fair hearings. Nina Gray from New Jersey, for example, wrote a letter of protest to her state welfare director: "Since I don't believe in your fair hearings it doesn't make sense to ask for one," she noted. "The object in [the welfare department office in] Paterson is, how fair is it to

Figure 18. By 1969, welfare rights activists who had once believed law supported their vision of human rights depicted Justice as narrow and bound by the rules. Courtesy George Wiley Papers, Wisconsin Historical Society.

the State not the human being."[61] The image on the cover of the Minnesota Welfare Rights Organization manual showed an all-female group of welfare recipients confronting a man in judicial robes who seemed to be a fair hearing referee. The women demanded basic items such as "food," "furniture," and "clothes," but the referee answered: "I'M SORRY, 'HUMAN RIGHTS' ISN'T MENTIONED IN THE MANUAL."[62] By the early 1970s, "legal civil disobedience" inspired both optimism and pessimism among welfare recipients. The rising conservative and antiwelfare mood called into question the idea that poor people could gain justice and protect their "human rights" by going to court.

In the federal courts, *Goldberg v. Kelly* represented the culmination of the expansive poverty law that had developed during the 1960s rather than the foundation for an expansion of welfare rights after 1970. Although it was a major departure from earlier statements about poverty and economic inequality by the Supreme Court, even in *Goldberg v. Kelly* the Court did not find a firm constitutional basis in either the "due process" clause or the "equal protection" clause of the Fourteenth Amendment for a citizen's right to a minimum standard of living.[63] Brennan's decision in *Goldberg v. Kelly* led to changes in fair hearing procedures, which may have afforded welfare clients protection against unjust benefit cuts and against reprisals for belonging to an activist organization.[64] They certainly imposed costs on state and local welfare administrations. But many jurisdictions fought the new fair hearing requirements within HEW and in the courts. Others treated welfare spending as zero-sum, and appear to have taken funds from cash grants to spend on implementing the new procedures.[65] New York City did not fight the requirements, but the city government may never have implemented them fully. Fair hearings were routinized and sped up, making it more difficult for recipients to challenge the bureaucracy by asserting their rights to appeal. A 1974 report sponsored by the American Bar Association observed that fair hearings in New York City were "scheduled at half-hour intervals, but rarely does the examiner meet the schedule. . . . The result tends to bring a kind of police court environment; a sense of hurry pervades the hearings."[66]

From the perspective of welfare rights activists, Justice Brennan's affirmation of the right to a pre-termination fair hearing came too late to do the work that they had planned for it. Although the hearings were a longstanding demand, the majority decision in *Goldberg v. Kelly* was overwhelmed by defeats that came at virtually the same moment. In *Dandridge v. Williams*, for example, the Justices let stand a Maryland statute mandating a maximum welfare benefit per family. Justice Stewart attempted to extricate the Court from its involvement in welfare issues, arguing that "the intractable economic, social, and even philosophical problems presented by public welfare assistance programs are not the business of this Court."[67] An article in the NWRO newspaper mentioned the *Goldberg* victory almost as an afterthought, and emphasized that it was meaningless without militancy at the grass roots.[68] George Wiley drew connections between the general antiwelfare context in the early 1970s, and a growing distaste among activists for court-based strategies, when he suggested in 1971 that welfare recipients "fight on many fronts. . . . We must . . . fight at State Capitals and in the courts. But most of all we must organize and fight at the grass roots level as we have never done before."[69]

Figure 19. Jack R. Goldberg, New York City Commissioner of Social Services and defendant in the U.S. Supreme Court case *Goldberg v. Kelly*. Courtesy George Wiley Papers, Wisconsin Historical Society.

How to Kill an Organization

The forces arrayed against Beulah Sanders and other welfare rights leaders were simply too great to overcome by hard work or clever strategies. Political changes in the early 1970s drained the life out of welfare rights efforts at the local and national levels. East Coast organizer Faith Evans

commented: "the problems are overwhelming even for the experts. . . .
From the Federal Gov[ernment] on down the kinds of legislative
Repression our people are facing is tremendous."[70] Even some of the
best local and statewide organizing efforts hit brick walls in the context
of intense polarization around issues of racial and economic justice.
Barely a year after the high point of Operation New York, for example,
the once powerful New York City welfare rights movement was reduced
to using contributions from neighborhood groups and loans from individual members to pay its bills.[71]

The political changes of the early 1970s undermined fundraising
efforts by NWRO. The group's most important funding source was the
Interreligious Foundation for Community Organization (IFCO). IFCO
began in late 1966 with backing from liberal mainline Protestant
denominations and a few Jewish congregations. In 1969, the foundation
became embroiled in controversy by supporting a Black Economic
Development Conference that approved the "Black Manifesto" written
by James Forman of the Student Nonviolent Coordinating Committee.
The Manifesto called for $500 million in reparations for African Ameri-
can militant organizations from "racist white churches and syna-
gogues."[72] Several IFCO member organizations, including the American
Jewish Committee, withdrew from the coalition. At roughly the same
time, IFCO came under scrutiny by the Internal Revenue Service, which
had become one of the leading weapons in the Nixon administration's
war against its perceived enemies.[73] To save their own organization, staff
members of IFCO demanded greater precision about the use of their
funds. "We are eager to help NWRO and its important work to the greatest extent possible," the executive director wrote to Wiley, "but we also
have a substantial obligation to IFCO and its members and donors to
ensure that we do not jeopardize our own tax exempt position."[74] IFCO
stopped funding welfare rights entirely in 1972.[75]

With the NWRO headquarters struggling, it was difficult for elected
leaders such as Beulah Sanders and the few remaining staff members
to support local organizing. NWRO hosted a "survival celebration and
auction" at which Sanders and others attempted to raise money by invit-
ing bids for one of Representative Abzug's signature hats and a puppy
named "FAP."[76] Staff members continued using the *Welfare Fighter* newspaper to share information and ideas about how to get counsel for legal
problems.[77] However, these small gestures were undermined by NWRO's
inability to support its local affiliates. Mamie McPherson from Florida
offered a glimpse of the situation when she wrote complaining that she
had called "4 or 5 times they told me that they was not taking any more
phone call on them" because NWRO could no longer afford to accept
the charges.[78] Sue Berta Martin from the People's Rights Group in Ala-

bama wrote in August 1972 because she had not received her newspaper since June, and was informed that this was so because "there haven't been any. NWRO is in an extremely severe financial crisis and there is no money for mailings and the printing costs of the Fighter."[79]

Under relentless external pressure, the welfare rights movement crumbled from within. Members of individual groups fought battles among themselves; elected welfare recipient leaders sniped at professional staff; and they became increasingly suspicious of middle-class "Friends."[80] The conflicts bared problems that had been present at the movement's creation, especially the tensions inherent in collaboration between people of different classes, sexes, and races. Ruth Welfield, a local activist, wrote apoplectically to a white man who was supposed to be a Friend to groups in her area but whom she suspected of playing favorites among them: "Is this any way to run an airline?" she demanded to know.[81] One frustrated member of a Philadelphia welfare recipients' group offered a list of suggestions on "HOW TO KILL AN ORGANIZATION," including one that sounded particularly as if it was drawn from experience: "WHEN YOUR OPINION ON ANY MATTER IS REQUESTED AT A MEETING, REPLY THAT YOU HAVE NOTHING TO SAY. BUT AFTER THE MEETING, TELL EVERYONE HOW THINGS SHOULD BE DONE."[82]

The problems that appeared at the local, citywide, and statewide levels of the organization were present at the national level as well. Faced with the same pressures, national officers held tightly to their leadership positions, fought with whites and men on the NWRO staff, and suspected middle-class allies of the worst possible motives. When the movement lost its footing, most of the middle-class staff and Friends moved on to other organizations or causes. New York's Hulbert James had already left the NWRO national staff by 1972, as had former Brooklyn organizer Rhoda Linton. Attorney Carl Rachlin withdrew quietly in favor of other legal work and teaching.[83] Internal conflicts among the elected leaders of NWRO drove Eastern Regional representative Faith Evans to announce his resignation in November 1972.[84] "I had promised myself and others in this organization," he wrote, "that if I had ever gotten to the position in this organization where I would find myself fighting within the organization more than fighting the establishment then I would leave. In the last few months, I have found myself doing just that, spending 90% of my time in conflict with the leadership."[85] Wiley resigned a month later, effective January 31, 1973. He confessed that the organization had been in a severe financial crisis since the Children's March and Democratic National Convention, to the point where every single member of the twenty-five person staff had been laid off except for the bookkeepers.[86]

The decline of the national welfare rights movement accelerated dramatically after George Wiley left. Johnnie Tillmon, who succeeded him as executive director of NWRO, and Sanders, who continued as the elected chair, lacked his political and fundraising contacts. As African American welfare mothers, they were indelibly linked to one of the most unpopular causes of the early 1970s. "Strategies for Survival" was the theme of the national welfare rights conference in 1973.[87] But few such strategies were on the horizon.

One sign of the deep divisions within the welfare rights movement, and a source of division in itself, was the resignation of New York's Jennette Washington and a few other movement veterans. Washington, Etta Horn from Washington, D.C., and recipient leaders from Boston, Philadelphia, and several cities in New Jersey disagreed with recent decisions by Faith Evans to remove them from their leadership positions. Evans claimed that they were not following democratic procedures and that their groups had devolved into factionalism, while they claimed that his actions were antidemocratic and unfair.

Shortly after Jennette Washington was dropped from the NWRO leadership roster, she announced her support for a new National Unemployed and Welfare Rights Organization. This organization was backed by the National Caucus of Labor Committees, which competed with the Communist Party-U.S.A. for the distinction of occupying the furthest left position on the U.S. political spectrum.[88] In making her move to the sectarian Left, Washington criticized NWRO for having abandoned the goal of adequate income and suggested, as Wiley had done, that organizers focus on recruiting low-wage workers. "A lot of people think that there's a difference between people on welfare and the unemployed," Washington wrote. "But anybody knows that the only reason why there are so many people on welfare is because there aren't enough decent jobs."[89] Welfare rights activists had insisted for years that even "decent jobs" were not the sole answer to recipients' problems. Washington (like Wiley before her) sidestepped questions about women's needs, the work mothers do when they raise children, and the limitations of waged labor as the basis of citizenship, which had animated Citywide and NWRO since their founding.

Welfare rights leaders faced more bad news in 1973. The most unexpected was George Wiley's death in August. Just forty-two, he fell while sailing in rough weather. His two children, his only passengers, saw him fall from the boat and disappear.[90] Executive Director Tillmon and Associate Director Faith Evans (who returned to NWRO after Wiley left) reported that the Internal Revenue Service was breathing down their necks for back taxes. Despite a heroic fundraising effort, they confessed, the organization's debt stood at about $50,000. Moreover, they admitted that the staff was back down to a total of eight, "four of whom are recipients and who have been working without pay," and that the *Welfare Fighter* had not appeared since the prior October.[91] Despite signs of continued activism, NWRO ran out of funds for good within the year.[92]

Fiscal Crisis of the City

After the closing of the NWRO headquarters, local organizers and groups were largely on their own in their efforts to sustain the movement. In New York City, there was not much of a local organization for leaders such as Beulah Sanders to come home to. Factions and sectarianism were only part of the problem. Far more serious than the public departure of Jennette Washington, and the quieter exits made by middle-class allies, was the city's political and economic situation. By 1974, John Lindsay had been succeeded in the mayor's office by Abe Beame, a conventional Democratic Party politician. Rockefeller had stepped down as governor. When scandal forced Vice President Agnew and President Nixon to resign, President Gerald Ford chose Rockefeller—who had supported Nixon at the time of the Cambodia invasion and received kudos from the White House for his crackdown at Attica prison—as his vice president. New York City was deeply in debt. By the end of 1974, the city owed $13 billion, an increase of more than 300 percent over a decade. With FAP dead, the oil crisis afire in the Middle East and at gas pumps in the United States, and the economy in the throes of the high inflation and high unemployment that would later be dubbed "stagflation," there was little chance that the city could avoid a fiscal day of reckoning.[93]

Everything got worse in 1975. New York City's debt continued to climb, fueled in part by the extraordinary responsibility the city continued to assume for welfare costs. The bankers who had made the city's indebtedness possible grew skittish about the safety of their investments and aggressive in asserting their ideas about how New York should spend its resources. Financial leaders such as Walter Wriston of Citicorp and David Rockefeller of the Chase Manhattan Bank (brother to the former governor) refused to continue lending unless New York City curtailed some of its generous social policies. They argued that municipal employees, including welfare department caseworkers, were costing the city too much money, and that an open admissions policy at free city universities was ill-advised. Mayor Beame went hat in hand to Washington, D.C., to ask the White House for financial help. President Ford refused, offering as support for his decision the data on supposed welfare frauds that had become common fodder in the city's political discourse. The *Daily News* summarized the occasion in the immortal headline: "Ford to City: Drop Dead!"[94]

The problem of the New York City financial crisis was framed as one of bloated welfare budgets, greedy public employees, and excessive higher education for the immigrant and nonwhite working class. "By now," economist William Tabb commented early in 1976, "everyone knows how to solve the New York City fiscal crisis: stop giveaway programs and well-meaning but ineffectual social experiments, cut spending, resist unreasonable union demands and roll back past contract gains."[95] The Municipal Assistance Corporation, a new entity created by Governor Hugh Carey to buy the city's debt by selling bonds of its own, which was controlled by Wall Street financiers, offered clear directions to the city government. The financiers demanded that Mayor Beame cut welfare benefits, fire hundreds of municipal workers, freeze wages, and impose tuition fees at the city universities for the first time in their history. By one account, two fifths of African American municipal employees, and half of the Latino/a employees, were dropped from the city payroll.[96] The bankers' pressure worked to impose the kind of retrenchment in social provision that the government alone had not been able to effect during the postwar heyday of social movements in New York City.

New York City in the middle of a fiscal crisis was a depressing place in which to organize welfare recipients. But Beulah Sanders remained politically active. As NWRO collapsed, she received a foundation grant to support herself. She published a guide to the new Talmadge Amendment work requirement for recipients.[97] Sanders also allied more closely with white women from the women's liberation movement, which remained strong in New York City in the 1970s. In 1975, she marched for International Women's Day, demanding child care available twenty-four hours a day regardless of a family's income, immediate ratification of the Equal Rights Amendment, and a reinvestment of the military budget in "human needs."[98] In the late 1970s, she helped organize the National Welfare Rights Union, a coalition of local groups that attempted to replicate NWRO's strength although it lacked the institutional infrastructure that had existed before 1974. Detroit's Marian Kramer, who headed the Welfare Rights Union, commented years later: "Working with women like Beulah and the others helped me deepen my development. These were the true fighters. They nurtured a movement."[99]

Conclusion

In 1975, the *New Yorker* began publishing a series of articles by journalist Susan Sheehan about a woman welfare recipient in the borough of Brooklyn. Sheehan offered her readers a portrait she claimed as both "singular and representative" of Puerto Rican mothers whose families received public aid. She described a woman who was "generous and lazy," and truthful "except when truthfulness conflicts with her economic interests."[1] According to Sheehan, the woman she referred to as Mrs. Santana had "no interest in national or international events"; she had never "seen a play or circus, visited a museum, or belonged to a social or political organization."[2] Although the largest and most militant welfare clients' movement in the history of New York City and of the United States had barely passed from the scene, readers of the *New Yorker* learned at length about a poor woman's passivity, isolation, political apathy, and intellectual weakness.[3]

By the time Sheehan's stories appeared in print, public assistance for women and children had become an almost universally unpopular program. Representations of low-income women who relied on government aid had reverted to familiar stereotypes, even though ten years of welfare rights politics had revealed poor people who were energetic, eager to engage in collective action, concerned about their own and their children's futures, passionate about political affairs, and both strategically and analytically acute. In little more than a decade, the antiwelfare rhetoric that had been developed in the middle 1960s by conservatives such as William F. Buckley had been adopted by the mainstream media and the overwhelming majority of politicians. The welfare rights era was over.

The shift, from the heyday of claims for welfare rights to the antiwelfare era, was fueled by a dramatic realignment in electoral politics. In New York, this began with a turnabout within the Republican Party. Social policy moderates Nelson Rockefeller and John Lindsay were shunted to the sidelines of a political party both had hoped to lead. Try as they did to blend into their new environment by renouncing their own historic support for welfare and other government programs, neither man ever fully regained his standing among Republicans. Rockefeller, the more successful of the two chameleons, was rewarded only by a brief tenure as Gerald Ford's vice president. Within the Democratic Party, both locally in New York and nationally, the shift at the end of the 1960s was so profound that the party's leaders stopped defending the public assistance programs their predecessors had created just three decades earlier.

Why did the politics of welfare change at the end of the 1960s? The black freedom movement transformed political and social life in every community in the country, North as well as South. The movement raised expectations, introduced new strategies, and built a record of concrete successes. Moreover, from New York City's welfare department head-quarters, to the marble halls of Congress, government expanded in the 1960s in ways that allowed poor people and communities of color to turn their grievances into effective campaigns of lobbying, litigation, and civil disobedience. However, from the standpoint of many observers, the appearance on the public stage of African Americans, other people of color, and poor women and men, was a problem in itself. New Yorker Irene Gibbs personified many working- and middle-class New Yorkers' worst nightmares when she vocally refused to participate in the "Opera-tion Compass" employment training program. Even worse was Beulah Sanders's penchant for taking over public agencies and assuming the titles of their chief bureaucrats. The electoral change that ultimately brought down Mayor Lindsay and Governor Rockefeller was a response to Gibbs, Sanders, and thousands of others in the 1960s who claimed full citizenship in the country of their birth.

Political strategists had recognized changes in voting patterns in New York City as early as 1964. However, the "revolt of the white lower mid-dle class" named by journalist Pete Hamill did not fully coalesce until the end of the decade. This revolt was not merely a response by whites to political demands made by African Americans, Puerto Ricans, and Mexican Americans. It was a sharp rejection of the ideology of the wel-fare rights movement and the other social movements of the era. The centerpiece of this ideology was a demand for full citizenship in post-World War II society. Full citizenship meant equality across lines of race and class, for example, in the treatment of African American and Latina mothers by government administrators who were used to offering help primarily to white families. In the postwar United States, citizenship included the right to participate in the affluent society and in all the legal and political institutions that structured public life.

In New York City, public policy shifted in the early 1970s not only because of long-term electoral trends but also because of the specific series of events that plunged the city into bankruptcy. The fiscal crisis in New York was as much a political as an economic fact. It occurred in part because the city carried an unsustainable burden of public assistance costs, a product of design flaws in the Social Security Act of 1935 and tight-fisted budgeting by New York State. Between the 1930s and the middle 1960s, city officials made these costs bearable by driving people away from welfare offices and sometimes from New York itself with residency requirements, one-way bus tickets "home," and scarce information for clients about the benefits for which they qualified. The northern civil rights and welfare rights movements publicized these tactics and made many of them unusable. *King v. Smith*, the first U.S. Supreme Court case won by lawyers associated with the welfare movement, established formal entitlement to public assistance benefits, which made it even more difficult for the city to keep poor people from receiving aid.[4]

Mayor Lindsay knew from the beginning of his term in office that the welfare budget posed serious financial and political problems for him. As the budget ballooned, he came to believe that the federal government would eventually make the largest share of public assistance costs disappear. The Lindsay administration made promises to its diverse constituencies at a time when the mayor believed the Family Assistance Plan (FAP) or some other national income-maintenance program would reduce the city's welfare costs. When FAP failed and the Nixon administration swung to the antiwelfare Right, a financial crisis in New York City became far more likely. When the crisis finally arrived and the federal government once again failed to save the city, financiers took the opportunity to roll back what historian Joshua Freeman has aptly described as a welfare state in the five boroughs of New York.[5]

The welfare rights era ended because social and historical factors that were not under the control of Beulah Sanders or any other leaders conspired to make it end. This is not to say that welfare rights organizing ceased entirely after the middle 1970s, or that the idea of a guaranteed income completely lost its hold on the imaginations of activists or intellectuals. Welfare rights organizations across the United States continued to agitate for their members. Some of these lasted through the end of the twentieth century. But the welfare rights campaign lost its mainstream legitimacy and visibility; public aid recipients lost most of their ability to place new ideas on the national agenda.

Historical forces far from Citywide and NWRO were responsible for the movement's demise. But individual actions and decisions shaped this history in critical ways. If members of Citywide and NWRO had not responded to political hostility by tearing up offices and calling each other names, then the movement might have lasted somewhat longer than it did. If white voters in New York City and elsewhere had reacted to the freedom movement of the 1960s with more equanimity—and pol-

Figure 20. The legacy NWRO hoped to leave. Courtesy Social Action Collection, Wisconsin Historical Society.

iticians ranging from Barry Goldwater and Richard Nixon, to Nelson Rockefeller and John Lindsay, had not reanimated old stereotypes in order to improve their careers—then the politics of social policy might have turned out very differently from the way it did. U.S. citizens might well have won a guarantee of income security, a minimum income that would have transformed their relationships with their employers, their national government, and their intimate partners.

The guaranteed income would have provided a cushion to protect women, men, and children against poverty when work and marriage failed to do so. By substituting a universal benefit, available to all citizens who were poor, for the particularistic benefits that had been the trademark of the U.S. welfare state, this income program would have made social policy less segregated and stigmatizing than it had ever been before. It might have provided the basis for the kind of social solidarity that has too often been lacking in this diverse and divided country. By protecting all citizens from the depths of poverty, the United States could have prevented some of the destruction caused by the storms of globalization, ecological degradation, and social strife at the end of the twentieth century and beginning of the twenty-first.[6]

The desire to impose a work requirement upon welfare recipients "has nothing to do with economics," political theorist Judith Sklar wrote late in the twentieth century. "It is about citizenship."[7] For Beulah Sanders and Jennette Washington, Irene Gibbs and Joan Sunderland, Johnnie Tillmon and Joyce Burson, Faith Evans and Hulbert James, Rhoda Linton and George Wiley, welfare too was about citizenship. The women and men of the City-Wide Coordinating Committee of Welfare Groups and the National Welfare Rights Organization asked legislators, judges, and everyone else to treat welfare recipients as full participants in postwar United States.

"When they cease to earn," Sklar observed, "whatever the character of their work, Americans lose their standing in their communities. It is irrational and unfair, but it is a fundamental fact of life constituted of enduring and deeply entrenched social beliefs."[8] Welfare rights activists challenged this fundamental feature of Anglo-American political ideology, insisting that income received from a government program was at least as dignified as income from a job that reminded one of slavery. They argued that parents' work in raising children was worthy of respect, and that mothers in particular deserved support from the government. Scores of welfare recipients asserted standing in their communities by bringing fair hearing appeals against their caseworkers and local officials. Others lobbied, petitioned, organized voters, sent letters, protested, and participated in landmark court cases. They enjoyed a string of successes, demonstrating that "enduring and deeply entrenched social beliefs" are more flexible in response to popular pressure than they may at first appear. Ultimately they were defeated, leaving behind so few traces that it became the job of historians to remember them.

Appendix: Oral History Interviews

Burson, Joyce, by Nick Kotz and Mary Lynn Kotz
Day, Edwin, by Nick Kotz and Mary Lynn Kotz
Duncan, Ruby, by Nick Kotz and Mary Lynn Kotz
Edelman, Peter and Marian Wright Edelman, by Nick Kotz and Mary Lynn Kotz
Espada, Frank, by Felicia Kornbluh, by telephone
Evans, Faith, by Nick Kotz and Mary Lynn Kotz
Farmer, James, by Nick Kotz and Mary Lynn Kotz
Ginsberg, Mitchell, by Nick Kotz and Mary Lynn Kotz
Glynn, Thomas, by Felicia Kornbluh, by telephone
Heard, Inez, by Nick Kotz and Mary Lynn Kotz
Henry, Marcia, by Felicia Kornbluh, Berkeley, California
Horn, Etta, by Nick Kotz and Mary Lynn Kotz
James, Hulbert, by Nick Kotz
Jermany, Catherine, by Nick Kotz and Mary Lynn Kotz
Kramer, Marian, by Robert Mast (published in *Detroit Lives*)
Kydd, Andrea, by Felicia Kornbluh, New York
Law, Sylvia, by Felicia Kornbluh, New York
Linton, Rhoda, by Felicia Kornbluh, by telephone
McCalpin, William, by Olavi Maru, American Bar Foundation
Pastreich, William, by Felicia Kornbluh, by telephone
Piven, Frances Fox, by Felicia Kornbluh, New York
Powell, Lewis, by Olavi Maru, American Bar Foundation
Rachlin, Carl, by Thomas Hilbink
Reich, Charles, by Felicia Kornbluh, San Francisco
Sampson, Timothy, by Felicia Kornbluh, 1998, by telephone, and 2001, Oakland, California
Sanders, Beulah, by Nick Kotz and Mary Lynn Kotz
Shea, Gerald, by Felicia Kornbluh, Washington, D.C.
Steinem, Gloria, by Nick Kotz and Mary Lynn Kotz
Stone, Alan, by Felicia Kornbluh, New York
Szpak, Terry, by Nick Kotz and Mary Lynn Kotz
Tillmon, Johnnie, by Sherna Berger Gluck, Los Angeles
Tillmon, Johnnie, by Nick Kotz and Mary Lynn Kotz
West, Guida, by Felicia Kornbluh, New York
Williams, Anna Mae, by Nick Kotz and Mary Lynn Kotz

Abbreviations

ACLU	American Civil Liberties Union papers, Seeley-Mudd Manuscript Library, Princeton University, Princeton, N.J.
ACORN	Arkansas Community Organizations for Reform Now
ACORN	Association of Community Organizations for Reform Now
ADC	Aid to Dependent Children
AFDC	Aid to Families with Dependent Children
AFSCME	American Federation of State, County, and Municipal Employees
Am. News	*Amsterdam News* newspaper, New York
ANC	Aid to Needy Children, California public assistance program
Bancroft	Bancroft Library, University of California at Berkeley
Becker	Dismas Becker papers, Wisconsin Historical Society, Madison
B-WAC	Brooklyn Welfare Action Council
CAP	Community Action Program
Citywide	City-Wide Coordinating Committee of Welfare Groups, New York City
Conf.	Confidential Subject Files, Mayoral Papers, New York City Municipal Archives
CORE	Congress of Racial Equality
CUSA	Christians United for Social Action
Dept.	Departmental Files, New York City Municipal Archives
FAP	Family Assistance Plan
Freedman	Henry Freedman personal papers, National Center for Law and Economic Justice, New York
Friedan	Betty Friedan papers, Schlesinger Library, Radcliffe Institute for Advanced Study, Cambridge, Mass.
GAI	Guaranteed Adequate Income
Groppi	Father James Groppi papers, Wisconsin Historical Society
HEW	U.S. Department of Health, Education, and Welfare

HRA	Human Resources Administration, New York City, combining functions of the former Welfare Department and local War on Poverty
IFCO	Interreligious Foundation for Community Organization
JDE	John D. Ehrlichman papers, Nixon Presidential Materials Project, National Archives and Records Administration II, College Park, Maryland
Kotz	Nick Kotz papers, Wisconsin Historical Society
LAW	League for Adequate Welfare
LAWMC	Los Angeles Women's Movement(s) Collection, Oral History Archives, California State University at Los Angeles
LCDC	Lawyers Constitutional Defense Committee
LDF	NAACP Legal Defense and Educational Fund
Lindsay	Mayor John V. Lindsay papers, New York City Municipal Archives
Linton	Rhoda Linton personal papers, privately held
MFY	Mobilization for Youth, New York
MWRO	Massachusetts Welfare Rights Organization papers, Wisconsin Historical Society
NAACP	National Association for the Advancement of Colored People
NASW	Library of the National Association of Social Workers, Washington, D.C.
NCC	National Coordinating Committee of the National Welfare Rights Organization
NCLEJ	National Center on Law and Economic Justice (formerly Center for Social Welfare Policy and Law), New York
NFB	National Federation of the Blind
Nixon	Richard Nixon Presidential Materials Project, National Archives and Records Administration II
NOW	National Organization for Women
NOW!	Newsletter of the National Welfare Rights Organization, 1966-69, Library, Wisconsin Historical Society
NWRO	National Welfare Rights Organization papers, Moorland-Spingarn Research Center, Howard University, Washington, D.C.
NYT	*New York Times*
OEO	U.S. Office of Economic Opportunity
Padwee	Michael Padwee papers, Tamiment Library and Robert F. Wagner Labor Archives, New York University, New York

Pamphlets	Pamphlets Collection, Library, Wisconsin Historical Society
PAT	Parents and Taxpayers
Piven	Frances Fox Piven personal papers, privately held
P/RAC	Poverty/Rights Action Center
Sampson	Tim Sampson papers, Center for Third World Organizing, Oakland, California (relocated to San Francisco State University)
Sampson (2)	Tim Sampson personal papers, privately held
SCLC	Southern Christian Leadership Conference
SEDFRE	Scholarship, Education, and Defense Fund for Racial Equality papers, Wisconsin Historical Society
SNCC	Student Nonviolent Coordinating Committee
Social Action	Social Action Vertical Files, Wisconsin Historical Society
Social Protest	Social Protest collection, Bancroft
SSEU	Social Service Employees Union papers, Tamiment Library and Robert F. Wagner Labor Archives
SSI	Supplemental Security Income
Subj.	Subject Files, Mayoral papers, New York City Municipal Archives
TLI	*Tell It Like It Is*, newsletter of the City-Wide Coordinating Committee of Welfare Groups, New York, Sampson
USDA	United States Department of Agriculture
VISTA	Volunteers in Service to America
Wagner	Mayor Robert F. Wagner, Jr., papers, New York City Municipal Archives
WECC	West End Community Council of Louisville, Kentucky, papers, Wisconsin Historical Society
Welfare Fighter	Newsletter of the National Welfare Rights Organization, 1969-1974, Wisconsin Historical Society
Welfare Righter	Newsletter of the City-Wide Coordinating Committee of Welfare Groups, New York, Sampson
WHCF	White House Central Files, Nixon Presidential Materials Project
WHSF	White House Special Files, Nixon Presidential Materials Project
Wickenden	Elizabeth Wickenden papers, Wisconsin Historical Society
Wiley	George Wiley papers, Wisconsin Historical Society
WIN/WIP	Work Incentive Program

Notes

Preface

1. Matthew Countryman, *Up South: Civil Rights and Black Power in Philadelphia* (Philadelphia: University of Pennsylvania Press, 2005); Rhonda Y. Williams, *The Politics of Public Housing: Black Women's Struggles Against Urban Inequality* (New York: Oxford University Press, 2005); Martha Biondi, *To Stand and Fight: The Struggle for Civil Rights in Postwar New York City* (Cambridge, Mass.: Harvard University Press, 2003); Robert O. Self, *American Babylon: Race and the Struggle for Postwar Oakland* (Princeton, N.J.: Princeton University Press, 2003); Jeanne Theoharis and Komozi Woodard, eds., *Freedom North: Black Freedom Struggles Outside the South, 1940–1980* (New York: Palgrave Macmillan, 2003); Heather Ann Thompson, *Whose Detroit? Politics, Labor and Race in a Modern American City* (Ithaca, N.Y.: Cornell University Press, 2001); Thomas J. Sugrue, *The Origins of the Urban Crisis: Race and Inequality in Postwar Detroit* (Princeton, N.J.: Princeton University Press, 1996); and Arnold Hirsch, *Making The Second Ghetto: Race and Housing in Chicago* (Cambridge: Cambridge University Press, 1983.

2. Sex and gender are central to Williams, *Politics of Public Housing*; Christina Greene, *Our Separate Ways: Women and the Black Freedom Movement in Durham, North Carolina* (Chapel Hill: University of North Carolina Press, 2005); and, on earlier periods, Sarah Deutsch, *Women and the City: Gender, Space, and Power in Boston, 1870–1940* (New York: Oxford University Press, 2000), and Christine Stansell, *City of Women: Sex and Class in New York, 1789–1860* (Urbana: University of Illinois Press, 1987). These concerns are also central to the work of historian Lisa Levenstein, who helped me to clarify the points in this section. Questions of sex, gender, and sexuality do not play a large role in Self, *American Babylon*; Sugrue, *Origins of the Urban Crisis*; or Hirsch, *Making the Second Ghetto*.

Introduction

1. "NWRO Takes Over . . . ," NWRO leaflet, n.d. [May 1970], 17/NWRO—Newsclips '70, Kotz. See also David Holmberg, "Protesters Occupy Finch's Office," *Evening Star* (Washington, D.C.), May 13, 1970, 1; Haynes Johnson, "Finch Takes Abuse Calmly as Protesters Seize Office," *Washington Post*, May 14, 1970, 1, A6; "NWRO Liberates Finch's Office," *Welfare Fighter* 1, 9 (May 1970): 12; "Angry Rally Backs H.E.W. Liberators," *Welfare Fighter* 1, 10 (June 1970): 1, 8; letter from George Wiley, Executive Director, National Welfare Rights Organization, to Editors, *Washington Post*, May 18, 1970, 17/FAP (Wiley Words) (NWRO Views 1970), Kotz; Beulah Sanders, interview with Nick Kotz and Mary Lynn Kotz, 1974, 7–8, 26/Beulah Sanders Interview, Kotz; Guida West, *The National Welfare Rights Movement: The Social Protest of Poor Women* (New York: Praeger,

1981), 303; and Nick Kotz and Mary Lynn Kotz, *A Passion for Equality: George A. Wiley and the Movement* (New York: Norton, 1977), 268.

2. Sanders, with Kotz and Kotz, 7.

3. For the income guarantee as a form of support especially for women see Anne Alstott, "Good for Women," in *What's Wrong with a Free Lunch?* ed. Philippe van Parijs (Boston: Beacon Press, 2001), 75–79. For other justifications and discussions see Guy Standing, ed., *Promoting Income Security as a Right: Europe and North America* (London: Anthem Press/International Labor Organisation, 2004), esp. Theresa Funiciello, "On a Path to Just Distribution: The Caregiver Credit Campaign," 359–64; and Standing, *Beyond the New Paternalism: Basic Security as Equality* (London: Verso, 2002). On the ways gender has structured social policies in the United States and modern Europe, see my "Women's History with the Politics Left In: Feminist Studies of the Welfare State," in *Exploring Women's Studies: Looking Forward, Looking Back*, ed. Carol Berkin, Judith Pinch, and Carole Appel (New York: Pearson Prentice-Hall, 2006), 236–55; Alice Kessler-Harris, *In Pursuit of Equity: Women, Men and the Quest for Economic Citizenship in 20th-Century America* (New York: Oxford University Press, 2001); Nancy J. Hirschmann and Ulrike Liebert, "Engendering Welfare, Degendering Care: Theoretical and Comparative Perspectives on the United States and Europe," in *Women and Welfare: Theory and Practice in the United States and Europe*, ed. Hirschmann and Liebert (New Brunswick, N.J.: Rutgers University Press, 2001), 1–19; Sonya Michel, *Children's Interests/Mothers Rights: The Shaping of America's Child Care Policy* (New Haven, Conn.: Yale University Press, 1999); Linda Kerber, *No Constitutional Right to be Ladies: Women and the Obligations of Citizenship* (New York: Hill and Wang, 1998); Joanne Goodwin, *Gender and the Politics of Welfare Reform: Mothers' Pensions in Chicago, 1911–1929* (Chicago: University of Chicago Press, 1997); Linda Gordon, *Pitied But Not Entitled: Single Mothers and the History of Welfare* (New York: Free Press, 1994); Molly Ladd-Taylor, *Mother-Work: Women, Child Welfare, and the State, 1890–1930* (Urbana: University of Illinois Press, 1994); Seth Koven and Sonya Michel, eds., *Mothers of a New World: Maternalist Politics and the Origins of Welfare States* (New York: Routledge, 1993); Theda Skocpol, *Protecting Soldiers and Mothers: The Political Origins of Social Policy in the United States* (Cambridge, Mass.: Belknap Press of Harvard University Press, 1992); Mimi Abramovitz, *Regulating the Lives of Women* (Boston: South End Press, 1988); Sylvia Law, "Women, Work, Welfare, and the Preservation of Patriarchy," *University of Pennsylvania Law Review* 131 (May 1983): 1251–1331; and Carol Brown, "Mothers, Fathers, and Children: From Private to Public Patriarchy," in *Women and Revolution*, ed. Lydia Sargent (Boston: South End Press, 1981), 239–67. For the general idea that welfare states stratify societies as much as they create social solidarity, see Gösta Esping Anderson, *The Three Worlds of Welfare Capitalism* (Princeton, N.J.: Princeton University Press, 1990).

4. For Beulah Sanders's opposition to the war in Vietnam, see Lacey Fosburgh, "Women's Unit Bids Congress Shun War to Aid Human Needs," *NYT*, June 17, 1969, 37; "Mrs. Sanders Speaks At DC Antiwar Rally," *Welfare Fighter* 1, 9 (May 1970): 1; John Herbers, "Big Capital Rally Asks U.S. Pullout in Southeast Asia," *NYT*, May 10, 1970, 1, 24; and C. Gerald Fraser, "Antiwar Leaders Plan Demonstrations at Prisons," *NYT*, September 29, 1971, 14. For the welfare rights movement and the war, see Doris Doughty, "April 15th Actions—New York," *Welfare Fighter* 1, 8 (April 1970): 1; "April 15th—National Priorities Day," *Welfare Fighter* 1, 7 (March 1970): 1; "Summary of Priorities Committee," *Welfare Fighter* 1, 6 (February 1970): 1; and NWRO Pamphlet, "STOP the WAR on us POOR," n.d. [March–April 1970], 7/11, Wiley.

5. For NWRO membership, see generally, Assorted membership tables, 8/4, Wiley. For the 540 groups, see "1971 Membership Lists, by Region," 1971/ Regional Group Lists—1971, NWRO. For NWRO and its local affiliates as black women's organizations, see Premilla Nadasen, *Welfare Warriors: The Welfare Rights Movement in the United States* (New York: Routledge, 2005); Christina Greene, *Our Separate Ways: Women and the Black Freedom Movement in Durham, North Carolina* (Chapel Hill: University of North Carolina Press, 2005), 99, 170; Deborah Gray White, *Too Heavy a Load: Black Women in Defense of Themselves* (New York: Norton, 1999), 223–42; and Paula Giddings, *When and Where I Enter: The Impact of Black Women on Race and Sex in America* (New York: Bantam, 1984), 312–13, 326.

6. For the terminology, see Jeanne Theoharis and Komozi Woodard, eds., *Freedom North: Black Freedom Struggles Outside the South, 1940–1980* (New York: Palgrave Macmillan, 2003); and Steven Lawson, "Freedom Then, Freedom Now: The Historiography of the Civil Rights Movement," *American Historical Review* 96 (April 1991): 456–71.

7. On African American feminism generally, see Winifred Breines, *The Trouble Between Us: An Uneasy History of White and Black Women in the Feminist Movement* (New York: Oxford University Press, 2006), 117–91; Kimberly Springer, *Living for the Revolution: Black Feminist Organizations, 1968–1980* (Durham, N.C.: Duke University Press, 2005); Benita Roth, *Separate Roads to Feminism: Black, Chicana, and White Feminist Movements in America's Second Wave* (Cambridge: Cambridge University Press, 2004); Jennifer Nelson, *Women of Color and the Reproductive Rights Movement* (New York: New York University Press, 2003); White, *Too Heavy a Load*, 212–22, 242–56; Giddings, *When and Where I Enter*, 337–48; and Michele Wallace, *Black Macho and the Myth of the Superwoman*, rev. ed. (1979; London: Verso, 1996).

8. For attempts to build bridges between NWRO and white feminists, see letter from George Wiley, Executive Director, NWRO, to Congresswoman Elect Bela [*sic*] Abzug, New York City, New York, November 16, 1970, 21/6, Wiley; letter from Aileen Hernandez, President, National Organization for Women, to Mr. George Wiley, Welfare Rights Organization, Washington, D.C., December 15, 1970, and attached statement, "WOMEN IN POVERTY," Adopted by the Executive Committee of the National Organization for Women, November 29, 1970, 21/6, Wiley; Frances Fox Piven, interview with Felicia Kornbluh, December 5, 1995, informal notes in possession of the author, n.p.; Gloria Steinem, Interview with Nick Kotz and Mary Lynn Kotz, January 25, 1975, 25/Gloria Steinem Interview, Kotz; Martha F. Davis, "Welfare Rights and Women's Rights in the 1960s," in *Integrating the Sixties: The Origins, Structures, and Legitimacy of Public Policy in a Turbulent Decade*, ed. Brian Balogh (University Park: Pennsylvania State University Press, 1996), 144-65; West, *National Welfare Rights Movement*, 256–58; and Kotz and Kotz, *Passion for Equality*, 289. For conflicts between white feminists and welfare rights leaders over the issue of waged work, see U.S. Congress, Joint Economic Committee, Subcommittee on Fiscal Policy, *Income Maintenance Programs—Hearings*, Ninetieth Congress, Second Session, June 11, 12, 13, 18, 19, 25, 26, 27, 1968, vol. 1, 76–79; and discussion in Chapter 4, below.

9. "Cuts Are Coming—Cuts Are Here," *Welfare Fighter* 2, 8 (October 1971): 2; and "Fighting Back at Cuts," ibid., 10.

10. A local case study is essential to the study of twentieth-century politics because much political power was exercised, and fought, at the local level. See discussions in Michael Willrich, *City of Courts: Socializing Justice in Progressive Era Chicago* (Cambridge: Cambridge University Press, 2003), esp. 314–15; and Thomas J. Sugrue, "All Politics is Local: The Persistence of Localism in Twenti-

eth-Century America," in *The Democratic Experiment*, ed. Meg Jacobs, William J. Novak, and Julian E. Zelizer (Princeton: Princeton University Press, 2003), 301–26. However, the local alone is not enough to fully illuminate U.S. political history, and so I combine local and national-level data.

11. William Stringfellow, *My People Is the Enemy: An Autobiographical Polemic* (New York: Holt, Rinehart, and Winston, 1964); Claude Brown, *Manchild in the Promised Land* (New York: Signet, 1965); Piri Thomas, *Down These Mean Streets* (New York: Vintage, 1967); Frank Gell (pseudonym), *The Black Badge: Confessions of a Caseworker* (New York: Harper and Row, 1969); James Graham, *The Enemies of the Poor* (New York: Random House, 1970); and Susan Sheehan, *A Welfare Mother* (New York: Mentor Books, 1977). The articles in Sheehan's book appeared originally in the *New Yorker* in 1975 and 1976.

12. See discussion in Chapters 4 and 7, below.

13. For assessments of the Nixon welfare reform proposal, see Chapter 6, below; Bruce Schulman, *The Seventies: The Great Shift in American Culture, Society, and Politics* (New York: Da Capo Press, 2002), 32–35; Alice O'Connor, *Poverty Knowledge: Social Science, Social Policy, and the Poor in Twentieth-Century U.S. History* (Princeton, N.J.: Princeton University Press, 2001), 222–26; Joan Hoff, *Nixon Reconsidered* (New York: Basic Books, 1994), 122–32; Vincent Burke and Vee Burke, *Nixon's Good Deed: Welfare Reform* (New York: Columbia University Press, 1974); and Daniel Patrick Moynihan, *The Politics of a Guaranteed Income: The Nixon Administration and the Family Assistance Plan* (New York: Vintage, 1973). On the President's Commission on Income Maintenance, see Michael B. Katz, *The Undeserving Poor: From the War on Poverty to the War on Welfare* (New York: Pantheon, 1989), 103–5; President's Commission on Income Maintenance Programs, *Poverty amid Plenty: The American Paradox* (Washington, D.C.: Government Printing Office [GPO], 1969); President's Commission, *Background Papers* (Washington, D.C.: GPO, 1970); and President's Commission, *Technical Papers* (Washington, D.C.: GPO, 1970). For the NWRO income plan, see "Adequate Income NOW!" *Welfare Fighter*, Special Edition (1970): 1; and National Welfare Rights Organization, "NWRO Adequate income plan—$5500 or Fight!" April 1970, 1, Pamphlets.

14. On McGovern and the "demogrant," see Alan Stone, interview with Felicia Kornbluh, New York City, February 11, 1997, 8, transcript in possession of the author; Mitchell Ginsberg, interview with Nick Kotz and Mary Lynn Kotz, n.d., 11, 24/Mitchell Ginsberg Interview, Kotz; Hunter S. Thompson, *Fear and Loathing: On the Campaign Trail '72* (New York: Warner Books, 1973), 262; and Jack Rosenthal, "Growth of an Issue: McGovern Dilemma," *NYT*, July 8, 1972, 10.

15. See discussion in Chapter 7, below. On public sector unions and the New York fiscal crisis, see Joshua Freeman, *Working-Class New York: Life and Labor Since World War II* (New York: New Press, 2000), 265. On the lawyers, see Martha Davis, *Brutal Need: Lawyers and the Welfare Rights Movement, 1960–1973* (New Haven, Conn.: Yale University Press, 1992).

16. For the feminist victories and near-victories, see Estelle Freedman, *No Turning Back: The History of Feminism and the Future of Women* (New York: Ballantine Books, 2002), 85; Ruth Rosen, *The World Split Open: How the Modern Women's Movement Changed America* (New York: Penguin, 2000), 88–90; and Sara Evans, *Born for Liberty: A History of Women in America* (New York: Free Press, 1989), 290–92. On the debate over the Equal Rights Amendment, see Kerber, *No Constitutional Right*, 382–87; Jane DeHart Matthews and Donald Matthews, *Sex, Gender,*

and the Politics of the ERA: A State and a Nation (New York: Oxford University Press, 1990); and Jane Mansbridge, *Why We Lost the ERA* (Chicago: University of Chicago Press, 1986).

17. James Patterson, *America's Struggle Against Poverty in the Twentieth Century*, rev. ed. (Cambridge, Mass.: Harvard University Press, 2000), 71–75; Michael B. Katz, *In the Shadow of the Poorhouse: A Social History of Welfare in America* (New York: Basic Books, 1986), 267–68; and Deborah A. Stone, *The Disabled State* (Philadelphia: Temple University Press, 1984), 119–22.

18. John Mica (R-Fl.), quoted in James Carville, *We're Right, They're Wrong: A Handbook for Spirited Progressives* (New York: Simon and Schuster, 1996), 31.

19. Gwendolyn Mink, *Welfare's End* (Ithaca, N.Y.: Cornell University Press, 1998). For analyses of the law, see Eileen Boris, "Scholarship and Activism: The Case of Welfare Justice"; Eva Feder Kittay, "Dependency, Equality, and Welfare"; Sonya Michel, "Childcare and Welfare (In)Justice"; Gwendolyn Mink, "The Lady and the Tramp (II): Feminist Welfare Politics, Poor Single Mothers, and the Challenge of Welfare Justice"; and Felicia Kornbluh, "The Goals of the National Welfare Rights Movement: Why We Need Them Thirty Years Later," all in *Feminist Studies* 24, 1 (Spring 1998): 27–78.

20. On the Kensington Welfare Rights Union, see David Zucchino, *Myth of the Welfare Queen: A Pulitzer Prize-Winning Journalist's Portrait of Women on the Line* (New York: Touchstone/Simon and Schuster, 1999). For other welfare rights activity after the heyday of NWRO, see Annelise Orleck, *Storming Caesar's Palace: How Black Mothers Fought Their Own War on Poverty* (Boston: Beacon Press, 2005); Catherine Pelissier Kingfisher, *Women in the American Welfare Trap* (Philadelphia: University of Pennsylvania Press, 1996); Teresa Funiciello, *Tyranny of Kindness: Dismantling the Welfare System to End Poverty in America* (New York: Atlantic Monthly Press, 1993); and Susan Handley Hertz, *The Welfare Mothers Movement: A Decade of Change for Poor Women?* (Washington, D.C.: University Press of America, 1981).

21. The legislation was drafted with the help of the Women's Committee of 100 advocacy group. Author's notes.

22. Institut de Drets Humans de Catalunya, Program, Seminar I, "The Right to a Basic Income: Egalitarian Democracy," Dialogue on Human Rights, Emerging Needs and New Commitments, Barcelona Forum 2004; and author's notes. Basic Income Guarantee advocates meet biennially and communicate regularly via the Basic Income Earth Network (BIEN), http://www.basicincome.org or bien@etes.ucl.ac.be (as of July 2006). For discussions of the basic income, see Standing, ed., *Promoting Income Security as a Right*; Standing, *Beyond the New Paternalism*; van Parijs, ed., *What's Wrong with a Free Lunch?*; Michael Hardt and Antonio Negri, *Empire* (Cambridge, Mass.: Harvard University Press, 2000), 403; Bruce Ackerman and Anne Alstott, *The Stakeholder Society* (New Haven, Conn.: Yale University Press, 1999); and Rik van Berkel, Harry Coenen, and Ruud Vlek, eds., *Beyond Marginality? Social Movements of Social Security Claimants in the European Union* (Brookfield, Vt.: Ashgate, 1998).

23. Erik Eckholm, "City by City, an Antipoverty Group Plants Seeds of Change," *NYT*, June 26, 2006, 12; Jon Gertner, "What Is a Living Wage?" *NYT Magazine*, January 15, 2006, 38–45; Rebecca Gordon, "Cruel and Usual: How Welfare 'Reform' Punishes Poor People," Applied Research Center, Oakland, Calif., 2001; GROWL Principles, Center for Third World Organizing, Oakland, Calif., n.d.; Tim Sampson, "The Welfare Rights Movement," *Social Policy* 30, 2 (Winter 1999): 51–53; Gary Delgado, *Organizing the Movement: The Roots and*

Growth of ACORN (Philadelphia: Temple University Press, 1986); and Frances Fox Piven, Wade Rathke, Hulbert James, Rhoda Linton, Bill Pastreich, Jackie Pope, Theresa Funiciello, and Delgado, "National Welfare Rights Organization: At the Crossroads of Race, Class, and Gender," Transcript, National Organizers Alliance National Gathering, Jekyll Island, Georgia, February 2, 1996.

24. I draw here upon scholarship that uses, and debates, the "Resource Mobilization" theory of the rise of social protest movements. See Robert Korstad, *Civil Rights Unionism: Tobacco Workers and the Struggle for Democracy in the Mid-Twentieth-Century South* (Chapel Hill: University of North Carolina Press, 2003), 7; William Gamson and Emilie Schmeidler, "Organizing the Poor: An Argument with Frances Fox Piven and Richard A. Cloward's *Poor People's Movements,*" in *The Breaking of the American Social Compact,* ed. Frances Fox Piven and Richard A. Cloward (New York: Free Press, 1999), 307–27; Piven and Cloward, "Disruption and Organization: A Reply to Gamson and Schmeidler," *Breaking of the Social Compact,* 329–44; Aldon Morris, *The Origins of the Civil Rights Movement: Black Communities Organizing for Change* (New York: Free Press, 1984), 275–86; and Linda Majka and Theo Majka, *Farm Workers, Agribusiness, and the State* (Philadelphia: Temple University Press, 1982). I have also learned from state-centered theories of social change, which emphasize the structure of the U.S. government to explain much of what has distinguished U.S. history from the history of comparably industrialized European countries. See, in particular, Skocpol, *Protecting Soldiers and Mothers;* Ira Katznelson and Aristide Zolberg, eds., *Working-Class Formation: Nineteenth-Century Patterns in Western Europe and the United States* (Princeton, N.J.: Princeton University Press, 1986); and Peter Evans, Dietrich Rueschemeyer, and Theda Skocpol, eds., *Bringing the State Back In* (Cambridge: Cambridge University Press, 1985).

25. I discuss NWRO and citizenship in Kornbluh, "The Goals of the National Welfare Rights Movement." The literature on citizenship, considered as a category of social membership rather than as a formal legal category, is vast. Among the sources on which I have drawn are Michael Katz, *The Price of Citizenship: Redefining the American Welfare State* (New York: Metropolitan Books, 2001); Shane Phelan, *Sexual Strangers: Gays, Lesbians, and Dilemmas of Citizenship* (Philadelphia: Temple University Press, 2001); Rogers Smith, *Civic Ideals: Conflicting Visions of Citizenship in U.S. History* (New Haven, Conn.: Yale University Press, 1997); Nancy Fraser, "From Redistribution to Recognition: Dilemmas of Justice in a 'Post-Socialist' Age," in her *Justice Interruptus: Critical Reflections on the "Postsocialist" Condition* (New York: Routledge, 1997), 11–39; Jeremy Waldron, "Social Citizenship and the Defense of Welfare Provision," in his *Liberal Rights: Collected Papers, 1981-1991* (Cambridge: Cambridge University Press, 1993), 271–308; Nancy Fraser and Linda Gordon, "Contract Versus Charity: Why Is There No Social Citizenship in the United States?" *Socialist Review* 22 (July–September 1992): 45–67; Judith N. Shklar, *American Citizenship: The Quest for Inclusion* (Cambridge, Mass.: Harvard University Press, 1991); John Rawls, *A Theory of Justice* (Cambridge, Mass.: Harvard University Press, 1971); and T. H. Marshall, "Citizenship and Social Class," in Marshall, *Citizenship and Social Class, and Other Essays* (Cambridge: Cambridge University Press, 1950), 1–85.

26. Pete Hamill, "The Revolt of the White Lower Middle Class," *New York Magazine,* April 14, 1969, 24–29.

27. Norman Atkins, "Governor Get-A-Job: Tommy Thompson," *NYT Magazine,* January 15, 1995, 22. For the welfare mothers' takeover of the Wisconsin state legislature, see Bernice Buresh, "Protestors Turn Decorum at Capitol into

Turmoil," *Milwaukee Sentinel*, September 30, 1969, n.p., 16/11, Groppi; [Liberation News Service], "Bayonets Against Mothers in Madison," *Welfare Fighter* 1, 2 (October 1969): 1; "Wisconsin Mothers Sit-In," *Welfare Fighter* 1, 2 (October 1969): 4; and Raymond Snyder, son of Phyllis (Mothers Forward WRO—Fond du Lac, Wisconsin), "Dissent—It's [*sic*] Place in America," reprinted in *Welfare Fighter* 1, 8 (April 1970): 5.

28. Charles Morris, *The Cost of Good Intentions: New York City and the Liberal Experiment, 1960–1975* (New York: Norton, 1980), esp. 67–71. For a similar argument, see Vincent J. Cannato, *The Ungovernable City: John V. Lindsay and His Struggle to Save New York* (New York: Basic Books, 2001), 540–42.

29. See especially Jim Sleeper, *Liberal Racism* (New York: Viking, 1997), 59; Sleeper, *The Closest of Strangers: Liberalism and the Politics of Race in New York* (New York: Norton, 1990), 91–94; Thomas B. Edsall with Mary Edsall, *Chain Reaction: The Impact of Race, Rights, and Taxes on American Politics* (New York: Norton, 1992), 72; and Moynihan, *Politics of a Guaranteed Income*, 226, 236–37. On FAP and NWRO, see also Katz, *In the Shadow*, 253–54; and Patterson, *America's Struggle*, 153, 180–81.

30. Mary Ann Glendon, *Rights Talk: The Impoverishment of Political Discourse* (New York: Free Press, 1991); Gerald Rosenberg, *The Hollow Hope: Can Courts Bring About Social Change?* (Chicago: University of Chicago Press, 1991); Nelson Lichtenstein, *State of the Union: A Century of American Labor* (Princeton, N.J.: Princeton University Press, 2002), 178, 181, 192; and Alan Brinkley, *The End of Reform: New Deal Liberalism in Recession and War* (New York: Knopf, 1995).

31. Nicholas Lemann, *The Promised Land: The Great Black Migration and How it Changed America* (New York: Knopf, 1991); Charles Murray, *Losing Ground: American Social Policy, 1950–1980* (New York: Basic Books, 1984), 181; and Daniel Patrick Moynihan, *Maximum Feasible Misunderstanding: Community Action in the War on Poverty* (New York: Free Press, 1969). For a more complete discussion of this literature, see my "Why Gingrich? Welfare Rights and Racial Politics, 1965–1995," in *Race Consciousness: African American Studies for the New Century*, ed. Jeffrey Tucker and Judith Jackson Fossett (New York: New York University Press, 1997), 193–207.

32. H. R. Haldeman, *The Haldeman Diaries: Inside the Nixon White House* (New York: Berkley Books, 1995), July 13, 1970, 218; and see discussion in Chapter 6, below.

33. Patricia Williams, *The Alchemy of Race and Rights* (Cambridge, Mass.: Harvard University Press, 1991). See also Kimberlé Crenshaw, Neil Gotanda, Gary Peller, and Kendall Thomas, eds., *Critical Race Theory: The Key Writings That Formed the Movement* (New York: New Press, 1995).

34. I have written on this point at greater length in "To Fulfill Their 'Rightly Needs': Consumerism and the National Welfare Rights Movement," *Radical History Review* 69 (Fall 1997): 76–113. For other discussions of consumerism as a basis for oppositional politics, see Lizabeth Cohen, *A Consumer's Republic: The Politics of Mass Consumption in Modern America* (New York: Knopf, 2003); Lawrence Glickman, "The Strike in the Temple of Consumption: Consumer Activism and Twentieth-Century American Political Culture," *Journal of American History* 99 (June 2001): 99–128; Dana Frank, *Buy American: The Untold Story of Economic Nationalism* (Boston: Beacon Press, 1999); Annelise Orleck, *Common Sense and a Little Fire: Women and Working-Class Politics in the United States, 1900–1965* (Chapel Hill: University of North Carolina Press, 1995); Frank, *Purchasing Power: Consumer Organizing, Gender, and the Seattle Labor Movement, 1919–1929*

(Cambridge: Cambridge University Press, 1994); and Glickman, "Inventing the 'American Standard of Living': Gender, Race and Working Class Identity, 1880–1925," *Labor History* 34, 2–3 (Spring–Summer 1993): 221–35. For discussions of consumption, gender, and citizenship, see Mary Louise Roberts, "Gender, Consumption, and Commodity Culture," *American Historical Review* 103, 3 (June 1998): 817–44; Victoria de Grazia, ed, *The Sex of Things: Gender and Consumption in Historical Perspective* (Berkeley: University of California Press, 1996), especially introductory essays by de Grazia and Belinda Davis, "Food Scarcity and the Empowerment of the Female Consumer in World War I Berlin," 287–310; and Jacqueline Dirks, "Complicating the Female Consumer," Berkshire Conference on the History of Women, June 9, 1996, in author's possession. For consumerism and the welfare rights movement, see, in addition to my work, Matthew Countryman, *Up South: Civil Rights and Black Power in Philadelphia* (Philadelphia: University of Pennsylvania Press, 2006), 272–73; and Nadasen, *Welfare Warriors*, 113–17.

35. Natalie Zemon Davis, *The Return of Martin Guerre* (Cambridge, Mass.: Harvard University Press, 1983), 125.

Chapter 1. Inventing Welfare Rights

1. Beulah Sanders, interview with Nick Kotz and Mary Lynn Kotz, 1974, 12, 26/Beulah Sanders Oral History, Kotz. For earlier examples of poor people's protest in New York City, see Franklin Folsom, *America Before Welfare* (New York: New York University Press, 1991), 108–25, 194–97, 469–71. On the national mobilization of the poor during the Depression of the 1930s, see Paul Dickson and Thomas B. Allen, *The Bonus Army: An American Epic* (New York: Walker and Company, 2004). On the most renowned mobilization in the late nineteenth century, see Carlos Schwantes, *Coxey's Army: An American Odyssey* (Lincoln: University of Nebraska Press, 1985).

2. Poverty/Rights Action Center, "Round-Up of June 30th Welfare Demonstrations," June 28, 1966, 2101/Round-up June 30th Demo. 1966—P/RAC, NWRO; Frances Fox Piven and Richard Cloward, "The Welfare Poor Organize," Draft, n.d. [1966], file titled "Welfare Poor Organize," Piven; Memorandum, from City-Wide Coordinating Committee on Welfare, to All interested organizations and individuals, May 12, 1966, Unnumbered Box/New York CCCWG Newsletters; Leaflets; Pamphlets, Sampson; Miss Beulah Sanders and Mr. Stephen Leeds, "Proposal for Staff Development of City-Wide Coordinating Committee of Welfare Groups," May 20, 1969, 3, Unnumbered Box/New York City-Wide Coordinating Committee of Welfare Groups, Sampson; "City-Wide Coordinating Committee of Welfare Groups, 1968 Prospectus," n.d., 1, ibid.; Larry Jackson and William Johnson, *Protest by the Poor: The Welfare Rights Movement in New York City* (New York: Rand Corporation, 1973), 126. On participants, see "Profile of a WRO: Mrs. Beulah Sanders, Chairman," *Welfare Fighter* 1, 4 (December 1969): 2; "Portrait of a WRO: Jennette Washington," *Welfare Fighter* 2, 6 (April–May 1971): 11; Frank Espada, interview with Felicia Kornbluh, by telephone, June 2004, transcript in possession of the author; and Frances Fox Piven, interview with Felicia Kornbluh, New York City, August 11, 1997, transcript in possession of the author, 12.

3. Poverty/Rights Action Center, "Round-Up of June 30th Welfare Demonstrations"; Homer Bigart, "Welfare Protest Made at City Hall," *NYT,* July 1, 1966, 44; Malcolm Nash, "Welfare Client Wants Changes," *Am. News,* July 23, 1966, 13; and Jackson and Johnson, *Protest by the Poor,* 127.

4. West Side Welfare Council, *Newsletter: The Voice of Poverty Midst Plenty* 1, 5 (September 1966): 1, 2167/Upper West Side Council, NWRO; Bigart, "Welfare Protest"; and Jackson and Johnson, *Protest by the Poor*, 127–28. On Ginsberg, see Mitchell Ginsberg, Curriculum Vitae, 1966, Subj. Ginsberg, 45/798, Lindsay; John V. Lindsay, Statement on Appointment of Mitchell Ginsberg, February 11, 1966, Dept. Welfare, 104/1314, Lindsay; and Mitchell Ginsberg, interview with Nick Kotz and Mary Lynn Kotz, n.d., 1–2, 24/Mitchell Ginsberg, Kotz.

5. Snipe quoted in Bigart, "Welfare Protest."

6. In April 1966, Cleveland had been the first Northern city investigated and visited by the United States Commission on Civil Rights. John Herbers, "Rights Hearing Focuses on Negro Ghetto in North," *NYT*, April 4, 1966, 17. On the Ohio protest, see AP, "1,000 in Ohio March in Welfare Protest," *NYT*, July 1, 1966, 2. Two years later, black residents of Cleveland engaged in an armed battle with local police. Louis H. Masotti and Jerome R. Corsi, for the National Commission on the Causes and Prevention of Violence, *Shoot-Out in Cleveland* (New York: Bantam Press, 1969).

7. Stokes quoted in Seymour Hersh, "Seek Welfare Power Bloc," *National Catholic Reporter* 2, 35 (June 29, 1966): 1, 56/Nat. Welfare Rights Organization (Poverty Rights Action Center), Social Action.

8. [Ohio Steering Committee for Adequate Welfare], "Tramp, Tramp, Tramp," Walk for Decent Welfare Song Sheet, 1953/Songs of Ohio, NWRO. The welfare rights movement remembered the Ohio march in its song, "Liberal's Lament": "Ohio mom[s] were discontent / With grants at se-ven-ty per-cent / They walked to see the governor / And he responded with this score: [Chorus] You're only hurting your cause this way / That's what all of us liberals say / Nobody likes things the way they are / But you go too fast and you go too far." Tim Sampson sang this song in *My Brother's Keeper*, a documentary on the welfare rights movement that was part of the series, "America's War on Poverty," produced by Harry Hampton for Blackside films and WGBH-TV, aired for the first time on November 25, 1994.

9. Poverty/Rights Action Center, "Round-up of June 30th Welfare Demonstrations," and "Cities Participating in June 30th Nationwide Welfare Demonstration," n.d. [July 1966], 2101/Round-up of June 30th Demo., NWRO; [George Wiley], transcript of notes from telephone conversation with Tim Sampson, California Center for Community Development, July 13, 1966, ibid.; [Jerry Sampson], California Center for Community Development, "What Is Happening in this New Movement for Welfare Rights?" *Welfare Rights News* 1 (July 30, 1966): 1, Pamphlets; "Los Angeles," *Welfare Rights News* 1, 2: ibid.; and Tim Sampson, interview with Felicia Kornbluh, Oakland, Calif., July 3, 1998, 9, transcript in possession of the author.

10. Poverty/Rights Action Center, "Round-up of June 30th Welfare Demonstrations."

11. Ibid. On Louisville, see also [West End Community Council (WECC)], "Welfare Complaints," [May–June 1966], 9/14, WECC; editorial, "Where More Help Is Needed To Live Poorly," *Louisville Courier-Journal*, May 13, 1966 (excerpted), ibid.; and [WECC], "Are you and your children constantly waiting on someone else to make the decision that will make your life better? Join the Demonstration for Decent Welfare! June 30," ibid.

12. James Ralph, Jr., *Northern Protest: Martin Luther King, Jr., Chicago, and the Civil Rights Movement* (Cambridge, Mass.: Harvard University Press, 1993), 1–42; Cleveland Sellers, with Robert Terrell, *The River of No Return: The Autobiography*

of a Black Militant and the Life and Death of SNCC (Jackson: University of Mississippi Press, 1990), 155–69; Clayborne Carson, *In Struggle: SNCC and the Black Awakening of the 1960s* (Cambridge, Mass.: Harvard University Press, 1981), 191–228; August Meier and Elliott Rudwick, *CORE: A Study in the Civil Rights Movement,* rev. ed. (1973, Urbana: University of Illinois Press, 1975); and Martin Luther King, Jr., *Where Do We Go from Here? Chaos or Community?* (New York: Harper and Row, 1967). For an explanation of the rejection of coalitions between black activists and whites, see Kwame Ture (Stokely Carmichael) and Charles Hamilton, *Black Power: The Politics of Liberation* (1967; New York: Vintage, 1992), 58–84.

13. Piven, with Kornbluh, 12.

14. The language of recognition comes from Nancy Fraser, "From Redistribution to Recognition: Dilemmas of Justice in a 'Post-Socialist' Age," from her *Justice Interruptus: Critical Reflections on the "Postsocialist" Condition* (New York: Routledge, 1997), 11–39. Welfare rights activists sought both the justice of "redistribution" and that of "recognition."

15. Anthropologist James Scott uses the term "infrapolitics" to refer to the everyday actions people take when they have little power but want to register dissent. What happened around 1963 in New York City may be seen as a move from the infrapolitical realm to formal politics. James C. Scott, *Domination and the Art of Resistance: Hidden Transcripts* (New Haven, Conn.: Yale University Press, 1990); and *Weapons of the Weak: Everyday Forms of Peasant Resistance* (New Haven, Conn.: Yale University Press, 1995). For historians' uses of Scott's concept of resistance, see Robin D. G. Kelley, *Race Rebels: Culture, Politics, and the Black Working Class* (New York: Free Press, 1994); and Linda Gordon, *Heroes of Their Own Lives: The Politics and History of Family Violence, Boston, 1880–1960* (New York: Penguin, 1988).

16. On the black freedom movement in the North, see Thomas J. Sugrue, *Sweet Land of Liberty: The Unfinished Struggle for Racial Equality in the North* (New York: Random House, forthcoming); Matthew Countryman, *Up South: Civil Rights and Black Power in Philadelphia* (Philadelphia: University of Pennsylvania Press, 2005); John D'Emilio, *Lost Prophet: The Life and Times of Bayard Rustin* (New York: Free Press, 2003), 59, 119, 239–40, 365–68, 382–84; Barbara Ransby, *Ella Baker and the Black Freedom Movement: A Radical Democratic Vision* (Chapel Hill: University of North Carolina Press, 2003), 148–69; Martha Biondi, *To Stand and Fight: The Struggle for Civil Rights in Postwar New York City* (Cambridge, Mass.: Harvard University Press, 2003); Robert O. Self, *American Babylon: Race and the Struggle for Postwar Oakland* (Princeton, N.J.: Princeton University Press, 2003); Jeanne Theoharis and Komozi Woodard, eds., *Freedom North: Black Freedom Struggles Outside the South, 1940–1980* (New York: Palgrave Macmillan, 2003); Heather Ann Thompson, *Whose Detroit? Politics, Labor and Race in a Modern American City* (Ithaca, N.Y.: Cornell University Press, 2001); Komozi Woodard, *A Nation Within a Nation: Amiri Baraka (LeRoi Jones) and Black Power Politics* (Chapel Hill: University of North Carolina Press, 1999); and Ralph, *Northern Protest.* For similar battles in the South, see Rhonda Y. Williams, *The Politics of Public Housing: Black Women's Struggles Against Urban Inequality* (New York: Oxford University Press, 2005); and Christina Greene, *Our Separate Ways: Women and the Black Freedom Movement in Durham, North Carolina* (Chapel Hill: University of North Carolina Press, 2005). For community-building and organizing in Puerto Rican communities, see Carmen Teresa Whalen, *From Puerto Rico to Philadelphia: Puerto Rican Workers and Postwar Economics* (Philadelphia: Temple University Press, 2001); Andrés Torres and

José E. Velázquez, eds., *The Puerto Rican Movement: Voices from the Diaspora* (Philadelphia: Temple University Press, 1998); and Virginia E. Sánchez Korrol, *From Colonia to Community: The History of Puerto Ricans in New York City*, rev. ed. (1983; Berkeley: University of California Press, 1994). For Mexican Americans, see Vicki Ruíz, *From Out of the Shadows: Mexican Women in Twentieth-Century America* (New York: Oxford University Press, 1998); David G. Guttiérrez, *Walls and Mirrors: Mexican Americans, Mexican Immigrants, and the Politics of Identity* (Berkeley: University of California Press, 1995); George J. Sánchez, *Becoming Mexican American: Ethnicity, Culture and Identity in Chicano Los Angeles, 1900–1945* (New York: Oxford University Press, 1993); and Linda C. Majka and Theo J. Majka, *Farm Workers, Agribusiness, and the State* (Philadelphia: Temple University Press, 1982).

17. Gertrude Samuels, "Even More Crucial Than in the South," *NYT Magazine*, June 30, 1963, 13.

18. Editorial, "The Anti-Welfare Drive," *NYT*, February 6, 1960, 18. On Newburgh, see Statement of the State Board of Social Welfare, July 18, 1961, 1/15, Wickenden; Joseph McDowell Mitchell, city manager of the City of Newburgh, N.Y., "The Newburgh Revolt," n.d. [1961], ibid.; letter from Loula Dunn, American Public Welfare Association, Chicago, to Elizabeth Wickenden, New York, July 28, 1961, ibid.; Elizabeth Wickenden, "Social Welfare and the Radical Right," January 26, 1962, 1/19, Wickenden; Eve Edstrom, "Newburgh Is a Mirror Reflecting on Us All, *Washington Post*, August 6, 1961, E 1, E 7; and Lisa Levenstein, "From Innocent Women to Unwed Mothers," *Journal of Women's History* 11, 4 (Winter 2000): 10–33.

19. *Report*, Moreland Commission on Public Welfare, January 15, 1963, 11, Dept. Welfare, 158/1812, Wagner. The Commission was created by an Executive Order signed by Governor Nelson Rockefeller, August 30, 1961.

20. Anonymous letter to Mayor Wagner, n.d. [received March 22, 1962], Dept. Welfare 158/1811, Wagner.

21. Martin Tolchin, "Relief Costs Laid to City's Policies," *NYT*, January 1, 1964, 25; Editorial, *NYT*, January 3, 1964, 22; and "Dumpson Assails Waste on Housing," *NYT*, January 6, 1964, 23.

22. Greenleigh Associates, "Report to the Moreland Commission on Welfare of Findings of the Study of the Public Assistance Program and Operations of the State of New York," November, 1962, 3, Dept. Welfare, 158/1812, Wagner.

23. Greenleigh for Moreland, 40, 45–47, 66, 72. For another view of caseworkers' negative attitudes, see Frank Gell, *The Black Badge: Confessions of a Caseworker* (New York: Harper and Row, 1969).

24. Letter from Fannie Blackwell, Brooklyn, N.Y., to Mayor Wagner, City Hall, New York City, n.d. [received Sept. 6, 1972], 5–6, Subj. Welfare, 157/1800, Wagner. See discussion of letters in Greenleigh for Moreland, 80, and Joseph P. Lyford, *The Airtight Cage: A Study of New York's West Side* (New York: Harper and Row, 1966), 301.

25. Letter from Edward Powers, New York City, to Mayor Wagner, October 27, 1962, 2–3, Subj. Welfare, 158/1809, Wagner; and letter from Powers to Wagner, November 11, 1962, ibid.

26. Letter from Albertha White, New York, to Mayor Wagner, n.d. [received November 1, 1962], 4–5, Subj. Welf, 157/1599, Wagner.

27. McCandish Phillips, "Harlem Tenants Open Rent Strike," *NYT*, September 28, 1963, 1; "Harlem Boycott on Rents Spreads," *NYT*, November 5, 1963, 23; Homer Bigart, "Rent Strike Gains Momentum Here," *NYT*, December 18, 1963, 33; and Martin Arnold, "Wagner to Urge Albany to Legalize Rent Strikes," *NYT*, January 6, 1964, 1, 29.

28. For discussions of urban renewal nationally and in other cities, see Arnold Hirsch, *Making The Second Ghetto: Race and Housing in Chicago* (Cambridge: Cambridge University Press, 1983), 112, 158, 269–75; Thomas J. Sugrue, *The Origins of the Urban Crisis: Race and Inequality in Postwar Detroit* (Princeton, N.J.: Princeton University Press, 1996), 48–51; Self, *American Babylon*, 139–44; Jon Rice, "The World of the Illinois Panthers," in *Freedom North*, ed. Theoharis and Woodard, 41–43; Williams, *Politics of Public Housing*, 101–2; and Greene, *Our Separate Ways*, 128–29.

29. Jane Jacobs, *The Death and Life of Great American Cities* (New York: Vintage, 1961). On urban renewal in Morningside Heights and Harlem, see George Todd, "Promise 117th St. Tenants Will Not Be Put in Street," *Am. News*, October 31, 1964, 4; James L. Hicks, "Columbia Gets a Warning," *Am. News*, January 9, 1965, 7, 30; "Columbia U Wants To Move You—Harlem Rejects Mayor's Plan—Would Displace Negroes," *Am. News*, April 24, 1965, 1–2; and editorial, "Does Anyone Care?" *Am. News*, March 19, 1966, 12.

30. Herbert Gans, "The Failure of Urban Renewal: A Critique and Some Proposals," in *Urban Renewal: People, Politics, and Planning: A Reader on the Political Controversies and Sociological Realities of Revitalizing the American City*, ed. Jewel Bellush and Murray Hausknecht (New York: Anchor Doubleday, 1967), 468. Also see in that volume Martin Anderson, "The Sophistry That Made Urban Renewal Possible," 52–66; Percival Goodman, "Lincoln Center, Emporium of the Arts," 406–12; and memorandum from Frances Piven to Sanford Kravitz, Office of Economic Opportunity, Re: "Resident Participation in Community Action Programs: An Overview," January 14, 1965, Piven.

31. Piven to Kravitz; Peter Meagher, Department of Real Estate, "Background and Statement of the West Side Urban Renewal Site Problem," n.d. [1965], Subj. Anti-Poverty—West Side Urban Renewal, 12/145, Wagner; Herman Badillo, Department of Relocation, "Dear Tenant" letter to residents of the Upper West Side Urban Renewal site, July 26, 1965, ibid.; Lyford, *Airtight Cage*, 118–30; Jennette Washington, Strycker's Bay Neighborhood Council, Testimony, *Examination of the War on Poverty, Part 6*, Senate Committee on Labor and Public Welfare, May 8–9, 1967, 1926; Rev. Henry Browne, Chairman, Housing Committee, Strycker's Bay Neighborhood Council, Testimony, *Housing Legislation of 1964*, Senate Committee on Banking and Currency, March 3, 1964, 968; Browne, President, Strycker's Bay, Testimony, *Federal Role in Urban Affairs*, Part 5, Senate Committee on Government Operations, August 29–30, 1966, 1116; and Jackson and Johnson, *Protest by the Poor*, 108.

32. Lyford, *Airtight Cage*, 125.

33. Steven V. Roberts, "City Trying to Ease Impact of Renewal on West Side," *NYT*, December 26, 1966, 1, 18.

34. Sanders and Washington quoted in Roberts, "City Trying to Ease Impact," 18.

35. Dr. Martin Luther King, Jr., "The School Boycott Concept," *Am. News*, April 1, 1964, 10. On the boycott generally, see "What a 'Fizzle.'" *Am. News*, February 8, 1964, 10; editorial, "The NYC School Crisis," *Am. News*, January 25, 1964, 1; Sara Slack, "We Can't Stop Now!—Galamison," *Am. News*, February 1, 1964, 1; and D'Emilio, *Lost Prophet*, 365–68, 375.

36. Samuels, "Even More Crucial," 24.

37. "New York Worlds Fair, 1964–1965," map, *NYT*, April 22, 1964, 21; Espada, with Kornbluh, 6–8; George Lipsitz, *A Life in the Struggle: Ivory Perry and the Culture of Opposition*, rev. ed. (Philadelphia: Temple University Press, 1995),

81–83; Meier and Rudwick, *CORE*, 252–53, 256–57; Unsigned Editorial, "The Stall-In," *NYT*, April 21, 1964, 36; Bayard Rustin, "Purpose of the Stall-In," letter, *NYT*, April 21, 1964, 36; and Fred Powledge, "CORE Chief Among Scores Arrested on Grounds," *NYT*, April 23, 1964, 28. The classic account of the World's Fair is Robert Caro's in *The Power Broker: Robert Moses and the Fall of New York* (New York: Vintage, 1975), 1082–1114.

38. Espada, with Kornbluh, 8. For Espada as community activist, see Philip Dougherty, "City Will Attack Slum in Brooklyn," *NYT*, February 5, 1966, 31; Dougherty, "Price Leads 'Mob' in Brooklyn Clean-Up Drive," *NYT*, February 12, 1966, 14; and Paul Montgomery, "East New York Peaceful, But Police Stay on Alert," *NYT*, July 25, 1966, 1, 3.

39. Martín Espada, "The Sign in My Father's Hands," from his *Imagine the Angels of Bread: Poems* (New York: Norton, 1996), 26–27.

40. James Booker, "As Jimmy Booker Saw the Rioting," *Am News*, July 25, 1964, 2. Also see "Harlem's Plea," *Am. News*, July 25, 1964, 1; Wendell Pritchett, *Brownsville, Brooklyn: Blacks, Jews, and the Changing Face of the Ghetto* (Chicago: University of Chicago Press, 2002), 192; and Jim Sleeper, *The Closest of Strangers: Liberalism and the Politics of Race in New York* (New York: Norton, 1990), 61.

41. "Manhattan Rioting Crosses Bridge, Spreads to Brooklyn," *Am. News*, July 25, 1964, 25.

42. Sanford Horwitt, *Let Them Call Me Rebel: Saul Alinsky, His Life and Legacy* (New York: Vintage, 1992), 452–56; Nick Kotz and Mary Lynn Kotz, A *Passion for Equality: George A. Wiley and the Movement* (New York: Norton, 1977), 124; and Les Matthews, "The People of Jersey City Speak," *Am. News*, August 8, 1964, 1.

43. Alice O'Connor, *Poverty Knowledge: Social Science, Social Policy, and the Poor in Twentieth-Century U.S. History* (Princeton, N.J.: Princeton University Press, 2001), 128–29; Eric Schneider, *Vampires, Dragons, and Egyptian Kings: Youth Gangs in Postwar New York* (Princeton, N.J.: Princeton University Press, 1999), 211–13; Piven and Cloward, "Echoes from the 'Old Left': A Comment on the Mobilization for Youth Fiasco," 2, Piven; and Minutes of the Meeting of the Committee on Social Issues and Public Policy, Mobilization for Youth, August 4, 1964, Subj. Anti-Poverty—Screvane, Paul, 11/139, Wagner. On the demand for civilian review of the police force, see "Harlem's Plea"; Vincent J. Cannato, *The Ungovernable City: John V. Lindsay and His Struggle to Save New York* (New York: Basic Books, 2001), 156–65; and Biondi, *To Stand and Fight*, 206, 277–78.

44. Memorandum from Julius C. C. Edelstein, executive assistant to the mayor, City of New York, to Hon. Paul R. Screvane, August 13, 1964, Subj. Anti-Poverty—Screvane, Paul, 11/139, Wagner. For the quotation, see William Federici, Edward O'Neill, and Henry Lee, "Anti-JD Agency Probed for Red Ties," *New York Daily News*, August 16, 1964, 2–3, plus banner headline, 1, Subj. Anti-Poverty: Mobilization for Youth—News Clips, 9/93, Wagner.

45. Jack Newfield, "Moynihan Says He Helped Extract Mobilization Reds," *Village Voice*, August 12, 1965, "Old Left," Piven; and "Moynihan Replies," *Village Voice*, August 19, 1965, ibid. On the MFY controversy, see also Junius Griffin, "2 in Youth Agency Are Communists, FBI Check Finds," *NYT*, August 24, 1964, 1, 12; Homer Bigart, "Youth United Aide Ran As a Leftist," *NYT*, August 27, 1964, 30; and Mobilization for Youth, Inc., Office of Public Relations and Information, Summary of Report by Phillip Haberman, special counsel appointed by the Board of Directors to review charges against MFY, November 25, 1964, 2–3, 7/23, Wickenden.

46. "MFYovitch," *National Review*, January 19, 1965, 2, 6. See also "On the

Left," *National Review,* September 5, 1964, 2; "MFY," *National Review,* December 1, 1964, 1045–46; and Richard Cloward and Frances Fox Piven, "Echoes from the 'Old Left': A Comment on the Mobilization for Youth Fiasco," unpublished typescript (Fall 1965), 1, "Old Left," Piven.

47. Alfonso Narvaez and Kenneth Gross, "Lower E. Side Seethes But the Rioting Is Over," *New York Post,* September 1, 1964, n.p., Subj. MFY, 9/93, Wagner; "13,500 Sign Petitions Backing MFY," *Daily News,* September 5, 1964, 5, ibid.; Selwyn Raab, "Youth Agency Probing Itself for Red Links," *New York World-Telegram and Sun,* August 24, 1964, n.p., ibid.; Jack Newfield, "Youth Agency Faces Purge by New Counsel," *New York Post,* August 25, 1964, n.p., ibid.; Piven and Cloward, "Echoes from the 'Old Left,'" 5; MFY Summary of Haberman Report, 3, 6, 7/23, Wickenden; and John Mallon, "MFY Probers Hook a Red Minnow," *Daily News,* October 19, 1964, 10, Subj. MFY, 9/95, Wagner.

48. Espada, with Kornbluh, 2–3; Jackson and Johnson, *Protest by the Poor,* 102–3; and James Graham, *Enemies of the Poor* (New York: Random House, 1970), 259–60.

49. Espada, with Kornbluh, 2.

50. Mobilization for Youth, "Program Fact Sheet," January 3, 1964, 29/Mobilization for Youth, Social Action; and Jackson and Johnson, *Protest by the Poor,* 94–95.

51. Frances Fox Piven and Richard Cloward, "The Weight of the Poor: A Strategy to End Poverty," *The Nation,* May 2, 1966, 511; and Piven, with Kornbluh, 5–6.

52. Statement of Beulah Sanders, U.S. Congress, Joint Economic Committee, Subcommittee on Fiscal Policy, *Income Maintenance Programs–Hearings,* Ninetieth Congress, Second Session, June 11, 12, 13, 18, 19, 25, 26, 27, 1968, vol. 1, 76–78. For background on the portions of the poverty programs that hired poor people as community workers, see Nancy Naples, *Grassroots Warriors: Activist Mothering, Community Work, and the War on Poverty* (New York: Routledge, 1998); and Frank Riessman and Arthur Perlstein, *New Careers for the Poor* (New York: Free Press, 1962).

53. Jackson and Johnson, *Protest by the Poor,* 108. For Sanders and Washington as leaders of the West Side Welfare Recipients League, see "Strycker's Bay," *Newsletter, West Side Welfare Council: The Voice of Poverty Midst Plenty* 1, 5 (September 1966): 3, 2167/Upper West Side Council, NWRO.

54. Letter from a "Mixed up mother" to the editor, *Am. News,* February 20, 1965, 8. For similar issues, see anonymous letter to the editor, *Am. News,* February 13, 1965, 8; and anonymous letter, *Am. News,* April 30, 1966, 14.

55. Letter from Marie Hatchett Gibbons, Staten Island, N.Y., to the editor, *Am. News,* July 16, 1966, 14.

56. "City-Wide Coordinating Committee of Welfare Groups, 1968 Prospectus"; "1969 Prospectus"; Beulah Sanders and Stephen Leeds, "Proposal for Staff Development of City-Wide Coordinating Committee of Welfare Groups," May 20, 1969, Unnumbered Box/New York City-Wide Coordinating Committee of Welfare Groups, Sampson; and Jackson and Johnson, *Protest by the Poor,* 122–24.

57. Organizational materials quoted in Jackson and Johnson, *Protest by the Poor,* 124–25.

58. City-Wide Coordinating Committee on Welfare, Report on First Meeting, May, 12, 1966, Unnumbered Box/New York CCCWG Newsletters; Leaflets; Pamphlets, Sampson; and Jackson and Johnson, *Protest by the Poor,* 125–26.

59. Social Service Employees Union, "To The New Caseworker," n.d. [1966], 4–5, 4/3, Padwee. On SSEU and public employees in New York City, see Daniel Walkowitz, *Working with Class: Social Workers and the Politics of Middle-Class Identity* (Chapel Hill: University of North Carolina Press, 1999), 265–75; Pritchett, *Brownsville, Brooklyn*, 179; Leon Fink and Brian Greenberg, *Upheaval in the Quiet Zone: A History of Hospital Workers Union, Local 1199* (Urbana: University of Illinois Press, 1989); and Jewel Bellush and Bernard Bellush, *Union Power and New York: Victor Gotbaum and District Council 37* (New York: Praeger, 1984), 112–16

60. Emanuel Perlmutter, "Welfare Strike Due in City Today in Spite of Writ," *NYT*, January 4, 1965, 1, 25; and Perlmutter, "9 Centers Closed—8,000 Strikers Facing Penalties—Accord Sought by Judge," *NYT*, January 5, 1965, 1, 21. SSEU, "To The New Caseworker," 6, claimed that 70 percent of supervisors and 90 percent of caseworkers stayed out of work for the entirety of the strike.

61. Brooklyn CORE, "People of New York—The Welfare Workers Strike is *Your* Fight!" 3/Welfare Strike 1965: Leaflets, Brochures and Reports, SSEU.

62. Perlmutter, "City Invokes Law and Ousts 5,398 in Welfare Tie-Up," *NYT*, January 6, 1965, 1, 26; Perlmutter, "3 Strike Leaders Given Jail Terms," *NYT*, January 21, 1965, 1, 26; Perlmutter, "16 More Go To Jail In Welfare Tie-Up," *NYT*, January 26, 1965, 1, 15; "Agreement," Between the City of New York, SSEU, and Local 371, n.d. [January 31, 1965] and Anna Rosenberg Hoffman, John A. Coleman and David Dubinsky, "Report of the Mayor's Task Force," n.d., 3/Welfare Strike 1965: Leaflets, Brochures and Reports, SSEU; Local 371, "This is Your Victory!!" Bulletin #14, February 1, 1965, 3/Bulletins, Leaflets, 1964–1966, SSEU; and Perlmutter, "Welfare Strike Ends As 2 Unions Accept Formula," *NYT*, February 1, 1965, 1, 11.

63. SSEU, "Contract," May 11, 1965, 1/C.B. Contract—1965, 1967, 1967–68, SSEU; Local 371, "FINALLY!" June 7, 1965, 3/Bulletins, Leaflets, 1964–1966, SSEU; SSEU, "To the New Caseworker," 6; and Charles Morris, *The Cost of Good Intentions: New York City and the Liberal Experiment, 1960–1975* (New York: Norton, 1980), 90.

64. Johnnie Tillmon, interview with Nick Kotz and Mary Lynn Kotz, November 26, 1974, 7, 26/Johnnie Tillmon interview, Kotz. See also Abigail Goldman, "Welfare Rights Pioneer Tillmon-Blackston Dies," *Los Angeles Times*, October 25, 1995, 22; and Tillmon, interview with Sherna Berger Gluck, February 3, 1984, preliminary transcript, 1–2, LAWC.

65. Tillmon, with Kotz and Kotz, 31–32, 34; and Hon. Augustus F. Hawkins, Extension of Remarks, U.S. House of Representatives, 90th Congress, 1st Session, *Congressional Record* 113/19 (February 8, 1967), Unnumbered Box/Goals—NWRO, Sampson.

66. Tillmon, with Kotz and Kotz, 6–7, 9, 15; and Tillmon, with Berger Gluck, 2.

67. Goldman, "Welfare Rights Pioneer"; Tillmon, with Berger Gluck, 2; Tillmon, with Kotz and Kotz, 38; and Kotz and Kotz, *Passion for Equality*, 221.

68. Tim Sampson, "The Rocking Chair," Los Angeles Chapter National Association of Social Workers *Record*, October 1963, 6–7, 2010/Social Workers Union 535 Calif. [L.A.], NWRO. See also Sampson, "Social Workers and Unions," Typescript of draft article for *The Record* [1964], ibid.; and Tim Sampson interview, with Felicia Kornbluh, July 3, 1998, Oakland, Calif., transcript in possession of the author, 6–7.

69. Sampson, with Kornbluh, July 3, 1998, 15.

70. H. Brett Melendy and Benjamin F. Gilbert, *The Governors of California, from*

Peter H. Burnett to Edmund G. Brown (Georgetown, Calif.: Talisman Press, 1965), 438–58; Stephen Ambrose, *Nixon: The Education of a Politician, 1913–1962* (New York: Simon and Schuster, 1987), 668–73; and Richard Nixon, *RN: The Memoirs of Richard Nixon* (New York: Touchstone, 1990), 246–47.

71. Kehoe quoted in "6:30 A.M. Welfare 'Bed-Check,'" *San Francisco Chronicle*, January 9, 1963, 1, reprinted in *Benny Max Parrish, petitioner and appellent, v. the Civil Service Commission of the County of Alameda, State of California, et al., respondents: appellant's opening brief, District Court of Appeal, First Appellate District Division Two* (San Francisco: Pernau Walsh, 1965), 2–3. For similar sources, see Parrish brief, 7, 10–11.

72. Parrish brief, 9–10.

73. Parrish brief; *Benny Max Parrish v. Civil Service Commission of Alameda County*, California Supreme Court #22429, Brief of Amici Curiae Edward Sparer, Martin Garbus, Carl Rachlin, et al., and Brief of Amicus Curiae, Congress of Racial Equality, 41/22, SEDFRE; decision in *Parrish v. Alameda*, California Supreme Court #22429, March 1967, ibid.; [Benny Parrish], "History of the Welfare Rights Organization," Funding Proposal, Alameda County Welfare Rights Organization, n.d., Unnumbered Box/Proposals for Welfare Rights Organizations, Sampson; and [Benny Parrish], "A Proposal to Organize Welfare Recipients in California," California Center for Community Development, September 1965, 7, ibid.

74. Tom Joe, interview with Nick Kotz and Mary Lynn Kotz, n.d., 1–2, 24/ Tom Joe interview, Kotz; Parrish brief; and Sampson, with Kornbluh, July 26, 2001, Oakland, Calif., transcript in author's possession, 6.

75. Sampson, with Kornbluh, 1998, 5–6; "Jacobus tenBroek—Synopsis," and Obituary, *San Francisco Chronicle*, March 28, 1968, both in *The Braille Monitor*, Voice of the National Federation of the Blind (inkprint edition), Berkeley, Calif., July 1968, Bancroft; and National Federation of the Blind, "Who Are the Blind Who Lead the Blind?" pamphlet, n.d. [1955–56], from binder titled *The National Federation of the Blind and the California Council for the Blind: Policies, Activities and Leaders*, University of California, Regional Cultural History Project (1956), Bancroft.

76. Jacobus tenBroek, "The Constitution and the Right of Free Movement," pamphlet (New York: National Travelers Aid Association, 1955), Doe Library, University of California at Berkeley; and Joel F. Handler, ed., *Family Law and the Poor: Essays by Jacobus tenBroek* (Westport, Conn.: Greenwood, 1971). The articles originally appeared in the *Stanford Law Review* 16: 257–317, 16: 900–81; 17: 612–82 (1964–1965).

77. See generally, 2/7, Wickenden. For evidence of the spread of Wickenden's ideas, see Edwin J. Lukas, "Social Welfare and the Rights of the Poor," in *Poverty in America*, ed. Louis Ferman, Joyce Kornbluh, and Alan Haber (Ann Arbor: University of Michigan, 1966), 192, and "Selected Bibliography," ibid., 258.

78. Letter from Elizabeth Wickenden, National Social Welfare Assembly, New York City, New York, to Jacobus tenBroek, chairman, California Social Welfare Board, Berkeley, Calif., April 1, 1963, 2/7, Wickenden; letter from Charles Reich, Professor, Yale Law School, New Haven, Conn., to Elizabeth Wickenden, New York, N.Y., March 4, 1963, ibid.; Charles Reich, interview with Felicia Kornbluh, San Francisco, January 10, 2002, transcript in possession of the author, 10–11; Reich, *The Sorcerer of Bolinas Reef* (New York: Random House, 1976), 20, 23–27, 42, 44–47; and Reich, "Mr. Justice Black and the Living Constitution," *Harvard Law Review* 76, 4 (February 1963): 673–754.

79. Charles Reich, "Midnight Welfare Searches and the Social Security Act," *Yale Law Journal* 72, 7 (June 1963): 1347–60; letter from Charles Reich, Professor of Law, Yale University Law School, New Haven, Conn., to Elizabeth Wickenden, New York City, November 2 [1963], 2/1, Wickenden; Eve Erdstrom, "Welfare Searches Called Illegal," *Washington Post*, October 13, 1963, n.p., 2/1, Wickenden; and letter from Norman Dorsen, New York University School of Law, New York, to Elizabeth Wickenden, New York, January 13, 1964, 7/1, Wickenden.

80. Charles Reich, "The New Property," *Yale Law Journal* 73, 5 (April 1964): 733–87. Reich became even more well known after publication of "The New Property" than he had been before. See letter from Elizabeth Wickenden to Charles A. Reich, October 13, 1964, 7/1, Wickenden.

81. "New Property," 785.

82. Letter from Jacobus tenBroek, president, American Brotherhood for the Blind, Berkeley, Calif., to Miss Elizabeth Wickenden, New York, June 25, 1964, 7/1, Wickenden. TenBroek was not an easy reader. He also found "problems in the analysis" offered by Reich, and took the opportunity in the same letter to "deplore [Wickenden's] misconception of the nature of the doctrine of equality."

83. Neil Bennett and Michael Austin, *The Roots of Community Organizing, 1917–1939* (Philadelphia: Temple University Press, 1990); Wini Breines, *Community and Organization in the New Left, 1962–1968: The Great Refusal* (New Brunswick, N.J.: Rutgers University Press, 1989); Harry C. Boyte, *The Backyard Revolution: Understanding the New Citizen Movement* (Philadelphia: Temple University Press, 1980); and Saul Alinsky, *Rules for Radicals: A Pragmatic Primer for Realistic Radicals* (New York: Vintage, 1972).

84. Wayne Hartmire, "Summary of Fred Ross's Presentation," Report on a Symposium on Community Development in California, Asilomar, California, July 9–12, 1963, 6, Sampson (2). For Ross, Chávez, and Huerta, see Majka and Majka, *Farm Workers, Agribusiness, and the State*, 170; and Ruíz, *From Out of the Shadows*, 132–34, 143.

85. Sampson, with Kornbluh, 1998, 27; and Majka and Majka, *Farm Workers, Agribusiness, and the State*, 171.

86. [Benny Parrish], California Center for Community Development, Del Rey, Calif., "A Proposal to Organize Welfare Recipients in California," September 1965, 5, Unnumbered Box/Proposals for Welfare Rights Organizations, Sampson; Tim Sampson, "Proposal for a Workshop with Welfare Recipients," November 22, 1965, ibid.; Benny Parrish, Remarks to a Combined Meeting of the National Association of Social Workers and California Social Workers Organization, Modesto, Calif., September 1966, Unnumbered Box/How Groups Started, Sampson; and Sampson, with Kornbluh, 1998, 7.

87. Sampson, with Kornbluh, 1998, 7; Parrish to the National Association of Social Workers and California Social Workers Organization, 1, 3; and Ed Day, interview with Nick Kotz and Mary Lynn Kotz, n.d., 10, 24/Wiley:Ed Day, Kotz.

88. Matthew Dallek, *The Right Moment: Ronald Reagan's First Victory and the Decisive Turning Point in American Politics* (New York: Oxford University Press, 2004); Ambrose, *Nixon: The Triumph of a Politician*, 119–20; Dan Carter, *The Politics of Rage: George Wallace, the Origins of the New Conservatism, and the Transformation of American Politics* (Baton Rouge: Louisiana State University Press, 1995), 313; and I. F. Stone, "A Widening Gulf and a Deepening Despair," October 10, 1966, from Stone, *In a Time of Torment, 1961–1967* (Boston: Little, Brown, 1967), 367.

89. "Participating Organizations in the Convention of the Poor," 5/25, Social Protest; Policies set forth by the Welfare Rights Organization group of the Convention of the Poor, [February 26–27, 1966], ibid.; Jerry Sampson, California Foundation, "Proceedings and Summary, First Statewide Convention of the Poor," March 1966, ibid.; Willie Thompson, Chairman pro-tem, "A Summary of the First State-Wide Convention of the Poor, Theme: Let's Unite," n.d., ibid.; and Sampson, "The Poor Unite in California," March 5, 1966, ibid.

90. Anna Mae Williams, interview with Nick Kotz and Mary Lynn Kotz, November 8, 1974, 9, 26/Anna Mae Williams Interview, Kotz.

91. James Farmer, interview with Nick Kotz and Mary Lynn Kotz, November 26, 1974, 1–3, 24/James Farmer Interview, Kotz; August Meier and Elliot Rudwick, *CORE*; D'Emilio, *Lost Prophet*, 53–54, 323–24; and Ed Day, with Kotz and Kotz, 1.

92. Williams, with Kotz and Kotz, 1–2, 4.

93. Day, with Kotz and Kotz, 2–3.

94. Farmer, with Kotz and Kotz, 2–3; and Day, with Kotz and Kotz, 5–6.

95. Day, with Kotz and Kotz, 10; Jane Whitney, CATC [Community Action Training Center, Syracuse University, School of Social Work], Syracuse, N.Y., to [Wiley?], 1966, 2167/Syracuse Welfare, NWRO; Jackson and Johnson, *Protest by the Poor*, 115–16; Horwitt, *Let Them Call Me Rebel*, 478–79; O'Connor, *Poverty Knowledge*, 171; Rhoda Linton, interview with Felicia Kornbluh, June 9, 1997, by telephone, transcript in possession of the author, 3; and William Pastreich, interview with Felicia Kornbluh, by telephone, February 26, 1997, informal notes, 1–2. For general, negative assessments of the Syracuse project, see Allen Matusow, *The Unraveling of America: A History of Liberalism in the 1960s* (New York: Harper Torchbooks, 1984), 248; Nicholas Lemann, *The Promised Land: The Great Black Migration and How it Changed America* (New York: Knopf, 1991), 169; and Daniel Patrick Moynihan, *Maximum Feasible Misunderstanding: Community Action in the War on Poverty* (New York: Free Press, 1970), 132–33.

96. Syracuse mayor quoted in Elizabeth Cobbs Hoffman, *All You Need Is Love: The Peace Corps and the Spirit of the 1960s* (Cambridge, Mass.: Harvard University Press, 1998), 196. See also Robert Levey, "The Organizer," *Boston Globe Sunday Magazine*, September 29, 1968, n.p., Pastreich; Jackson and Johnson, *Protest by the Poor*, 116; O'Connor, *Poverty Knowledge*, 171; and Matusow, *Unraveling*, 248.

97. Crusade for Opportunity in Syracuse, *Joint Neighborhood News: Voice of the People*, n.d., 2167/Syracuse, New York, NWRO; Crusade for Opportunity Fact Sheet, May 3, 1967, ibid.; and letter from [Jane Whitney] to George Wiley, February 14 [1967], ibid. On the controversy, see also Matusow, *Unraveling*, 252; Horwitt, *Let Them Call Me Rebel*, 481; Frances Fox Piven, "Professionalism as a Political Skill: The Case of a Poverty Program," January 25–27, 1966, 35, Folder titled "Prof. as Political Skill," Piven; Samuel Kaplan, "Syracuse Group Fighting Shriver: Private Antipoverty Program Protests Shift in Funds," *NYT*, December 3, 1965, 26; and Joseph A. Loftus, "Shriver Rejects Syracuse Plea: Refuses to Promise Group Continued Direct Funds," *NYT*, December 9, 1965, 58. For Alinsky's reflections on the poverty programs, based in part on his Syracuse experience, see Saul Alinsky, "The War on Poverty–Political Pornography," *Journal of Social Issues* 21 (January 1965): 41–47.

98. Pastreich, with Kornbluh, 1. Pastreich's role in welfare rights is documented in Lawrence Bailis, *Bread or Justice: Grassroots Organizing in the Welfare Rights Movement* (Lexington, Mass.: D.C. Heath, 1974); Levey, "The Organizer"; and Austin Scott, "The Plight of an Organizer," *Washington Post*, August 14, 1972, 1, 6.

99. Linton, with Kornbluh, 8. For Linton's contribution to welfare rights, see Jacqueline Pope, *Biting The Hand That Feeds Them: Organizing Women on Welfare at the Grassroots Level* (New York: Praeger, 1989).

100. Linton had first tried to get a job at one of the "neighborhood city halls" established by the Lindsay administration to make urban government more responsive to its constituents. As she and I discussed, "I finally ended up at City Hall [and] . . . it was like in the last cut and this guy wanted me to sleep with him (laugh) FK: That was the Lindsay administration, right? RL: Yeah . . . jeez, I couldn't believe it! . . . So I got this other job and then I started right away to organize . . . I went to that first demonstration [on June 30] '66." Linton, with Kornbluh, 12–13.

101. Pastreich, with Kornbluh, 5.

102. Sanders, with Kotz and Kotz, 1; Jackson and Johnson, *Protest by the Poor*, 117–18; and Kotz and Kotz, *Passion for Equality*, 181.

103. Kotz and Kotz, *Passion for Equality*, 125–76; Meier and Rudwick, *CORE*, 154, 198, 334–7, 408; and Matusow, *Unraveling*, 252–53. A similar strategy to the one that interested Wiley was outlined by CORE cofounder Bayard Rustin, in "From Protest to Politics: The Future of the Civil Rights Movement" *Commentary* 39, 2 (February 1965): 25–31. See discussion in D'Emilio, *Lost Prophet*, 397–403.

104. Kevin Boyle, *The UAW and the Heyday of American Liberalism 1945–1968* (Ithaca, N.Y.: Cornell University Press, 1995), 190. Also see discussion in Nelson Lichtenstein, *The Most Dangerous Man in Detroit: Walter Reuther and the Fate of American Labor* (New York: Basic Books, 1995), 389–90. Thanks to Eileen Boris for alerting me to the link between Reuther and the Citizens Crusade.

105. Boyle, *UAW*, 193.

106. Tillmon, with Kotz and Kotz, 44.

107. Boyle, *UAW*, 217; Tillmon, with Kotz and Kotz, 44–45; Nan Robertson, "Shriver Defends Program to the Poor, but He is Booed," *NYT*, April 15, 1966, 1, 21; Lemann, *Promised Land*, 168; and Kotz and Kotz, *Passion for Equality*, 185.

108. Social welfare consultant Elizabeth Wickenden, who had been a Vice Chairman of the organization, quit the Executive Committee of the Citizens Crusade after the Shriver incident. A statement to the press by another Vice Chairman admitted to being "embarrassed" but not "discouraged." Memorandum from Elizabeth Wickenden to C. F. O'Neil, Subject: Officers' Meeting of Citizens Crusade Against Poverty, April 19, 1966, and Statement to the Press by Dr. Eugene Carson Blake, Vice Chairman of the Citizens' Crusade Against Poverty, April 14, 1966, both 2/27, Wickenden.

109. Kotz and Kotz, *Passion for Equality*, 185.

110. Richard A. Cloward and Frances Fox Piven, "Organizing the Poor—How It Can Be Done," First Draft, February 1966, File titled "Organizing the Poor," Piven; Piven, with Kornbluh, 9–11; and O'Connor, *Poverty Knowledge*, 128. On Wiley and Cloward, see Wiley, notes on "mtg. w/Cloward at my apt. at 15 Montgomery St. in N.Y.C. Feb. 1966," 7/6, Wiley; and George Wiley, Comment, "Strategy of Crisis: A Dialogue," *The American Child* 48, 3 (Summer 1966), in Cloward and Piven, *The Politics of Turmoil: Poverty, Race, and the Urban Crisis* (New York: Vintage, 1975), 111.

111. Piven, with Kornbluh, 9.

112. Richard Cloward and Frances Fox Piven, "The Weight of the Poor: A Strategy to End Poverty," *The Nation*, May 2, 1966, 510–17.

113. Cloward and Piven, "Organizing the Poor," III-c, and generally, III-a-d, I-a, I-c; Wiley notes on meeting with Cloward, February 1966; and Piven, with Kornbluh.

114. Piven, with Kornbluh, 10; and Kotz and Kotz, *Passion for Equality*, 183. Piven added that, despite his initial skepticism, Bayard Rustin was "actually good when [the welfare rights movement] started." See also D'Emilio, *Lost Prophet*, 451.

115. Day, with Kotz and Kotz, 20.

116. George Wiley, "Prospectus for the Establishment of an Anti-Poverty/Civil Rights Action Center," May 1, 1966, and "Poverty Rights Action Center-Welfare Rights Organization," Freedman. For similar language, see Poverty/Rights Action Center, "Philosophy-History-Operation," September 29, 1966, 1953/Untitled File, NWRO.

117. [Wiley/Day], "What Is The Poverty/Rights Action Center?" n.d. [September 1966?], 36/Nat. Welfare Rights Org. (Poverty Rights Action Center), Social Action.

118. On Ed Day's trip around the country, see Tillmon, with Kotz and Kotz, 49–51; and Day, with Kotz and Kotz, 31–33. On the conference and its organizers, see George Martin and Elinor Paulson, "The Ad Hoc Committee for a Guaranteed Income," *Guaranteed Annual Income Newsletter* 1, 1 (June 1966): 1, Arlene Eisen, "The Ad Hoc Committee's Leadership Conference on the Guaranteed Income, *Guaranteed Annual Income Newsletter* 1, 2 (July 1966): 1, and Ad Hoc Committee for a Guaranteed Income, "The Guaranteed Income: A Selected Bibliography, 17/No File, Kotz. On the School of Social Service Administration and its long engagement with social welfare reform, see Robyn Muncy, *Creating a Female Dominion in American Reform, 1890–1935* (New York: Oxford University Press, 1991), 66–92.

119. Poverty/Rights Action Center, "Summary Report: Welfare Action Meeting," May 21, 1966, 2, 7/7, Wiley. For participation, see also Espada, with Kornbluh, 12; Sampson, with Kornbluh, 1998, 8–9; Sanders, with Kotz and Kotz, 1; Anna Mae Williams, with Kotz and Kotz, 3; and Notes from P/RAC Founding Meeting, titled "Wiley's Mtg.," [May 1966], 3, 7/8, Wiley.

120. "Summary Report," 3–4; Notes from P/RAC Founding, 3; Kotz and Kotz, *Passion for Equality*, 187; and City-Wide Coordinating Committee of Welfare Rights Groups, Report on First Meeting of City-Wide Coordinating Committee, May 12, 1966, Unnumbered Box/New York CCCWG Newsletters; Leaflets; Pamphlets, Sampson.

121. [Ed Day and George Wiley], "The Birth of a Movement—June 30, 1966," 16/NWRO—Newsletters, '68–'72, Kotz; and Sampson, with Kornbluh, 1998, 9. For other proclamations of the birth of a movement, see Poverty/Rights Action Center, "Round-Up of June 30th Welfare Demonstrations"; and Piven and Cloward, "The Welfare Poor Organize."

Chapter 2. Citizens of the Affluent Society

1. Lily Mae Robinson, "What It Was Like on the Inside," *TLI* 1, 7 (September 23, 1966): 3. Emphasis hers.

2. Poverty/Rights Action Center, "Round-Up of June 30th Welfare Demonstrations," June 28, 1966, 2101/Round-up June 30th Demo. 1966—P/RAC, NWRO; Larry Jackson and William Johnson, *Protest by the Poor: The Welfare Rights Movement in New York City* (New York: Rand Corporation, 1973), 127; "17 Arrested for a Welfare Sit-In over Demand for More Clothes," *NYT*, September 15, 1966, 45; "Welfare Protest Planned," *NYT*, August 31, 1966, 31; "School Clothes Sept. 1st or School Boycott Sept. 12th," *TLI* 1, 4 (August 5, 1966): 1;

"Welfare Families Demand $100 Semi-Annual School Clothing Grant—Pickets & School Boycott Planned for September," *TLI* 1, 5 (August 19, 1966): 1; and "Citywide Committee Outlines Demands for Sept. 12 Picket," *TLI* 1, 6 (August 26, 1966): 1.

3. Lizabeth Cohen, *A Consumer's Republic: The Politics of Mass Consumption in Postwar America* (New York: Knopf, 2003).

4. Jennette Washington, "The Good Life," *TLI* 1, 18 (March 17, 1967): 1.

5. On African American women claiming the public space of the consumer market, see my "To Fulfill Their 'Rightly Needs': Consumerism and the National Welfare Rights Movement," *Radical History Review* 69 (Fall 1997): 76–113; and Regina Austin, "A Nation of Thieves: Consumption, Commerce, and the Black Public Sphere," *Public Culture* 7, 1 (Fall 1994): 225–48. For a theory of citizenship that includes the idea of living at a socially determined minimum level, see T.H. Marshall, *Citizenship and Social Class and Other Essays* (Cambridge: Cambridge University Press, 1950), 1–85.

6. Robinson, "What It Was Like."

7. "Clients Storm 250 Church St.," *TLI* 1, 7 (September 23, 1966): 1–2.

8. "Clients Storm"; A.L. Faltz, "On the Outside of the Inside," *TLI* 1, 8 (September 30, 1966): 2–3; Poverty/Rights Action Center, Excerpt from Welfare Leaders Newsletter, October 31, 1966, 40/Poverty Rights Action Center, Social Action; and "17 Arrested for a Welfare Sit-In."

9. John Sibley, "Welfare Agency Faces 2 Revolts," *NYT*, September 19, 1966, 25.

10. Sibley, "2 Revolts"; Martin Tolchin, "Work Load Spurs Welfare Protest," *NYT*, September 20, 1966, 57; Tolchin, "Relief Caseloads Reduced by City," *NYT*, September 21, 1966, 49; "Ginsberg Promises Albany Push; City-Wide Steps Up Its Total Demands," *TLI* 1, 7 (September 23, 1966): 2; "Welfare Negotiations On! Some Points Were Won; Now Let's C[h]eck Up!" *TLI* 1, 8 (September 30, 1966): 1; and "Negotiations," *TLI* 1, 11 (October 28, 1966): 1.

11. Letter from Catherine Kerwin (Mrs. Thomas Kerwin), Brooklyn, N.Y., to Honorable Robert F. Wagner, mayor of New York, November 14, 1962, Subj. Welfare, 158/1810, Wagner. For similar appeals, see letter from Mrs. Bernice Inge to Mayor Wagner, April 3, 1962, Subj. Welfare, 157/1800, Wagner; letter from Evelyn Forbes to Mayor Wagner, n.d., Subj. Welfare, 158/1809, Wagner; letter from Maria Ramos to Mayor Wagner, n.d. [received August 16, 1962], Subj. Welfare, 157/1800, Wagner; letter from Mrs. Clementine Allen to Mayor Wagner, October 30, 1962, Subj. Welfare, 158/1808, Wagner; and letter from Miss Mildred Newett to Mayor Wagner, [received November 8, 1962], Subj. Welfare, 158/1808, Wagner.

12. Lawrence Podell, "Families on Welfare in New York City," The Center for the Study of Urban Problems, City University of New York, 1968, quoted in Jackson and Johnson, *Protest by the Poor*, 77.

13. Kerwin to Wagner, November 14, 1962.

14. Letter from Mrs. Theresa Vasta, Brooklyn, N.Y., to Mayor Wagner, City Hall, New York City, November 12, 1962, Subj. Welfare, 158/1809, Wagner.

15. Maria Ramos to Mayor Wagner; and Julia Harrison, Queens, N.Y., to Mayor Wagner, n.d., Subj. Welfare, 158/1808, Wagner. Also see letter from Justina Rivera, Brooklyn, N.Y., to Mayor Wagner, October 12, 1962, ibid.

16. For references to the language of "minimum standards" and "decency" in the New York State social security law, see Christina Mann Fair Hearing, New York City, N.Y., September 18, 1967, 13–14, Case of Christina Mann, 48/142,

SEDFRE; and Draft Fair Hearing Questions for Miriam Stevenson Fair Hearing, November 1, 1968, 4, Case of Miriam Stevenson, 47/58, SEDFRE. All the names of clients of the Scholarship, Education, and Defense Fund for Racial Equality (SEDFRE) have been changed. For an example of how the minimum standards language was used in welfare rights organizing, see, D.C. Citywide Alliance, flyer, "Should we get money for school clothes? YES," 1952/No file, NWRO. On "benefit-based" organizing, see discussion in Chapter 1 above.

17. On "Friendly Visiting," I rely on my own unpublished research in the case records of the Charity Organization Society of New York, Community Service Society papers, Butler Rare Books and Manuscripts Library, Columbia University. On welfare practices between the 1930s and 1960s, see Boxes 1–2, Wickenden; Winifred Bell, *Aid To Dependent Children* (New York: Columbia University Press, 1965); and Jennifer Mittelstadt, *From Welfare to Workfare: The Unintended Consequences of Liberal Reform, 1945–1965* (Chapel Hill: University of North Carolina Press, 2005). On postwar spending, see U.S. Department of Commerce, Bureau of the Census, *Historical Statistics of the United States, Colonial Times to 1970, Part I* (Washington, D.C.: GPO, 1975), 225, Series F 17–30, "Per Capita Income and Product for Selected Items in Current and Constant (1958) Prices: 1929 to 1970" and Part II, 688–89, Series P 231–300, "Physical Output of Selected Manufactured Commodities: 1860 to 1970—Women's Misses' and Juniors' Dresses (in thousands)" and 692–93, Series P 231–300, "Shoes Produced (except athletic)—Women's (in millions of pairs)." Also see discussions in Cohen, *Consumers' Republic*; Daniel Horowitz, *The Anxieties of Affluence: Critiques of American Consumer Culture, 1939–1979* (Amherst: University of Massachusetts Press, 2004); Elaine Tyler May, *Homeward Bound: American Families in the Cold War Era* (New York: Basic Books, 1988), 162–82; and David Potter, *People of Plenty: Abundance and the American Character* (Chicago: University of Chicago Press, 1964).

18. Theodore H. White, *The Making of the President 1964* (New York: Signet Books, 1966), 365.

19. Public Welfare Amendments of 1962 (July 25, 1962), [76 Statutes at Large 172]; John F. Kennedy, "Presidential Statement Upon Approving the Public Welfare Amendments Bill," in *Statutory History of the United States: Income Security*, ed. Robert B. Stevens (New York: Chelsea House), 652.

20. Testimony of Philip H. Vogt, welfare administrator, Omaha, Nebr., from "Restricted Payments—Discussion in 19[6]0 Before the Senate Finance Committee," Excerpts from Hearings Before the Committee on Finance, United States Senate, Eighty-First Congress, Second Session, on H.R. 6000, 282–83, 1/28, Wickenden.

21. Public Welfare Amendments of 1962, Section 107(a). On the origins and meaning of the "best interests of the child" see Michael Grossberg, *A Judgment for Solomon: The D'Hauteville Case and Legal Experience in Antebellum America* (Cambridge: Cambridge University Press, 1997), 55, 231. On the money payment principle, see Jane Hoey, Director, Bureau of Public Assistance, "The Significance of the Money Payment In Public Assistance," *Social Security Bulletin* 7, 9 (September 1944): 3–5.

22. W[inifred] Bell, "Dangers of Restricted Cash Payments or Voucher Payments or Restricted Practices," n.d., 1/28, Wickenden.

23. Elizabeth Wickenden, "Public Welfare Amendments of 1962—Memo #2: The Issue of the Civil Rights of Assistance Recipients," confidential draft August 17, 1962, 4, 1/28, Wickenden.

24. The 1962 amendments reached poor people in New York City through comparable changes in state and local law and regulations. See New York State Regulations 381.2 (a) and New York City Regulations Section 221 (p. 121), discussed in Draft Document on Spending Restrictions, marked "Hearing, 11/1/68—Mrs. Miriam Stevenson," 5, from Case of Miriam Stevenson, 47/58, SEDFRE.

25. In 1962, the title of the largest public assistance program changed from Aid to Dependent Children to Aid to Families with Dependent Children. See *Statutory History of the United States—Income Security*, 652–54. Old Age Assistance (OAA) was a federal program for the low-income elderly who were not covered by the Old-Age Insurance ("Social Security") program. Home Relief was the term in many states for the assistance program for adults who had no children or who did not qualify for AFDC. For the origins of individualized casework practices in the early twentieth century, see Linda Gordon, "Social Insurance and Public Assistance: The Influence of Gender in Welfare Thought in the United States, 1890–1935," *American Historical Review* 97, 1 (February 1992): 19–54.

26. City of New York—Department of Welfare, "Half-Monthly Budget Plan—Miller, Louise," February 16, 1966, Case of Louise Miller, 48/73, SEDFRE.

27. Social Service Employees Union, "Tables of Minimum Standards from Information Found in the Handbook for Case Units in Public Assistance," n.d., Basic clothing chart, "Woman," n.p., "Household Furnishings and Equipment (not included in the regular check)," n.p., SSEU manual, 2010/SSEU-NY, NWRO. See discussion of the standards in Charles Morris, *The Cost of Good Intentions: New York City and the Liberal Experiment, 1960–1975* (New York: Norton, 1980), 69.

28. SSEU manual, 13.

29. Memorandum, City of New York, Department of Welfare, "Subject: Determining Need for Household Furniture, Furnishings, Supplies and Equipment, To: Administrative Group, Case Unit, Home Economist," October 24, 1966, 2101/Basic Needs Campaign, NWRO.

30. Beulah Sanders, interview with Nick Kotz and Mary Lynn Kotz, 1974, 2, 24/Beulah Sanders interview, Kotz.

31. Espada, quoted in Jackson and Johnson, *Protest by the Poor*, 103.

32. Frank Espada, interview with Felicia Kornbluh, by telephone, June 23, 2004, 2, 23, transcript in possession of the author; Jackson and Johnson, *Protest by the Poor*, 103; and Frances Fox Piven and Richard Cloward, *Poor People's Movements: How They Succeed, Why They Fail* (New York: Vintage, 1977), 286–87. On Birnbaum, see Hulbert James, interview with Nick Kotz, October 30, 1974, 4, 24/Hulbert James Interview, Kotz; and A. L. Faltz, "On the Outside of the Inside."

33. Washington quoted in Jackson and Johnson, *Protest by the Poor*, 108.

34. Greenleigh Associates study cited in Richard Cloward and Frances Fox Piven, "The Weight of the Poor: A Strategy to End Poverty," *The Nation*, May 2, 1966, 511.

35. Jackson and Johnson, *Protest by the Poor*, 129–39; Mobilization for Youth, "Synopsis of Programs (1966)" and "Summary Report of Progress (1966)" (Glen Rock, N.J.: Microfilming Corporation of America, 1976); and Executive Board, City-Wide Coordinating Committee of Welfare Groups, "Here Is the Straight Story on the Negotiations with Ginsberg and Costello," *TLI* 1, 1 (July 15, 1966): 1.

36. Sydelle Moore, quoted in Jackson and Johnson, *Protest by the Poor*, 109.

37. Executive Board, "Here Is the Straight Story," 2; "Citywide Meeting

Decides on Local Action," *TLI* 1, 2 (July 22, 1966): 1; "Pressure Welfare Ctrs. for Clients Rights," *TLI* 1, 4 (August 5, 1966): 1; and "Brooklyn Group Pickets Welfare Center Every Week," *TLI* 1, 5 (August 19, 1966): 2.

38. "New Brooklyn Group," *TLI* 1, 10 (October 14, 1966): 2; and "Coney Island Welfare Clients Organization," *TLI* 1, 11 (October 28, 1966): 2. For other examples of minimum standards success, see "Victory List," *TLI* 1, 5 (August 19, 1966): 2; and "Bedford-Stuyvesant Unit of Project Enable," *TLI* 1, 11 (October 28, 1966): 2.

39. "Coney Island"; and Hudson Neighborhood Conservation Project, "Questions for Welfare Rights Groups and Individuals in Relation to the Poverty Rights Newsletter," n.d. [Received by P/RAC, October 21, 1966], 2167/Upper West Side Council, NWRO.

40. Espada was still the chairman of the City-Wide Coordinating Committee in October 1966. See "Radio-WBAI: A Puerto Rican Leader Views New York," *NYT*, October 14, 1966, 87; and Espada, with Kornbluh, 9. For Sanders as chair, see "New Arrangement," *TLI* 2, 1 (May 26, 1967): 1; and "Clients Speak Out," *TLI* 2, 7 (August 4, 1967): 2. For the outcome of negotiations with the city, see "Victory List"; "City Welfare Fund to Give Penniless a Private Burial," *NYT*, August 14, 1966, 16; and reprint of *NYT* piece in Upper West Side Welfare Council *News Letter: The Voice of Poverty Midst Plenty* 2, 1 (January 1967): 4, 2167/Upper West Side Council, NWRO. For Citywide organizing based on minimum standards, see "Call for Volunteers for July 28th," *TLI* 1, 2 (July 22, 1966): 2; "Welfare Rights Manual Here," *TLI* 1, 5 (August 19, 1966): 2; "Training Sessions Begin for Organizers & Leaders," *TLI* 1, 6 (August 26, 1966): 1; and no title, notice of continuing training sessions, *TLI* 1, 8 (September 30, 1966): 2.

41. "Nationwide Meeting of Welfare Groups Aug. 6–7," *TLI* 1, 2 (July 22, 1966): 2; "Area Delegates To Go to Nationwide Meeting in Chicago, Aug. 6&7," *TLI* 1, 3 (July 29, 1966): 1; "Citywide Now Part of Nationwide Movement," *TLI* 1, 5 (August 19, 1966): 1; Poverty Rights Action Center [Wiley/Day], "National Welfare Rights Meeting," n.d. [July 1966], 1953/W.R. Mtg. Call, NWRO; Poverty/Rights Action Center, "National Welfare Rights Meeting, Chicago, Illinois—Tentative Agenda," August 3, 1966, 1953/Chicago Rights Meet. Tentative Addenda (sic), NWRO; and Poverty/Rights Action Center, "Press Release—National Welfare Rights Meeting," for release August 4, 1966, 1953/Press Release 8/4 Chicago Meeting, NWRO.

42. Johnnie Lea Tillmon, interview with Nick Kotz and Mary Lynn Kotz, November 26, 1974, 59, 24/Johnnie Tillmon Interview, Kotz.

43. [George Wiley and Edwin Day], Poverty/Rights Action Center, "Summary Report on National Welfare Rights Meeting held in Chicago, Illinois, on August 6 and 7, 1966," August 11, 1966, 36/Nat.Welfare Rights Org. (Poverty/Rights Action Center), Social Action; Tillmon, with Kotz and Kotz, 57, 59, 61; P/RAC, "Summary Report," August 11, 1966, 1–2; and "Citywide Now Part of Nationwide Movement," *TLI* (August 19, 1966): 1.

44. James, with Kotz and Kotz, 1–2; Institute for Religious and Social Studies, Notes on an Interview with Hulbert James, February 6, 1970, 11/18, Wiley; and Gail Evans, "East Kentucky, Negro Women Push Welfare," *Louisville Courier-Journal*, June 28, 1968, n.p., 8/7, WECC.

45. John Kenneth Galbraith, *The Affluent Society* (Cambridge, Mass: Riverside Press, 1958), 315. On Galbraith and other critics of post-World War II affluence, see my "A Right to Welfare? Poor Women, Professionals, and Poverty Programs, 1935–1975" (PhD dissertation, Princeton University, 2000), chapter 1; and

Horowitz, *Anxieties of Affluence*, 102–8. For the longer history of anxiety over work and spending, see Horowitz, *The Morality of Spending: Attitudes Toward the Consumer Society in America, 1875–1940* (Baltimore: Johns Hopkins University Press, 1985); and Daniel T. Rodgers, *The Work Ethic in Industrial America, 1850–1920* (Chicago: University of Chicago Press, 1978).

    46. Galbraith, *Affluent Society*, 293.

    47. Galbraith, *Affluent Society*, 2nd ed. (Boston: Houghton Mifflin, 1969), 266–67.

    48. Galbraith, *Affluent Society*, 1st ed., 289–90.

    49. Ibid., chapter 21, "The Divorce of Production from Security."

    50. Milton Friedman, with Rose Friedman, *Capitalism and Freedom* (Chicago: University of Chicago Press, 1962), 178. Friedman and Friedman remembered their support for the guaranteed income, and later disenchantment with policy proposals based on this idea, in Milton Friedman and Rose D. Friedman, *Two Lucky People: Memoirs* (Chicago: University of Chicago Press, 1998), 381–82.

    51. Friedman, with Friedman, *Capitalism and Freedom*, 192.

    52. Robert Theobald, *Free Men and Free Markets* (New York: Anchor, 1963), 3. Italics his. Prior to formulating the guaranteed income proposal, Theobald had written an investment handbook titled *Profit Potential in the Developing Countries*, among other works, and was an economic consultant to private firms. *Free Men and Free Markets*, x, and jacket copy; and Theobald, testimony before the U.S. Senate, Committee on Labor and Public Welfare, "Nation's Manpower Revolution," part I, May 20–23, 1963, 118–50. James, with Kotz and Kotz, remembered that Theobald attended the national welfare rights meeting (2).

    53. Theobald, *Free Men*, 6.

    54. Ibid., 8, emphasis his.

    55. Ibid., 8–9.

    56. Galbraith, *Affluent Society*, 2nd ed., 266. George Wiley had begun thinking about the guaranteed income idea when he was still a leader of the civil rights group CORE. Piven and Cloward had included the idea in their essay "The Weight of the Poor," 511, 516, and Piven and Cloward participated in *The Guaranteed Income*, special issue *American Child* 48, 3 (Summer, 1966), 17/No File, Kotz. James, with Kotz and Kotz, noted that the most vocal advocates of the minimum income idea at the National Welfare Rights Meeting were members of the Social Service Employees Union from New York City and other progressive social workers from Chicago (2). See Ad Hoc Committee for a Guaranteed Income, *Guaranteed Annual Income Newsletter*, July 1966–February 1967 and Ad Hoc Committee, "The Guaranteed Income: A Selected Bibliography," 17/No File, Kotz.

    57. M. S. Handler, "Screvane Report Scored as Unfair," *NYT*, November 15, 1964, 58; Clayton Knowles, "Screvane Report Scores Practices of Youth Agency," *NYT*, November 10, 1964, 1, 43; Homer Bigart, "Screvane and U.S. to Evaluate F.B.I. Report on Youth Agency," *NYT*, August 22, 1964, 22; Homer Bigart, "City Hunts Reds In Youth Project on the East Side," *NYT*, August 17, 1964, 1, 12; James, with Kotz and Kotz, 2; and see discussion in chapter 1.

    58. Transcript, telephone conversation between George Wiley and Ed Day, 8:30 p.m., September 15, 1966, 2101/Poor People's March on Wash.—Sept. 27, 1966, NWRO; Espada, with Kornbluh, 9–11; Poverty/Rights Action Center, *Bulletin*, July 19, 1966, 1953/Bull. Pov. Program Analysis, NWRO; P/RAC, "War on Poverty Appropriations Bulletin Number 2," July 26, 1966, 1953/War on Pov. $ Bull #2, NWRO; P/RAC, "Analysis of War on Poverty Appropriations," July 26, 1966, 1953/Pov. Prog. $ Analysis, NWRO; [Espada, et al.], press release, "The

Poor People's March on Washington," September 17, 1966, 2101/Poor People's March on Wash.—Sept. 27, 1966, NWRO; Marjorie Hunter, "Democrats Unite on Poverty Bill," *NYT*, September 27, 1966, 1, 29; and Nan Robertson, "Powell Faces House Move To Strip Him of Powers," *NYT*, September 16, 1966, 1, 26.

59. Transcript, Wiley and Day, September 15, 1966, 1.

60. Ibid., 4–5; and John D'Emilio, *Lost Prophet: The Life and Times of Bayard Rustin* (New York: Free Press, 2003), 394, 410, 426–28, 440–71.

61. P/RAC, "Summary Report," 1953/No File, NWRO; Ed Day, "Interim Report—Attendance at Poor People's March on Washington, Sept. 27, 1966," n.d., 2101/Poor People's March on Wash.—Sept. 27, 1966, NWRO; and James, with Kotz and Kotz, 2.

62. Letter from Baltico S. Erias, deputy director, Niagara Community Action Program, Niagara Falls, New York, to George Wiley, Poverty/Rights Action Center, Washington, D.C., September 26, 1966, with attachment, "Petition for Funding Target Areas In Niagara Falls, New York," 2101/Poor Peoples March Sept 66, NWRO.

63. Poverty/Rights Action Center, "Strategy for Support of Anti-Poverty Legislation," September 27, 1966, in Manual for Marchers: Poor People's March on Washington, 1953/No File, NWRO.

64. Poverty/Rights Action Center, "Summary Report: Poor People's March on Washington: September 27, 1966," 1953/No file, NWRO.

65. John Kifner, "U.S. Aid for Poor In City May Drop," *NYT*, October 22, 1966, 16. For the evolution of the debate, see Joseph Loftus, "House Republicans Call for Shriver's Resignation," *NYT*, September 28, 1966, 36; Loftus, "House Votes Poverty Bill; Mandates Role for Poor," *NYT*, September 30, 1966, 1, 20; "The Nation—Everybody's in The Poverty Act," *NYT*, October 2, 1966, 204; and Loftus, "Congress Passes Poverty Program With New Curbs," *NYT*, October 21, 1966, 1, 25.

66. Mitchell Ginsberg, interview with Nick Kotz and Mary Lynn Kotz, n.d., 3, 24/Mitchell Ginsberg Interview, Kotz.

67. James, with Kotz and Kotz, 5.

68. Ibid., 3.

69. "Get your group ready to move on your Welfare Center," *TLI* 1, 14 (December 2, 1966): 1, with attached Minimum Standards forms in Spanish and English; and "City Groups Hit Centers in Winter Clothing Campaign," *TLI* 1, 15 (December 19, 1966): 1.

70. Jacqueline Pope, *Biting the Hand That Feeds Them: Organizing Women on Welfare at the Grassroots Level* (New York: Praeger, 1980), 1–3. Rhoda Linton estimated the membership figure as significantly lower, perhaps 5,000 at the high point of B-WAC. However, she agreed with Pope that the Brooklyn welfare rights coalition was far more successful than other groups in attracting members, and she noted that this caused resentment within the national welfare rights movement. Linton personal communication, June 21, 2006.

71. The national group, Christians United for Social Action, had formed to support the civil rights movement. The Brooklyn activists called themselves Christians and Jews United for Social Action. See Wendell Pritchett, *Brownsville, Brooklyn: Blacks, Jews, and the Changing Face of the Ghetto* (Chicago: University of Chicago Press, 2002), 212; James Graham, *The Enemies of the Poor* (New York; Random House, 1970), ix, 167, 259 167; Espada, with Kornbluh, 5; Jackson and Johnson, *Protest by the Poor*, 106–7; Pope, *Biting the Hand*, 55; and Morris, *Cost of Good Intentions*, 59. On Espada's career, see Espada, with Kornbluh, 11; "Puerto

Ricans Press Plea for Espada in New Post," *NYT,* June 24, 1967, 24; "50 Demonstrators at Sviridoff's Office," *NYT,* June 29, 1967, 39; and "Urban Coalition Here Appoints Two Vice Presidents," *NYT,* May 22, 1968, 21.

72. Pope, *Biting the Hand,* 41–42, 44; Jackson and Johnson, *Protest by the Poor,* 106–7; and Graham, *Enemies of the Poor,* 64: "Brooklyn by accident has raised a generation of radical priests who refuse to quit their ministry. They remain to annoy the bishop with their tactics and to reproach him by their example with the silent accusation that he has lost his own vocation to cater to the poor."

73. Joyce Burson, interview with Nick Kotz and Mary Lynn Kotz, 1974, 9–12, 24//Joyce Burson Interview, Kotz. The presence of War on Poverty personnel in Brooklyn points to the significance of the federal programs in building the welfare rights movement, even as movement activists devoted most of their energy to local organizing rather then to lobbying Congress. For more on the role of VISTA's in welfare rights, see Piven and Cloward, *Poor People's Movements,* 292–93.

74. Burson, with Kotz and Kotz, 11. Also see Graham, *Enemies,* 277–78; and Jackson and Johnson, *Protest by the Poor,* 106–7.

75. Burson, with Kotz and Kotz, 11; and Pope, *Biting the Hand,* 44.

76. Pope, *Biting the Hand,* 55.

77. Both quotations from Rhoda Linton, interview with Felicia Kornbluh, June 9, 1997, by telephone, 17, transcript in author's possession.

78. Burson, with Kotz and Kotz, 17. On the growth of CUSA and B-WAC, see Graham, *Enemies of the Poor,* 165; Jackson and Johnson, *Protest by the Poor,* 106–7; and Pope, *Biting the Hand,* vii.

79. Burson, with Kotz and Kotz, 21.

80. Poverty/Rights Action Center, "Welfare Rights Organizations," December 1, 1966, Unnumbered Box/List of Welfare Rights Organizations, Sampson; and Poverty/Rights Action Center, "Welfare Rights Organizations," February 15, 1967, ibid. The St. Louis LAW groups started in June 1966, and grew directly out of the local offices of the federally funded poverty programs. See (Miss) Earline Ingram, consultant, Project Description (Prospectus), Union-Sarah Chapter of the League for Adequate Welfare, St. Louis, Missouri, n.d. [late 1966], Unnumbered Box/How Group Started, Sampson.

81. Marian Hall, the chairman of the Ohio Welfare Rights Coalition, became a paid staff member of the Akron War on Poverty Agency in late 1966. Gary Sampson, "Mrs. Hall Keeps Fighting for Poor," *Akron Beacon-Journal,* December 2, 1966, n.p., 2167/Akron, NWRO.

82. "Around the State—Columbus," 2167/Ohio Steering Committee for Adequate Welfare, NWRO; Mary Spurlock, Columbus Welfare Rights Organization, "Poem," *Ohio Adequate Welfare News,* January 9, 1967, 1, ibid.; and Spurlock, "The Bad Months," *Ohio Adequate Welfare News,* February 14, 1967, 4, ibid.

83. Ed Day, interview with Nick Kotz and Mary Lynn Kotz, n.d., 48, 24/Wiley: Ed Day, Kotz.

84. Tillmon, with Kotz and Kotz, 66.

85. Ibid., 67–68.

86. George Wiley, letter to Welfare Leaders and Organizers, *NOW!* 1, 8 (March 20, 1967): 2–3. The February meeting approved a set of legislative goals. See "Legislative Goals: What Congress Should Do to Improve Welfare!!!!!" *NOW!* 1, 16 ([August ?] 1967): 11.

87. Tillmon, with Kotz and Kotz, 75.

88. Tim Sampson, interview with Felicia Kornbluh, Oakland, Calif., July 26, 2001, 22–23, transcript in author's possession; Day, with Kotz and Kotz, 10, 49, 58, 24; and Tillmon, with Kotz and Kotz, 78, 85.

89. Sampson, with Kornbluh, July 26, 2001, 8. Ed Day also claimed credit for the slogan, "More Money NOW!" which he, too, half regretted. Day, with Kotz and Kotz, 46.

90. Johnnie Tillmon, chairman, National Coordinating Committee, and George Wiley, director, National Headquarters of the Welfare Rights Movement, "Convention Call," *NOW!* 1, 15 ([July 24?], 1967): n.p.

91. "National Convention August 25th to 28th—Convention Details," *NOW!* Supplement, n.d., 2.

92. Alan Stone, interview with Felicia Kornbluh, New York City, NY, February 11, 1997, 4, transcript in possession of the author.

93. "National Convention August 25th to 28th—Convention Details," *NOW!* Supplement, 1; and "First Annual National Welfare Rights Convention—Program and Journal," *NOW!* Supplement, 1–2.

94. Tillmon, with Kotz and Kotz, 121.

95. Ibid., 91. Announcements of the rally and march to HEW appeared in "National Convention August 25th to 28th—Convention Details"; and "National Convention August 25th to 28th," *NOW!* 1, 16 ([August ?] 1967): 4.

96. "1,400 March on Capitol," *TLI* 2, 9 (September 27, 1967): 2.

97. Sampson, with Kornbluh, July 21, 1998, 12. For the lock-out (or, as the author for *Tell It Like It Is* termed it, the "lock-in"), see also "1,400 March on Capitol"; and Tillmon, with Kotz and Kotz, 92.

Chapter 3. Legal Civil Disobedience

1. All the names of the people whose fair hearing records were used have been changed. For this woman's role in the New York City welfare rights movement, see "Citywide Elections," *TLI* 3, 1 (January 15, 1968): 2, and "New Executive Board Members," ibid.; "Borough & Group News—Bronx," *TLI* 3, 7 (May 22, 1968): 1; and "Borough News," *TLI* 3, 10 (July 1968): 1.

2. Sunderland fair hearing, October 24, 1967, New York City, case of Joan Sunderland, 49/1, SEDFRE.

3. Sunderland hearing, 80–82, case of Joan Sunderland. For thoughtful discussion of a legal proceeding similar to that of Joan Sunderland, see Lucie White, "Subordination, Rhetorical Survival Skills, and Sunday Shoes: Notes on the Hearing of Mrs. G.," *Buffalo Law Review* 38, 1 (Winter 1990): 1–58.

4. *NOW!* 1, 20 (October 20, 1967), cover.

5. Martha Davis, *Brutal Need: Lawyers and the Welfare Rights Movement, 1960– 1973* (New Haven, Conn.: Yale University Press, 1992). On welfare rights and law, see also William Forbath, "The New Deal Constitution in Exile," *Duke Law Journal* 51 (October 2001): 165; Forbath, "Constitutional Welfare Rights: A History, Critique, and Reconstruction," *Fordham Law Review* 69 (April 2001): 1821; Frank Michelman, "A Comment on Forbath," *Fordham Law Review* 69 (April 2001): 1893; Elizabeth Bussiere, *(Dis)Entitling the Poor: The Warren Court, Welfare Rights, and the American Political Tradition* (University Park: Pennsylvania State University Press, 1997); Hartley Dean, *Welfare, Law, and Citizenship* (New York: Prentice Hall, 1996); Shep Melnick, *Between the Lines: Interpreting Welfare Rights* (Washington, D.C.: Brookings Institution Press, 1994); Susan E. Lawrence, *The Poor in Court: The Legal Services Program and Supreme Court Decision Making* (Princeton, N.J.: Princeton University Press, 1990); and Aryeh Neier, *Only Judgment: The Limits of Litigation in Social Change* (Middletown, Conn.: Wesleyan University Press, 1982), 127–40. For additional views of poor people's uses of law,

see Rebecca Zietlow, "Two Wrongs Don't Add Up to Rights: The Importance of Preserving Due Process in Light of Recent Welfare Reform Measures," *American University Law Review* 45, 4 (April 1996): 1111–49; Louise Trubek, "The Worst of Times . . . And the Best of Times: Lawyering for Poor Clients Today," *Fordham Urban Law Journal* 20 (1995): 1123–40; Sally Engle Merry, *Getting Justice and Getting Even: Legal Consciousness Among Working-Class Americans* (Chicago: University of Chicago Press, 1990); and Austin Sarat, "The Law Is All Over: Power, Resistance, and the Legal Consciousness of the Welfare Poor," *Yale Journal of Law and the Humanities* 2, 2 (Summer 1990): 343–79.

6. Ted Seaver, "The Care and Feeding of Southern Welfare Departments," in *The Mississippi Experience: Strategies for Welfare Rights Action*, ed. Paul Kurzman, foreword George Wiley (New York: Association Press, 1971), 54, 58.

7. *Shelley v. Kramer* (334 U.S. 1); and *Brown v. Board of Education of Topeka* (347 U.S. 483). On the NAACP Legal Defense and Educational Fund, see Mark Tushnet, *Making Civil Rights Law: Thurgood Marshall and the Supreme Court, 1936–1961* (New York: Oxford University Press, 1994), 27, 310–11; Tushnet, *The NAACP's Legal Strategy Against Segregated Education, 1925–1950* (Chapel Hill: University of North Carolina Press, 1987); and Richard Kluger, *Simple Justice: The History of Brown v. Board of Education and Black America's Struggle for Equality* (New York: Vintage, 1975), esp. 221.

8. There has been substantial scholarly debate about the efficacy of this litigation. For overviews, see Kevin Gaines, Clayborne Carson, Mary Dudziak, Adam Fairclough, Scott Kurashige, Daryl Michael Scott, Charles M. Payne, and Lani Guinier, "Round Table: *Brown v. Board of Education*, Fifty Years After," *Journal of American History* 91, 1 (June 2004): 19–118; and David Garrow, "Why *Brown* Still Matters," *The Nation*, May 3, 2004, 45–50. For critiques of civil rights litigation, see Derrick Bell, *Silent Covenants: Brown v. Board of Education and the Unfulfilled Hopes for Racial Reform* (New York: Oxford University Press, 2004); Daryl Michael Scott, *Contempt and Pity: Social Policy and the Image of the Damaged Black Psyche, 1880–1996* (Chapel Hill: University of North Carolina Press, 1997); Michael Klarman, "How *Brown* Changed Race Relations: The Backlash Thesis," *Journal of American History* 81 (June 1994): 81–118; and Gerald Rosenberg, *The Hollow Hope: Can Courts Bring About Social Change?* (Chicago: University of Chicago Press, 1991). On the difficult battles to implement civil rights decisions, see Charles Clotfelter, *After Brown: The Rise and Retreat of School Desegregation* (Princeton, N.J.: Princeton University Press, 2004); and James Patterson, *Brown v. Board of Education: A Civil Rights Landmark and Its Troubled Legacy* (New York: Oxford University Press, 2001). For a wrenching view of African American institutions destroyed by desegregation initiatives, see David Cecelski, *Along Freedom Road: Hyde County, North Carolina, and the Fate of Black Schools in the South* (Chapel Hill: University of North Carolina Press, 1994).

9. On the organizations pursuing civil rights and poverty law, see Tushnet, *Making Civil Rights Law*, 44–45; Davis, *Brutal Need*, 18–19, 51, 57; and Thomas M. Hilbink, "Filling The Void: The Lawyers Constitutional Defense Committee and the 1964 Freedom Summer," senior thesis, Columbia College, New York City, May 1994, 10–25. On Rachlin's career, see August Meier and Elliott Rudwick, *CORE: A Study in the Civil Rights Movement* (Urbana: University of Illinois Press, 1975), 226, 335–36; "Right-Wing Union for Social Agents," *NYT*, July 16, 1948, 20; "Witness Disputes U.S. Reds' 'Break,'" *NYT*, February 21, 1957, 13; "Red Session Here Held Democratic," *NYT*, February 25, 1957, 14; Anthony Lewis, "Army Risk Rules Face New Attack," *NYT*, March 23, 1958, 36; and Peter Kihss, "Hearing Is Urged on Security Code," *NYT*, January 18, 1960, 17.

10. Rachlin quoted in Hilbink, "Filling the Void," 4, 11.

11. For public benefits cases brought by LCDC, see Maggie Gordon, Holmes County, Mississippi, welfare claim, reel 25; Mose Patterson, Alcora County, Miss., Social Security claim, reel 56; and Ora Wilson, Sunflower County, Miss., A.F.D.C. claim, reel 72. Also see the cases LCDC brought against welfare departments, such as Hinds County, Miss., Welfare Department case, reel 36; Opelousas Welfare case, St. Landry Parish, La., reel 54; and Sunflower County, Miss., fair hearings litigation, reel 67, all from "Southern Civil Rights Litigation of the 1960s," ed. Clement Vose, microfilm from the collections of Fisk University, prepared for filming in the Collection on Legal Change, Wesleyan University, Middletown, Conn. Martha Davis (*Brutal Need*, 61) also argues that LCDC attorneys took on more poverty-related cases after Freedom Summer.

12. Walter Goodman, "The Case of Mrs. Sylvester Smith," *NYT Magazine*, August 25, 1968, SM 67; and Martin Garbus, *Ready for the Defense* (New York: Farrar, Straus, and Giroux, 1971), 146. For *King v. Smith* generally, see "Complaint, Smith, Sylvester, Ruben King v.," December 2, 1966; "Plaintiffs' Trial Brief of Fact and Law, Civil Action No. 2495-N, U.S. District Court for the Middle District of Alabama, Northern Division," April 1967; and "Decree Filed in Case of *Smith v. King*, U.S. District Court for the Middle District of Alabama, Northern Division," November 8, 1967, from Vose, "Southern Civil Rights Litigation of the 1960s," reel 65.

13. Goodman, "The Case of Mrs. Sylvester Smith," 64; and Garbus, *Ready for the Defense*, 148–49.

14. Smith quoted in Goodman, "The Case of Mrs. Sylvester Smith," 29, 62.

15. Robert Semple, Jr., "Alabama Loses Welfare Appeal," *NYT*, June 18, 1968, 33; *King v. Smith* (392 U.S. 309) (1968); and the perceptive discussion in Gwendolyn Mink, *Welfare's End*, (Ithaca, N.Y.: Cornell University Press, 1998), 51–53.

16. Letter from Carl Rachlin, general counsel, CORE, to Hon. James Scheuer, member of Congress, Washington, D.C., December 21, 1966, and letter from Carl Rachlin to Armand Derfner, Esquire, Covington and Burling, Washington, D.C., December 9, 1966, 29/24, SEDFRE. For Rachlin's connection to the school clothing protest, see assorted affidavits and correspondence, 41/12, SEDFRE. Rachlin switched from working on the black freedom movement in the south to working increasingly with the welfare rights movement in 1966, when he saw that the Lawyers Constitutional Defense Committee "was proceeding very well" and would not suffer if he shifted his emphasis. Carl Rachlin, interview with Thomas Hilbink, October 13, 1992, transcript in possession of author, 17.

17. For Rachlin and Citywide, see "Condolences," *TLI* 1 (May 1–9, 1967): 2; and letter from Jacqueline Pitts, City Wide Coordinating Committee of Welfare Groups, to Mr. Carl Rachlin, SEDFRE, April 1, 1968, 30/52, SEDFRE. For Rachlin and Wiley, see Rachlin, with Hilbink, 16–17.

18. Letter from Gloria Arce (Gloria Arce Perez), New York City, to Department of Welfare, Albany, N.Y., October 22, 1962, 158/1809, Wagner. The Welfare Department reopened her case.

19. Letter from Charles Simmons, New York, to Mayor R. Wagner, October 14, 1962, 157/1599, Wagner.

20. William Stringfellow, *My People Is the Enemy: An Autobiographical Polemic* (New York: Holt, Rinehart, and Winston, 1964), 44.

21. Stringfellow, *My People Is the Enemy*, 60–61. See also James Finney, "The Harlem Experience," U.S. Department of Health, Education, and Welfare,

Office of Juvenile Delinquency and Youth Development, *The Extension of Legal Services to the Poor—Conference Proceedings, November 12, 13, and 14, 1964* (Washington, D.C.: U.S. Government Printing Office, 1964), 109.

22. Jerome Carlin, *Lawyers' Ethics: A Survey of the New York City Bar* (New York: Russell Sage Foundation, 1966), xxvii, 178. On racial and class biases by New York lawyers, see Carlin, 9, 13, 16, 178; Jonathan Randall, "Legal Profession Here Accused of Not Meeting Ethical Criteria," *NYT*, June 12, 1966, 112; and Joseph P. Lyford, *The Airtight Cage: A Study of New York's West Side* (New York: Harper and Row, 1966), xxii.

23. Reginald Heber Smith, *Justice and the Poor* (1919; New York: Arno Press, 1971), 134–35, 149; Earl Johnson, Jr., *Justice and Reform: The Formative Years of the O.E.O. Legal Services Program* (New York: Russell Sage Foundation, 1974), 4–5, 9, 13–14; Harrison Tweed, *The Legal Aid Society of New York City, 1876–1951* (New York: Legal Aid Society, 1954); and Davis, *Brutal Need*, 11–17. In 1964, the eleven Legal Aid lawyers in Harlem handled sixteen thousand applications for legal assistance. James R. Dumpson, Maxwell Lehman, and Herman Badillo, Anti-Poverty Operations Board, "Suggested Objectives and Criteria for Program Selection—Draft," January 7, 1965, Subj. Anti-Poverty-Legal Services, Community Action Programs, 8/84, Wagner.

24. Richard A. Cloward and Richard M. Elman, "The Storefront on Stanton Street: Advocacy in the Ghetto," in *Community Action Against Poverty: Readings from the Mobilization Experience*, ed. George A. Brager and Francis P. Purcess (New Haven, Conn.: College & University Press, 1967), 268. On the MFY Legal Unit, see Charles Grosser, "The Need for Neighborhood Legal Services and the New York Experience," U.S. Department of Health, Education, and Welfare, *Extension of Legal Services to the Poor*, 73; Michael Appleby, "Overview of Legal Services," in *Justice and the Law in the Mobilization for Youth Experience*, ed. Harold Weissman (New York: Association Press, 1969), 1; and Johnson, *Justice and Reform*, 23. On Strycker's Bay and legal aid, see Lyford, *Airtight Cage*, 118, 125–26.

25. Memorandum from Anne Roberts to Julius C.C. Edelstein, "Legal Services Under the CAP Proposal," February 11, 1965, Subj. Anti-poverty–Legal Services, Community Action Programs, 8/84, Wagner; Fred Powledge, "$9,183,626 U.S. Aid Given City To Open Poverty Program," *NYT*, June 6, 1965, 1; Powledge, "A Basic Question Stalls Legal Aid—Program Held Up Here over Representation of Poor," *NYT*, December 12, 1965, 62; editorial, "Lawyers for the Poor," *NYT*, December 12, 1966, 46; and Johnson, *Justice and Reform*, 92. On the arrival of legal services in New York City, see Johnson, *Justice and Reform*, 93, 99; Fred Samuel, "Free Legal Services to the Poor Program," *Am. News*, February 3, 1968, 4; "Community Law Office Opens in East Harlem," *Am. News*, June 29, 1968, 6; and "Able Legal Services Free in Brownsville," *Am. News*, August 31, 1968, 19. For the MFY Legal Unit as a model, see Johnson, *Justice and Reform*, 22; and Davis, *Brutal Need*, 32–33.

26. For the founding of the Center on Social Welfare Policy and Law, see "Center Will Advise Welfare Lawyers," *NYT*, December 6, 1965, 37; and letter from Edward Sparer, legal director, CSWPL, New York, New York, to "Dear Friend," December 1, 1965, 49/66, SEDFRE. On other providers of legal assistance to poor people in New York City, see letter from Gabe Kaimowitz, Center on Social Welfare Policy and Law, to Carl Rachlin, SEDFRE, New York City, April 16, 1968, 30/52, SEDFRE; letter from Gabe Kaimowitz to Stephen Nagler, SEDFRE, May 7, 1968, ibid.; and letter from Alan Levine, New York Civil Liberties Union, to Gabe Kaimowitz, June 19, 1968, ibid. On the pro bono practices of

private firms, see Deborah Rhode, *Access to Law* (New York: Oxford University Press, 2004). Thanks to Catherine Fisk and Erwin Chemerinsky for this reference.

27. Prospectus, Project on Social Welfare Law, Arthur Garfield Hays Civil Liberties Program, New York University School of Law, n.d. [1965], 7/9, Wickenden; Elizabeth Wickenden, "Legal and Constitutional Issues Affecting the Rights of Individuals Seeking or Receiving Welfare and Related Public Benefits," September 1, 1965, 49/66, SEDFRE; Edward Sparer, draft proposal for a Center for the Study of Legal and Policy Problems in Public Welfare, February 4, 1965, ibid.; and [Wickenden?], draft prospectus, Project on Social Welfare Law, April 28, 1965, 7/29, Wickenden. Norman Dorsen points out that, although the NYU center did not sponsor litigation, he was personally involved in litigation related to poverty and public benefits during the period when he headed the NYU center. Dorsen personal communication, September 27, 2006.

28. A. Delafield Smith, "Public Assistance as a Social Obligation," *Harvard Law Review* 63, 2 (December 1949): 266–88.

29. Charles Reich, "Individual Rights and Social Welfare: The Emerging Legal Issues," *Yale Law Journal* 74, 7 (June 1965), 1246.

30. On the origins of fair hearings in welfare rights, see Davis, *Brutal Need*, 31, 47–48; and David Gilman and Ezra Birnbaum, "New York City Minimum Standards-Fair Hearing Campaigns—June to December 1967," January 1968, 1, 2101/Basic Needs Campaign, NWRO. On Gilman himself, see Jackson and Johnson, *Protest by the Poor*, 183; and Rhoda Linton, interview with Felicia Kornbluh, June 9, 1997, by telephone, transcript in possession of author, 74. Birnbaum was a left-leaning social worker, a member of the New York group Social Work Action for Welfare Rights and, later, of the Revolutionary New Left Caucus of the national Social Welfare Workers Movement. See Social Work Action for Welfare Rights, leaflet, "Welfare and the Ghetto," n.d., 4/18, Padwee; "SWAWR Position Paper," May 1970, ibid.; membership list, "Revolutionary New Left Caucus of SWWM," n.d., ibid.; and Social Welfare Workers Movement, "Why We Are and Why We Are Here," May 25, 1969, ibid. On the Center on Social Welfare Policy and *King v. Smith*, see Garbus, *Ready for the Defense*, 146, 166, 173–74.

31. Jill Jackson fair hearing March 30, 1967, 67–68, case of Jill Jackson, 48/22, SEDFRE. For other Mount Vernon clients of Rachlin's, see letter from Marian Wilson, Mt. Vernon, N.Y., to Carl Rachlin, SEDFRE, n.d. [September 1967?], case of Marian Wilson, 47/92, SEDFRE; decision after fair hearing, State of New York Department of Social Services, in the Matter of the Appeal of Thomasina Lewis, from a determination by the Westchester County Department of Social Services, n.d., case of Thomasina Lewis, 47/16, SEDFRE; and George K. Wyman, Commissioner, State of New York Department of Social Services, "Decision After Hearing, in the Matter of the Appeal of Alice Farmer, from a determination by the Westchester County Department of Social Services," October 26, 1967, case of Alice Farmer, 47/128, SEDFRE.

32. Jackson fair hearing, 70–71.

33. Ibid.

34. Ibid., 6–7. On changes in social casework during the 1960s, particularly around illegitimacy, see Winifred Bell, *Aid to Dependent Children* (New York: Columbia University Press, 1965).

35. Jackson fair hearing, 49–50. On boyfriend issue, see also 57, 64.

36. "National Action Campaign—GET READY," *NOW!* 1, 12 (May 2, 1967): cover, 2; "Citywide and Nationwide Minimum Standards, Membership & Action

Campaign," *TLI* 2, 1 (June 1, 1967): n.p.; Sydney Zion, "Welfare Clients Press to Collect Thousands 'Owed' Them," *NYT*, October 23, 1967, 1, 34; and Jackson and Johnson, *Protest by the Poor*, 183.

37. "Lower East Side," *TLI* 1, 18 (March 17, 1967): 2.

38. Gilman and Birnbaum, 1.

39. Ibid. For the tactic of jamming the courts and jails in the black freedom movement, see Martin Luther King, Jr., *Why We Can't Wait* (New York: Penguin, 1964), 30; John D'Emilio, *Lost Prophet: The Life and Times of Bayard Rustin* (New York: Free Press, 2003), 332–36; and Maurice Isserman and Michael Kazin, *America Divided: The Civil War of the 1960s* (New York: Oxford University Press, 2004), 90–91.

40. "Fair-Hearing," *TLI* 2, 7 (August 4, 1967): 1. On the public meeting at which the hearing requests were submitted, see "Clients Speak Out!" *TLI* 2, 7 (August 4, 1967): 2. On the hearing campaign in the summer of 1967 generally, see "Action Campaign—Step #2—Fair Hearings to Be Demanded," *NOW!* 1, 14 ([July 3–10?], 1967): 7; "Summer Action Continues," *NOW!* 1, 15 ([July 24?], 1967): 1; and "More and More Clients Demanding Fair Hearings," *TLI* 2, 9 (September 27, 1967): 1.

41. Gilman and Birnbaum, 2. On the "massive campaign," see also press release, "Havoc in Welfare Department," September 22, 1967, Unnumbered Box/C.C.C.W.G. Newsletters; Leaflets; Pamphlets, Sampson; and Jackson and Johnson, *Protest by the Poor*, 185.

42. The highest estimate came from the *New York Times*. See Sydney Zion, "Welfare Clients Press"; Gilman and Birnbaum, 1; Jackson and Johnson, *Protest by the Poor*, 186; and "More and More Clients Demanding Fair Hearings," *TLI* 2, 9 (September 27, 1967): 1–2. NWRO estimated that Citywide members had filed for "thousands" of fair hearings ("WRO's Use New Weapon"). A fair hearing referee noted with chagrin that Citywide had delivered "approximately 763" hearing requests on August 16, 1967 alone. See Mary Sellors fair hearing, September 25, 1967, New York City, Frederick Goldfeder, Esq., referee, case of Mary Sellors, 48/154, SEDFRE.

43. Zion, "Welfare Clients Press"; Jackson and Johnson, *Protest by the Poor*, 188, 190–92; and "WRO's Use New Weapon."

44. Gilman and Birnbaum, 2.

45. As noted previously, I borrow the language of recognition from feminist philosopher Nancy Fraser, "From Redistribution to Recognition? Dilemmas of Justice in a 'Postsocialist' Age," from her *Justice Interruptus: Critical Reflections on the "Postsocialist" Condition* (New York: Routledge Press, 1997), 11–39.

46. Letter from Mary Louise Sellors, Bronx, N.Y., to Stephen Nagler, SEDFRE, n.d., case of Mary Sellors, 48/154, SEDFRE.

47. Christina Mann fair hearing, September 18, 1967, New York City, 11, case of Christina Mann, 48/142, SEDFRE. For similar issues, see Mary Sellors fair hearing, September 25, 1967, New York City, 55–56, case of Mary Sellors.

48. Ann Freeman fair hearing, October 16, 1967, New York City, 15–16, case of Ann Freeman, 49/14, SEDFRE.

49. "Welfare Clients Press"; Jackson and Johnson, *Protest by the Poor*, 190; and [Department of Health, Education, and Welfare], "Specific Instances In Which States Are Presently Out Of Conformity."

50. "For Immediate Release to The Press," *TLI* 2, 5, n.d. [June 22–23, 1967]: 1.

51. For examples, see Sarah Harrison fair hearing, March 27, 1968, 44, case

of Sarah Harrison, 48/4, SEDFRE; Gertrude Small fair hearing, July 31, 1967, 49, 47/100, SEDFRE; and, on people who were supposed to testify being on strike, Small hearing, July 31, 1967, 42.

52. Office of the Mayor, "Statement by Mayor John V. Lindsay on the Threatened Work Stoppage of the Social Services Employees Union Against the Welfare Department," June 17, 1967, Dept. Welfare, NYC Department Of—1967, 104/1315, Lindsay. See also Office of the Mayor, statement by Mayor John V. Lindsay, June 23, 1967, ibid.; telegram from Henry Foner, president, Joint Board, Fur, Leather, and Machine Workers, AFL-CIO, to Mayor John Lindsay, June 15, 1967, ibid.; Damon Stetson, "Mayor Contends Protest is 'Dying,'" *NYT*, June 30, 1967, 17; and Ruth Kling fair hearing, October 30, 1967, New York City, 42, case of Ruth Kling.

53. Letter from Beulah Sanders to Joseph Rogoff, Welfare Local 371, New York City, August 16, 1967, 3/President's Files—Tribute to Martin Luther King, SSEU. For Citywide responses to the strike, see also strike notice (no title), *TLI* 2, 5, n.d. [June 22–23, 1967]: 1; and "Summer Action Continues," *NOW!* 1, 15 ([July 24?], 1967): 1. For union support of welfare rights, see "Community Action and Client Organizations," *SSEU Rank and File Committee Newsletter*, December 14, 1966, 3, 4/12, Padwee; and Social Service Employees Union, "Community Action Committee Directory," n.d., 9, 4/3, Padwee.

54. Gilman and Birnbaum, 6; Zion, "Welfare Clients Press"; and Jackson and Johnson, *Protest by the Poor*, 190.

55. Letter from (Mrs.) Eleanor Blakely, senior Welfare consultant, New York City Department of Social Services, to Carl Rachlin, June 14, 1967, case of Ann Freeman, 49/14, SEDFRE. See also letter from Harry Brown, senior Welfare representative, Family Services, New York City Department of Social Services, to Stephen Nagler, SEDFRE, October 11, 1967, in case of Martha Dickerson, 48/157, SEDFRE; correspondence between Stephen Nagler and Frances B. Lewis, senior Welfare representative, Family Services, State of New York Department of Social Welfare, New York City office, February-March, 1967, in case of Louise Litvak, 48/40, SEDFRE; and letter from Esther Kvanvik, senior Welfare representative, State of New York, Department of Social Services, New York City area office, to Carl Rachlin, September 12, 1967, in case of Karen McIver, 48/74, SEDFRE.

56. Letter from (Miss) Miriam Mitchell, Brooklyn, N.Y., to the New York State Dept. of Social Services, New York City, March 26, 1968, case of Miriam (Timothy) Mitchell, 49/2, SEDFRE; notice of change in grant, City of New York Department of Welfare, Linden Welfare Center, Brooklyn, N.Y., for Mr. Timothy Mitchell, May 27, 1968, ibid.; notice of special grant, New York Department of Social Services, Linden W[elfare] C[enter], Brooklyn, N.Y., May 27, 1968, ibid.; New York City Department of Social Services-Linden Center, 250 Church Street, NYC, summary of issues to be raised at fair hearing, n.d., ibid.; and notice of change in grant, City of New York Department of Welfare, Linden Welfare Center, for Mr. Timothy Mitchell, Brooklyn, June 17, 1968, ibid.

57. See, for examples, Jean Younger fair hearing, October 23, 1967, New York City, case of Jean Younger, 49/35, SEDFRE; Ruth Kling fair hearing, October 30, 1967, New York City, 5, case of Ruth Kling; and Ilene Money fair hearing, September 27, 1967, New York City, 11, case of Ilene Money, 47/52, SEDFRE. Gilman and Birnbaum, 5, noted that, although most clients received what they wanted prior to a hearing, "Of the 10% who did show for their hearing, at least half received a settlement on their hearing date that covered substantially all the requests made."

58. Martha Dickerson fair hearing, 19–20, case of Martha Dickerson.

59. Letter from Carl Rachlin, legal director, SEDFRE, to Mitchell Ginsberg, commissioner, New York City Department of Welfare, March 7, 1967, case of Estelle Perry, 48/51, SEDFRE.

60. For all these reasons, Rhoda Linton remembered, Brooklyn welfare rights activists were sometimes hesitant to participate in fair hearings. Linton, with Kornbluh, 28–29.

61. Ann Freeman fair hearing, 14, case of Ann Freeman.

62. Joan Sunderland fair hearing, 76–77, case of Joan Sunderland.

63. Linton, with Kornbluh, 29; Gilman and Birnbaum, 5; and Jackson and Johnson, *Protest by the Poor*, 190.

64. Letter from (Mrs.) Delores Monta, Chairman, Binghamton Welfare Rights, Binghamton, N.Y., to NWRO, Washington, D.C., March 12, 1968, 2167/ Binghamton N.Y. WRO, NWRO; telephone contact record, Marcia [Henry?], NWRO, to Sarah Jones, Rochester, N.Y., November 22, [1968], and report from Mrs. Sarah Jones, chairman, on the activities of Rochester Action for Welfare Rights, n.d., 2167/Rochester, N.Y., NWRO; Poverty/Rights Action Center, Basic Needs Campaign questionnaire, completed by Cuyahoga County Welfare Rights Movement, n.d. [July–August 1967], 2167/Cleveland WRM, NWRO; "Profile of Alden Brown," *Welfare Fighter* 1, 10 (June 1970): 8; Alden Brown, Pike County, Ohio, reports to NWRO headquarters, 26/6, Wiley; [J. B. ?], notes on conversation with Rebecca Smith, Bridgeport Moms, November 28, 1971, 2101/Bridgeport MOMS, NWRO; letter from Sander Karp, Greenberg and Karp, Attorneys at Law, Madison, Wisconsin, to Tim Sam[p]son, NWRO, Washington, D.C., November 20, 1968, 2063/Legal Network, NWRO; "High Society Area," *Milwaukee County Welfare Rights Organization Newsletter*, April [1971]: 2, 56/Milw. Welfare Rights Org., Social Action; and Dan Adams, "Fair Hearings and Your Welfare Rights," [Milwaukee County] *Welfare Rights Organization Newsletter*, September 1969: 8–10, Pamphlets.

65. David Diaz, Jr., "Welfare Agency Takes New View of Its Clients," *Louisville Times*, November 15, 1967, n.p., 9/15, WECC.

66. Letter from Edward T. Donnelly, New Haven, Conn., to NWRO, Washington, D.C., November 6, 1971, 2101/Connecticut, NWRO.

67. Letter from Mrs. Elvira Jorgensen, Wichita, Kans., to NWRO, Washington, D.C., July 7, 1969, 2063/Complaints-Misc., NWRO. Jorgensen included a State of Kansas "Request for a Fair Hearing."

68. Letter from David Hensley, Ontario, Calif., to NWRO, Washington, D.C., 1971/California, NWRO. Also see letter from Dorothy G. Hughes, Montclair, Calif., to Debby Vajda, NWRO, December 9, 1971, ibid.

69. Stephen Wexler, "The Poverty Lawyer as Radical," in *Radical Lawyers: Their Role in the Movement and in the Courts*, ed. Jonathan Black (New York: Avon Books, 1971, orig. *Yale Law Review*, 1970), 216. For similar sentiments, see [Tim Sampson?], NWRO, "House Lawyer Memo," n.d. [late 1967?], 2063/Legal Network, NWRO.

70. On available attorneys, see House Lawyer Memo and attached "Report on Lawyers currently interested in work with NWRO"; and Jim Hoagland, "Legal Services Agency: Champion of the Poor," *Washington Post*, July 3, 196[7], ibid. On Neighborhood Legal Services, see Legal Services Program, "First Annual Report of the Legal Services Program of the Office of Economic Opportunity to the American Bar Association at Annual Convention" (Washington, D.C.: OEO, August 1966), 11.

71. Tim Morrison, summer legal intern, NWRO Attorney Listings, August 21, 1969, 2063/Legal Network, NWRO; House Lawyer Memo; and "Some Things Lawyers and Law Students Can Do."

72. George A. Wiley, notice to Reginald Heber Smith Fellows, n.d., 2063/ Legal Network, NWRO. See attached response by Jeffrey B. Schwartz, New Orleans Legal Assistance Corporation, who reported that he was working with the New Orleans WRO. On Sparer and the "Reggies," see "Report on Lawyers Currently Interested in Work with NWRO," attached to House Lawyer Memo.

73. "Some Things Lawyers and Law Students Can Do," 2. For one example of an NWRO attorney using his contacts to get legal assistance for local welfare activists, see letter from Carl Rachlin to Armand Derfner. Derfner had worked with Rachlin in the Lawyers Constitutional Defense Committee. Thanks to Thomas Hilbink for this information.

74. Hoagland, "Legal Services Agency."

75. Linton, with Kornbluh, 48.

76. Poverty/Rights Action Center, "*Summary Report*: Welfare Action Meeting," Saturday Evening, May 21, 1966, YMCA Hotel, Chicago, Illinois, May 27, 1966, 7/7, Wiley.

77. Linton, with Kornbluh, 27; Rhoda Linton, "Leadership Training Project of Brooklyn Welfare Action Council," February, 1968, Linton; and letter to B-WAC Groups from Rhoda Linton, about a second semester of Leadership Training classes, April 19, 1968, ibid. Leadership Training materials also appear in 2022/Brooklyn B-WAC, NWRO.

78. Linton, with Kornbluh, 27, 31.

79. Center on Social Welfare Policy and Law, "Welfare Handbooks," *NOW!* 1, 11 (April 19, 1967), 3–5; and Center on Social Welfare Policy and Law, "Guidelines for the Preparation of Welfare Rights Handbooks," n.d. [1967], file titled "NWRO," NCLEJ. On Newark, see letter from Marvin Rich, executive director, SEDFRE, New York, New York, to Mrs. Deborah Cole, executive director, Aaron Norman Fund, Inc., New York, New York, September [?] 1966, 12/3, SEDFRE. On Mississippi guide, see Poverty/Rights Action Center, Welfare Leaders Newsletter, October 31, 1966: 2, 40/Poverty Rights Action Center, Social Action. For other state and local handbooks, see Welfare Rights Committee, Alameda County, Calif., "The Welfare Rights Handbook," 27/3, Wiley; Massachusetts Welfare Rights Organization, "Welfare Rights Handbook," n.d. [January 1970], ibid.; and Welfare Rights Committee of Monongalia County, West Virginia, "Your Welfare Rights," n.d. [February 1968], ibid.

80. [Shirley Lacy], "Report on the Welfare Program," May 1, 1967, 12/3, SEDFRE.

81. Wayne Williams, "Our Lawyer Speaks," *People Power*, newsletter of the Clark County, Nevada (Las Vegas) Welfare Rights Organization, n.d. [1971]: 3, 56/Clark County (Nev.) Welfare Rights Organization, Social Action; Steve Baridge, MWRO lawyer, "Welfare Law Corner (Esquina de Ley del Welfare)," *Adequate Income Times*, number 1, published by the Massachusetts Welfare Rights Organization, November 14, 1969: 3, 2/6, MWRO; and "Legally," *Upper West Side Welfare Council News Letter: The Voice of Poverty Midst Plenty*, March–April 1967: 4, 2167/Upper West Side Council, NWRO. For Wiley quotation, see George Wiley, report to the Interreligious Foundation for Community Organization, 1968, 11/18, Wiley.

82. For an NWRO workshop with legal content, see [George Wiley], revised draft, N[ational] C[oordinating] C[ommittee] Meeting, Jackson, Miss., Feb 21–

24, 1969, 7/11, Wiley. For local examples, see Rhoda Linton, report on trip to upstate New York, August 14, 1968, 2167/New York-Old Contacts, NWRO; Louisville Welfare Rights Org., Louisville, Ky., "Getting It Together in '71—Workshop Schedule for April 17, 1971," 56/Louisville Welfare Rights Organization, Social Action; JOIN Community Union, Chicago, "JOIN Fights for Better Welfare," n.d., 23/JOIN-Uptown Community Union—Chicago, Social Action; and West End Community Council, Louisville, Ky., schedule of Welfare Workshop, December 3, 1967, 9/14, WECC. On leaflets, see Welfare Grievance Committee of Ohio, "How to Organize a Welfare Rights Local Group," June 1967, 56/Welfare Rights Org., Social Action.

83. On the hearings generally and the use of lay advocates, see Jonathan Marsh, "Fair Hearings & You," *TLI* 3, 11 (August 16, 1968): 2; "Regular Fair Hearings for Minimum Stand.," *TLI* (August, 16, 1963): 1; and "Apply for a Job with Citywide," *TLI* 3, 16 ([December?] 1968): 1. On costs to New York City, see Michael Clendenin, "Legislators' Howl Stops Welfare Income Plan," *New York Daily News*, July 4, 1968, 30; and Peter Kihss, "Monthly City Cost for Extra Relief Put At $10 Million—Ginsberg Says Increase in Special Aid Shows Need for Flat-Grant System," *NYT*, July 15, 1968, 1. Citywide leaders used the $300 figure. See "Telephone Campaign Continues," *TLI* 3, 13 (September 27, 1968): 1.

84. Letter from Toni Stret, Brooklyn, New York, to Mayor Lindsay, Comm. Ginsbergs [sic], and Comm. J. Louchermin [sic], August 28, 1967, case of Toni Stret, 47/118, SEDFRE. For other fair hearings from this period, see Sarah Harrison fair hearing, March 27, 1968, case of Sarah Harrison; Linda Winterson fair hearing, March 28, 1968, case of Linda Winterson, 47/60, SEDFRE; and case of Frances Garnet, 47/21, SEDFRE.

85. Letter from Toni Stret to Mayor Lindsay, et al.

86. Toni Stret fair hearing, March 26, 1968, New York City, 8–9, case of Toni Stret.

87. "Telephone Campaign for Welfare Clients," press release, August 13, 1968, Unnumbered Box/C.C.C.W.G. Newsletters; Leaflets; Pamphlets, Sampson. See also City-Wide Coordinating Committee of Welfare Groups, "Telephone Application Form," n.d. [Summer 1968], Linton; and "Seek Phones For Those On Welfare," *New York Post*, August 14, 1968, n.p., 10/City-Wide Coordinating Committee of Welfare Groups, Social Action.

88. "Telephone Campaign," press release.

89. [Health, Education, and Welfare], "Specific Instances In Which States Are Presently Out Of Conformity"; "Telephone Campaign: Get all our Fair Hearing forms to Citywide," *TLI* 3, 12 (September ?, 1968): 1; "Telephone Campaign Continues," *TLI* 3, 13 (September 27, 1968): 1; "Fight Flat Grant – Get a Phone!/ Pelea 'Flat Grant'—Pida Un Telefono!" *TLI* 3, 14 (October 18, 1968): 3; and "Phone Campaign Climax," *TLI* 3, 15 (November 7, 1968): 2.

90. Clendenin, "Legislators' Howl."

91. On Ginsberg, see Kihss, "Monthly City Cost." For more on Lindsay and proposals for a national takeover of the welfare system, see chapter 4 below.

92. See Tomiko Brown-Nagin, "Elites, Social Movements, and the Law: The Case of Affirmative Action, *Columbia Law Review* 105 (June 2005): 1436–528; Bell, *Silent Covenants*; Clotfelter, *After Brown*; Rosenberg, *Hollow Hope*; Scott, *Contempt and Pity*; Klarman, "How *Brown* Changed Race Relations"; and Patterson, *Brown v. Board of Education*. For a range of views, see Gaines, Scott, Payne, and Guinier contributions to "Round Table: *Brown v. Board of Education*, Fifty Years After." For a less gloomy view of the efficacy of law, as applied to economic

rights, see Forbath, "New Deal Constitution" and "Constitutional Welfare Rights." For optimistic assessments of women's gains from legal strategies, see Nancy MacLean, *Freedom Is Not Enough: The Opening of the American Workplace* (Cambridge, Mass.: Harvard University Press, 2006); and Michael McCann, *Rights at Work: Pay Equity Reform and the Politics of Legal Mobilization* (Chicago: University of Chicago Press, 1994).

93. Rosenberg, *Hollow Hope.*

Chapter 4. On a Collision Course

1. City-Wide Coordinating Committee of Welfare Groups, press release, "Statement, Mrs. Beulah Sanders," July 3, 1968, Unnumbered Box/New York C.C.C.W.G. Newsletters; Leaflets; Pamphlets, Sampson. The release was referenced in John Kifner, "Welfare Protest Group Warns Mayor That Drive Will Continue," *NYT*, July 4, 1968, 7; and "The Welfare Situation is a Mess," *Am. News*, July 13, 1968, 3.

2. Sanders quoted in Kifner, "Welfare Protest Group."

3. Irene Gibbs, "Irene Gibbs Tells Goldberg Like It Is," *TLI* 3, 8 (July 3, 1968): 3.

4. "100's Carry Demands from U.N. to 250 Church/ Beulah Sanders New Commissioner Welfare/ Sit-Ins End in Arrests—State Welfare 'Visited,' " *TLI* 3, 8 (July 3, 1968): 1–2.

5. Hulbert James, interview with Nick Kotz, October 30, 1974, 22, 24/Hulbert James Interview, Kotz; "Brutality at City Hall," *NOW!* 2, 13 (October 1968): 14–15; Peter Kihss, "Relief Recipients and Police Clash," *NYT*, August 28, 1968, 1, 50; Larry Jackson and William Johnson, *Protest by the Poor: The Welfare Rights Movement in New York City* (New York: Rand Corporation, 1973), 203–5; and Jacqueline Pope, *Biting the Hand That Feeds Them: Organizing Women on Welfare at the Grassroots Level* (New York: Praeger, 1989), 95–96.

6. What was new in this period was the open retreat from the original justification of the New Deal program Aid to Dependent Children, which was to support children in their own (meaning their mothers') homes. Work requirements were not new, although a *national* mandatory work program was new. For work requirements at the state level prior to the late 1960s, see Jennifer Mittelstadt, *From Welfare to Workfare: The Unintended Consequences of Liberal Reform, 1945–1965* (Chapel Hill: University of North Carolina Press, 2005).

7. Nancy Gooding, "Poem," *Welfare Righter* 1, 2 (March 28, 1969): 3.

8. On PAT and resistance to integration in New York City, see Joshua Freeman, *Working-Class New York: Life and Labor Since World War II* (New York: New Press, 2000), 198–99; and Martha Biondi, *To Stand And Fight: The Struggle for Civil Rights in Postwar New York City* (Cambridge, Mass.: Harvard University Press, 2003), 246.

9. On the role of the public sector in helping whites get ahead, see Ira Katznelson, *When Affirmative Action Was White: An Untold Story of Racial Inequality in Twentieth-Century America* (New York: Norton, 2005); and Felicia Kornbluh, "Why Gingrich? Welfare Rights and Racial Politics, 1965–1995," in *Race Consciousness: African American Studies for the New Century,* ed. Judith Jackson Fossett and Jeffrey Tucker (New York: New York University Press, 1997), 193–207. For the reactions of white residents of New York, Detroit, and Chicago to African Americans' efforts to share their neighborhoods and benefits, see Thomas J. Sugrue, *The Origins of the Urban Crisis: Race and Inequality in Postwar Detroit* (Princeton, N.J.:

Princeton University Press, 1996); Jonathan Rieder, *Canarsie: The Jews and Italians of Brooklyn Against Liberalism* (Cambridge, Mass.: Harvard University Press, 1985); and Arnold Hirsch, *Making the Second Ghetto: Race and Housing in Chicago, 1940–1960* (Cambridge: Cambridge University Press, 1983). For an astute analysis of white attitudes toward public welfare, which emphasizes race as well as waged work, see Martin Gilens, *Why Americans Hate Welfare: Race, Media, and the Politics of Antipoverty Policy* (Chicago: University of Chicago Press, 1999).

10. Kevin Phillips, *The Emerging Republican Majority* (New Rochelle, N.Y.: Arlington House, 1969), 167–68. Phillips emphasized that the Goldwater voters, many of them former Democrats, were Catholic. Jews, although "white ethnics," continued to vote for Democrats in overwhelming numbers.

11. Sam Tanenhaus, "How William F. Buckley's '65 Run for Mayor Changed America," *NYT Magazine*, October 2, 2005, 68–73; Jonathan Schoenwald, *A Time For Choosing: The Rise of Modern American Conservatism* (New York: Oxford University Press, 2001), 168–88; Vincent J. Cannato, *The Ungovernable City: John V. Lindsay and His Struggle to Save New York* (New York: Basic Books, 2001), 40, 73; Freeman, *Working-Class New York*, 209; and William F. Buckley, *The Unmaking of a Mayor* (New York: Viking, 1966), 67, 122–68, 173–227.

12. Buckley, *Unmaking*, 93.

13. Tanenhaus, "How Buckley's Run Changed America," 106; Cannato, *Ungovernable City*, 36, 56; Schoenwald, *Time for Choosing*, 169, 179–80; and Buckley, *Unmaking*, 178.

14. Phillips, *Emerging Republican Majority*, 168. Again, Phillips emphasized that the new conservative voters were Catholic. See also Cannato, *Ungovernable City*, 69; and Schoenwald, *Time for Choosing*, 186.

15. Freeman, *Working-Class New York*, 165.

16. Charles Brecher, *Where Have All The Dollars Gone? Public Expenditures for Human Resource Development in New York City, 1961–1971* (New York: Praeger, 1974), 35. On wages, see Bureau of Labor Statistics, United States Department of Labor, *Occupational Wage Survey—New York, New York*, esp. Table A-4, "Maintenance and Powerplant Occupations" and Table A-5, "Custodial and Material Movement Occupations," April 1962, April 1964, April 1966, April 1968, April 1972 (Washington, D.C.: U.S. Government Printing Office, 1962–1972).

17. On women's labor-force participation, see Miriam Cohen, *Workshop to Office: Two Generations of Italian Women in New York City, 1900–1950* (Ithaca, N.Y.: Cornell University Press, 1992); Barbara F. Reskin and Patricia A. Roos, *Job Queues, Gender Queues: Explaining Women's Inroads into Male Occupations* (Philadelphia: Temple University Press, 1990), 3–18; Kathy Peiss, *Cheap Amusements: Working Women and Leisure in Turn-of-the-Century New York* (Philadelphia: Temple University Press, 1986), 34–36; and Alice Kessler-Harris, *Out to Work: A History of Wage-Earning Women in the United States* (New York: Oxford University Press, 1982), 228–30, 254–59, 296–97, 300–303.

18. John V. Lindsay, *The City* (New York: Norton, 1969), 147.

19. For migration as a political act, see Nell Irvin Painter, *Exodusters* (New York: Norton, 1979). On recent migrants as welfare recipients, see Greenleigh Associates, "Report to the Moreland Commission on Welfare of Findings of the Study of the Public Assistance Program and Operations of the State of New York," November 1962, 39, 158/1812, Dept. Welfare, 158/1812, Wagner.

20. Greenleigh for Moreland, 40; and Moreland Commission report, "Public Welfare in the State of New York," January 15, 1963, 21, 158/1812, Dept. Welfare, Wagner.

21. Office of Statistical Coordination, "Table G-23—Public Assistance, Monthly Average Number of Cases and Persons, by Program and County, 1966," *New York Statistical Yearbook, 1967* (New York State Capitol: Albany, N.Y., February 1968), 87; Office of Statistical Coordination, "Table J-12—Public Assistance, Monthly Average Numbers of Cases and Persons, by Program and by County, 1967," and "Table J-14, Number of Medical[ly] Needy Authorized and Public Assistance Recipients Compared with Total Population As of December 31, 1967," *New York Statistical Yearbook, 1968–1969*, 191, 193; Peter Kihss, "City Relief Rolls Pass 900,000 Mark," *NYT*, October 17, 1968, 1; Francis X. Clines, "Record $1.7 Billion Asked for Welfare Budget Here," *NYT*, January 3, 1969, 1, 17; and *Annual Report of Mayor John V. Lindsay* (New York: Office of Administration, Central Publications Office, December 1968), 20.

22. Jackson and Johnson, *Protest by the Poor*, 280–81.

23. For Mitchell Ginsberg's thoughts on this trend, see Clines, "Caseload Rises Again," *NYT*, January 3, 1969, 17.

24. Jackson and Johnson, *Protest by the Poor*, vi, viii, 278–79.

25. Office of Statistical Coordination, "Table J-11, Amount and Percent of Personal Income Spent for Public Assistance or Work Relief Benefits, 1932–1967," *New York Statistical Yearbook, 1968–1969* (New York State Capitol: Albany, N.Y., March 1969), 190.

26. "Table G-24, Total Public Assistance Expenditures from All Sources, 1951 to 1966 (thousands)," *Statistical Yearbook, 1967*, 88.

27. U.S. Department of Commerce, Bureau of the Census, "Table 6, Compendium of City Government Finances—Finances of the 43 Largest Cities, in Detail—General Expenditure—Public Welfare," 1949, 1961 to 1973–74 (Washington, D.C.: U.S. Government Printing Office, 1950, 1962–1975), various pages.

28. Peter Kihss, "Welfare Budget Asks $1.4-Billion, Biggest City Item," *NYT*, January 6, 1968, 1; and Clines, "Caseload Rises Again," *NYT*, January 3, 1969, 1.

29. Memorandum from James R. Carberry, assistant to the mayor, to Mayor John V. Lindsay, April 21, 1966, "Why Welfare Costs Can't Be Reduced—Much," Dept. Welfare, 104/1314, Lindsay.

30. Memorandum from Mayor John V. Lindsay to Mitchell Sviridoff, Human Resources administrator, November 22, 1966, Dept. Human Resources Administration, 1966, 47/609, Lindsay.

31. [NYC government], "Facts on Welfare Financing," Source: National Center for Social Statistics, n.d. [1969 data], Subj. Welfare, 117/2219, Lindsay.

32. Even without fully financing the rise in welfare costs, the Lindsay administration increased taxes on city residents, instituting the first personal income tax in the city's history and increasing taxes on business and real estate revenues. Woody Klein, *Lindsay's Promise: The Dream That Failed* (New York: Macmillan, 1970), 130, 167.

33. *Annual Report, 1967, of Mayor John Lindsay to the City Council and the People of New York City* (City of New York, 1967), 29.

34. Lindsay annual report, 1967, 30. For positive commentary on the Lindsay program, see Carl McCall, "The Fight on Poverty—Welfare in Focus," *Am. News*, May 20, 1967, 17.

35. Lindsay annual report, 1967, 30–31.

36. On the longer history of debate among African American and working-class women about out-of-home child care, see Sonya Michel, *Children's Interests/ Mothers' Rights: The Shaping of America's Child Care Policy* (New Haven, Conn.: Yale University Press, 1999), 38, 67–71, 380n68.

37. Neither the statute nor the regulations implementing it specified the conditions under which mothers would be considered suitable for employment. See letter from Marian E. Wright, for Dr. Ralph David Abernathy, president, Southern Christian Leadership Conference, to Honorable Wilbur Cohen, secretary, Department of Health, Education, and Welfare, Washington, D.C., June 12, 1968, 1988/HEW Demands, NWRO. For other specifics on WIN/WIP, see Vincent Burke and Vee Burke, *Nixon's Good Deed: Welfare Reform* (New York: Columbia University Press, 1974), 27, 35. On NWRO activists demanding support so that they could work for wages, see [Committee for Adequate Welfare], "Are you and your children constantly waiting on someone else to make the decision that make will your life better?" 9/14, WECC; Ohio Steering Committee for Adequate Welfare, "Work Incentive," *Adequate Welfare News*, February 14, 1967, 3, 2167/Ohio Steering Committee for Adequate Welfare, NWRO; and Cornelia Olive, "Welfare Workers Hear Clients," *Durham Morning Herald*, November 15, 1968, n.p., 2167/North Carolina, NWRO.

38. Hulbert James explained the provision in James, with Kotz, 8, 11. For the "freeze" language, see, "Congress Declares 'War' on Poor—H.R. 12080 Now Law," *TLI* 2, 10 (December 1967): 1; Jennette Washington, "An Open Letter from a Mad Mother," ibid.; and "Position of the National Welfare Rights Organization on the Proposed Welfare Amendments to the Social Security Act—H.R. 12080 and H.R. 5710," *NOW!* 1, 18 (September 18, 1967): 4a.

39. "Congress Declares 'War' on Poor"; and "Position of the National Welfare Rights Organization on the Proposed Amendments." The ambiguity of the legislation was discussed and resolved by the U.S. Supreme Court in *Rosado v. Wyman* (397 U.S. 397) (1970).

40. [NWRO staff], "Fight The Anti-Welfare Bill, H. R. 12080," *NOW!* 1, 17 (August 15, 1967): cover, 2, 4; "Fight Against the Anti-Welfare Bill Continues," *NOW!* 1, 18 (September 8, 1967): 3; and "Resolution on the Anti-Welfare Bill H.R. 12080," adopted unanimously August 27, 1967 (summarized), *NOW!* 1, 18 (September 8, 1967): 7. On Wilbur Mills, see Julian Zelizer, *Taxing America: Wilbur D. Mills, Congress, and the State* (Cambridge: Cambridge University Press, 1998).

41. Beulah Sanders, interview with Nick Kotz and Mary Lynn Kotz, 1974, 12–13, 26/Beulah Sanders Interview, Kotz.

42. Nick Kotz and Mary Lynn Kotz, *A Passion for Equality: George A. Wiley and the Movement* (New York: Norton, 1977), 220. For Sanders's perspective on domestic work, see Sanders, with Kotz and Kotz, 13. On African American women as domestic workers, see Elizabeth Clark-Lewis, *Living In, Living Out: African-American Domestics in Washington, D.C., 1910–1940* (Washington, D.C.: Smithsonian Institution Press, 1994); Jacqueline Jones, *Labor of Love, Labor of Sorrow: Black Women, Work, and the Family from Slavery to the Present* (New York: Basic Books, 1985), 235–37, 256–60; Paula Giddings, *When and Where I Enter: The Effect of Black Women on Race and Sex in America* (New York: Bantam: 1984), 232, 237–38, 256; and. Kessler-Harris, *Out To Work*, 279, 311–12.

43. On claims for greater access to waged work in the making of the Second Wave women's movement, see Betty Friedan, *The Feminine Mystique* (1963; New York: Laurel, 1983); anonymous letter to Mrs. Friedan, 6 September 1963, 19/682, Friedan; anonymous letter from Sucasunna, N.J., to Betty Friedan, New York, May 20, 1964, 19/682, Friedan; and anonymous letter, April 24, 1964, to Betty Friedan, 19/690, Friedan. For conflicts over waged work between black and white women in the feminist Second Wave, see Giddings, *When and Where I*

Enter, 299, 305–11. For African American women's efforts to create new organizations to speak to needs neither white feminists nor black leaders of the freedom movement addressed fully, see Deborah Gray White, *Too Heavy a Load: Black Women in Defense of Themselves, 1894–1994* (New York: Norton, 1999), 212–56. For an overview of women's efforts to combine waged work with mothering, see Estelle Freedman, *No Turning Back: The History of Feminism and the Future of Women* (New York: Ballantine Books, 2002), 170–99.

44. U.S. Congress, Joint Economic Committee, Subcommittee on Fiscal Policy, *Income Maintenance Programs—Hearings*, Ninetieth Congress, Second Session, June 11, 12, 13, 18, 19, 25, 26, and 27, 1968, vol. 1, 76. For Griffiths as an advocate of aggressive action on issues of women's rights to employment, see letter from Martha W. Griffiths, member of Congress, to Betty Friedan, May 17, 1967, 49/1799, Friedan; Griffiths to Friedan, June 21, 1967, ibid.; and copy of letter from Griffiths to Mrs. W. M. Simpson, Birmingham, Ala., July 12, 1967, forwarded to Friedan, ibid.

45. Hearings on Income Maintenance, 77–78.

46. Ibid., 78–79. For similar conflicts concerning mandatory work among middle-class white feminists, welfare recipients, and welfare advocates, see Gwendolyn Mink, *Welfare's End* (Ithaca, N.Y.: Cornell University Press, 1998), 2–4, 6–7, 23–27, 69–101; and Felicia Kornbluh, "Feminists and the Welfare Debate: Too Little? Too Late?" *Dollars and Sense* (November/December 1996): 25.

47. "The Welfare WIP Program and YOU," *NOW!* (June 17, 1968): cover.

48. Quoted in "Marchers, Mills Meet," *Washington Evening Star*, May 28, 1968, reprinted in *NOW!* (June 17, 1968): back page.

49. "NWRO Battles Welfare Rights Enemy Number 1, Wilbur Mills," *NOW!* 2, 9 (June 17, 1968): cover; "Wanted for Conspiracy to Starve Children, Destroy Families, Force Women into Slavery and Exploit Poor People Public Enemy Number 1, Alias Congressman Mills," *NOW!* 2, 10 (August 1, 1968): cover; and "Testimony of the National Welfare Rights Organization Before the Platform Committee," 2.

50. For the number of groups, see Poverty/Rights Action Center, "Welfare Rights Organizations," February 15, 1967, 8/4, Wiley; City-Wide Coordinating Committee of Welfare Groups, "Havoc in Welfare Department—Clients Begin Month Of Massive Action as Welfare Dept. Refuses to Issue School Clothing," press release, September 11, 1967, Unnumbered Box/New York C.C.C.W.G. Newsletters; Leaflets; Pamphlets, Sampson; "List of Affiliated Groups," January 1968, 8/4, Wiley; "Join Us—Bread, Justice, Dignity—NOW!" *TLI* 3, 7 (May 22, 1968): 3; Jackson and Johnson, *Protest by the Poor*, 5, 192, 207; and Pope, *Biting the Hand*, 2.

51. Washington, "Letter from a Mad Mother." For the governor's position on WIN/WIP, see Nelson Rockefeller, "Announcement by the Governor that New York State Will Participate Fully in a New Federal-State Work Incentive Program," State of New York Executive Chamber, April 1, 1968, *Public Papers of Nelson A. Rockefeller* (Albany: New York State Government, 1968), 1026–28.

52. On NWRO skepticism, see letter from George Wiley to Rev. Dr. Martin Luther King, Jr., October 15, 1966, 36/Nat. Welfare Rights Org. (Poverty Rights Action Center), Social Action; and James, with Kotz, 9, 11. On the meeting, see Edith Doering, minutes, National Coordinating Committee Meeting, Feb. 3, 4, 5, 1968—Chicago, Ill., YMCA Hotel, 7/11, Wiley; National Welfare Rights Organization, Officers and State Representatives, National Coordinating Committee

Meeting, Chicago, February 3–5, 1968, 7/11, Wiley; "Martin Luther King Backs NWRO Fight Against Anti-Welfare Law," *TLI* 2, 2 (February 23, 1968): 5–6; Faith Evans, interview with Nick Kotz and Mary Lynn Kotz, n.d., 43, 24/Faith Evans Interview, Kotz; James, with Kotz, 9; Giddings, *When and Where I Enter,* 312; and Gray White, *Too Heavy a Load,* 214.

53. James, with Kotz, 9; and Doering minutes, 1.

54. Doering minutes, 11; and "Martin Luther King Backs NWRO Fight."

55. Doering minutes, 11.

56. Ibid., 11–12; and "Martin Luther King Backs NWRO Fight."

57. Eve Edstrom, "Women Hit 'Welfare Brutality'," *New York Post,* February 8, 1968, 22, 2101/Spring Press 1968, NWRO; "Dr. King Issues A Warning on Dems' Parley—Backs March if His Demands Fail," *Chicago Tribune,* February 6, 1968, 2101/Spring Press 1968, NWRO; James, with Kotz, 10, 12; and "Martin Luther King Backs NWRO Fight."

58. Beulah Sanders, "Poor People's Campaign," *TLI* 3, 4 (March 29, 1968): 1.

59. Quoted in C. Gerald Fraser, "Dr. King Takes 'Poor People's Campaign' to Groups in Harlem and Queens," *NYT,* March 27, 1968, 24. See also "National-Citywide Campaign to Repeal 12080–New York City Action Plans," *TLI* 3, 4, (March 2, 1968): 1; "Nonviolence Tactic Defended by King In Reply to Powell," *NYT,* March 25, 1968, 46; and Wil Haygood, *King of the Cats: The Life and Times of Adam Clayton Powell, Jr.* (Boston: Houghton Mifflin, 1993), 373.

60. Jose Yglesias, "Dr. King's March on Washington, Part II," *NYT Magazine,* March 31, 1968, SM 30. King had begun speaking openly against the War in Vietnam in the Spring of 1967. His position was controversial within the civil rights movement and among such advocates for African American progress as the editors of New York's *Amsterdam News.* See editorial, "Where We Stand," *Am. News,* April 15, 1967, 1; "War-Rights Link Brings About Break," *Am. News,* April 22, 1967, 1; and Coretta Scott King, *My Life with Martin Luther King, Jr.* (New York: Avon Books, 1969), 293–98.

61. James, with Kotz, 14.

62. James Patterson, *Grand Expectations: The United States, 1945–1974* (New York: Oxford University Press, 1996), 685–86. Novelist and journalist Norman Mailer, a New Yorker, claimed that Harlem and Brooklyn *were* among the places where violence, fire, and looting broke out after the assassination. Norman Mailer, *Miami and the Siege of Chicago* (New York: Signet, 1968), 10.

63. Beulah Sanders, "Dr. King Will Cary On—And Win," *TLI* 3, 5 (April 12, 1968): 1.

64. Wiley, quoted in Kotz and Kotz, *Passion for Equality,* 256. See also Carolyn Lewis, "Welfare Head Asks for King Memorial," *Washington Post,* April 12, 1968, C1.

65. "Proposals For A LIVING MEMORIAL" to Martin Luther King, Jr., 2101/King Memorial—Apr 68, NWRO; "The NWRO Proposals for a Living Memorial," *NOW!* 2, 6 (April 15, 1968): 6; Carolyn Lewis, "Welfare Head Asks for King Memorial"; and Hon. Richard L. Oettinger (D-N.Y.), "Extension of Remarks—A Living Memorial to Dr. King," *Congressional Record,* April 9, 1968, E2870–71, 2101/King Memorial—Apr 68, NWRO.

66. "NCC Vigil on Capitol Hill Results in 39 Arrests," *TLI* 3, 6 (April 26, 1968): 1; NWRO, statement on bias demonstrated by General Sessions Judge Charles W. Hallack, April 23, 1968, 33/1, Wiley; "Persons Arrested in the National Welfare Rights Organization Vigil for Dr. Martin Luther King Jr. April

22, 1968 at Capitol Hill," 33/1, Wiley; George Wiley, letter to Welfare Rights Leaders and Friends, *NOW!* 2, 7 (May 6, 1968): 1; "NWRO Leaders Jailed for King Vigil at U.S. Capitol," ibid., 2–3, 5–6; and Kotz and Kotz, *A Passion for Equality*, 257.

67. Interview with Beulah Sanders, "NCC Vigil on Capitol Hill," 2. See also Sanders, with Kotz and Kotz, 20.

68. Interview with Irene Gibbs, "NCC Vigil on Capitol Hill," 3. See also interview with Mamie Hall, "NCC Vigil on Capitol Hill," 3.

69. "Mother's Day Caravan to Washington to Join NWRO & Mrs. King in National Demand to Repeal 12080," *TLI* 3, 6 (April 26, 1968): 1; City-Wide Coordinating Committee of Welfare Groups, "Citywide Emergency Bulletin— Three Pronged Mother's Day Action," May 2, 1968, 2101/Mothers Day Mar. 68, NWRO; "Mrs. Martin Luther King, Jr., Leads 'Mother's Day' March for Welfare Mothers," NWRO press release, May 4, 1968, ibid.; flyer, "Join With Mrs. Martin Luther King," ibid.; Elsie Carper, "3000 March in Opening of Drive by Poor," *Washington Post*, May 13, 1968, 1; Leonard Downie, Jr., "1st Caravan of Marchers Reaches City," *Washington Post*, May 13, 1968, 1; Ben A. Franklin, "5,000 Open Poor People's Campaign in Washington," *NYT*, May 13, 1968, 1, 37; Lillian Wiggins, "Marchers Sing Songs of Freedom," *Washington Afro-American* and the *Washington Tribune*, May 14, 1968, 1–2, 2101/Mothers Day Clips, NWRO; Joseph R. L. Sterne, "King Widow Leads Trek by Mothers—Asks 'Woman Power' Use as Poor March Opens First Phase," *Baltimore Sun*, May 13, 1968, 1, 33/1, Wiley; and letter from George Wiley to Welfare Rights Leaders and Friends, *NOW!* 2, 8 (June 6, 1968): 1, 1952/Women, *NOW*, NWRO.

70. Mrs. Martin Luther King, Jr., "Woman Power," Speech given May 12, 1968, *NOW!* 2, 8 (June 6, 1968): 6; and Ben A. Franklin, "5,000 Open Poor People's Campaign."

71. [Washington, D.C., Citywide Welfare Alliance], n.d., flyer, Mother's Day March, 2101/Mothers Day Mar. 68, NWRO; Elsie Carper, "3000 March in Opening of Drive," 10; and Lillian Wiggins, "Marchers Sing Songs of Freedom."

72. Jennette Washington, "Solidarity Day for Poor People's Campaign," *TLI* 3, 8 (July 3, 1968): 3; "Solidarity Day Programme," June 19, 1968, 2101/Poor People's Campaign—Solidarity Day, NWRO; National Mobilization Office for Solidarity Day, "June 19th Solidarity Day Fact Sheet," ibid; and "Johnny Socks It to 'Em," *NOW!* 2, 10 (June 28, 1968): 2.

73. Carolyn Lewis, "She Marched To Change Children's Future," *Washington Post*, reprinted in *NOW!* 2, 8 (June 6, 1968): 17–18.

74. Anonymous letter to Carolyn Lewis, *Washington Post*, n.d., 21/4, Wiley.

75. Letter from "A Disgusted Reader," to Carolyn Lewis, *Washington Post*, n.d., 21/4, Wiley.

76. I. F. Stone, "Billions for Missiles and Pennies for Poverty," July 8, 1968, from Stone, *Polemics and Prophecies, 1967–1970* (Boston: Little, Brown), 99.

77. For the end of the Poor People's Campaign and assessments of it, see "Everything, Everybody Gone," Resurrection City photograph, *Am. News*, June 29, 1968, 1; Nick Kotz, *Judgment Days: Lyndon Baines Johnson, Martin Luther King, Jr., and the Laws that Changed America* (Boston: Houghton Mifflin, 2005), 422; Adam Fairclough, *To Redeem the Soul of America: The Southern Christian Leadership Conference and Martin Luther King, Jr.* (Athens: University of Georgia Press, 1987), 368–88; and David J. Garrow, *Bearing the Cross: Martin Luther King, Jr., and the Southern Christian Leadership Conference* (New York: William Morrow, 1986), 590– 601. On media treatment of the Campaign, I have learned from Gordon Man-

tler, "Plague after Plague: Race, Class, and Media in the Poor People's Campaign," unpublished paper in possession of the author, April 28, 2003.

78. Nick Kotz, *Let Them Eat Promises: The Politics of Hunger in America* (Englewood Cliffs, N.J.: Prentice-Hall, 1969), 154–92; and Mailer, *Miami and the Siege of Chicago*, 55.

79. Jackson and Johnson, *Protest by the Poor*, 203; and Michael Clendenin, "Legislators' Howl Stops Welfare Income Plan," *Daily News*, July 4, 1968, 30, reprinted in special *TLI*, 10/City-Wide Coordinating Comm. of Welfare Groups, Social Action.

80. "100's Carry Demands from U.N. to 250 Church"; "11 Demonstrators at Welfare Office Taken into Custody," *NYT*, July 1, 1968, 66; and Jackson and Johnson, *Protest by the Poor*, 198–99.

81. "Welfare Recipients Protest Legislation," *Am. News*, June 29, 1968, 2; "The Welfare Situation is a Mess," *Am. News*, July 13, 1968, 3; and "100's Carry Demands," 2.

82. "100's Carry Demands," 2–3; Michael Clendenin, "Welfare Clients Try to Crash Joint Talks," *Daily News*, July 3, 1968, n.p., reprinted in special *TLI*, 10/City-Wide Coordinating Comm. Of Welfare Groups, Social Action; and "Meeting Harassed by Welfare Clients," *NYT*, July 3, 1968, n.p., reprinted in special *TLI*.

83. Clendenin, "Legislators' Howl"; and John Kifner, "The Deepening Welfare Crisis—News Analysis," *NYT*, August 1, 1968, 23.

84. "Special Message from Mrs. Martin Luther King, Jr. to Mrs. Beulah Sanders and Leaders of Women's Organizations in the New York Area," July 23, 1968, 1952/Women, NWRO. Also see Jackson and Johnson, *Protest by the Poor*, 204.

85. Mailer, *Miami and the Siege of Chicago*, 36; Theodore H. White, *The Making of the President, 1968* (New York: Atheneum, 1969), 231, 238; I. F. Stone, "The GOP Convention Was Not Without Its Cheering Aspects," August 19, 1968, *Polemics and Prophecies*, 43; and Garry Wills, *Nixon Agonistes: The Crisis of the Self-Made Man* (New York: Signet, 1971), 197, 206. For the general phenomenon of the rise of conservatism, and the geographic and ideological shifts within the Republican Party, see Lisa McGirr, *Suburban Warriors: The Origins of the New American Right* (Princeton, N.J.: Princeton University Press, 2001); Alan Brinkley, "The Problem of American Conservatism," *American Historical Review* 99 (April 1994): 409–29; and Joshua Freeman, "Putting Conservatism Back into the 1960s," *Radical History Review* 44 (1980): 94–99.

86. *Report of the National Advisory Commission on Civil Disorders* (Washington, D.C.: U.S. GPO, 1968); and Cannato, *Ungovernable City*, 204–8.

87. White, *Making of the President*, 251–52; Wills, *Nixon Agonistes*, 190, 263, 270; Mailer, *Miami and the Siege of Chicago*, 73, 75; and Cannato, *Ungovernable City*, 381–85.

88. George Wiley, Mrs. Etta Horn, and Mrs. Beulah Sanders, "Testimony of the National Welfare Rights Organization Before the Platform Committee of the Democratic National Convention, Aug. 19, 1968," 2101/Demo Platform Aug 19, 1968, NWRO. The NWRO appearance before the Platform Committee was described as "the closest thing . . . to a demonstration" that occurred in the days just prior to the opening of the 1968 convention. United Press International, "Welfare Mothers Tell Democrats 'How It Is'," *NYT*, August 23, 1968, n.p., 2101/Demo Platform. Also see "Welfare Mothers Unite!" *NOW!* 2, 13 (October 1968): 22.

89. Mrs. Juliet Greenlaw, "Statement of National Welfare Rights Organiza-

tion to the Democratic Platform Hearing," August 16, 1968, 2101/Demo Platform, NWRO.

90. For general discussions of Chicago in 1968, see Wills, *Nixon Agonistes,* 295–327; David Farber, *Chicago '68* (Chicago: University of Chicago Press, 1988); and Patterson, *Grand Expectations,* 694–97.

91. "'. . . Equal Justice Under Law Shall Be Denied to No One'," excerpts from the Democratic Platform, *Washington Post,* August 28, 1968, D2–3.

92. James, with Kotz, 21.

93. Jackson and Johnson, *Protest by the Poor,* 204–5; and Peter Kihss, "City Will Simplify Payments System in Welfare Cases—U.S. and State Approve $100 a Year in 4 Installments to Cover Special Grants," *NYT,* August 27, 1968, 1, 46.

94. Quoted in Peter Kihss, "City Will Simplify Payments System," 1. For details of the "simplified payments" system, see Jackson and Johnson, *Protest by the Poor,* 204–5.

95. City-Wide Coordinating Committee of Welfare Groups, press release, "Welfare Recipients to Fight New System," August 26, 1968, Unnumbered Box/ New York C.C.C.W.G. Newsletters; Leaflets; Pamphlets, Sampson. On the demonstration, see Peter Kihss, "City Will Simplify Payments System"; and Jackson and Johnson, *Protest by the Poor,* 205.

96. Peter Kihss, "Relief Recipients and Police Clash," *NYT,* August 28, 1968, 1, 50; "Brutality at City Hall," *NOW!* 2, 13 (October 1968): 14–15; James, with Kotz, 22; Jackson and Johnson, *Protest by the Poor,* 205; and Pope, *Biting the Hand that Feeds Them,* 95–96.

97. Rachlin and the women quoted in Kihss, "Relief Recipients and Police," 50. Other reports of the incident appear in James, with Kotz, 22; Peter Millones, "Behind the Clash at City Hall," *NYT,* September 1, 1968, n.p., reprint *NOW!* 2, 13 (October 1968): 17; and "Brutality at City Hall."

98. Citywide Coordinating Committee of Welfare Groups, press release, Beulah Sanders statement on the Flat Grant, August 30, 1968, Unnumbered Box/ New York C.C.C.W.G. Newsletters; Leaflets; Pamphlets, Sampson. See also Peter Kihss, "18 Arrested Here in 2d Day of Relief Recipient-Police Clashes," *NYT,* August 30, 1968, 30; "Brutality at City Hall," 14–15; and Kihss, "Relief Recipients and Police," 50.

99. Press release, Sanders on the Flat Grant, August 30, 1968; Peter Millones, "Behind the Clash at City Hall"; James, with Kotz, 22; John Kifner, "Welfare Protest Enters 2d Week—6 Centers Here Hindered by Demonstrations by Clients," *NYT,* September 4, 1968, 96; "Welfare Protests Slacken Off Here," *NYT,* September 7, 1968, 58; "Pressure Rising on Relief Agency," *NYT,* September 20, 1968, 54; and Jackson and Johnson, *Protest by the Poor,* 207.

100. Joyce Burson, interview with Nick Kotz and Mary Lynn Kotz, 1974, 46–47, 24/Joyce Burson Interview, Kotz.

101. John Kifner, "Welfare Protest Enters 2d Week"; "75 Welfare Recipients Go on Rampage, Closing 3 Brooklyn Centers," *NYT,* September 18, 1968, 1, 94; Jackson and Johnson, *Protest by the Poor,* 206; and James, with Kotz, 22.

102. Quoted in "75 Welfare Recipients Go on Rampage," 94.

103. James, with Kotz, 22.

104. "75 Welfare Recipients Go on Rampage," 1, 94. For concerns about destruction of property and bodily harm to welfare center employees, see letter from Maurice Hunt, acting commissioner of Social Services, to Honorable John V. Lindsay, mayor, City of New York, n.d. [stamped received Jan. 23, 1968], Dept. Welfare, NYC Dept. of Social Services, 1968, 104/1316, Lindsay.

105. Letter from "A Concerned Fulton Staff Member," Brooklyn, N.Y., to Mayor Lindsay, June 21, 1968, Dept. Welfare, NYC Dep: Welfare, NYC Dept. of Social Services, 1968, 104/1316, Lindsay.

106. Editorial, "Welfare Center Arrests," *NYT*, September, 27, 1968, 46. See also "2 Women Arrested At Welfare Center While Testing Rule," *NYT*, September 27, 1968, 18.

107. Letter from George Wiley to Welfare Rights Leaders and Friends, *NOW!* 2, 13 (October 1968): 2; James, with Kotz, 21–22; Francis X. Clines, "Welfare Clients Renew Protests—Hold Sit-Ins At Six Centers Against New System," *NYT*, December 6, 1968, 43; Clines, "3 Welfare Sit-Ins Cut Short on Threat of Arrest," *NYT*, December 7, 1968, 43; Richard Reeves, "Welfare Clients Plan Rent Revolt—Organizers Say Checks for Housing Will Be Used for Food and Clothing," *NYT*, October 26, 1968, 1, 62; "Welfare Groups Drop Rent Action—Resistance Among Clients Causes Strategy Shift," *NYT*, December 8, 1968, 42; Edward C. Burks, "Welfare Clients Sue To Void Flat Grants," *NYT*, November 23, 1968, 1, 41; and City-Wide Coordinating Committee of Welfare Groups, press release, "New York City Welfare Clients Seek Injunction Against Flat Grant Payments System," November 22, 1968, Unnumbered Box/New York C.C.C.W.G. Newsletters; Leaflets; Pamphlets, Sampson.

108. "Good Grief! Snoopy Makes Macy's Parade," *NYT*, November 29, 1968, 48. Plans for the parade demonstration were mentioned in Burks, "Welfare Clients Sue."

109. City-Wide Coordinating Committee of Welfare Groups, press release, "A Statement about the New Welfare Legislation," Unnumbered Box/C.C.C.W.G. Newsletters; Leaflets; Pamphlets, Sampson; Jennette Washington, "April 15 Rally," *Welfare Righter* 2, 3 (April-May 1969): 1; editorial (Jackie Pope), *Welfare Righter* 1, 3 (April-May 1969): 2; and Francis X. Clines, "15 Seized Near Grand Central After 5th Ave. Welfare March," *NYT*, April 16, 1969, 1, 28.

110. On the proposed cuts, see "Governor Proposes [$]125 Cut in Welfare Check, Robbing Poor to Balance Budget," *TLI* 3, 1 (January 17, 1969):1; "Rocky's War on Poor," *TLI* 3, 2 (January 31, 1969): 2; Sylvia Law and Jonathan Marsh, "Bills Before Legislature," *Welfare Righter* 1, 1 (February 21, 1969): 2; and Eladio Mendez, "Atencion Hispanos," ibid.. For other responses to welfare rights activism, see Richard Reeves, "A 15-Man Inquiry in Poverty Fraud Voted by Council—Payments to Ineligibles and Illegal Sending of Yippies to Chicago Are Charged," *NYT*, October 11, 1968, 1, 25; Peter Kihss, "City Relief Rolls Pass 900,000 Mark," *NYT*, October 17, 1968, 1, 22; and "U.S. To Begin Review of Welfare Monday," *NYT*, November 27, 1968, 35.

111. Lindsay, *The City*, 21.

112. Ibid.; and Nat Hentoff, *A Political Life: The Education of John V. Lindsay* (New York: Knopf, 1969), 261, 302–03. On the school strike, see Wendell Pritchett, *Brownsville, Brooklyn: Blacks, Jews, and the Changing Face of the Ghetto* (Chicago: University of Chicago Press, 2002), 222–37.

113. Pete Hamill: 'The Revolt of the White Lower Middle Class," *New York Magazine*, April 14, 1969, 24–26. For similar themes, see Peter Schrag, "The Forgotten American," *Harper's Magazine*, 239, 1431 (August 1969): 27–34; and "Man and Woman of the Year: The Middle Americans," *Time Magazine*, 95, 1 (January 5, 1970): 10–17.

114. Peter Kihss, "City Sees Saving in Welfare Costs," *NYT*, September 15, 1969, 1, 38; Martin Tolchin, "Lindsay Reports New Relief Cases Show Sharp Drop," *NYT*, September 18, 1969, 1, 38; Tolchin, "Relief Applications Rise, But

Fewer Are Accepted," *NYT*, September 19, 1969, 1, 38; and "Welfare Charge Rebutted By City," *NYT*, September 20, 1969, 1, 17. For welfare and the politics of the mayoral race, see also Clayton Knowles, "Overhaul of Relief To Cut Rising Cost Proposed by Marchi," *NYT*, September 25, 1969, 1, 40; Richard Severo, "Marchi Urges Ginsberg to Quit Because of Welfare Disclosures," *NYT*, September 27, 1969, 18; William E. Farrell, "Procaccino Urges Congress to Hold Welfare Hearing," *NYT*, October 5, 1969, 1, 79; and Emanual Perlmutter, "Procaccino Offers Job Program To Cut Relief Rolls by 200,000," *NYT*, October 29, 1969, 1, 50.

115. Lindsay, *The City*, 25. For the perspectives of Citywide and NWRO on the mayoral race, see excerpt from transcript, 1969 NWRO Organizers' Meeting, 15/NWRO Organizer Meeting (1969?) N.Y. Mayor Race, Kotz; Mrs. Henrietta Rice/Sherill Covain, press release, "The 'Welfare Game' Must End," Unnumbered Box/New York C.C.C.W.G. Newsletters; Leaflets; Pamphlets, Sampson; and City-Wide Coordinating Committee of Welfare Groups, "Statement About the New Welfare Legislation." On the election generally, see Freeman, *Working-Class New York*, 235–37; and Cannato, *Ungovernable City*, 389–441.

116. Michael Kramer and Sam Roberts, *I Never Wanted to be Vice-President of Anything! An Investigative Biography of Nelson Rockefeller* (New York: Basic Books, 1976), 333. On the 1968 election generally, see Phillips, *Emerging Republican Majority*.

117. Phillips quotation in Wills, *Nixon Agonistes*, 249.

118. On the convention and Nixon's choice of Agnew over Lindsay, see the newspaper clippings from Lindsay's own files: editorial, "Richard Nixon's Battle Plan," *New York Post*, August 9, 1968, 40, Subj. Nixon (1), 79/1498, Lindsay; Edward O'Neill, "Lindsay Cooled Off On Nixon & Agnew By Thurmond Role," *Daily News*, August 14, 1968, 28, Subj. Nixon (2), 79/1499, Lindsay; and Robert Bartlett, "Nixon and the 'Forgotten Americans'," *Wall Street Journal*, September 5, 1968, n.p., Subj. Nixon (2), 79/1499, Lindsay. See also Wills, *Nixon Agonistes*, 182–84, 190–92, 195–206.

119. Linda Kerber, *No Constitutional Right To Be Ladies: Women and the Obligations of Citizenship* (New York: Hill and Wang, 1998), 47–80; Mink, *Welfare's End*, 23–30; Dorothy Roberts, "The Value of Black Mothers' Work," *Connecticut Law Review* 26 (Spring 1994): 871–73; and Jones, *Labor of Love, Labor of Sorrow*, 201, 263.

120. Freeman, *Working-Class New York*, 143, 164–65, 209, 256.

121. Frances Fox Piven and Richard Cloward, *Poor People's Movements: How They Succeed, Why They Fail* (New York: Vintage, 1977), 306, 309, 317, 325, 329–30. About the flat grant in New York, they argue that welfare recipients had three potential strategies, including one of continuing "to mount militant demonstrations in the local centers," which "was attempted, but half-heartedly" and another, which Piven and Cloward favored, the "spend the rent campaign," which was announced but never implemented. "Instead," they write, "the recipient leadership opted for a lobbying campaign in Albany, the state capital" (306). I read this history differently then they do. It appears to me that welfare recipients attempted militant and disruptive tactics over a fairly sustained period, but were completely rebuffed. They retreated from the "spend the rent" idea because they were afraid that families would be evicted from their homes (a reasonable fear in the increasingly antiwelfare climate of the time). And their efforts at legislative lobbying in Albany were minimal. For an analysis of NWRO's decline that mirrors their analysis of the decline of Citywide, see, in addition

to *Poor People's Movements,* Piven and Cloward, "Strategy of Crisis: A Dialogue," *American Child* 48, 3 (Summer 1966): 20–32, reprinted in Cloward and Piven, *The Politics of Turmoil: Poverty, Race, and the Urban Crisis* (New York: Vintage, 1975), 106–26; and Piven and Cloward, *The Breaking of the American Social Contract* (New York: New Press, 1997), 267–308, 329–44.

Chapter 5. Give Us Credit for Being American

1. Jackie Pope, "Credit Cards Burn at Sears," *Welfare Righter* 1, 4 (June 27, 1969): 1. For the relationship between the NCSW and NWRO, see "An Important Issue Before the Membership," n.d., 2079/NCSW, NWRO; proposals to NCSW from dissident groups, including NWRO, [1968], ibid.; and letter from Arthur Flemming, president, National Council of Social Welfare, Columbus, Ohio, to George Wiley, NWRO, June 28, 1969, with attached pamphlet, "This Is the National Conference on Social Welfare," n.d., ibid.

2. Joyce Burson, interview with Nick Kotz and Mary Lynn Kotz, 1974, 48, 24/ Joyce Burson Interview, Kotz. Brooklyn organizer Rhoda Linton agreed that the credit card campaign originated with rank-and-file members. "I really hated that campaign," she recalled. "I didn't have a credit card until I was 40 or something." Rhoda Linton, interview with Felicia Kornbluh, June 9, 1997, by telephone, 68, transcript in possession of the author.

3. "Sears Action Oct. 23rd," *Welfare Fighter* 1, 2 (October 1969): 1.

4. Hearings on Family Assistance Plan, H.R. 16311, Thursday, November 19, 1970, Washington, D.C., 178, 17/NWRO—FAP Testimony Before Clean Gene, Kotz.

5. David Caplovitz, *The Poor Pay More: Consumer Practices of Low-Income Families* (Glencoe, N.Y.: Free Press, 1963), 81. Other studies of consumer practices in postwar black neighborhoods include Federal Trade Commission, "Economic Report on Installment Credit and Retail Sales Practices of District of Columbia Retailers," in *Consumerism: Search for the Consumer Interest,* ed. David Aaker and George Day (New York: Free Press, 1971), 374–81; and Eric Schnapper, "Consumer Legislation and the Poor," *Yale Law Journal* 76 (1967): 745–92.

6. This was true until the U.S. Congress in 1968 expressly forbade firing employees on account of wage garnishment. 82 Stat. 146, Act of May 29, 1968, cited in Justice Douglas's opinion in *Sniadach v. Family Finance Corporation of Bay View, et al.* (395 U.S. 340) (1969).

7. Caplovitz, *Poor Pay More,* 37, 41.

8. Ibid., 47.

9. Ibid., 9, 30, 50.

10. See Allison Dunham, "Consumer Credit Problems of the Poor—Legal Assistance as an Aid in Law Reform," National Conference on Law and Poverty, June 23–25, 1965 (Washington, D.C.: Government Printing Office), 9–14; Office of Economic Opportunity, *The Poor Seek Justice* (Washington, D.C.: GPO, 1966), *Guidelines for Legal Services Programs* (Washington, D.C.: Community Action Program, 1966, and GPO, 1967), and *Evaluation Manual* (Legal Services Program, 1966); and Harry Stumpf, *Community Politics and Legal Services: The Other Side of the Law* (Beverly Hills, Calif.: Sage Publications, 1975), 137.

11. See the definition of unconscionability in Henry Campbell Black et al., *Black's Law Dictionary,* 6th ed. (Saint Paul, Minn.: West Publishing Company, 1991), 1059.

12. *Williams v. Walker-Thomas Furniture Company* (351 F. 2d 447) (D.C. Circuit,

1965). For the significance of the case, see Stewart Macaulay, "Bambi Meets Godzilla: Reflections on Contracts Scholarship and Teaching vs. State Unfair and Deceptive Trade Practices and Consumer Protection Statutes," *Houston Law Review* 26, 4 (July 1989): 575–601. For similar issues among the clients of welfare rights counsel Carl Rachlin, see SEDFRE, Summary of Mary Dandridge's Installment Purchasing Experiences, n.d. [Summer/Fall 1968], 3, Case of Mary Dandridge, 47/98, SEDFRE; Case of Ellen D'Amico, 47/82, SEDFRE; Case of Sarah Harrison, 48/4, SEDFRE; and Case of Doris Brown, 47/141, SEDFRE. The names of all of Rachlin's clients have been changed.

13. *Williams v. Walker-Thomas*, 448–50.

14. For a theory of consumption as a form of work women perform, see Batya Weinbaum and Amy Bridges, "The Other Side of the Paycheck: Monopoly Capital and the Structure of Consumption," in *Capitalist Patriarchy and the Case for Socialist Feminism*, ed. Zillah Eisenstein (New York: Monthly Review Press, 1979), 190–205. On women as consumers of welfare state services, see Laura Balbo, "Crazy Quilts: Rethinking the Welfare State Debate from a Woman's Point of View," in *Women and the State*, ed. Anne Showstack Sassoon (London: Unwin Hyman, 1987), 45–71.

15. For the significance of African American protests over "the right to shop and the right . . . to sell," see Regina Austin, "A Nation of Thieves: Consumption, Commerce, and the Black Public Sphere," *Public Culture* 7, 1 (Fall 1994): 225–48; and Patricia Williams, "The Death of the Profane," in Williams, *The Alchemy of Race and Rights* (Cambridge, Mass.: Harvard University Press, 1991), 44–51.

16. See Evelyn Brooks Higginbotham, *Righteous Discontent: The Women's Movement in the Black Baptist Church, 1880–1920* (Cambridge, Mass.: Harvard University Press, 1993); Jacqueline Jones, *Labor of Love, Labor of Sorrow: Black Women, Work, and the Family from Slavery to the Present* (New York: Basic Books, 1985), 68–70; and Paula Giddings, *When and Where I Enter: The Impact of Black Women on Race and Sex in America* (New York: Bantam Books, 1984), 22–23. On the claim of African American women to ladyhood at the turn of the twentieth century, see Giddings, 49, 178; Kevin Gaines, *Uplifting the Race: Black Leadership in the Twentieth Century* (Chapel Hill: University of North Carolina Press, 1996); and Gaines, "Rethinking Race and Class in African-American Struggles for Equality, 1885–1941," *American Historical Review* 201, 2 (April 1997): 378–87.

17. Linda Majka and Theo Majka, *Farm Workers, Agribusiness, and the State* (Philadelphia: Temple University Press, 1982), 174–99, 205–7. On women in the UFW boycotts, see Vicki Ruíz, *From Out of the Shadows: Mexican Women in Twentieth-Century America* (New York: Oxford University Press, 1998), 119, 132; and Margaret Rose, "'From the Fields to the Picket Line': Huelga Women and the Boycott, 1965–1975," *Labor History* 31, 3 (Summer 1990): 271–93. On NWRO and the UFW, see chapter 1 and Tim Sampson, interview with Felicia Kornbluh, July 26, 2001, Oakland, Calif., 27–30, transcript in author's possession.

18. Rachel Carson, *Silent Spring* (New York: Fawcett Crest, 1962), esp. 161–78; Carson, *Always, Rachel: The Letters of Rachel Carson and Dorothy Freeman, 1952–1964*, ed. Martha Freeman (Boston: Beacon Press, 1995), 247–420; Charles McCarry, *Citizen Nader* (New York: Saturday Review Press, 1971); and Ralph Nader, *Unsafe at Any Speed* (1965; New York: Pocket Books, 1968).

19. Estelle Freedman, *No Turning Back: The History of Feminism and the Future of Women* (New York: Ballantine, 2002), 183–84; and Flora Davis, *Moving the Mountain: The Women's Movement in America Since 1960* (New York: Simon and Schuster, 1991), 147–48.

20. For early twentieth-century women's protests, see Annelise Orleck, *Common Sense and a Little Fire: Women and Working-Class Politics in the United States, 1900–1965* (Chapel Hill: University of North Carolina Press, 1995), 200–221; and Dana Frank, "Housewives, Socialists, and the Politics of Food: The 1917 New York Cost-of-Living Protests," *Feminist Studies* 11, 2 (Summer 1985): 255–56. For "Don't Buy Where You Can't Work" in Harlem, see Wil Haygood, *King of the Cats: The Life and Times of Adam Clayton Powell, Jr.* (New York: Houghton Mifflin, 1993), 75–77; Jim Sleeper, *The Closest of Strangers: Liberalism and the Politics of Race in New York* (New York: Norton, 1990), 48–50; and Gilbert Osofsky, *Harlem: The Making of a Ghetto* (New York: Harper and Row, 1966), 121. On Ella Baker, see Barbara Ransby, *Ella Baker and the Black Freedom Movement: A Radical Democratic Vision* (Chapel Hill: University of North Carolina Press, 2003), 82–90; and Charles Payne, *I've Got the Light of Freedom: The Organizing Tradition and the Mississippi Freedom Struggle* (Berkeley: University of California Press, 1995), 82. On the immediate postwar period, see Martha Biondi, *To Stand and Fight: The Struggle for Civil Rights in Postwar New York City* (Cambridge, Mass.: Harvard University Press, 2003), 89–93.

21. Cathy Aldridge, "Harlem Housewives Join Pickets Over Food Prices," *Am. News*, November 5, 1966, 3. For co-ops, see "Consumer Plan for Harlemites," *Am. News*, September 24, 1966, 22; "Human Rights Through Consumer Cooperation," program, Harlem Consumer Education, Inc., 6th Annual Conference, n.d. [1968], 51/19, SEDFRE; "E. Harlem Furniture Co-Op Opens Friday," *Am. News*, December 21, 1968, 4; and George Todd, "Housewives Form Own Food Co-op in Bed-Stuy," *Am. News*, February 21, 1970, 23.

22. Leaflet, "The Black Forum Invites You to Hear a Discussion on '*Installment Buying* and *Black People*'," n.d., 51/19, SEDFRE; "Don't Buy and Sign in Haste," *Am. News*, May 22, 1965, 10; "Seeking Credit Gyp Legislation," *Am. News*, September 16, 1966, 25; Whitney Young, "Consumer Frauds," *Am. News*, June 17, 1967, 16; and "Credit Dealings in City's Ghettos Come Under Fire," *Am. News*, January 20, 1968, 1. For "Operation Lambchop" and similar protests, see "War Is Opened on Overchargers—Boro Combats Fleecing," *Am. News*, November 6, 1965, 27; "Milk Cost 20 Cents More in Harlem Stores," *Am. News*, April 16, 1966, 48; Simon Anekwe, "Operation Lambchop Hits Harlem Markets," *Am. News*, May 14, 1966, 1–2; and Floyd McKissick, "The High Cost of Being Poor," *Am. News*, February 14, 1970, 7.

23. "CORE Wins Hiring Pact in Bank Drive," *Am. News*, September 26, 1964, 7. See also Oakland Chapter, CORE, "Selma, Alabama and Bogalousa, Louisiana . . . Here in Oakland?" [1965], 3/44, Social Protest; "They Think You're a 98 lb. Weakling . . . Picket & Sip-In Hy's Restaurant" [1965], ibid.; and August Meier and Elliott Rudwick, *CORE: A Study in the Civil Rights Movement* (Urbana: University of Illinois Press, 1975), 30, 47, 57, 59, 234.

24. Letter from Carl Rachlin, General Counsel, CORE, to Mr. Peter Darrow, University of Chicago Law Review, Chicago, Illinois, December 1, 1965, 12/20, SEDFRE; memorandum from Carl Rachlin to Messrs. [James] Farmer, [George] Wiley, [Alan] Gartner, [Marvin] Rich, Re: Follow up on Memorandum on Unconscionable Retail Practices to the Poor, November 29, 1965, 50/41, SEDFRE; and [Rachlin?], draft press release, on the report, "Unprincipled Exploitation of the Poor," n.d. [1965], 50/42, SEDFRE. Rachlin assessed Section 2-302 of the Uniform Commercial Code in letter from Rachlin to Robert F. Drinan, S.J., dean, Boston College Law School, Brighton, Mass., September 19, 1966, 12/23, SEDFRE.

25. Martin Luther King, Jr., *Where Do We Go from Here? Chaos or Community* (New York: Harper and Row, 1967), 38.

26. Ibid., 116. On consumer demands by SCLC and other major civil rights groups, see Clayborne Carson, David Garrow, Gerald Gill, Vincent Harding, and Darlene Clark Hine, eds., *The Eyes on the Prize Civil Rights Reader* (New York: Penguin, 1991), 291–303; Clayborne Carson, *In Struggle: SNCC and the Black Awakening of the 1960s* (Cambridge, Mass.: Harvard University Press, 1981), 103, 172, 255, 269; and Meier and Rudwick, *CORE*, 187, 234, 262.

27. Operation Breadbasket began in Philadelphia. It built on the initiative of Reverend Leon Sullivan, who began a campaign of "selective patronage" by African American consumers. See Matthew Countryman, *Up South: Civil Rights and Black Power in Philadelphia* (Philadelphia: University of Pennsylvania, 2006), 101.

28. Southern Christian Leadership Conference, New York City, flyer about A&P boycott, February 1971, 33/14, Social Action. See also Dick Edwards, "Operation Breadbasket: Total Involvement—NOW!," *Am. News*, May 18, 1968, 23; editorial, "Operation Breadbasket," *Am. News*, April 18, 1970, 16; and Rev. William A. Jones, chairman, Operation Breadbasket of Greater New York, "Not a Press Release," on the A&P Protest, n.d. [February 1971], 33/14, Social Action. On Operation Breadbasket generally, see Negro Ministers of Atlanta, "Selective Buying Campaign Enters Second Phase," January 23, 1963, 38/Operation Breadbasket, Social Action.

29. National Advisory Commission on Civil Disorders, *Report of the National Advisory Commission on Civil Disorders* (New York: Bantam, 1968), 274–75.

30. Joan Hoff, *Nixon Reconsidered* (New York: Basic Books, 1994), 95–97. One recipient of Nixon Administration funds for the promotion of "black capitalism" was Floyd McKissick, who had defeated George Wiley in the 1966 contest for the presidency of CORE. Community Relations Service, U.S. Department of Justice, "New Minority Enterprises" (Washington, D.C.: Department of Justice, [1971?]), 55, lists McKissick as president of a for-profit "economic development corporation" involved in developing a new town of 18,000 persons called Soul City. See also Meier and Rudwick, xi. Writer James Baldwin called black capitalism "a concept demanding yet more faith and infinitely more in schizophrenia than the concept of the Virgin Birth." Baldwin, *No Name in the Street* (New York: Dell/Laurel, 1972), 48.

31. Statement by Senator William Proxmire on the introduction of S. 2146, the Community Credit Expansion Act, in the Senate of the United States, *Congressional Record*, May 13, 1969, 2038/Retail Stores—Other Than Sears, NWRO.

32. See discussion of postwar labor-force participation rates in Alice Kessler-Harris, *Out to Work: A History of Wage-Earning Women in the United States* (New York: Oxford University Press, 1982), 301–3. On postwar gender relations and consumption, see Elaine Tyler May, *Homeward Bound: American Families in the Cold War Era* (New York: Basic Books, 1988), 162–82.

33. On the role of VISTA's in the Philadelphia welfare rights movement, see Countryman, *Up South*, 277. On the credit campaign, see Countryman, 279–80; Felicia Kornbluh, "Black Buying Power: Welfare Rights, Consumerism, and Northern Protest," in *Freedom North: Black Freedom Struggles Outside the South, 1940–1980*, ed. Komozi Woodard and Jeanne Theoharis (New York: Palgrave/Macmillan, 2005), 199–222; Kornbluh, "To Fulfill Their 'Rightly Needs': Consumerism and the National Welfare Rights Movement," *Radical History Review* 69 (Fall 1997): 76–113; Nick Kotz and Mary Lynn Kotz, *A Passion for Equality: George*

A. Wiley and the Movement (New York: Norton, 1977), 235–36; and Larry R. Jackson and William A. Johnson, *Protest by the Poor: The Welfare Rights Movement in New York City* (Lexington, Mass.: D.C. Heath and Rand Corporation, 1974), 41. Roxanne Jones was later elected to the Pennsylvania State House, where she served until her death in 1996. See Linda Loyd, et al., "State Sen. Roxanne H. Jones Dies at 68," *Philadelphia Inquirer*, May 20, 1996, A1.

34. Quoted in "Wanamaker and Lerner Agree To Give Relief Clients Credit," *Philadelphia Tribune*, August 20, 1968, n.p., "NWRO ACTION Leadership Packet No. 3," file titled "NWRO," NCLEJ.

35. [Tim Sampson?], "Nationwide Sears Credit Campaign," notice from NWRO to all WRO's, n.d. [March 1969?] 2038/NWRO Sears Materials, NWRO.

36. "NWRO Winter Action Campaign—WRO's 'Get It'—New York," *NOW!* 2, 14 (December 1968): 8. On Brooklyn, see Jacqueline Pope, *Biting the Hand That Feeds Them: Organizing Women on Welfare at the Grass Roots Level* (New York: Praeger, 1989), 62, 105–10; and Kotz and Kotz, *A Passion for Equality*, 236.

37. "I played a game with the man," Burson added, "and that's the way we always did." Burson, with Kotz and Kotz, 48.

38. "NWRO Winter Action Campaign—New York"; and Pope, *Biting the Hand*, 105–6.

39. Pope, *Biting the Hand*, 108–9; "Credit Offered to Welfare Recipients," *TLI*, 4, 1 (January 17, 1969): 1; Jackson and Johnson, *Protest by the Poor*, 41; and Sadie Jackson, "Sears Demonstration," *B-WAC Newsletter*, April 4, 1969, 2038/Local WRO Sears Material, NWRO.

40. Mamie Hall, "Heat on in July," *Welfare Righter* 1, 5 (July 31, 1969): 2. Hall and Sadie Jackson, mentioned above, were both members of B-WAC as well as Citywide. Rhoda Linton, personal communication, June 21, 2006.

41. Isadore Barmash, "3 Big Stores Agree on Extending Credit to Relief Recipients," *NYT*, July 23, 1969, 1, 78; and notice on credit, *NOW!* (July 1969), 10.

42. Pope, *Biting the Hand*, 106–8. For the shop-in as a tactic in places other than New York City, see "Call to Action" on Sears campaign, n.d. [March 1969?], 2038/NWRO Sears Materials, NWRO.

43. Pope, *Biting the Hand*, 106–7; and "Call to Action."

44. Pope, *Biting the Hand*, 106–7.

45. Barmash, 78; Notice on Credit, *NOW!*; and summary of NWRO credit agreements, n.d., 2038/Sears Correspondence, NWRO.

46. Typical callers quoted in Isidore Barmash, "As Those on Relief Get an Offer of Credit," *NYT*, July 20, 1969, E2.

47. Pete Hamill, "The Revolt of the White Lower Middle Class," *New York Magazine*, April 14, 1969, 24.

48. Institute for Religious and Social Studies, New York, notes on an interview with Hulbert James, February 6, 1970, 2–3, 11/18, Wiley.

49. Press release on National Coordinating Committee Meeting, Jackson, Mississippi, February, 24, 1969, 36/Nat. Welfare Rights Org. (2), Social Action. For Sanders and Olivo as leaders at this time, see "NWRO Action—Negotiate NOW! with Sears," 2038/Sears, NWRO.

50. Tim Sampson, interview with Felicia Kornbluh, February 12, 1996, by telephone, informal notes in author's possession, n.p. Also see Kotz and Kotz, *Passion for Equality*, 236; press release on NCC meeting in Jackson; Paul Harvey, "Conversation Piece— Poverty Pays as Welfare Demands More," *Wheeling (West Virginia) News-Register*, n.d. [March? 1969], n.p., attached to letter from U.S. Sen-

ator Jennings Randolph, D-West Virginia, to Mrs. Johnnie Tillmon, April 8, 1969, 21/5, Wiley; and Etta Horn, "Credit Given by Montgomery Ward," *Welfare Fighter* 1, 4 (December 1969): 1.

51. Horn, "Credit Given by Montgomery Ward."

52. On legal efforts to encode income discrimination in constitutional doctrine, see Martha Davis, *Brutal Need: Lawyers and the Welfare Rights Movement, 1960–1973* (New Haven, Conn.: Yale University Press, 1993); Aryeh Neier, *Only Judgment: The Limits of Litigation in Social Change* (Middletown, Conn.: Wesleyan University Press, 1982), 127–40; Laurence H. Tribe, *American Constitutional Law* (Mineola, N.Y.: Foundation Press, 1978), 1098–1136; Frank Michelman, "The Supreme Court 1968 Term—Forward: On Protecting the Poor Through the Fourteenth Amendment," *Harvard Law Review* 83, 7 (1969): 7–59; and A. Delafield Smith, *The Right to Life* (Chapel Hill: University of North Carolina Press, 1955).

53. Mrs. Etta Horn, statement, *WRO's in ACTION*, 1, 1 (April 1969): 2, 2038/Sears, NWRO.

54. Letter from Eugene May, president, Pike County Citizens Association, Hellier Kentucky, to Manager, Sears Roebuck & Company, Pikeville, Kentucky, June 15, 1969, 2038/Sears Correspondence, NWRO.

55. List of possible slogans for the Sears campaign, n.d., 2038/NWRO Sears Materials, NWRO.

56. Chicago Welfare Rights Organization, "Press Release," April 7, 1969, 2038/Local WRO Sears Material, NWRO.

57. Dorothy Perry, "Composition—'Welfare Rights'," April 8, 1969, 2038/Local WRO Sears Material, NWRO.

58. *WRO's in ACTION* 1, 1 (April 1969): 8, 2038/Sears, NWRO.

59. "Nationwide Sears Credit Campaign," NWRO ACTION Leadership Packet No. 3, File titled "NWRO," NCLEJ.

60. "Nationwide Sears Credit Campaign"; NWRO notice to local WROs, n.d., 2038/NWRO Sears Materials, NWRO.

61. "Call to Action [on Sears campaign]," n.d., 2038/NWRO Sears Materials, NWRO. For the campaign as outreach to the middle class, see letter from Betty Younger, Pittsburgh, Pa., to Johnnie Tillmon, president, National Welfare Rights Organization, Washington, D.C., May 9, 1969, 2038/Correspondence with People About Sears, NWRO; Pima County (Tucson, Ariz.) Welfare Rights Organization, "NOW! Don't Buy Sears," n.d., 2038/Local WRO Sears Material, ibid.; and [George Wiley], "Sears Action Group," n.d., 2038/Sears—To Write, ibid.

62. Letter from Better Younger to Johnnie Tillmon and letter from Mrs. Wayne W. Harrington, president, Women's Division of the Methodist Church, to Arthur M. Woods [sic], president, Sears, Roebuck Company, Chicago, March 18, 1969, 2038/Sears Correspondence, NWRO.

63. See letter from Mrs. S. N. Levens, Rutherford, N.J., to Dr. George Wiley, c/o T.V. station 13, March 29, 1969, 2038/Correspondence With People About Sears, NWRO; letter from Neil Witting, Alexandria, Virginia, to NWRO, April 25, 1969, ibid.; and letter from M. Kling to George Wiley, n.d. [marked received April 3, 1969], ibid.

64. Mail-in cards on the Sears campaign, 2038/Correspondence With People About Sears, NWRO.

65. Letter from "An outspoken wage earner" to the National Welfare Rights Organization, July 20, 1969, postmarked Buffalo, N.Y., 2038/Sears Correspondence, NWRO.

66. Ibid.

67. [Tim Sampson?], "Summary of NWRO Credit Agreements," n.d., 2038/ Sears Correspondence, NWRO.

68. On quiet extensions of credit to low-income people, see Pam [?], "Pontiac's Agreement with Sears," n.d., 2038/Local WRO Sears Material, NWRO. For Montgomery Ward agreement, see press release, Montgomery Ward Company, on its Agreement with the National Welfare Rights Organization, December 8, 1969, 2038/Montgomery Ward, NWRO; memorandum of Agreement between the National Welfare Rights Organization and the Montgomery Ward Company for a Pilot Program Extending Credit to Welfare Recipients, September 10, 1969, 21/5, Wiley; Kotz and Kotz, *Passion for Equality*, 237; and Jackson and Johnson, *Protest by the Poor*, 41.

69. "NWRO Sears Action," n.d. [March, 1969?], 2038/Consumer Credit, NWRO; and "Sears Boycott Action List," April 9, 1969, 15/2, Wiley.

70. Memo to: All WROs, From: Etta B. Horn, chairman, NWRO Ways and Means Committee and George A. Wiley, executive director, Subject: Sears Action, n.d. [March–April 1969], 2038/Sears Correspondence, NWRO.

71. On European family allowances, see Susan Pedersen, *Family, Dependence, and the Origins of the Welfare State: Britain and France, 1914–1945* (Cambridge: Cambridge University Press, 1993), 13, 326, 415–17; Jane Jenson, "Representations of Gender: Policies to 'Protect' Women Workers and Infants in France and the United States," in *Women, the State, and Welfare*, ed. Linda Gordon (Madison: University of Wisconsin Press, 1990), 158; and Alva Reimer Myrdal, *Nation and Family: The Swedish Experiment in Democratic Family and Population Policy* (New York: Harper & Brothers, 1941), 134–35.

72. National Welfare Rights Organization, "NWRO Private Sector/Family Allowance Plan," n.d., 2038/ NWRO Sears Stuff, NWRO.

73. Letter from Mrs. Johnnie Tillmon and George Wiley, National Welfare Rights Organization, Washington, D.C., to Mr. J. F. McFarland, president, General Mills, Inc., Minneapolis, Minn., December 16, 1968, 2038/Consumer Credit, NWRO.

74. Ibid.

75. The suggestion of such an "honor roll" probably bore with it the implicit threat of a boycott of firms that failed to participate. For an explicit threat, see letter from (Mrs.) Etta Horn, chairman, Committee on Ways and Means, and George Wiley, executive director, National Welfare Rights Organization, Washington, D.C., to Mr. H. J. Morgens, president, The Proctor & Gamble Company, Cincinnati, Ohio, May 16, 1969, 2038/Proctor and Gamble, NWRO.

76. "NWRO Private Sector/Family Allowance Plan."

77. Letter from Thomas L. Olson, manager of Community Relations, General Mills, to Mrs. Johnnie Tillmon, December 31, 1968, 2038/Consumer Credit, NWRO.

78. See letter from Johnnie Tillmon and George Wiley to Mr. D.J. Fitzgibbons, president, the Sterling Drug Company, New York, N.Y., December 16, 1968 (same text as General Mills letter), 2038/Consumer Credit, NWRO. On high-priority targets for NWRO's private-sector program, see note [from Tim Sampson] to Joyce [Burson], n.d., ibid.

79. Jane Hoey, director, Bureau of Public Assistance, "Significance of the Money Payment in Public Assistance," *Social Security Bulletin* 7, 9 (September 1944): 3–5. See discussion in Chapter 2, above.

80. Letter from Thomasina Lewis, Mount Vernon, N.Y., to Carl Rachlin, legal

director, Scholarship, Education, and Defense Fund for Racial Equality, New York, N.Y., August 3, 1967, case of Thomasina Lewis, 47/16, SEDFRE; memorandum from E. Dahlgren, B. Wolf, M. Barlow, and E. Shapiro, to Mrs. Mae Feinstein, Re: Younger, Jean, November 10, 1967, and George W. Chesbro, acting commissioner, New York State Department of Social Services, decision after fair hearing, in the Matter of the Appeal of Jean Younger from a determination by the New York City Department of Social Services, May 28, 1968, 2–3, case of Jean Younger, 49/35, SEDFRE; letter from Stephen Nagler, SEDFRE, New York, to Hon. Joseph Louchheim, deputy commissioner, State of New York Department of Social Services, New York, N.Y., November 6, 1967, and [Louchheim?], decision after fair hearing, in the Matter of the Appeal of Miriam Stevenson, May 1, 1969, case of Miriam Stevenson, 47/58, SEDFRE; Ann Freeman, reasons for requesting a fair hearing, November 2, 1967, case of Ann Freeman, 49/14, SEDFRE; and George K. Wyman, commissioner, New York State Department of Social Services, decision after fair hearings, in the Matter of the Appeal of Toni Stret, from a determination by the New York City Department of Social Services, October 25, 1967, March 26, and May 8, 1968, 4, Case of Toni Stret, 47/118, SEDFRE.

81. Letter from Thomasina Lewis to Carl Rachlin, case of Thomasina Lewis. Also see letter from Stephen Nagler, SEDFRE, to Honorable Max Waldgeir, Westchester, N.Y., August 11, 1967, ibid.

82. Letter from Nelly Peissachowitz, ACSW, Neighborhood Service Center No. 1, Bronx, N.Y., to Carl Rachlin, SEDFRE, May 16, 1967, 46/19, SEDFRE. See also letter from Marjorie Nazel, Forest Neighborhood House, Inc., Bronx, New York, to Stephen Nagler, SEDFRE, n.d., 46/19, SEDFRE.

83. Michael B. Katz, *In The Shadow of the Poorhouse: A Social History of Welfare in America* (New York: Basic Books, 1986), 266; Maurice McDonald, "Food Stamps: An Analytical History," *Social Service Review* 51 (December 1977), 643; and Nick Kotz, *Let Them Eat Promises: The Politics of Hunger in America* (Englewood Cliffs, N.J.: Prentice-Hall, 1969), 48, 178–89, 229–38.

84. Mitchell Ginsberg, interview with Nick Kotz and Mary Lynn Kotz, n.d., 4–5, 24/Mitchell Ginsberg Interview, Kotz.

85. Beulah Sanders, "Food Stamp Trick," *TLI* 3, 3 (March 14, 1968): 3. For other arguments against food stamps from Sanders and Citywide, see Beulah Sanders, testimony, hearings on Family Assistance Plan, H.R. 16311, November 18, 1970, Washington, D.C., 44, 65, 17/NWRO–FAP Testimony Before Clean Gene, Kotz; and press release, May 1, 1969, Unnumbered Box/New York C.C.C.W.G. Newsletters; Leaflets; Pamphlets, Sampson.

86. "Discurso de Socurro Martin al Rally de Junio 30," *TLI* 3, 8 (July 3, 1968): 1; and Celia Paul, "Anti-Food Stamp Action," *TLI* 3, 7 (May 22, 1968): 2.

87. Mrs. Marty Green, "Food Stamps = Hunger Stamps," *NOW!* (July 1969): 10.

88. "Complaints Against Food Stamps," *Welfare Fighter* 1, 6 (February 1970): 6; and Hon. Allard Lowenstein, "Transcript of a Meeting Between Poor People of Beaufort and Jasper Counties, S.C., and Representative Allard K. Lowenstein," extension of remarks, *Congressional Record*, April 3, 1969, p. E2774, 21/2, Wiley.

89. Mrs. Annie Smart, southern regional representative, NWRO, testimony, hearings on Family Assistance Plan, H.R. 16311, Thursday, November 19, 1970, Washington, D.C., 108–9, 17/NWRO—FAP Testimony Before Clean Gene, Kotz.

90. Lowenstein, extension of remarks, E2774. On the meeting, see also

"NWRO News from Across the Nation," *Welfare Righter* 1, 2 (March 28, 1969): 4. On Lowenstein generally, see William Chafe, *Never Stop Running: Allard Lowenstein and the Struggle to Save American Liberalism* (New York: Basic Books, 1993).

91. "Brooklyn WRO Demands Voter Registration," *NOW!* (August 1968): 9.

92. City-Wide Coordinating Committee of Welfare Groups, press release, August 14, 1969, Unnumbered Box/New York C.C.C.W.G. Newsletters; Leaflets; Pamphlets, Sampson; and Jennette Washington, "Food Surplus Action."

93. Ron Pollack, "Food Stamp Hoax," *Welfare Righter* 1, 3 (April–May 1969): 7; Beulah Sanders, "Legitimate Chanels vs. Governmental Repression," April 16, 1969, press release, Unnumbered Box/New York C.C.C.W.G. Newsletters; Leaflets; Pamphlets, Sampson; and "A Statement by Mrs. Beulah Sanders," June 27, 1969, press release, ibid.

94. Francis X. Clines, "25% Here Eligible for Food Stamps," *NYT*, August 15, 1970, 1, 30; letter from John V. Lindsay, mayor, City of New York (by Bob Carroll), to Mr. Harold Larsen, regional director, United States Post Office, New York, N.Y., August 28, 1970, Conf.—S.S. (3), 17/203, Lindsay; Peter Kihss, "Food Stamp Plan Under Way Here," *NYT*, September 1, 1970, 1, 26; and letter from John V. Lindsay, mayor, City of New York, to Honorable Clifford M. Hardin, secretary of Agriculture, U.S. Department of Agriculture, Washington, D.C., September 2, 1970, Conf.—HRA (4), 11/133, Lindsay.

95. For welfare departments having "cheated" by not paying full utility costs, see "Citywide Action on Utilities," *TLI* 3, 1 (January 15, 1968): 1. On the campaign generally, see "The Poor Pay More for Utilities," report from *Congressional Record*, May 15, 1968, 2063/Utility Campaign, NWRO; letter from Roger Rice, staff attorney, NWRO, Washington, D.C., to Mr. Steve Herzberg, National Consumer Law Center, Boston College Law School, Boston, Mass., December 24, 1969, ibid.; and Carol McMurrough, "Utility Hike Halt Hearing Slated," *Denver Post*, November 16, 1969, n.p., ibid.

96. "School Lunch Rights Campaign," *Welfare Fighter* 1, 4 (December 1969): 3; "Demands of the Utah State Board of Education in Behalf of Utah Welfare Rights Organization Members," n.d., 1959/Legal Title I—Harvard & Columbia Center Stuff, NWRO; George Wiley, report to the Interreligious Foundation for Community Organization, covering January 1 to December 31, 1969, 11/18, Wiley; letter from Ron Pollack, Center on Social Welfare Policy & Law, New York, N.Y., to Attorney, December 16, 1968, 2063/Legal Network, NWRO; and memorandum from Pollack to Tim Sampson, January 31, 1969, ibid.

97. Center on Social Welfare Policy & Law, "Legal Approaches to the Provision of a Meaningful Public School Education in the City of New York," n.d., 1959/Legal Title I—Harvard & Columbia Center Stuff, NWRO; letter from Mr. and Mrs. Bernard Strassberg, Brooklyn, N.Y., to Dr. Seymour Lachman, New York City Board of Education, Brooklyn, N.Y., February 10, 1970, ibid.; memorandum from Gabe Kaimowitz, Center on Social Welfare Policy and Law, to Gentlemen, Re: *Freemen, et al. v. Nyquist, et al.*, January 1970, ibid.; and list of people attending the Title I Litigation Conference, New Orleans, La., April 17–18, 1970, ibid.

98. Memorandum from the Center on Social Welfare Policy & Law, to National Welfare Rights Organization, Re: Action on issues linking education to welfare, especially through the utilization of Title I of the Elementary and Secondary Education Act of 1965, n.d., 1959/Legal Title I—Harvard & Columbia Stuff, NWRO.

Chapter 6. Nixon, Moynihan, and Real Live Welfare Moms

1. Memorandum from Mitchell I. Ginsberg, adviser on Human Resources, to John V. Lindsay, mayor of New York, September 15, 1970, 4, Conf. HRA (4), 11/133, Lindsay. On Ginsberg's time in Washington, see Ginsberg, interview with Nick Kotz and Mary Lynn Kotz, n.d., 10–11, 24/Mitchell Ginsberg Interview, Kotz; and James Welsh, "Welfare Reform: Born, Aug. 8, 1969; Died, Oct 3, 1972, A Sad Case Study of the American Political Process," *NYT Magazine,* January 7, 1973, 17.

2. For data on costs, see [Office of Program Planning Evaluation and Planning, Social Security Administration, Department of Health, Education, and Welfare (HEW)], "Welfare Reform Fact Sheet: Background Material, August 8, 1969," from binder titled, "The President's Proposals for Welfare Reform, October 2, 1969," WHSF—Staff Member and Office Files, JDE, 38/[Welfare Book] [President's Proposals for Welfare Reform, Oct. 2, 1969], 5–6, Nixon; and Warren Weaver, Jr., "Nixon Aides Push Welfare Reform," *NYT,* July 2, 1970, 24.

3. On the departure of jobs from New York City to its suburbs, see Joshua Freeman, *Working-Class New York: Life and Labor Since World War II* (New York: New Press, 2000), 143.

4. City-Wide Coordinating Committee of Welfare Groups, "Law and Order Means Rights for Everyone," June 18, 1969, Unnumbered Box/New York C.C.C.W.G. Newsletters; Leaflets; Pamphlets, Sampson; press release, "A Statement by Mrs. Beulah Sanders," June 27, 1969, ibid.; *Rosado, et al. v. Wyman, Commissioner of Social Services of New York, et al.* (397 U.S. 397); "Know Your Welfare Rights," *Welfare Fighter* (April 1970): 3; "No-Cut Welfare Checks Till Ruling," *Am. News,* May 3, 1969, 3; "Cuts in Welfare, Medicaid," *Am. News,* June 12, 1969, 12; "News of the Week—Local," *Am. News,* June 28, 1969, 2; and Martha Davis, *Brutal Need: Lawyers and the Welfare Rights Movement, 1960–1973* (New Haven, Conn.: Yale University Press, 1993), 126–27, 131.

5. "Union Warns State on Cuts in Welfare," *NYT,* August 9, 1969, 9; Sylvan Fox, "142 Arrested in Sit-Ins for School Clothes Grants," *NYT,* September 5, 1969, 4D; Leonard Buder, "Welfare Recipients and Police Clash in School Row," *NYT,* September 11, 1969, 37; City-Wide Coordinating Committee of Welfare Groups, "Welfare Recipients Demand Release of $40 Million," October 14, 1969, Unnumbered Box/New York C.C.C.W.G. Newsletters; Leaflets; Pamphlets, Sampson; and "NWRO Hope of the 70's," *Welfare Fighter* 1, 5 (January 1970): 1.

6. Washington and Brooklyn activists quoted in Buder, "Welfare Recipients and Police Clash."

7. "School Clothing for Welfare Children," *Welfare Fighter* 1, 1 (September 1969): 7.

8. Miriam Davis, "Congressional Families Live on a Welfare Budget," *NOW!* (July 1969), 12; William Pastreich, interview with Felicia Kornbluh, February 26, 1997, by telephone, n.p., notes in possession of the author; Jacqueline Pope, *Biting the Hand That Feeds Them: Organizing Women on Welfare at the Grassroots Level* (New York: Praeger, 1989), 112; and Guida West, *The National Welfare Rights Movement: The Social Protest of Poor Women* (New York: Praeger, 1981), 184, 189.

9. Craig Claiborne, "Even a Food Expert Can Stretch a Welfare Budget Only So Far," *NYT,* July 31, 1969, 34M, 1952/Newspaper Articles, NWRO.

10. Ibid.

11. "Mrs. Bingham Tells of Welfare Diet," *NYT,* July 28, 1969, 1952/Newspaper Articles, NWRO.

12. On Pope and Burson, see Hulbert James, interview with Nick Kotz, October 30, 1974, 27, 24/Hulbert James Interview, Kotz; and West, *National Welfare Rights Movement*, 108. On the Brooklyn leadership curriculum, see Rhoda Linton, "Leadership Training Project of Brooklyn Welfare Action Council" [1968] and "Description of Classes," February 1968, Linton; Pope, *Biting the Hand That Feeds Them*, 88–89; and Larry Jackson and William Johnson, *Protest by the Poor: The Welfare Rights Movement in New York City* (New York: Rand Corporation, 1973), 169–75. On Linton's departure, I rely on Linton personal communication, June 21, 2006; and Linton, interview with Felicia Kornbluh, June 9, 1997, by telephone, 32, transcript in possession of the author.

13. For Burson in the national office, see Joyce Burson, interview with Nick Kotz and Mary Lynn Kotz, n.d., 26–27, 31–32, 24/Joyce Burson Interview, Kotz; and Linton, with Kornbluh, 47. For Pope as editor, see *Welfare Righter* 1, 1 (February 21, 1969); "WRO Members Give Eyewitness Reports on June 30th Action," compiled by Jackie Pope, *NOW!* (July 1969), 2; and editorials, *Welfare Fighter* 1, 4 (December 1969): 2. For Day as the original editor of the NWRO newspaper, see Edwin Day, interview with Nick Kotz and Mary Lynn Kotz, n.d., 53–56, 24/Wiley: Ed Day, Kotz.

14. [Hulbert James], press release, February 6, 1969, Unnumbered Box/New York C.C.C.W.G. Newsletters; Leaflets; Pamphlets, Sampson; "A Beginning + An Ending," *TLI* 3, 2 (January 31, 1969): 2; Concerned Parents for Adequate Welfare, "Goodbye Hulbert," *Welfare Righter* 1, 1 (February 21, 1969): 3; and "Local Reports—New York City," *NOW!* February 14, 1969, n.p. For James in Washington, D.C., and his departure from NWRO in 1969, see George Wiley, "Director's Corner," *Welfare Fighter* 1, 2 (October 1969): 2; Wiley, "Director's Corner," *Welfare Fighter* 1, 4 (December 1969): 2; James, with Kotz, 25–26; Tim Sampson, interview with Felicia Kornbluh, July 27, 2001, Oakland, Calif., 3–4, transcript in possession of the author; and West, *National Welfare Rights Movement*, 108.

15. "New Orleans," *NOW!* (December 1968), 3; "School Clothing for Welfare Children," *Welfare Fighter* 1, 1 (September 1969): 7; "Pima County WRO," *Welfare Fighter* 1, 2 (October 1969): 6; "Arizonians Fight Cuts—An Open Letter by the Pima County Welfare Rights Organization," *Welfare Fighter* 1, 9 (May 1970): 9; "140 Moms & Children Protest," *Welfare Fighter* 1, 6 (February 1970): 6; "The States—Kansas," *Welfare Fighter* 1, 7, (March 1970): 8; and Bertha Cavanaugh, "Rhode Island WRO's Win Incentive Battle," *Welfare Fighter* 1, 9 (May 1970): 9.

16. Ethel Mae Mathews, N[ational] C[oordinating] C[ommittee] member, Atlanta, Ga., to Mrs. Bertha Cavanaugh, NWRO, January 11, 1972, 1971/Georgia, NWRO.

17. "Marchers Not Liked, But Doors Stay Open," *Milwaukee Journal*, September 27, 1969, n.p., 16/11, Groppi; Bernice Buresh, "Marchers to Pressure Legislators," *Milwaukee Sentinel*, Sept. 29, 1969, 12, ibid.; and "NWRO Hope of the 70's," *Welfare Fighter* 1, 5 (January 1970): 1. On Father Groppi, see editorial, "'An Evil Man'," *Boston Globe*, October 6, 1969, n.p., 15/10, Groppi.

18. Bernice Buresh, "Protestors Turn Decorum at Capitol Into Turmoil," *Milwaukee Sentinel*, September 30, 1969, n.p., 16/11, Groppi; "Bayonets Against Mothers in Madison," *Welfare Fighter* 1, 2 (October 1969): 1; "Wisconsin Mothers Sit-In," *Welfare Fighter* 1, 2 (October 1969): 4; "Power to the People" [October 1969], 56/Welfare Rights Org., Social Action; "Support the Welfare Mothers" [October 1969], ibid.; "Welfare Protesters Clash With Police, 20 Arrested—

Injured as Officers Use Clubs," *Milwaukee Journal,* October 4, 1969, 1–2, 16/11, Groppi; and John Keefe, "A Week of Protest, a Week of Shame," *Wisconsin State Journal,* October 5, 1969, section 1, 16, ibid.

19. For one writer who made a leap of sympathy from her own life to the lives of welfare recipients, see letter from Carol Peters to Father Groppi, October 3, 1969, 4/6, Groppi.

20. Anonymous letter to Father Groppi, Milwaukee, Wis. [Nov. 11, 1969], 11/1, Groppi.

21. Letter from V. M. Madden, Muskeogon, Mich., to Reverend James Groppi, Madison, Wis., October 8, 1969, 11/1, Groppi.

22. Letter from Mrs. McCarthy, RN, Mass., to Father J. Gropie, August 30, 1969, 8/1, Groppi. On the Second Vatican Council, see Michael B. Katz, *The Undeserving Poor: From the War on Poverty to the War on Welfare* (New York: Pantheon, 1989), 180–83; Pope, *Biting the Hand,* 41; and discussion of Brooklyn in Chapter 2.

23. Letter from Maria C. Betnor, [Green] Bay, Wis., to Father Groppi, [October 3, 1969], 8/1, Groppi.

24. Anon. Letter to Gropi, [October 4, 1969], 11/1, Groppi. For other examples, see Anon. letter for Father James Groppi, [October 30, 1969], ibid.; Post Card from James Q. Roop, Wildwood, Florida, to Father?? Groppi, City Jail, Madison, Wis., October 4, 1969, ibid.; and anonymous letter, Chicago, Ill., to Father James Groppi, n.d., ibid.

25. Anonymous letter, to "You James Groppi," [October 7, 1969], 8/1, Groppi.

26. Letter from "A Real Christian and a Child of God," to Reverend James Groppi, Oct 3, 1969, 8/1, Groppi; letter from V. M. Madden; and letter from Joyce M. Thurston, Jefferson, Wis., to Father James Groppi, [October 9, 1969], 11/1, Groppi.

27. Letter from "A Quiet Sideline Observer," to Mr. James Groppi, Milwaukee, Wis., September 30, 1969, 8/1, Groppi.

28. "NCC Exec Board Plan for Future," *Welfare Fighter* 1, 3 (November 1969): 1.

29. "Adequate Income NOW!" *Welfare Fighter* (Special Edition 1970): 1.

30. "NWRO Adequate Income Plan—$5500 or Fight!" April 1970, 1, Pamphlets.

31. Ibid., 5.

32. Ibid., 3.

33. "NWRO's Adequate Income Plan—21 Congressmen Support H.R. 7257."

34. "Adequate Income Plan," 4.

35. See comparison with California in memorandum from Edward K. Hamilton, budget director, City of New York, to Honorable John V. Lindsay, Subject: California Welfare Arrangements, February 10, 1971, Conf. Social Services (3), 17/203, Lindsay.

36. John V. Lindsay, *The City* (New York: Norton, 1969), 15. On the origins of this relationship between New York City and New York State, see Hendrik Hartog, *Public Property and Private Power: The Corporation of the City of New York in American Law, 1730–1870* (Chapel Hill: University of North Carolina Press, 1983).

37. Lindsay, *The City,* 160.

38. Statement of Hon. John V. Lindsay, mayor, City of New York, accompanied by Mitchell I. Ginsberg, commissioner, Department of Social Services, August 24, 1970, from *Family Assistance Act of 1970—Hearings Before the Committee*

on Finance, United States Senate, part 3 (Washington, D.C.: Government Printing Office, 1970), 1305.

39. Moynihan recalled: "As the delegates to Governor Rockefeller's 1967 Conference on Public Welfare came down the mountain road from Arden House they found waiting for them at the gates a straggle of demonstrators, mostly women, many black, identifying themselves as welfare recipients and protesting that *they* had not been invited to join the discussions, as indeed they had not." Daniel Patrick Moynihan, *The Politics of a Guaranteed Income: The Nixon Administration and the Family Assistance Plan* (New York: Vintage Books, 1973), 236-37. Linton, communication June 21, 2006, remembered that she and other welfare rights activists protested at Rockefeller's conference.

40. Vincent Burke and Vee Burke, *Nixon's Good Deed: Welfare Reform* (New York: Columbia University Press, 1974), 50; Moynihan, *Politics of a Guaranteed Income*, 57, 63–64; statement of Governor Rockefeller, April 4, 1968, *Public Papers of Nelson A. Rockefeller, 53rd Governor of the State of New York, 1968* (Albany: New York State Government, 1968), 1298–1300; and statement of Governor Rockefeller, Announcing Establishment of a Governor's Steering Committee on Social Problems, State of New York—Exec Chamber, Albany, December 7, 1968, *Public Papers, 1968*, 1246–47.

41. Governor Nelson Rockefeller, testimony before the House Committee on Ways and Means, October 31, 1969, *Public Papers of Nelson A. Rockefeller, 1969*, 1417.

42. In this overall assessment of President Nixon, I join Allen Matusow, *Nixon's Economy: Booms, Busts, Dollars, and Votes* (Lawrence: University Press of Kansas, 1998), 1.

43. [Richard Nathan], "Task Force on Public Welfare: Programs to Assist the Poor—Report to President-Elect Richard M. Nixon," December 28, 1968, Transitional Task Force Report #13, Nixon.

44. Ibid., 1.

45. In 1968, candidate Nixon considered offering Finch the vice presidency before he offered it to Spiro Agnew. Joan Hoff, *Nixon Reconsidered* (New York: Basic Books, 1994), 121; Stephen Ambrose, *Nixon: The Triumph of a Politician 1962–1972* (New York: Simon and Schuster, 1989), 173–74; Garry Wills, *Nixon Agonistes* (New York: Signet, 1971), 350, 376–80; and Rowland Evans, Jr., and Robert D. Novak, *Nixon in the White House: The Frustration of Power* (New York: Vintage, 1971), 15–16.

46. [Moynihan], "Report of the Committee on Welfare," April 4, 1969. On Moynihan and Finch as architects of the plan, see editorial, *Roanoke (Virginia) Times*, April 20, 1970, *Editorials on File: Newspaper Educational Reference Service, 1970* (New York: Facts on File, 1970), 464; and editorial, *St. Louis Globe-Democrat*, April 20, 1970, ibid.

47. "Report of the Committee on Welfare," 6.

48. Ibid., 8–9.

49. Ibid., 9.

50. Ibid., 13.

51. Ibid., 11.

52. Daniel P. Moynihan, memorandum for the President, June 26, 1969, Staff Member and Office Files, WHSF, JDE, 38/[Welfare Book] [Family Security System, 1969] [1 of 2], Nixon.

53. Memorandum from Secretary of the Treasury David Kennedy, For The President, [July 31, 1969], 2, 6, WHSF, JDE, 38/[Family Security System, 1969]

[2 of 2], Nixon, contained an alternative to the Family Security proposal endorsed by four other officials, including Agnew. Its key points were a national welfare minimum, increased job training and child care, "unemployed father" benefits in every state, and stiffer work requirements. For more opposition to the Moynihan/Finch plan, see "Conservative Union Scores Relief Plan," *NYT*, January 11, 1970, 46; and editorial, *Charlotte Observer*, April 19, 1970, *Editorials on File*, 459.

54. On Roosevelt's Second Inaugural, see Blanche Weisen Cook, *Eleanor Roosevelt*, vol. 2, *1933–1938* (New York: Viking, 1999), 416–18.

55. Nixon, "New Welfare Plan," 49, 51.

56. Ibid., 51. The President argued that the welfare system "stagnates enterprise and perpetuates dependency. What began on a small scale in the depression '30s has become a huge monster in the prosperous '60s. . . It breaks up homes. It often penalizes work. It robs recipients of dignity. And it grows."

57. Moynihan, *Politics of a Guaranteed Income*, 153–54; and memorandum from Stephen Hess to Bryce Harlow, cc: John Ehrlichman and Daniel Patrick Moynihan, August 29, 1969, WHSF, JDE, 31/355, Domestic Policy [1 of 2], Nixon.

58. On the "silent majority" idea, see H. R. Haldeman, *The Haldeman Diaries: Inside the Nixon White House* (New York: Berkley Books, 1995), 125–26, 141–44, 212, 242–43.

59. John D. Ehrlichman, notes on meetings with the President, [June–July, 1969], WHSF, JDE, 3/1969 JDE Notes of Meetings with the President, Nixon. The White House inner circle considered calling the program "LIFT" (for Labor/Incentive/Family/Training), "UPLIFT," or "CLIMB." See discussion of name change in Richard Reeves, *Richard Nixon: Alone in the White House* (New York: Touchstone, 2001), 112.

60. "The President's Proposals for Welfare Reform," October 2, 1969, WHSF, JDE, 38/[Welfare Book] [President's Proposals for Welfare Reform, Oct. 2, 1969], Nixon.

61. [HEW?], Family Assistance Act of 1969, Sec. 442 (a) (1–2), 7–10; Richard M. Nixon, "President's Message on Welfare Reform," 5, Office of the White House Press Secretary, August 11, 1969 and, attached, "Appendix: Proposed Benefit Schedule"; [Office of Program Planning Evaluation and Planning, Social Security Administration, HEW], "Welfare Reform Fact Sheet: Background Material, August 8, 1969, all from WHSF, JDE, 38/[Welfare Book] [President's Proposals for Welfare Reform, October 2, 1969], Nixon.

62. On state supplementation of the FAP grant, see Tom Joe, "Book Review, *The Politics of a Guaranteed Income*," *Social Work* 18, 3 (May 1973): 5; "The New Nixon Welfare Plan," n.d., 17/FAP (NWRO Views) 1969, Kotz; "Why NWRO Opposes the Nixon Family Assistance Plan," November 5, 1970, ibid; memorandum to members of the Senate from George Wiley, December 4, 1970, 17/FAP (Wiley Words) (NWRO Views 1970), Kotz; and Ginsberg to Lindsay, March 23, 1970, "Priorities for Senate Amendment of HR 16311," Conf. HRA (4), 11/133, Lindsay.

63. President's Message, 9; William Safire, "2nd Draft: FAMILY SECURITY," July 11, 1969, 12: "From Welfare to Workfare," and Safire 8th Draft, August 5, 1969, WHSF, JDE 38/[Welfare Book] [Family Security System, 1969] [2 of 2], Nixon.

64. "Summary of Family Assistance Act," 3; Family Assistance Act, 20; Finch, 5; and President's Message, 2. For comparison to the 1967 WIN program, see Burke and Burke, *Nixon's Good Deed*, 35.

65. President's Message, 6–8, promised 450,000 child care slots, which would be "more than custodial."

66. President's Message, 5.

67. Finch Statement, 3.

68. Ibid., 5.

69. President's Message, 5–6, 9; Finch Statement, 6; and Burke and Burke, *Nixon's Good Deed*, 9, 53, 66, 104.

70. Editorial, *Los Angeles Times*, April 27, 1970, *Editorials on File*, 460. See also editorials, *Charlotte Observer*, April 19, 1970, ibid., 459; *Minneapolis Tribune*, April 20, 1970, ibid.; and *Deseret (Salt Lake City) News*, April 17, 1970, ibid., 462.

71. Ginsberg to Lindsay, March 23, 1970, 1, Conf. HRA (4), 11/133, Lindsay.

72. Russell Long quoted in Timothy J. Sampson, *Welfare: A Handbook for Friend and Foe* (New York: United Church Press, 1972), 152.

73. Evans and Novak, *Nixon in the White House*, 232; Burke and Burke, *Nixon's Good Deed*, 154–55; Weaver, "Nixon Aides," *NYT*, 24; and Welsh, "Welfare Reform," 16–17.

74. Moynihan, *Politics of a Guaranteed Income*, 451–52.

75. On the Nixon administration and civil rights, see Congressional Quarterly, *Nixon: The Second Year of His Presidency* (Washington, D.C.: Congressional Quarterly, Inc., 1971), 67–72; Leon Panetta and Peter Gall, *Bring Us Together: The Nixon Team and the Civil Rights Retreat* (Philadelphia: J.P. Lippincott, 1971); and Reeves, *Richard Nixon*, 116–17. On Carswell and Haynsworth, see Laura Kalman, *Abe Fortas: A Biography* (New Haven, Conn.: Yale University Press, 1990), 327–75; *Haldeman Diaries*, 176; and Melvin Urofsky and Paul Finkelman, *A March of Liberty: A Constitutional History of the United States*, vol. 2 (New York: Oxford University Press, 2002), 896–97. On school desegregation, see *Swann v. Charlotte-Mecklenburg Board of Education* (402 U.S. 1) (1970); Lawrence Friedman, *American Law in the Twentieth Century* (New Haven, Conn.: Yale University Press, 2002), 395; and *Haldeman Diaries*, 151–55, 159 ("Friday, February 25, 1970—Wants E[hrlichman] to move fast on developing a constitutional amendment about schools. Feels we should bite the bullet now and hard, if it's called racism, so be it!"), 224–25, 249.

76. Richard M. Nixon, "Explaining the 'Secret War' in Laos," in *Vietnam and America: A Documented History*, ed. Marvin Gettleman, Jane Franklin, Marilyn Young, and H. Bruce Franklin (New York: Grove Press, 1985), 442–47; Marilyn Young, *The Vietnam Wars, 1945–1990* (New York: HarperPerennial, 1991), 234–36, 248; and *Haldeman Diaries*, 191.

77. Quoted in Freeman, *Working-Class New York*, 238.

78. Editorials, *Detroit Free Press, St. Louis Post-Dispatch, Chicago Sun-Times*, and *Des Moines Tribune*, April 30, 1970, *Editorials on File, 1970*, 469–71; editorials, *Portland Oregonian, Salt Lake City Tribune*, and *Chicago Tribune*, May 5, 1970, ibid., 491–93; editorial, *Memphis Commercial Appeal*, May 15, and *San Francisco Chronicle*, May 13, ibid., 526–27; and William Safire, *Before the Fall: An Inside View of the Pre-Watergate White House* (New York: Da Capo Press, 1975), 193, 195.

79. Moynihan, *Politics of a Guaranteed Income*, 498. Moynihan, 500, noted that Nixon ceased to press for the welfare proposal.

80. John D. Ehrlichman, notes on a meeting with President Nixon and George Shultz, August 19, 1970, 12:50 p.m., WHSF, JDE, 4/3, Nixon.

81. Geoffrey Hodgson, *The Gentleman from New York: Daniel Patrick Moynihan* (Boston: Houghton Mifflin, 2000), 175–80; Ehrlichman, "The White House," 130; *Haldeman Diaries*, May 21, 1970, 202, and June 5, 1970, 206; and Ambrose, *Nixon*, 173–74, 297, 365.

82. See, generally, inventory, WHCF—Staff Member and Office Files, Materials of Robert H. Finch; and Kenneth Cole, Jr., deputy assistant to the president for Domestic Affairs, memorandum for the Domestic Council, September 17, 1970, ibid.

83. Safire, *Before the Fall,* 316, 323; and *Haldeman Diaries,* July 8, 1970, 216; November 7, 1970, 249; November 12, 1969, 128; and September 9, 1970, 230.

84. *Haldeman Diaries,* July 13, 1970, 218.

85. Welsh, "Welfare Reform," 17; Ehrlichman notes on State of the Union Messages, WHSF, JDE, Alphabetical Subject File, 26/1970 State of the Union and 26/State of the Union—1971. For details of the amended FAP, see Hoff, *Nixon Reconsidered,* 131.

86. Ehrlichman notes on 1972 State of the Union, in WHSF, JDE, Alphabetical Subject File, 26/1972 State of the Union [1 of 2]; Hodgson, *Gentleman from New York,* 180; and editorial, *Minneapolis Tribune,* October 5, 1972, *Editorials on File, 1972,* 1245.

87. According to speechwriter William Safire, Buchanan wrote an important memorandum in January 1971: "Rather than draw up our own yardstick of success and failure," he charged, "the administration cravenly attempted to out-do liberals on racial integration and guaranteed incomes." Safire believed that FAP was effectively "abandoned by a Nixon who heard Buchanan loud and clear." Safire, *Before the Fall,* 545, 548.

88. Theodore H. White, *The Making of the President 1972* (New York: Atheneum, 1973), 120, 126, 128; Welsh, "Welfare Reform," 21; Ginsberg, with Kotz and Kotz, 11; and editorial, *Minneapolis Tribune,* October 5, 1972.

89. Ginsberg, with Kotz and Kotz, 11. Tom Joe remembered the critical moment as one shortly after Nixon's return from Russia, when Secretary Richardson finally got to meet with the President. Joe, interview with Nick Kotz and Mary Lynn Kotz, n.d., 9, 24/Tom Joe Interview, Kotz.

90. Ginsberg, with Kotz and Kotz, 12–13.

91. Ibid., 13; "Congress kills FAP," *Welfare Fighter* 3, 8 (October 1972): 1, 3; editorial, *Toledo Blade,* October 8, 1972, *Editorials on File,* 1248; *NYT,* October 8, 1972, ibid., 1249; *Nashville Tennessean,* October 14, 1972, ibid.; and *Minneapolis Tribune,* October 5, 1972.

92. Editorial, *Washington Post,* October 6, 1972, *Editorials on File,* 1246.

93. Editorial, *NYT,* October 8, 1972.

94. Editorial, *Nashville Tennessean,* October 14, 1972. Also see editorial, *Akron Beacon Journal,* October 2, 1972, ibid., 1246.

95. NWRO press release, National Coordinating Council Meeting in Jackson, Mississippi, February 24, 1969, 36/Nat. Welfare Rights Org. (2), Social Action.

96. Sanders statement, *Social Security and Welfare Proposals: Hearings Before the Committee on Ways and Means, Part 3* (Washington, D.C., Government Printing Office, 1970), 1014; and "Sanders Testifies Before the House."

97. George Wiley, statement, *Social Security and Welfare Proposals,* 1014. See also Sanders, Wiley, and Carl Rachlin, "Statement to the House Ways and Means Committee," 8.

98. Question-and-answer on the NWRO testimony, *Social Security and Welfare Proposals,* 1033.

99. NWRO, "$5500 or Fight!" 7.

100. Letter from Carl Rachlin, legal director, Scholarship, Education and Defense Fund for Racial Equality, New York City, to Dr. George Wiley, January 10, 1969, 33/3, Wiley.

101. Center on Social Welfare Policy and Law, notes From the Emergency Conference On Welfare Litigation, May 21–22 [1970], 2017/Columbia Center Conference, NWRO.

102. James quoted in Kotz and Kotz, *Passion for Equality*, 265.

103. James, with Kotz, 31.

104. Haynes Johnson, "Finch Takes Abuse Calmly as Protesters Seize Office," *Washington Post*, May 14, 1970, 1, A6. See also David Holmberg, "Protesters Occupy Finch's Office," *Evening Star*, May 13, 1970, 1; "NWRO Liberates Finch's Office," *Welfare Fighter* 1, 9 (May 1970): 12; and "Angry Rally Backs H.E.W. Liberators," *Welfare Fighter* 1, 10 (June 1970): 1, 8. Wiley responded to the negative articles by claiming that Finch had "promised to consult" with NWRO about new welfare legislation but had reneged on his promise. He argued that the NWRO action was a response to "the overriding question of the war." Letter from George Wiley to editor, *Washington Post*, May 18, 1970, 17/FAP (Wiley words) (NWRO Views 1970), Kotz; and letter from George Wiley to "Friend," n.d., Pamphlets.

105. *Welfare Fighter* 1, 10 (June 1970): 8.

106. Editorial, "Can I Help You?" *Washington Post*, May 16, 1970, A12.

107. Douglas Chevalier, photograph to accompany "Finch Takes Abuse Calmly," *Washington Post*, May 14, 1970, 1; and Pete Schmick, photograph to accompany "Protesters Occupy Finch's Office."

108. On Sanders's candidacy, see City-Wide Coordinating Committee of Welfare Groups, press release, July 29, 1968, Unnumbered Box/New York C.C.C.W.G. Newsletters; Leaflets; Pamphlets, Sampson; "List of the Candidates in the City Who Will Be Voted On in Tomorrow's Elections," *NYT*, November 14, 1968, 39; and "Profile of a WRO: Mrs. Beulah Sanders, Chairman," *Welfare Fighter* 1, 4 (December 1969): 2. On her opposition to the war in Vietnam, see Lacey Fosburgh, "Women's Unit Bids Congress Shun War to Aid Human Needs," *NYT*, June 17, 1969, 37; "Mrs. Sanders Speaks At DC Antiwar Rally," *Welfare Fighter* 1, 9 (May 1970): 1; John Herbers, "Big Capital Rally Asks U.S. Pullout In Southeast Asia," *NYT*, May 10, 1970, 1, 24; and C. Gerald Fraser, "Antiwar Leaders Plan Demonstrations at Prisons," *NYT*, September 29, 1971, 14.

109. "Mrs. Sanders Speaks at DC Antiwar Rally"; and Herbers, "Big Capital Rally Asks U.S. Pullout," 24.

110. Doris Doughty, "April 15th Actions—New York," *Welfare Fighter* 1, 8 (April 1970): 1.

111. NWRO pamphlet, "STOP the WAR on us POOR," n.d. [March–April 1970], 7/11, Wiley. See also, NWRO model leaflet, "Everyone has a Right to Welfare," n.d. [1970], ibid.; NWRO, "Stop the War and Feed the Poor—3 seconds off the war would give one family of four $5500," Pamphlets; "April 15th—National Priorities Day," *Welfare Fighter* (March 1970): 1; and "April 15th Rallies Support Adequate Income," *Welfare Fighter* (April 1970): 1–2.

112. "NWRO's Adequate Income Bill," 22/4, Wiley; Sen. Eugene McCarthy, "X. 3780—Introduction of a Bill To Provide An Adequate Income For All American Citizens," *Congressional Record—Senate*, April 1970: S6386, reprint as NWRO leaflet, 17/FAP—NWRO Views (1970), Kotz; and "The Nixon Plan Is Getting Worse," *Welfare Fighter* (July 1970): 3.

113. "NWRO Position on the Nixon Welfare Plan," July 25, 1970, 1959/No file, NWRO. See also "How the Nixon Plan Hurts Poor People," July 28, 1970, 36/National Welfare Rights Organization, Social Action. On the convention, see "Getting It Together in the '70s: Conference 70, Program," 7/8, Wiley.

114. "NWRO Position on the Nixon Welfare Plan."

115. "ZAP FAP," *Welfare Fighter* 2, 2 (October 1970): 3; "ZAP FAP," October 6, 1970, Pamphlets; cartoon, "Zap FAP," *Welfare Fighter* 2, 3 (November 1970): 1; and "ZAP FAP," *Welfare Fighter* 2, 5 (February 1971): 12.

116. Hearings on Family Assistance Plan, H.R. 16311, November 18–19, 1970, Washington, D.C., 45, 17/NWRO–FAP Testimony Before Clean Gene, Kotz. On the hearings, see also "NCC's Meet in Atlanta," *Welfare Fighter* 2, 3 (November 1970): 2; and "Hearings Turn The Tide—NWRO Plays Leading Role in Zapping FAP," *Welfare Fighter* 2, 4 (December 1970–January 1971): 6.

117. Hearings on Family Assistance Plan, day 1, 48.

118. Ibid., 71.

119. Ibid., 49–50.

120. Hearings on Family Assistance Plan, day 2, 169.

121. Hearings on Family Assistance Plan, day 1, 45.

122. Ibid., 73.

123. Ibid., 78–79.

124. Tom Joe, with Kotz and Kotz, 12; "President Losing Welfare Support," *NYT,* November 20, 1970, 1, 30; and Ginsberg, with Kotz and Kotz, 12–13: NWRO "clearly had an influence on Fred Harris. . . . deeply troubled by their opposition. And to some extent Senator McCarthy . . . N[ick] K[otz]: The influence was on the liberals. M[itchell] G[insberg]: That's right. It sure wasn't on the others."

125. Lowell Beck, executive director, Common Cause, telegram to George Wiley, November 16, 1970, 17/FAP (Wiley Words) (NWRO Views 1970), Kotz; copy of Telegram from Johnnie Tillmon and George Wiley to Honorable Elliot Richardson, secretary of Health, Education, and Welfare, November 16, 1970, ibid; and "Welfare Rights Demand Stalls Citizens' Lobby," *Evening Star* (Washington, D.C.), November 17, 1970, 1, A-7.

126. Office of Congressman Charles Rangel, "Press Conference Announcement," n.d. [April 5, 1971], 17/FAP—NWRO Views (1971), Kotz; Representative Bella Abzug, extension of remarks, House of Representatives, 92d Congress, 1st Session, June 22, 1971, *Congressional Record,* n.p., reprint in 4/17, Wickenden; and memorandum from George Wiley to Congressman Charles Diggs and members of the Congressional Black Caucus, May 27, 1971, 17/FAP—NWRO Views (1971), Kotz. On the 1971 convention, see Mrs. Audrey Williams, notes on the General Session, NWRO Convention '71, August 1, 1971, 7/8, Wiley; "Welfare Not Warfare: NWRO Convention '71," 7/8, Wiley; and "NWRO Convention '71," *Welfare Fighter* 2, 7 (August 1971): 1, 8.

127. Letter from Elizabeth Perry, D.C. Family Rights Organization, Washington, D.C., to Mrs. [Marion] Kidd, NWRO, Washington, D.C., December 13, 1971, 1971/District of Columbia, NWRO. For further use of the slavery analogy, see Faith Evans, "Back to Slavery?" *Welfare Fighter* 2, 8 (October 1971): 1.

128. Memo from Mrs. Catherine Jermany, president, California Welfare Rights Organization, to All Local Welfare Rights Groups of California, Subject: CWRO Legislative Action Training Conference, n.d., 2061/No file, NWRO.

129. George Wiley claimed that the defeat was "a monument to good organization and strategy" on the part of grassroots welfare rights activists and their allies in Washington. Wiley, remarks at the National Conference of Health, New Orleans, October 19, 1972, in "Congress Kills FAP," *Welfare Fighter* 3, 8 (October 1972): 4.

130. "Cuts Are Coming—Cuts Are Here," *Welfare Fighter* 2, 8 (October 1971): 2; and "Fighting Back at Cuts," ibid., 10.

131. Moynihan, *Politics of a Guaranteed Income*, esp. 247–48.

132. Hoff, *Nixon Reconsidered*, 130; Melvin Small, *The Presidency of Richard Nixon* (Lawrence: University Press of Kansas, 1999), esp. chapter 7; and Joan Hoff-Wilson, "Outflanking the Liberals on Welfare," in *Richard M. Nixon: Politician, President, Administrator* (Westport, Conn.: Greenwood Press, 1991), ed. Leon Friedman and William Leventrosser, 85–106, esp. 102. On Nixon and civil rights, see Dean Kotlowski, *Politics, Principles, and Policy* (Cambridge, Mass.: Harvard University Press, 2002). For discussion of the "liberal Nixon" thesis, see Stanley Kutler, "Richard Nixon: Man and Monument," in *Nixon: An Oliver Stone Film*, ed. Eric Hamburg (New York: Hyperion, 1995), 43; and David Greenberg, *Nixon's Shadow: The History of an Image* (New York: Norton, 2003), 304–37. Works that discuss FAP without describing Nixon as a "liberal" include Bruce J. Schulman, *The Seventies: The Great Shift in American Culture, Society, and Politics* (New York: DaCapo Press, 2002), 23–42; Alice O'Connor, *Poverty Knowledge: Social Science, Social Policy, and the Poor in Twentieth-Century History* (Princeton, N.J.: Princeton University Press, 2001), 191–92, 223–25; Michael Brown, *Race, Money, and the American Welfare State* (Ithaca, N.Y.: Cornell University Press, 1999), 295–322; and Jill Quadagno, *The Color of Welfare: How Racism Undermined the War on Poverty* (New York: Oxford University Press, 1994), 117–18, 123.

133. See colloquy between Beulah Sanders and NWRO staff member John Kaufman, minutes of National Coordinating Council Executive Committee Meeting, December 5, 1970, 8/3, Wiley.

134. Sanders, with Kotz and Kotz, 23.

Chapter 7. End of an Era

1. [Faith Evans?], Minutes of N[ational] C[oordinating] C[ommittee] Meeting, October 15, 1971, 2061/Eastern Regional Folder II, NWRO; George Wiley, "Director's Corner," *Welfare Fighter* 2, 8 (October 1971): 3; and "Operation New York," *Welfare Fighter* 2, 9 (November 1971): 9.

2. Beulah Sanders, "Message from the Chair," *Welfare Fighter* 2, 8 (October 1971): 3.

3. Fact Sheet on New York State Welfare Cuts, as of April 1971, 56/Welfare Rights Org., Social Action; "Rockefeller Wins His Stars****," *Welfare Fighter* 2, 6 (April–May 1971): 3; Minutes of N.C.C. Meeting, October 15, 1971; "Operation New York"; and Faith Evans, "Back to Slavery?" *Welfare Fighter* 2, 9 (October 1971): 1, 14.

4. Letter from Carl Rachlin, Hunter College, City University of New York, to Dr. George Wiley, NWRO, Washington, D.C., January 19, 1971, 33/3, Wiley.

5. Paul Delaney, "Welfare-Job Law stirs Bitterness and Confusion," *NYT*, October 9, 1972, 1, 46; "The States Report—New York State," *Welfare Fighter* 3, 6 (August–September 1972): 14; "More States Report—Philadelphia," *Welfare Fighter* 3, 6 (August–September 1972): 16; "Talmadge Exploitation of Welfare Recipients," *Tioga Welfare Rights Community Newsletter*, August/September 1972: 1, 2061/No file, NWRO; Editorial, "Welfare Muddle," *NYT*, August 1, 1972, 34; and Vincent Burke and Vee Burke, *Nixon's Good Deed: Welfare Reform* (New York: Columbia University Press, 1974), 164.

6. On legal changes, see Martha Davis, *Brutal Need: Lawyers in the Welfare Rights Movement, 1967–1973* (New Haven, Conn.: Yale University Press, 1993), 128–34; Laurence H. Tribe, *American Constitutional Law*, 2nd ed. (New York: Foundation Press, 1988), 1663–64; Daniel Jay Baum, *The Welfare Family and Mass Administra-*

tive Justice (New York: Praeger, 1974), 20; and discussion below. On state cuts, see "States Report—Indiana," *Welfare Fighter* 2, 10 (December 1971): 6; "More States Report—Missouri," *Welfare Fighter* 3, 2 (March 1972): 16; "Ohioans Protest New Welfare Law," *Welfare Fighter* 3, 3 (April 1972): 19; "The States Report—Connecticut," *Welfare Fighter* 3, 5 (June 1972): 13; and "The States Report—District of Columbia," *Welfare Fighter* 3, 6 (August–September 1972): 15.

7. Tim Sampson, "Brief History of the National Welfare Rights Movement," n.d. [1982?], National Welfare Rights Organization—Welfare Rights Organizations, Freedman. For the closing of the Citywide office in Harlem in 1975, I rely on New York Telephone, *Manhattan Telephone Directory, 1974–75*, 309; *Manhattan Telephone Directory, 1975–76*, 313; and Frances Fox Piven, personal communication, August 25, 2005.

8. On "open admissions" at CUNY, see Tomas Lopez, "An American Necessity: The Politics of Survival at Hostos Community College" (senior thesis, Duke University, spring 2006), 12–15; Vincent Cannato, *The Ungovernable City: John Lindsay and his Struggle to Save New York* (New York: Basic Books, 2001), 457–58; and Charles Morris, *The Cost of Good Intentions: New York City and the Liberal Experiment, 1960–1975* (New York: Norton, 1980), 156–57.

9. Human Resources Administration, "FY 1971–1972 Budget," Subj. HRA, 52/950, JVL; Peter Kihss, "Rise in Relief Roll Triples Lindsay Budget Forecast," *NYT*, December 13, 1970, 1, 42; and Martin Tolchin, "Sugarman Sees No Ebbing of Welfare Rise Till 1972," *NYT*, December 29, 1970, 1, 22. For the legal action, see *The City of New York, John V. Lindsay as Mayor, Jule Sugarman as Commissioner of Social Services, and Plaintiffs, v. Elliott L. Richardson, as Secretary of Health, Education and Welfare of the United States, et al., Defendants*, Complaint, U.S. District Court, Southern District, n.d. [February 1971], Subj. Welfare (1971), 117/2219, JVL; Peter Kihss, "Lindsay Rejects Record Request by Welfare Unit," *NYT*, December 30, 1970, 1, 22; Robert McFadden, "City Will Sue U.S. on Welfare Costs," *NYT*, January 3, 1971, 1, 58; Martin Tolchin, "Suit on Welfare Filed by Lindsay," *NYT*, February 25, 1971, 1, 44; and Larry Jackson and William Johnson, *Protest by the Poor: The Welfare Rights Movement in New York City* (New York: Rand Corporation, 1973), 1.

10. Lindsay, "Text of Rejection of the Welfare Budget"; memorandum from Edward K. Hamilton, budget director, to Honorable John V. Lindsay, Subject: California Welfare Arrangements, February 10, 1971, Conf. Social Services (3), JVL; Project Management Staff, Department of Social Services, "Work Plan: Reorganization of Operating Functions," February 19, 1971, Conf. Social Services (2), 17/202, JVL; and Department of Social Services, "Separation of Income Maintenance From Social Services in Social Service Centers," n.d. [Spring 1971], Conf. HRA (3), 11/132, JVL.

11. "Work Plan: Reorganization of Operating Functions," 3; and "Separation of Income Maintenance From Social Services": "The advantages of a separated system are: 1. Clerical workers' salaries are, on average, lower than caseworkers' salaries. 2. The concept of caseload per caseworker no longer exists which means as the public assistance caseload increases fewer additional staff is required. Number of cases per caseworker had in the past been written into the union contract."

12. Peter Kihss, "Welfare Study For 1969 Reports 60,000 Ineligible," *NYT*, August 9, 1971, 1, 33; Peter Kihss, "6% on Relief Here Called Ineligible," *NYT*, December 12, 1971, 1, 32; "Operation New York"; and "Legal," *Welfare Fighter* 3, 8 (October 1972): 5. For the local economy and welfare, see Francis X. Clines,

"263,500 Workers in City Called Eligible for Welfare," *NYT*, September 22, 1970, 1, 53; Peter Kihss, "Rise in Relief Roll Triples Lindsay Budget Forecast," 42; and Kihss, "City Notes Jump in Welfare Rolls as Jobs Decline," *NYT*, May 9, 1971, 1, 31.

13. [NWRO], Fact Sheet on New York State Welfare Cuts; "Rockefeller Wins His Stars"; memorandum from Catherine Boddie, chairwoman, Upstate Welfare Rights Organization, to All Upstate WRO's, September 2, 1971, 2061/No File, NWRO; memorandum from Gordon Davis, assistant to the mayor, City of New York, to Jule Sugerman, administrator of Human Resources, Re: HRA Priority Matters, April 14, 1971, Dept. HRA, 1971, 48/617, JVL; memorandum from Gordon Davis to John V. Lindsay, et al., Re: Follow-Up on HRA Administrator Meeting—May 13, May 14, 1971, Conf. HRA (4), 11/133, JVL; statement by Mayor John V. Lindsay, May 18, 1971, Subj. Welfare, 117/221, JVL; and Evans, "Back to Slavery?"

14. Memorandum from Georgia L. McMurray, special assistant for Child Development, through Mr. Jule Sugarman, administrator, HRA, To: The Honorable John V. Lindsay, February 18, 1971, Dept. HRA 1971, 48/617, JVL. Also see press release, Office of the Mayor, City Hall, for release November 22, 1971, Subj. HRA—Day Care, 52/947, JVL; and McMurray, commissioner, Agency for Child Development, First Report to the Mayor of the Agency for Child Development of the HRA, November 22, 1971, Subj. HRA—Day Care, 52/947, JVL. Mayor Lindsay and his staff believed that their efforts would be supplemented by federal funds, since Congress passed a child care bill in 1971. When President Nixon vetoed the bill, Lindsay trimmed the sails of the New York program. See Sonya Michel, *Children's Interests/Mothers' Rights: The Shaping of America's Child Care Policy* (New Haven, Conn.: Yale University Press, 1999), 248–51. For Lindsay's opposition to the residency requirement, see statement by Mayor John V. Lindsay, May 18, 1971, Subj. Welfare, 117/2219, JVL.

15. Memorandum from Max Waldgeir, acting commissioner of Social Services, to Mayor John V. Linsday, Subject: Progress report on referrals to the Employment Service and to Public Works Projects, August 12, 1971, Dept. HRA, 48/617, JVL; memorandum from Anton Adams [?] to Ed Hamilton, director of the Budget, Re: Work Relief Project Referrals to Maintenance Jobs, August 26, 1971, Conf. HRA (3), 11/132, JVL; and memorandum from Edward K. Hamilton, director of the Budget, to Honorable John V. Lindsay, Subject: Placement of Work Relief People in Visible Maintenance Jobs, August 27, 1971, ibid. For the political importance of city compliance with the program, see Edward Ranzal, "City Reports Welfare Frauds by 20,000," *NYT*, August 27, 1971, 1, 67. City officials referred to this article in Hamilton to Lindsay, et al., August 27, 1971, and to another article critical of the city on this point in Adams to Hamilton, August 26, 1971.

16. Waldgeir to Linsday, August 12, 1971.

17. Hamilton to Lindsay et al., August 27, 1971. A handwritten note on the document reads: "Ed is clearly right. Keep pushing—you've got my full support. J.V.L."

18. Some welfare recipients did pretend to lose checks in order to get more money; others were accused unjustly. Fraud Control Program, Department of Social Services, HRA, "Project Status Report—Check Duplication Analysis and Systems Development," April 28, 1972, Dept. HRA 1972 48/618, JVL; and memo from Jule Sugarman, administrator, HRA, to Honorable John V. Lindsay, et al., Subject: DSS Fraud Control Program—Program Status Report, May 5, 1972, Dept. HRA 1972, 48/618, JVL.

19. Memorandum from Joan Leiman, special adviser to the mayor, to John V. Lindsay, Re: Briefing memorandum for June 16 meeting on Department of Social Services Staffing and on Community Social Services Program, June 15, 1972, Conf. Social Services (Dept of) (1), 17/201, JVL; memorandum from Art Spiegel and Bob Carroll, HRA, to Mayor John V. Lindsay, Subject: Mayoral Orders to HRA/DSS, August 16, 1972, Conf. HRA (2), 11/131, JVL; and letter from Arthur Schiff, assistant administrator, HRA, to Hon. John V. Lindsay, July 12, 1973, Dept. HRA 1973, 48/619, JVL.

20. Letter from John V. Lindsay, mayor, City of New York, to Hon. Jule Sugarman, Human Resources administrator, May 15, 1973, Subj. HRA-1973, 48/619, JVL. For the Nixon administration defunding Community Action Programs, which set the stage for New York City sunsetting the programs, see Hoff, *Nixon Reconsidered*, 60–65.

21. Cannato, *Ungovernable City*, 494–99, 517, 555–57; Martin Shefter, *Political Crisis/Fiscal Crisis: The Collapse and Revival of New York City* (New York: Basic Books, 1985), 97–98; and Fred Ferretti, *The Year The Big Apple Went Bust* (New York: G.P. Putnam's Sons, 1976), 56.

22. "Rockefeller Wins His Stars"; and Jennette Washington, "Attica—from an Anguished Welfare Mother," *Welfare Fighter* 2, 8 (October 1971): 3. Also see George Wiley, "Director's Corner," *Welfare Fighter* 2, 8 (October 1971): 3; and, on Attica generally, Heather A. Thompson, *Attica: Race, Rebellion, and the Rise of Law and Order in America* (New York: Knopf, forthcoming 2007) and Henry Hampton, prod., "A Nation of Law? 1968–1971," episode 6, from the series *Eyes on the Prize II: America at the Racial Crossroad* (Boston: Blackside Productions, 1990).

23. "Welfare Hotels—A Grim, Tragic Mess," *Welfare Fighter* 2, 5 (February 1971): 3; Murray Schumach, "Welfare Cases in Hotels Called a Modern Horror," *NYT*, November 23, 1970, 1, 42; and Schumach, "Official's Dismissal Asked in 'Welfare Hotel' Dispute," *NYT*, November 25, 1970, 1, 46.

24. "Welfare Hotels—A Grim, Tragic Mess"; and C. Gerald Fraser, "10 Are Arrested in Relief Protest," *NYT*, February 27, 1971, n.p., Unnumbered Box/ New York C.C.C.W.G. Newsletters; Leaflets; Pamphlets, Sampson.

25. Evans, "Back to Slavery?"; "Rockefeller Wins His Stars"; and Minutes of National Coordinating Council Meeting, October 15, 1971, 2061/Easter Regional Folder II, NWRO.

26. George Wiley, "Director's Corner," *Welfare Fighter* 2, 8 (October 1971): 3. See also "Operation New York," *Welfare Fighter* 2, 9 (November 1971): 9; National Coordinating Committee, October 15, 1971; and Nick Kotz and Mary Lynn Kotz, *A Passion for Equality: George A. Wiley and the Movement* (New York: Norton, 1977), 288.

27. "Operation New York," 9. On the Brownie Point system, see also Evans, "Back to Slavery?"; and "NWRO Sues HEW," *Welfare Fighter* 2, 9 (November 1971): 2.

28. Statement quoted in "Operation New York Starts Moving," *Welfare Fighter* 2, 10 (December 1971): 1.

29. See, generally, Box 2061, NWRO. The letters are not arranged in files.

30. Eliza Williams, Connecticut WRO, Waterbury, Conn., report to Bertha Cavanaugh, NWRO, November 1971, 2061/No file, NWRO; letter from Mrs. Eliza Williams to HEW, Washington, D.C., September 6, 1972, ibid.; and Eliza Williams and James Pach, NCC's Connecticut, report to NWRO, n.d. [received February 24 1972], ibid.

31. Letter from Ms. Cassie Downer, chairwoman, Milwaukee County Welfare Rights Organization, to "Dear Friend," December 1972, 56/Milw. County Welfare Rights Org., Social Action; letter from Mattie Richardson, chairman, Finance Committee, Milwaukee County Welfare Rights Organization, to Chairs of Local Groups in Milwaukee, January 17, 1972, 1/5, Becker; and Minutes, general meeting, Milwaukee County Welfare Rights Organization, August 21, 1972, 1/8, Becker. Also see the book the Milwaukee group produced, with help from Thomas Tarantino and Reverend Dismas Becker, *Welfare Mothers Speak Out: We Ain't Gonna Shuffle Anymore* (New York: Norton, 1972).

32. [Alabama WRO], 2061/No file, NWRO; letter from Mrs. Ruby Williams, Birmingham, Ala., to Bertha Cavanaugh, November 11, 1971, ibid.; and agenda, statewide meeting, South Carolina Welfare Rights Organization, Zion Baptist Church, Columbia, S.C., January 11, 1972, ibid. See also Sullivan County (Tennessee) Food Stamp and Welfare Rights Manual, March 1972, 2061/No file, NWRO; letter from Jon Hunter, W.Va. WRO, Morgantown, W.Va, to Debbie Vajda, NWRO, May 26, 1972, ibid.; memorandum from John Due, Miami, Fla., to Florida Welfare Rights Organization & Florida Tenant Organization, February 19, 1972, ibid.; and report from Mrs. Ethel Mathews, Atlanta, Ga., to Mrs. Bertha Cavanaugh, NWRO, April 10, 1972, ibid.

33. William Pastreich, interview with Felicia Kornbluh, by telephone, February 26, 1997, n.p., notes in possession of the author.

34. Johnnie Tillmon, interview with Nick Kotz and Mary Lynn Kotz, November 26, 1974, 113–14, 26/Johnnie Tillmon Interview, Kotz; West, *National Welfare Rights Movement*, 116; and Frances Fox Piven and Richard Cloward, *Poor People's Movements: How They Succeed, Why They Fail* (New York: Vintage, 1977), 313–14.

35. Pastreich, with Kornbluh; Tillmon, with Kotz and Kotz, 109–13, 120; and Rhoda Linton, interview with Felicia Kornbluh, June 9, 1997, by telephone, 53–54. Also see Austin Scott, "The Plight of an Organizer," *Washington Post*, August 14, 1972, A6; "Profile of a Welfare Fighter—Annie Smart," *Welfare Fighter* 2, 4 (December 1970–January 1971): 11; and Gary Delgado, *Organizing the Movement: The Roots and Growth of ACORN* (Philadelphia: Temple University Press, 1986). On the reactions of the elected leadership, see Beulah Sanders, interview with Nick Kotz and Mary Lynn Kotz, 1974, 17, 26/Beulah Sanders Interview; and Tillmon, with Kotz and Kotz, 109. Piven and Cloward argue that it was a conscious strategy on Wiley's part to spur organizing outside of the usual NWRO channels, since leaders such as Sanders and Tillmon had little incentive to bring new kinds of people into the organization (*Poor People's Movements*, 314).

36. Letter from George Wiley to Welfare Rights Leaders, Members, Friends and Supporters, December 17, 1972, WRO's/MEJ, NCLEJ; Austin Scott, "Wiley Quitting as Head of National Welfare Rights Group," *Washington Post*, December 17, 1972, A2; and Ronald Smothers, "Welfare Activist Plans New Group," *NYT*, December 17, 1972, 43B. For the conflicts that preceded his departure, see Sanders, with Kotz and Kotz, 18–19; and Catherine Jermany, interview with Mary Lynn Kotz, n.d., 22–23, 25/Catherine Jermany Interview, Kotz.

37. Wiley to Welfare Rights Leaders, Members, Friends.

38. "And the Wall Came Tumbling Down," *Welfare Fighter* 2, 7 (August 1971): 2; memo from Bill Briggs to January Peace Conference, Re: Proposed April Solidarity Action, January 9, 1971, 36/Nat. Welfare Rights Org. (1), Social Action; Dr. Ralph David Abernathy, President SCLC, and Dr. George A. Wiley, "Declaration of War Against Repression—A Call to Action," February 24, 1971, 36/Nat. Welfare Rights Org. (3), Social Action; and NWRO, "Join the Spring Offensive

to End the War Against Poor People At Home and Abroad!" April 19, 1971, 33/16, Wiley.

39. Beulah Sanders, chair's report, *Welfare Fighter* 3, 5 (June 1972): 9; "WROs Exercise Political Muscle," *Welfare Fighter* 3, 5 (June 1972): 10; "NWRO Plans March At Democratic Convention," *Welfare Fighter* 3, 5 (June 1972): 1; and Dr. George Wiley, "NWRO Strives Forward," *Welfare Fighter* 3, 6 (July 1972): 1. On what happened at the convention, see Austin Scott, "Miami 'Poor' Coalition Burgeons," *Washington Post*, July 7, 1972, A12; Scott, "Poor Win Right to Negotiate for Seats," *Washington Post*, July 8, 1972, A7; and Edward Zuckerman, "The Poor Can Play the Media Game," *Village Voice*, July 13, 1972, 9–10.

40. "Poor People's Platform," *Welfare Fighter* 3, 5 (June 1972): 8. On the process of writing the Platform, see "NWRO, SCLC, NTO form united front," *Welfare Fighter* 3, 6 (July 1972): 3.

41. Tim Sampson, "Brief History of the National Welfare Rights Movement"; Wiley to Welfare Rights Leaders, Members, Friends; and "Wiley Addresses Democratic Platform Committee," *Welfare Fighter* 3, 6 (July 1972): 5.

42. "Why The Children Must March," *Welfare Fighter* 3, 2 (March 1972): 6; George Wiley, "Words out of Wiley," *Welfare Fighter* 3, 3 (April 1972): 3; "Marcha de Los Ninos," *Welfare Fighter* 3, 1 (January–February 1972): 1; "50,000 Say No to FAP and Yes to Children," *Welfare Fighter* 3, 3 (April 1972): 1, 7–9; and Kotz and Kotz, *A Passion for Equality*, 289. On the child care legislation, see Ruth Rosen, *The World Split Open: How The Modern Women's Movement Changed America* (New York: Penguin, 2000), 90–91; and Michel, *Children's Interests/Mothers' Rights*, 250–51. On Abzug, see letter from George Wiley to Congresswoman-Elect Bela [sic] Abzug, New York City, November 16, 1970, 21/6, Wiley; and Amy Swerdlow, *Women Strike for Peace* (Chicago: University of Chicago Press, 1993), 143–47.

43. Social Service Employees Union, Local 371, District Council 37, AFSCME, AFL-CIO, "Make Bus Reservations for Children's March Now," March 14, 1972, 56/Welfare Rights Org., Social Action. For local actions, see "16 Cities Join National Crusade for Children's Rights," *Welfare Fighter* 3, 3 (April 1972): 13.

44. Hulbert James, interview with Nick Kotz, October 30, 1974, 39, 24/Hulbert James Interview, Kotz.

45. Tim Sampson, interview with Felicia Kornbluh, July 27, 2001, Oakland, Calif., 1, transcript in possession of the author.

46. Letter from Aileen Hernandez, president, National Organization for Women, to Mr. George Wiley, December 15, 1970, and attached statement, "Women in Poverty," adopted by the Executive Committee of the National Organization for Women, November 29, 1970, 21/6, Wiley; Gloria Steinem, Interview with Nick Kotz and Mary Lynn Kotz, January 25, 1975, 25/Gloria Steinem Interview, Kotz; West, *National Welfare Rights Movement*, 256–58; and Martha Davis, "Welfare Rights and Women's Rights in the 1960s," *Integrating the Sixties*, ed. Brian Balogh (University Park: Pennsylvania State University Press, 1996), 144–65. For other efforts to link NWRO with white feminists and majority-white feminist organizations, see Kotz and Kotz, *A Passion for Equality*, 289. Frances Fox Piven commented on the 1971 NWRO convention, at which Gloria Steinem addressed the membership, that "welfare mothers find it condescending when a glamour queen like that stands up and calls them 'sister'." Piven, interview with Felicia Kornbluh, December 5, 1995, informal notes in possession of the author, n.p.

47. Decision, *Catherine Boddie, et al., v. George K. Wyman, et al.*, in the U.S. Dis-

trict Court for the Northern District of New York, filed Oct. 13, 1970, 70 Civ. 200 ORDER, 1952/No file, NWRO; and George Wiley, report to the Interreligious Foundation for Community Organization, 1970, 11/18, Wiley. For Boddie as head of the Upstate group, see memorandum from Catherine Boddie, chairwoman, Upstate Welfare Rights Organization, to All Upstate WRO's, September 2, 1971, 2061/No File, NWRO.

48. "The States Report—New York City," *Welfare Fighter* 3, 7 (August–September 1972): 14.

49. Charles Reich, "The New Property," *Yale Law Journal* 73, 5 (April 1964): 733–87.

50. *Goldberg v. Kelly* (25 L Ed 2d 287) (1970), 295.

51. Ibid., 297.

52. *National Welfare Rights Organization, et al., Appellants, v. The Honorable Robert Finch, Secretary, United States Department of Health, Education, and Welfare, et al.*, U.S. Court of Appeals for the District of Columbia Circuit (1319 U.S. App. D.C. 46) (1970); "Legal Notes," *Welfare Fighter* 1, 4 (December 1969): 2; and "Legal Notes," *Welfare Fighter* 1, 6 (February 1970): 2.

53. *NWRO v. Finch* (1970), lexis-nexis.com/universe/doc, 16; and "Legal Notes," February 1970.

54. "HEW Plans Compliance Hearings," *Welfare Fighter* 2, 1 (July 21, 1970): 7; memorandum from Elliot Richardson, secretary of HEW, to the Honorable Robert H. Finch, n.d., WHCF, Staff Member and Office Files, Robert H. Finch, Subject/Name File, 7/5, Nixon; John H. Twiname, administrator, Social and Rehabilitation Service, HEW, to All Parties, In the matter of the Indiana Conformity Hearing, January 18, 1971, ibid.; and decision of John Twiname, In the Matter of the Continuance of Grants for the State of Nebraska's Program for Aid to Families with Dependent Children under Title IV)Part A) of the Social Security Act, September 10, 1970, ibid.

55. Letter from John D. Twiname, administrator, to the Secretary of HEW, [Re:] California Conformity Hearing, July 28, 1970, WHCF, Staff Member and Office Files, Robert H. Finch, Subject/Name File, 7/5, Nixon.

56. Twiname to Finch.

57. Jermany, with Mary Lynn Kotz, 7, notes the participation of the California Welfare Rights Organization in the California conformity hearing.

58. Social and Rehabilitation Service, HEW, In the Matter of: The Continuance of Grants to the State of California under Titles I, IV (Part A), X, and XIV of the Social Security Act, August 25, 1970, before Hearing Examiner J. Andrew Brooks, "Recommended Findings and Proposed Decision," October 6, 1970, 5, WHCF, Staff Member and Office Files, Robert H. Finch, Subject/Name File, 7/5, Nixon.

59. Brooks, "Recommended Findings and Proposed Decision"; "HEW Examiner Rules California Didn't Obey Federal Regulations," *Wall Street Journal*, October 6, 1970, WHCF, Staff Member and Office Files, Robert H. Finch, Subject/Name File, 7/5, Nixon; and memorandum to the Honorable Robert Finch, from John D. Twiname, Administrator, Social and Rehabilitation Service, HEW, October 6, 1970, ibid. The Nixon Administration briefly cut off public assistance payments to the states of Indiana and Nebraska. See letter from Twiname to Honorable Edgar D. Whitcomb, governor of Indiana, Indianapolis, Indiana, n.d.; Twiname to Honorable J.J. Exon, governor of Nebraska, Lincoln, Nebraska, n.d.; and "HEW News," January 19, 1971, ibid.

60. For trends in Legal Services, see Isidore Silver, "Is Poverty Illegal? An

Opportunity for a Quiet Revolution," *Commonweal*, February 19, 1971, 488–92, 2044/Right to Live, NWRO; "Movement Spotlight," *Welfare Fighter* 2, 4 (December 1970–January 1971): 10; and Thomas Hilbink, "The Creation of the Legal Services Corporation and the Battle over Public Interest Law," unpublished paper in possession of author, presented at the New York University Legal History Colloquium, New York, N.Y., February 25, 1998. For the effects of these changes on legal careers, see Davis, *Brutal Need*, 119–41.

61. Letter from (Mrs.) Nina Gray, Paterson, N.J., to Mr. Irving Engelman, director, State of New Jersey Division of Public Welfare, Trenton, N.J., July 26, 1969, 2017/Letters of Complaint, NWRO.

62. Minnesota Welfare Rights Organization, *Minnesota Welfare Rights*, 1969, 27/3, Wiley.

63. For the vision of the lawyers, see Edward Sparer, "The Right to Welfare," in *The Rights of Americans: What They Are—What they Should Be*, ed. Norman Dorsen (New York: Pantheon, 1971), 65–93; Sparer, "The Illegality of Poverty," *Social Policy* (March/April 1971): 49–53; and A. Delafield Smith, *The Right to Life* (Chapel Hill: University of North Carolina Press, 1955). For an alternative vision of constitutional welfare rights, see Frank Michelman, "The Supreme Court 1968 Term—Forward: On Protecting the Poor Through the Fourteenth Amendment," *Harvard Law Review* 83 (1969): 7.

64. Baum, *Mass Administrative Justice*, 20.

65. Ibid., 18–23.

66. Ibid., 39–40.

67. *Dandridge v. Williams* (25 L Ed 2d 503) (1970). Jermany, with Mary Lynn Kotz, 26, emphasized the negative effects of a third case, *Jefferson v. Hackney*. Also see *Rosado v. Wyman* (397 U.S. 455) (1970).

68. "Know Your Welfare Rights," *Welfare Fighter* 1, 7 (April 1970): 3.

69. "Words Out of Wiley," *Welfare Fighter* 2, 10 (December 1971): 3.

70. Draft letter from Faith Evans, Eastern Regional representative, NWRO, to Brothers and Sisters, [1972], 2061/Eastern Regional Folder II, NWRO.

71. Georgia L. Ware, Chairlady, [City-Wide Coordinating Committee of Welfare Groups], minutes of executive board meeting, June 12, 1972, 2061/No file, NWRO.

72. IFCO Annual Report, January 1970, 11/18, Wiley; and James Forman, *The Making of Black Revolutionaries* (Seattle: University of Washington Press, 1985), 545–50. On IFCO and NWRO, see Kotz and Kotz, *A Passion for Equality*, 245; and George Wiley, notes on the IFCO Black Caucus Meeting, December 9, 1969, 11/18 Wiley.

73. Stanley I. Kutler, ed., *Abuse of Power: The New Nixon Tapes* (New York: Simon and Schuster, 1997), 31–33, 112–13, 119, 176. Kotz and Kotz, *A Passion for Equality*, 247, quote the IFCO executive director as saying that the IRS "used NWRO as the main hammer" to bring down IFCO: "IRS spent three years examining our books. They practically lived in our office and disrupted our work." Also see West, *National Welfare Rights Movement*, 369.

74. Letter from Lucius Walker, Jr., executive director, IFCO, New York, N.Y., to Dr. George Wiley, April 29, 1971, 11/18, Wiley. Also see letter from Ann Douglas, director of Administration, IFCO, to George Wiley, October 14, 1971, ibid.; and Wiley draft letter to Reverend Lucius Walker, IFCO, n.d. [December 1971], ibid.

75. Kotz and Kotz, *A Passion for Equality*, 291.

76. ". . . And There Was a Survival Celebration and Auction," *Welfare Fighter* 3, 3 (April 1972): 14.

77. Form for Staff Wishing to Work for Welfare Rights Groups, n.d. [1971–1972], 2061/No file, NWRO; "Legal—Finding Non-Welfare Legal Help," *Welfare Fighter* 3, 2 (March 1972): 4; and "Legal—Youth and the Law," *Welfare Fighter* 3, 5 (June 1972): 11.

78. Letter from Mrs. Mamie McPherson, Broward WRO, Florida, to Mrs. Annie Smart, via NWRO, Washington, D.C., May 3, 1972, 2061/No file, NWRO.

79. Letter from Sue Berta Martin, secretary, the People's Rights Group, Hazel Green, Alabama, to NWRO, Washington, D.C., August 10, 1972, 2061/No file, NWRO; and response from Debby Vajda, NWRO staff, August 31, 1972, ibid.

80. Letter from Debby Vajda, NWRO, to Jackie Eldridge, Billings, Montana, July 26, 1972, 2061/No file, NWRO; letter from Elizabeth Perry, National Coordinating Committee representative, D.C. Family Welfare Rights Organization, to Mrs. Marie Ratagick, May 10, 1972, ibid.; Corethea Saxon, New Jersey National Coordinating Committee Report, n.d. [received, 11/22/71] and Saxon, NCC Monthly Report, New Jersey, n.d. [received 12/20/71], ibid; memo from Faith Evans, Eastern regional representative, NWRO, to All Chairmen of Baltimore Citywide WRO's, November 14, 1972, and report from Shirley McNeill, Baltimore City WRO, to NWRO, May 3, 1972, ibid.

81. Letter from Ruth Welfield, chairman, [illeg], New Jersey, WRO, to Murray Klein, action chairman of CC [Camden City?] Welfare Rights Organization, cc: NWRO, Washington, D.C., June 24, 1972, 2061/No file, NWRO.

82. *Tioga Welfare Rights Community Newsletter*, August/September 1972: 4.

83. George Wiley, "Director's Corner," *Welfare Fighter* 1, 4 (December 1969): 2 (on Hulbert James departure); Rhoda Linton, interview with Felicia Kornbluh, June 9, 1997, by telephone, 55, transcript in possession of the author; letter from Rachlin to Wiley, January 19, 1971; and Pastreich, with Kornbluh. Davis, *Brutal Need*, 135, discusses the departures of the lawyers.

84. On Wiley's departure, see Sanders, with Kotz and Kotz, 18; Faith Evans, interview with Nick Kotz and Mary Lynn Kotz, n.d. [1974–75], 23–24, 24/Faith Evans Interview, Kotz; West, *National Welfare Rights Movement*, 121; and Kotz and Kotz, *A Passion for Equality*, 290.

85. Faith Evans, Eastern regional representative, NWRO, to All Executive Board Members and National Coordinating Committee Members, November 21, 1972, Nat'l Welfare Rts. Org.—Welfare Rts. Orgs., Freedman.

86. Wiley to Welfare Rights Leaders, Members, Friends; Scott, "Wiley Quitting"; and Smothers, "Welfare Activist Plans New Group."

87. See, generally, file of material on the 1973 National Convention, 7/10, Wiley.

88. "Operation Mop Up the Class Struggle Is for Keeps," *Organizer* (National Caucus of Labor Committees) 1, 2 (April 1973): 2. For conflict between Faith Evans and local leaders, see memo from Evans to All Chairmen of Baltimore Citywide WRO's; report from Shirley McNeill; and Corethea Saxon, Monthly Report. For the ousters as reasons to join the National Caucus of Labor Committees, see "Rebuild NWRO! Convention March 31," *Organizer*, 1, 1 (February 1973): 1; and "Organizers Map Slave-Labor Fight; Plan NWRO Meet," *Organizer*, 1, 1 (February 1973): 1.

89. "Jennette Washington Urges Recipients, Vets & Unemployed To Join in Building New WRO," *Organizer*, 1, 1 (February 1973): 8. For Washington's support of the new organization, see also "Organizers Map Slave-Labor Fight," 1; and "Organizers Defy Nixon; Forge NU-WRO," *Organizer*, 1, 2 (April 1973): 1.

90. "Dr. George Wiley Feared Drowned," *NYT*, August 10, 1973, 13; letter

from Ms. Johnnie Tillmon, executive director, and Mr. Faith Evans, associate director, NWRO, to All WRO's & Friends, August 16, 1973, Poverty Rights Action Center—Welfare Rights Organizations, Freedman; and Bert De Leeuw, coordinator, Movement for Economic Justice, "In Memoriam: George A. Wiley," Movement for Economic Justice—Welfare Rights Organizations, Freedman.

91. Letter from Tillmon and Evans to All WRO's & Friends.

92. Notes from National, November 1973, Poverty Rights Action Center—Welfare Rights Organizations, Freedman; attached memo, To: All Welfare Rights Advocates and Groups, Re: Supplemental Security Income Program, November 6, 1973, ibid.; and Tyrone Chapman, "How an SSI Campaign Can Be Used to Build a Local Group," November 1973, ibid.

93. David Harvey, *A Brief History of Neoliberalism* (New York: Oxford University Press, 2005), 44–48; Joshua Freeman, *Working-Class New York: Life and Labor Since World War II* (New York: New Press, 2000), 256; Robert Zevin, "New York City Fiscal Crisis: First Act in a New Age of Reaction," in *The Fiscal Crisis of American Cities*, ed. Robert Alcaly and David Mermeltsein (New York: Vintage, 1977), 24; Ferretti, *Year the Big Apple Went Bust*; and Shefter, *Political Crisis/Fiscal Crisis.* For Rockefeller's ascent, see Joseph E. Persico, *The Imperial Rockefeller: A Biography of Nelson A. Rockefeller* (New York: Simon and Schuster, 1982), 243–45.

94. Banner headline, "Ford to City: Drop Dead—Vows He'll Veto Any Bail-Out," *New York Daily News*, October 30, 1975, 1; and William K. Tabb, "Blaming the Victim" in *Fiscal Crisis of American Cities*, 315.

95. Tabb, "Blaming the Victim," 315. For examples of this advice being given to city officials, see *NYT*, "Urban Experts Advise, Castigate and Console the City on its Problems," *Fiscal Crisis of American Cities*, 5–10 (originally July 30, 1975); and Edward M. Gramlich, *The New York City Fiscal Crisis: What Happened and What Is to Be Done?* (Washington, D.C.: Brookings Institution, 1977).

96. Freeman, *Working-Class New York*, 263; Zevin, "New York City Fiscal Crisis," 27; and Piven and Cloward, *Poor People's Movements*, 356.

97. Evans, with Kotz and Kotz, 67; and " 'Making it' in the Ghetto: The Man's Game," *Organizer* 1, 3 (June 1973): 1.

98. Judy Klemesrud, "March and Rally Celebrate First International Women's Day," *NYT*, March 9, 1975, 1.

99. Marian Kramer oral history, from *Detroit Lives*, compiled and edited by Robert H. Mast (Philadelphia: Temple University Press, 1994), 105.

Conclusion

1. Susan Sheehan, *A Welfare Mother* (1975–1976; New York: Mentor Books, 1977), esp. 3, 23, 133.

2. Ibid., 2, 100. For more on the welfare mother's ignorance of politics, see p. 54.

3. Michael B. Katz has described a similar contradiction in the postwar period between the African American freedom movement and movements elsewhere in the world for decolonization, and social science theories that treated communities of color as passive or stagnant. See Katz, *The Undeserving Poor: From the War on Poverty to the War on Welfare* (New York: Pantheon, 1989), 167–73.

4. *King v. Smith* (392 U.S. 309) (1968). The Supreme Court decision in *Shapiro v. Thompson* (394 U.S. 618) (1969) made it more difficult for states or localities to save money by denying benefits to people who had recently moved into the state.

5. Joshua Freeman, *Working-Class New York* (New York: New Press, 2000), 208.

6. One set of people who might have benefited from an income guarantee were the victims of Hurricane Katrina and other similar disasters. See Michael Ignatieff, "The Broken Contract," *NYT Magazine*, September 25, 2005, 15–17. As I have mentioned previously, late twentieth- and early twenty-first-century conditions bred renewed calls in the United States and elsewhere for a guaranteed income, or a Basic Income Grant. See Guy Standing, ed., *Promoting Income Security as a Right: Europe and North America* (London: Anthem Press/International Labour Organization, 2004); and the Basic Income Earth Network (BIEN) Website, http://www.basicincome.org or bien@etes.ucl.ac.be.

7. Judith N. Shklar, *American Citizenship: The Quest for Inclusion* (Cambridge, Mass.: Harvard University Press, 1991), 14.

8. Ibid., 98.

Index

Acknowledgments

Many of my most important colleagues in recent years have been the scholars, writers, and activists with whom I have worked on welfare policy issues. The women of the Women's Committee of 100, a volunteer campaign to preserve public assistance programs for women and children, shaped this work in every way. I owe special thanks to Gwendolyn Mink, Eva Kittay, Frances Fox Piven, Guida West, Cynthia Harrison, Ruth Brandwein, Mimi Abramovitz, Eileen Boris, Maureen Lane and the Welfare Rights Initiative at Hunter College, Heidi Hartmann, Pat Reuss, Martha Davis, and Barbara Ehrenreich. Sonya Michel deserves special mention for bringing me into this activist network and helping me find the NWRO papers at Howard University.

In the final stages of preparing this work for publication, my most engaged interlocutors have been Thomas Sugrue and Peter Agree, who shepherded the book through the production process at the University of Pennsylvania Press, and Grey Osterud, who read the entire manuscript with great care. For help with particular chapters, I thank Louis Anthes, Adina Back, Brian Balogh, Felica Batlan, Eileen Boris, Joyce Burson, George Chauncey, Nancy Cott, Martha Davis, Jane DeHart, Peter Edelman, Dan Ernst, Catherine Fisk, William Forbath, Joshua Freeman, Kevin Gaines, Bryant Garth, Gary Gerstle, Linda Gordon, Robert Gordon, Tom Green, Joel Handler, Dirk Hartog, Thomas Hilbink, Daniel Horowitz, Anore Horton, Thomas Jackson, Ira Katznelson, Karen Krahulik, Claudia Koonz, Stanley Kutler, Gerda Lerner, Lisa Levenstein, Elizabeth Lunbeck, Kate Masur, Scott Messinger, Sonya Michel, Andy Morris, Kevin Murphy, William Nelson, Alice O'Connor, Anneliese Orleck, Nell Irvin Painter, Frances Fox Piven, Dorothy Roberts, Daniel Rodgers, Timothy Sampson, Rickie Solinger, Susan Sterett, John Thompson, Jeanne Theoharis, Chris Tomlins, Kate Torrey, Danny Walkowitz, Guida West, Vicky Saker Woeste, Peter Wood, and Komozi Woodard.

Among my colleagues at Duke University, I am especially indebted to Bill Chafe, Sally Deutsch, Catherine Fisk, Lisa Hazirjian, Cynthia Herrup, Margaret Humphreys, Reeve Huston, Claudia Koonz, Robert Korstad, Ian Lekus, Gerda Lerner, Charles McKinney, Kristen Neuschel, Charles Payne, Gunther Peck, Anne Scott, John Thompson, Susan

Thorne, and Peter Wood. I also thank my students, especially those in my lecture course, "History and Public Policy: The 1960s in America," and in my seminars on "Women and Welfare" and "Law and American Society."

For permission to quote from archival materials and images under their care, I thank Leonora Gidlund and Kenneth Cobb of the New York City Municipal Archives, Joellen El-Bashir of the Moorland-Spingarn Research Center at Howard University, Harry Miller and Lisa Hinzman of the Wisconsin Historical Society, Mark Greek of the Washington, D.C., Public Library, Henry Freedman of the National Center for Law and Economic Justice, and the helpful staffs of the Bancroft Library, the Schlesinger Library, the Tamiment and Bobst Libraries at New York University, the Seeley-Mudd manuscripts library at Princeton University, and the Nixon Presidential Materials Project at the National Archives. I especially thank Rhoda Linton for permission to quote from materials in her possession (and for her generous reading of the completed manuscript), Nancy Sampson for allowing me to read Tim Sampson's papers before they were archived, and Marilyn Cervino of the *New York Times* for finding archived photographs on short notice. Last, but not least, I thank the staffs of the Duke University libraries, especially Ann Miller, Carson Holloway, and Danette Patchner, for being unfailingly helpful and pleasant to work with.

For financial assistance, I thank Duke University for granting me a semester's leave from teaching in which I was able to write full-time. I also thank the American Bar Foundation for two years of generous support; the New York University School of Law for a Samuel Golieb fellowship in legal history; the University Center for Human Values and Woodrow Wilson Society of Fellows at Princeton University; the American Historical Association for a Littleton-Griswold research award; the Wisconsin Historical Society for an Amy Louise Hunter award; and the Woodrow Wilson Foundation for a Women's Studies Dissertation Fellowship.

For sharing their time with me in oral history interviews, and for helping me locate sources, I thank Charles Reich, Frank Espada, Tim Sampson, Rhoda Linton, William Pastreich, Gerry Shea, Guida West, Frances Fox Piven, Henry Freedman, Marcia Henry, Martha Davis, Andrea Kydd, Alan Stone, and Sylvia Law. For helping me with research assistance of every conceivable kind, I thank Leila Nesson, Ian Shedd, Alexis Morant, and the incomparable Felicity Turner.

Traveling to archives and taking research fellowships in strange cities affords many opportunities for gratitude. In Berkeley, I relied on the kindness of Tim and Nancy Sampson, Kristin Luker and Jerry Karabel, and Julia Query. In Chicago, I was sustained by Bruce Aaron, Eric Arnesen and Catherine Shulteiss, Alix Feinberg Sherman and Jon Sherman, Paula Kamen, Amie Wilkinson, Amy Randall, Alex Pollack, Amy Johnson, Mary Rose, Brian Roraff, Martha Phillips, Christie Tate, Ann Stanford, Karen Yates, Kathleen Glennon, and many others. From my time in Madison, I owe debts to Tracey Deutsch and David Chang, Bethel Saler, Colleen Dunlavy, Jeanne Boydston, Louise Trubek, Ann Shola Orloff, Jennifer Frost, and Linda Gordon. In Washington, D.C., I benefited from the generosity of Karen Kornbluh and Jim Halpert and Samuel and Daniel Halpert, Deepak Bhargava, Justin Leites, Deborah Cohen, and Eileen Boris. In New York, I have balanced time in the archives with time talking about the 1960s and 1970s with Cynthia Nixon, Daniel Moses, Aaron Retica, and Sarah Basset.

I thank my family, especially my sisters, Karen Kornbluh and Rebecca Kornbluh, and my parents, Beatrice Braun and David Kornbluh. My mother taught me about labor relations and administrative law from her position as a retired attorney for the National Labor Relations Board. My father has taught me about urban politics from his multiple positions as community leader and city bureaucrat. My late stepfather, Irwin Braun, shared my love of history and provided the financial base that allowed me to live in reasonable comfort while researching this book. My stepmother, Lorayne Losch, has shared stories from her time as a case worker for the New York City Department of Social Services in the late 1960s and helped me gain perspective on the social work profession.

Above all, I thank my partner Anore Horton, who has helped me with every aspect of this project and has made my life outside the project worth living.